SILVER SCREEN
SAUCERS

SILVER SCREEN SAUCERS

SAUCERS

Sorting Fact from Fantasy in Hollywood's UFO Movies

by

ROBBIE GRAHAM

www.whitecrowbooks.com

For information, contact White Crow Books
at 3 Hova Villas, Hove, BN3 3DH United Kingdom,
or e-mail to info@whitecrowbooks.com.

Cover Design: David Sankey © Spectre Artwork Studio
Cover Production: Butterfly Effect
Interior design by Velin@Perseus-Design.com

Paperback ISBN 978-1-910121-11-5
eBook   ISBN 978-1-910121-12-2

Non Fiction / Body, Mind & Spirit / UFOs & Extraterrestrials

www.whitecrowbooks.com

PRAISE FOR
SILVER SCREEN SAUCERS

'It would be a tragic mistake to assume *Silver Screen Saucers* is a book about UFO movies. It isn't. It is a hard-edged, well-documented, and thoroughly entertaining look at the evolution of the UFO mystery, as seen through the prism of UFO and alien films. What UFOlogy needs more than anything else, more than new cases or leaked documents or fuzzy photos, is a fresh pair of eyes, a new way of looking at this enduring enigma. That is exactly what Robbie Graham brings to the table. This is an important book.'

George Knapp
Emmy and Peabody Award-winning Investigative
Reporter, KLAS TV

'At last we have a full history and critical analysis of the multiple ways that the UFO phenomenon has influenced, and been influenced by, its representations in film and television. Skilled in the methods of film criticism and media studies, Robbie Graham sets a new standard and gives us a new guide with *Silver Screen Saucers*.'

Jeffrey J. Kripal

J. Newton Rayzor Chair of Philosophy and Religion, Rice
University, Texas.
Author of *'Mutants and Mystics: Science Fiction,*
Superhero Comics and the Paranormal'

'Graham's exploration of the relationship between UFOs and movies is encyclopedic, profoundly revealing, and a dramatic, riveting account of military and intelligence professionals, film-makers, UFOlogists and ordinary people who experienced extraordinary things. His discussion is fair, judicious, and eminently sane. This book is a must-read for anyone interested in UFOs, the influence of films, and the often hidden powers that manipulate the mind of society so effectively.'

Richard Thieme
Author of *Mind Games* and contributor to *UFOs and Government: A Historical Inquiry*

'Robbie Graham is on the cutting edge of thought on the UFO phenomenon. In this innovative history of representations of UFOs and extraterrestrials in movies and television, Graham keeps us fully grounded in the recognition that Hollywood's spectacular productions are inspired by real events reported by real people. He reveals how movies and media about UFOs influence what we believe about them, yet he also uncovers the existence of interpretations less beholden to Hollywood and more accurate to what is reported by people who have experienced UFO events. *Silver Screen Saucers* is an exciting contribution to the cultural history of UFOs and is a must-read for anyone interested in the subject.'

Diana Walsh Pasulka
Professor, University of North Carolina Wilmington.
Author of *Stellar Visions: UFO Events, E.T.s, Belief and Religion* (forthcoming)

'Robbie Graham's scholarship informs the dialogue between actual UFOlogical experience and its depiction in film and popular culture. That half-perceived, half-created relationship drives a significant part of the consumable entertainment market. *Silver Screen Saucers* is an important book for students of film and flying saucers alike.'

Kenn Thomas
Steamshovel Press

"Graham takes us on a captivating journey through the vaults of UFO and alien films. He shows that movies can and do shape our reality, but he also reveals an underlying truth behind Hollywood's UFO entertainment products. Fact truly is stranger than fiction."

Ben Hansen
Lead Investigator and Host of Syfy's *Fact or Faked:* *Paranormal Files*

'I've waited all my adult life to read this book presented in this manner, and, finally, here it is... the most comprehensive and detailed thesis on the symbiotic connection between Hollywood and aliens... brilliant and definitive.'

From the Foreword by Bryce Zabel

Co-Creator of NBC's *Dark Skies,* **former Chairman of the Academy of Television Arts and Sciences**

CONTENTS

———⟫◆⟪———

DEDICATION

For Tamasine,

My support, my encouragement, my joy, my love, my life

ACKNOWLEDGEMENTS

This book is the product of around nine years of research on my part, seven of which, off and on, have been dedicated to the writing process. It has been a long journey, fascinating and frustrating in equal measure. A number of individuals have made significant contributions to my work, either as interviewees or as sources of much needed critique, encouragement, and inspiration. With this in mind I would like to thank the following people:

My brother, Jamie, my parents, Alan and Glennis, Matthew Alford, Bryce Zabel, Mike Clelland, Diana Walsh Pasulka, Jeffrey J. Kripal, Andrea Springer, Claire McGauley (Pandora Spocks), Franky Ma, Anthony Beckett, Miguel Romero, Grant Cameron, Dawn Lilgé, Søren Hyldgaard, Joe Alves, Ben Hansen, Don Ecker, Linda Moulton Howe, Christopher Bledsoe Sr., Bret Oldham, Brigitte Barclay, Steven Jones, Anne Ashley Jones, Peter Faust, Tracy Tormé, Paul Davids, Joe Dante, Paul Meehan, Andy Fickman, Robert Emenegger, Leanne Jones, John Ellis, Nick Redfern, Robert Baer, Ika Willis, Kristian Moen, Kenn Thomas, Paul Mayo, Jason Colavito, Will Bueché, Scott Ross, George Knapp, Richard Thieme, Daniel Myrick, Andrew Thomas.

And a special thank you to my publisher, Jon Beecher of White Crow Books, for his patience and belief, and to David Sankey, who created the wonderful cover art for this book.

ABOUT THE AUTHOR

Robbie Graham is a leading authority on the cultural and political interplay between UFOs and Hollywood. He has been interviewed on these subjects for BBC Radio, Coast to Coast AM, Canal+ TV, and Vanity Fair, among others. His articles have appeared in a variety of publications including The Guardian, New Statesman, Filmfax, Fortean Times, and the peer-reviewed Journal of North American Studies, 49th Parallel. He holds a First Class Honors Degree in Film, Television, and Radio Studies from Staffordshire University, and a Masters Degree with Distinction in Cinema Studies from the University of Bristol.

'UFO MOVIE'

Any movie that taps directly into any aspect of UFO mythology or draws notable inspiration from UFOlogical literature, incorporating into its plot references to frequently debated UFOlogical phenomena, events, and locales, as well as specialized UFOlogical terminology. A UFO movie need not be about UFOs, per se, nor feature traditional UFOlogical iconography, but will often devote a respectable amount of its running time to the dramatization of imagined human-alien interactions, usually, though not always, in the context of a 'first contact' scenario in which the aliens assume the role of visitor/ invader. In other words, the UFO movie typically is concerned with the problems inherent from a human perspective in earthly encounters with alien lifeforms.

FOREWORD

BY BRYCE ZABEL

Which came first, the chicken or the egg? Flying saucer sightings or Hollywood's depiction of them?

These questions hang over the subject like heavy clouds and they have rarely been addressed. Robbie Graham has spent many years sorting the fact from the fantasy and he's written the brilliant and definitive book on the subject with *Silver Screen Saucers*.

If the 1947 Roswell incident is a true example of alien contact, for example, then that would easily explain how Hollywood made a batch of 1950s invasion films like *Earth vs. the Flying Saucers*. They could have been, as has so often been speculated, pushed forward as a kind of acclimation project for a population that was about to make a huge adjustment.

If *Close Encounters of the Third Kind* was just a flight of fantasy from the creative genius of Steven Spielberg, on the other hand, it could still explain the prevalence of reports of gray aliens with big heads and spindly arms that came in the decades that followed. People would have gotten the idea from the director of a generation that this is what alien contact looks like.

I'm so glad that Robbie Graham has tackled this subject with the academic credentials he possesses, and has treated it with the importance and seriousness it deserves. I've waited all my adult life to read this book presented in this manner, and, finally, here it is.

What we know for sure at this point in history, is that probably more than 75% of Americans believe in the existence of UFOs, even as the media makes fun of people that do and the government denies all knowledge. This is a top-level disconnect if ever I've heard of one.

There's no doubt that ET-themed films, documentaries, and TV shows have always been among the most popular and financially successful of Hollywood's products. Are they reflecting an honest reality that suggests "we are not alone in the universe," or are they deliberately creating a public misconception to make people believe something that isn't true? If that's the case, then why? And why are there more alien-themed film and TV projects than ever before?

Personally, I don't buy the 'Hollywood-helping-acclimate' story at all anymore, even if it was ever true. From my personal experience, the entertainment industry makes alien films because they're full of conflict and cater to the fanboy crowd. It's show-me-the-money time.

Still, this mix between Hollywood product and facts-on-the-ground can't be denied from my own personal experience either. My creative partner Brent Friedman and I certainly mixed the concept into our NBC series *Dark Skies* by saying that a Majestic-12 agent asked us to create a series so we could get the truth out "under the cover of fiction," and then we returned the favor by making him our main character. It was a Mobius strip of reality if ever there was one.

It got more complicated. During our production, we were watched and approached by several people who claimed that they were part of a UFO group operating with the Office of Naval Intelligence and they wanted to give us some notes on the series. This would be laughable, except that these men were not funny at all. They were dead serious, military-sounding types who had a coherent, detailed, and powerfully odd account of alien contact that they wanted to share with us.

So, for me, the jury is still out. I just don't know.

I also don't know if Robbie Graham knows. What I do know, however, is that he has assembled the most comprehensive and detailed thesis on the symbiotic connection between Hollywood and aliens. After you read his book, you will be able to assess for yourself with clear-eyed insight what you think is the best theory to explain it all.

And this book excels in another way. If you simply want to understand UFOlogy and its history, then that is all here for you. Or, if you want to know more about the behind-the-scenes anecdotes and context of some culturally powerful and important films about UFOs, alien contact, and the nature of reality, then that is here too.

At least we all know that as we read this wonderful book together, it will be an experience that binds us, and proves that, for us anyway, we are not alone.

Bryce Zabel
Los Angeles, California
June 30, 2015

CHAPTER ONE

SETTING THE SCENE

"Hollywood fills the gaps in our knowledge of the world."

– KEN RUSSELL

~ THE SILVER SCREEN ~

In the years 1895 and 1896, crowds in several French cities gathered to witness a new technological marvel. Unsure of what was about to unfold, they were startled by the sudden appearance of a hulking, steam-spewing locomotive hurtling directly toward them. Fearing for their lives, men, women, and children scrambled desperately for safety, their screams piercing the air.[1] So goes the popular accounting of what transpired at the earliest screenings of one of history's first motion pictures: *Arrival of a Train at La Ciotat*. This primitive movie, comprised of one fifty-second static shot, showed the arrival of a train at a station. Nothing more. The crowds, of course, were cinemagoers, and the technological marvel was cinema itself, the miracle of moving pictures. The directors of this terrifying movie, the legendary Lumière brothers, had placed their camera on the platform at such an angle as to create

1

the illusion that the train was on a collision course with the viewer. It was simple, but effective.

Fast-forward some eleven decades to 2009 when, following the release of James Cameron's epic 3D adventure *Avatar*, many cinemagoers became afflicted with a cinematically induced melancholy that cultural commentators have since referred to as "post-Avatar depression."[2] Cameron's special effects extravaganza was so immersive, its lush alien world of Pandora so vividly detailed and appealing, that men and women from all walks of life spiralled into a state of despair within days or even hours after having watched the movie. Real life, it seemed, could not hold a candle to Cameron's extraterrestrial fantasy.

Within a month of *Avatar*'s theatrical release a fan site dedicated to the movie, 'Avatar Forums,' had generated more than a thousand posts under a topic thread titled "Ways to cope with the depression of the dream of Pandora being intangible." The topic became so popular that the forum's administrator was forced to create a second thread so people could continue to share their feelings about the movie in what became a sort of virtual group therapy. One forum member named 'Mike' posted:

> Ever since I went to see *Avatar* I have been depressed. Watching the wonderful world of Pandora and all the Na'vi [the movie's aliens] made me want to be one of them. I can't stop thinking about all the things that happened in the film and all of the tears and shivers I got from it... I even contemplated suicide thinking that if I do it I will be rebirthed in a world similar to Pandora and that everything is the same as in Avatar.[3]

Mike's reaction to *Avatar* was extreme, but it was not unique. A post by forum user Ivar Hill also expressed an obsessive relationship with the movie:

> When I woke up this morning after watching *Avatar* for the first time yesterday, the world seemed... gray. It was like my whole life, everything I've done and worked for, lost its meaning. It just seems so... meaningless. I still don't really see any reason to keep... doing things at all. I live in a dying world.[4]

The movie's 3-D performance capture and CGI effects were so lifelike that, for the 162 minutes of its running time, viewers became virtual inhabitants of Pandora. When the credits rolled, separation anxiety kicked in.

Arrival of a *Train at La Ciotat* and *Avatar* are testaments, past and present, to the tangible power of cinema. Even in today's world of tablet devices and TV on demand, cinema remains a wondrous, almost magical medium. Its continued popularity after over a century should come as little surprise, however, because what cinema offers that our PCs, Macs, iPads, and even our televisions do not, is an expansive communal experience, the chance to gather in a public space with dozens or sometimes hundreds of other human beings, all of whom are strangers to one another, but who, for ninety minutes at least, are united on an emotional journey.

There is something undeniably special about sitting in a darkened cinema and being able to hear a pin drop as 'they' finally kiss in a romance, as a mystery finally unravels in a crime thriller, or as that breathless yet inevitable decision is made in an action movie: red wire or blue wire? The silence that falls over a movie theatre like a blanket in these moments is confirmation to all of us present that we are not so dissimilar after all; that we all experience love, fear, and hope, and that we all share a desire to experience these emotions in a communal environment, to reach out to our brothers and sisters, albeit from the confines of our cinema seats, enveloped in darkness, and say, "I feel it, too."

A magic window

In his book, *In the Blink of An Eye*, Oscar-winning sound-designer and editor, Walter Murch, (*The Godfather, Apocalypse Now*) likens the act of cinemagoing to passing through a magic window:

> With a theatrical film, particularly one in which the audience is fully engaged, the screen is not a surface, it is a magic window, sort of a looking glass through which your whole body passes and becomes engaged in the action with the characters on the screen. If you really like a film, you're not aware that you are sitting in a cinema watching a movie. Your responses are very different than they would be with television. Television is a 'look-at' medium, while cinema is a 'look-into' medium.[5]

Philosophy professor Colin McGinn, of the University of Miami, is similarly intrigued by the enduring appeal of cinema, so much so that he has written an entire book on the subject. *The Power of Movies: How*

Screen and Mind Interact poses hundreds of questions about the essence of the spell movies cast upon us, but ultimately fails in its quest to provide a single satisfactory answer – which isn't to say it doesn't come close and provide much food for thought.

Like Walter Murch, McGinn considers cinema a 'look-into' medium, referring to the movie screen as a window-like structure: "It appears as a bright window on a dark wall, and through it we can be the spectators of an entire new world. Yet, it is a one-way window, since no one on the other side can see us as we drink them in with our eyes."[6]

McGinn also observes that movie-watching and TV-watching are less alike than one might assume:

> There remains a significant point of difference between the two types of screen [cinema and TV], arising simply from the physical nature of the TV screen. For the TV itself – a piece of rectangular glass sitting in front of the viewer – is an object that can all too easily become a visual surface in its own right, as when light from the window or a lamp falls across its glassy face... We can never quite make a TV screen go away. We are always looking at a bulky piece of hardware that is on the brink of gaining our attention. The TV set is uncomfortably close to being a piece of furniture – not an impalpable window onto another world.[7]

Television, then, despite its ability to 'beam' directly into our homes twenty-four hours a day, seven days a week, cannot match the immersive power of cinema. And, despite having tremendous *reach,* in terms of its physical dimensions, TV is dwarfed by the cinema screen. This gargantuan cinematic 'window' swallows our immediate physical environment and invites us, indeed, *pulls* us, into another world. It is only as the credits finally role and the houselights fade-up that our own world floods back to us. This is not to say that TV is not a remarkably powerful medium, but merely that it lacks cinema's essential mystical ability to completely detach us from our physical environment.

Still, regardless of the medium through which it is screened, a movie is a movie, and movies are imbued with the power to impact our reality and transport us to other realms of perception. Perhaps I am over-complicating the matter. Perhaps the appeal of movies is simpler and more primal. Perhaps, as the great director Martin Scorsese has suggested, it stems from our subconscious desire "to share a common memory."[8] Memory, as it happens, is of particular interest to the author of this book – what we remember about the movies we see, where and how dominantly those memories reside in the collective experience of our lives, and, crucially, how easily we're able to separate our cinematic memories from our everyday reality.

~ THE SAUCERS ~

Of course, this book is also about UFOs. One of the most compelling mysteries of all time, Unidentified Flying Objects have been reported in Earth's skies dating back to the biblical age (see Chapter Six). Even before written records began, prehistoric cave paintings and petroglyphs from around the world were depicting strange disc-shaped objects and beings with bulbous heads and large black eyes. Some of these beings appear to be wearing clothing resembling our astronauts' space suits, complete with helmets and antennae.

The first sightings in the modern era of what we now refer to as "UFOs" were reported by Air Force pilots during the Second World War when anomalous balls of light and disc and cigar-shaped objects were sighted so frequently keeping pace with planes that the US military even coined a name for the phenomena, "Foo Fighters."[9] It was not until after the war had ended, however, that UFOs lodged themselves firmly and forever into the popular consciousness and that UFO secrecy began to metastasize behind the most impenetrable layers of America's national security state.

The US government's interest in UFOs dates back to the summer of 1947 when America's national security apparatus was besieged by hundreds of reports from concerned citizens and military personnel of what appeared to be metallic disc-shaped objects traversing the nation's skies, sometimes in formation and often at impossible speeds. On 24 June 1947, a private aviator and businessman, Kenneth Arnold, reported seeing a chain of nine unusual objects over the Cascade Mountains in Washington State. He described the objects' movement as being "like a saucer if you skip it across the water," inspiring the press to dub the mystery objects "flying saucers."[10] Many hundreds of saucer sightings were reported worldwide in the months to follow.

In 1948 the US Air Force produced its top secret and highly controversial "Estimate of the Situation," an official report concluding flying saucers to be "interplanetary" in origin.[11] Other factions within the Air Force, however, favored the more palatable idea that the saucers were the product of technological innovations in the Soviet Union. Either way, secrecy regarding the issue was of paramount importance as the question of whether the objects were physically real had already been affirmatively answered in the minds of America's military leaders. In a once secret letter to Air Force Headquarters dated 23 September 1947, General Nathan Twining, head of Air Materiel Command (AMC), stated that flying saucers were "real and not visionary or fictitious," that they had "metallic or light reflecting surface[s]," were "circular or elliptical in shape, flat on bottom and domed on top," and were sometimes sighted in "well-kept formation flights varying from three to nine objects."[12] In a previously top secret Canadian government document dating from 1950, Wilbert Smith, head of the Canadian government's UFO research project, Magnet, noted of UFOs that "The matter is the most highly classified subject in the United States government, rating higher even than the H-bomb."[13]

Today, numerous governments worldwide maintain dedicated and costly UFO study projects, collating and often investigating what collectively amount to thousands of UFO sighting reports made annually to authorities. In South America alone, the governments of Argentina,[14] Uruguay,[15] Peru,[16] Chile,[17] and Brazil,[18] either operate UFO investigations units or actively collect UFO sighting reports through their militaries. Other governments, including those of France,[19] New Zealand,[20] Denmark,[21] Canada,[22] and Russia,[23] have in recent years released to the public thousands of pages of previously classified UFO files.

The UK government has engaged with its citizenry through a process which has seen the release of thousands of previously classified UFO files through the National Archives.[24] According to the UK Ministry of Defence (MoD), UFOs (or UAPs – Unidentified Aerial Phenomena – as the MoD refers to them) "certainly exist," but are "still barely understood."[25] In a formerly secret 400-page assessment of the UFO phenomenon released in 2006 under the Freedom of Information Act, the UK Defence Intelligence Staff acknowledged that:

> The phenomena occur on a daily, world-wide basis. That UAP exist is indisputable. Credited with the ability to hover, land, take-off, accelerate to exceptional velocities, and vanish, they can reportedly alter their direction of flight suddenly and clearly can exhibit aerodynamic characteristics well beyond those of any known aircraft or missile - either manned or unmanned.[26]

The report also notes that "attempts by other nations to intercept the unexplained objects, which can clearly change position faster than an aircraft, have reportedly already caused fatalities," and warns that, with the increasing density of UAP reports in the UK air defence region, "a small possibility may exist... of a head-on encounter with a UAP."[27]

There appears, then, to be a broad consensus among the governments cited above: UFOs are objectively real, albeit currently not fully understood by science. They are worthy, at best, of focused study, and, at the very least, of sustained monitoring in the interests of aviation safety and national security.

This book takes its cue from officialdom that UFOs, regardless of their precise nature and origin, are objectively real. Moreover, it works from the logic that at least *some* UFOs are the product of non-terrestrial intelligences and that various governments, or military and intelligence groups within them, are well aware of this fact. Let us address this preceding sentence in two parts. First, why should we assume some UFOs are otherworldly in nature?

We are not alone

In April 2015, NASA Chief Scientist, Ellen Stofan, announced her conviction that signs of primitive alien life will be discovered within just ten years from now. "We know where to look. We know how to look," she said while speaking at a panel discussion broadcast on Nasa TV. "In most cases we have the technology and we're on a path to implementing it. And so I think we're definitely on the road."[28]

Stofan was discussing the discovery of rudimentary alien life-forms. However, renowned theoretical physicist Professor Mickio Kaku goes considerably further with his suggestion that alien life may already be visiting us and that some UFOs could indeed be extraterrestrial spacecraft.[29] According to Kaku, considering the age of the universe (13.82 billion years), many, if not most extraterrestrial civilizations will be technologically thousands or even millions of years more advanced than our own (ours is so young it barely registers on the cosmic timeline). If such civilizations exist, certain physicists, including Kaku, consider it likely that they will have developed hyperspatial technologies that enable their spacecraft to circumvent the lightspeed barrier, thereby opening the gates for interstellar travel.[30]

The popular assumption in the UFO community is that true UFOs are extraterrestrial vehicles – an assumption undoubtedly reinforced by Hollywood, which prefers a simplistic approach. However, while the Extraterrestrial Hypothesis (ETH) is appealing on many levels, some have argued that it fails to account for all aspects of UFO phenomena as reported by witnesses. Certainly, it has been my own experience that the closer one looks at UFOs, the harder it becomes to reconcile the phenomenon solely with visits from outer space. Indeed, in a puzzling amount of cases, the phenomenon seems to tailor its manifestations to the expectations of the individual perceiver based on spiritual or ideological values. Extraterrestrial intelligences may play some role in all of this, but it would be a mistake to consider ETs as a definitive solution to the UFO riddle.

Still, the ETH has considerable merit on the face of it. Extraterrestrial life in primitive forms *almost certainly* exists. If it exists, then the laws of evolution dictate that extraterrestrial intelligences far in advance of our own *probably* exist. As will be shown in this book, UFOs in the form of structured craft exhibiting performance characteristics well beyond Earth's most advanced technologies *definitely* exist, and have been studied and (reluctantly) acknowledged by governments around the world. It seems not unreasonable, then, to suggest that at least *some* UFOs *may* be of extraterrestrial origin, despite official assertions to the contrary.

As for my suggestion that various governments or 'rogue' military and intelligence groups within them are quietly aware of the non-human nature of UFOs, this is a logic based not on Hollywood movies or TV shows such as *Men In Black* or *The X-Files*, but on tens-of-thousands of pages of declassified government documentation which, collectively, paints a surprisingly clear (though certainly not explicit) picture of a decidedly unearthly phenomenon that for over six decades has held, vice-like, the attention of the powers that be, not only in the United States, but around the world.

The real X-Files: UFOs and officialdom

On 31 January 1949, the FBI issued a memo on UFOs entitled "Protection of Vital Installations." The classified document was sent to the Army's G-2, the Air Force Office of Special Investigations, the Office of Naval Intelligence, and FBI Director J. Edgar Hoover. The memo reveals that a meeting between these authorities had recently taken place concerning UFOs, and states that "the matter of 'Unidentified Aircraft' or 'Unidentified Aerial Phenomena,' otherwise known as 'Flying Discs,' 'Flying Saucers,' and 'Balls of Fire,' is considered top secret by intelligence officers of both the Army and the Air Forces."[31] The FBI document catalogues a list of incursions by unknown objects into restricted airspace surrounding the Atomic Energy Commission's highly sensitive research installation at Los Alamos, New Mexico, throughout December 1948 and into early 1949.

The memo goes on to explain that "the unidentified phenomena travel at the rate of speed estimated at a minimum of three miles per second and a maximum of twelve miles per second, or a mean calculated speed of seven and one-half miles per second, or 27,000 miles per hour."[32] Needless to say, such speeds are well beyond the capability of any terrestrial aircraft of the 21st Century, never mind the 20th. Even more eye-popping are the memo's statements that "on two separate occasions a definite vertical change in path was indicated," and that the appearance of the object was "round in a point of light with a definite area to the light's source." Some of the lights were "a diamond shape," while others were "elongated."[33]

It should be noted that this memo came at a time when the US government was insisting to the public that flying saucers were of no defense significance and that all UFOs could be explained away either as conventional aircraft, hallucinations, misidentifications of natural phenomena, or outright hoaxes. And yet, as the document makes clear, behind the scenes, the phenomenon was deemed to be of extreme defense significance and considered "top secret."

Almost four years later, on 2 December 1952, another jaw-dropping UFO-related document was produced, not by the FBI, but the by CIA. In a secret memo to CIA Director, General Walter Bedell Smith, the Agency's Director of Scientific Intelligence, H. Marshall Chadwell, wrote of UFOs:

> At this time, the reports of incidents convince us that there is something going on that must have immediate attention.... Sightings of unexplained objects at great altitudes and travelling at high speeds in the vicinity of major U.S. defense installations are of such nature that they are not attributable to natural phenomena or known types of aerial vehicles.[34]

In other words, in the absence of other satisfactory explanations, these objects were, in all likelihood, intelligently controlled craft not belonging to the United States government, nor presumably, to any other terrestrial power. Reading between the lines, it seems that Chadwell was seriously considering the possibility that these objects were of non-terrestrial origin, but he knew better than to state so explicitly in official documentation. Such discussions are better held in a quiet office, face-to-face.

To this day, for reasons outlined below and in the chapters to follow, the United States government remains reluctant to publicly acknowledge the underlying exotic nature of the UFOs. Other governments, however, have been relatively vocal about the phenomenon and are becoming more so with each passing year.

South American officials in particular have been especially forthright regarding military encounters with UFOs. Speaking on the direct authority of the President of Ecuador, Rafael Correa, Colonel Wilson Salgado of the Ecuadorian Air Force stated in an interview for the 2010 documentary *UFOs in South America: Disclosure Has Begun*:

> The information we have available – not just our information, but also that coming from abroad, in particular the United States – makes me confident that we are dealing with... Unidentified Flying Objects. In real terms, these are extraterrestrial objects, and I'm sure of it. We share the universe with other beings.[35]

More recently, in February 2012, Colonel Ariel Sanchez, head of the Uruguayan Air Force's Commission for the Reception and Investigation of UFO Reports (known as "Cridovni"), told American journalist Billy Cox of the *Sarasota Herald Tribune*, "I believe that Uruguay, as well as Argentina, Chile, Peru, Ecuador, and of course, Brazil, all have declassified only the smallest part of their files." Sanchez said that the UFO information thus far released by these governments is but "the tip of a huge iceberg."[36]

Some of the most remarkable statements from military officers on UFOs have come from France, a country in which these phenomena been actively investigated at an official level since 1977. In 1999, the Institute of Higher Studies for National Defense – a military think tank – prepared a ninety-page report detailing the results of an independent study on UFOs. The white paper, now commonly referred to as The COMETA Report, was compiled by a group of thirteen retired top-tier generals, admirals, and government scientists (including the former head of the French Tactical Air Force, General Bernard Norlain, and the former head of CNES [the French equivalent of NASA]), Andre Lebeau. The report documented the existence of unidentified flying objects and their implications for national security.[37] Copies were received by President Jacques Chirac and Prime Minister Lionel Jospin. The report concluded that, for a small percentage of UFO sightings, the extraterrestrial hypothesis was valid. It stated that some UFOs represent "completely unknown flying machines with exceptional performances that are guided by natural or artificial intelligence"[38] and noted that, although the extraterrestrial hypothesis "has not been categorically proven... strong presumptions exist in its favor."[39] The report then goes on to consider in detail the likely consequences of open extraterrestrial contact for politics, science, and religion.

Concerning the US government's historical UFO research, the CO-META report states:

> It is clear that the Pentagon has had, and probably still has, the greatest interest in concealing, as best it can, all of this research, which may, over time, cause the United States to hold a position of great supremacy over terrestrial adversaries, while giving it a considerable response capacity against a possible threat coming from space. Within this context, it is impossible for them to divulge the sources of this research and the goals pursued, because that could immediately point any possible rivals down the most beneficial avenues. Cover-ups and disinformation (both active as well as passive) still remain, under this hypothesis, an absolute necessity. Thus it would appear natural in the minds of U.S. military leaders, secrecy must be maintained as long as possible.[40]

In addition to the reams of official documents and scholarly white papers hinting at an extraterrestrial origin for UFOs, there are also many retired, and in some cases serving, government, military, and intelligence officials who have testified publicly to their own knowledge of UFOs and/or the intelligences behind them, and to the extreme secrecy surrounding these issues. Notable among these individuals are former CIA Director, Roscoe Hillenkoetter;[41] former Special Assistant to Deputy CIA Director Richard Helms, Victor Marchetti;[42] Senator Barry Goldwater;[43] Gemini astronaut, Col. Gordon Cooper;[44] former UK Chief of Defence Staff and Chairman of the NATO Military Committee, Admiral of the Fleet, The Lord Hill Norton;[45] billionaire financier,

Lawrence Rockefeller;[46] Apollo astronaut, Edgar Mitchell;[47] former Deputy Prime Minister of Canada, Paul Hellyer;[48] former Governor of Arizona, Fife Symington;[49] and Japanese Defense Minister, Shigiru Ishiba.[50] Presidential Counsellor, John Podesta, also has strongly hinted at a UFO cover-up. Speaking at the National Press Club in Washington DC in 2002, Podesta stated:

> I think it's time to open the books on questions that have remained in the dark on Government investigations of UFOs. It's time to find out what the truth really is that's out there. We ought to do it, really, because it's right; we ought to do it because the American people quite frankly *can* handle the truth; and we ought to do it because it's the law.[51]

And all of this is to say nothing of the literally millions of individuals from all walks of life and from every corner of the globe who, over the past six decades, have reported seeing not only structured craft unlike anything known to have been built by man, but also – and crucially – non-human entities in the vicinity of and inside said craft. It is the sheer number of UFO sightings reported worldwide that compels so many governments and militaries to continue to closely monitor the UFO phenomenon.

~ THE SAUCERS AND THE SILVER SCREEN ~

UFOs are naturally cinematic. These sleek, unearthly objects are seen performing remarkable aerial manoeuvres. They shimmer, they glow, they glide majestically. Though factual, UFOs are also the stuff of great science-fiction, and so it is no surprise that they have always sold well at the box-office. Recent years have seen an explosion in the popularity of the UFO subgenre, and audiences now stand little chance against what amounts to a full-scale alien invasion of our popular culture.

This book asks the reader to consider the effects of this invasion and to ponder cinema's transcendent power to both fictionalize and actualize its subject matter. Several years ago I was enjoying coffee with a friend. She had no particular interest in UFOs, no UFOlogical knowledge of which to speak. I asked her, "Have you heard of men in black?" I was referring to the factual historical accounts of UFO witnesses suffering intimidation by ominous black-clad mystery men in the days and weeks following their sightings. This very real phenomenon dates back to the late-1940s-early-1950s and has been the subject of many factual books over the decades. My friend replied immediately, "Of course, everyone's seen *Men in Black!*" Naturally, she was referring to the 1997 sci-fi blockbuster. Decades' worth of lived history had been consumed in its entirety by a 98 minute Will Smith movie. All my friend knew of men in black... was *Men in Black.* This is the power of cinema.

For my friend, a little-known reality had been fictionalized through its fantastical representation onscreen. And yet, cinema also has the power to actualize. *Men in Black* and other UFOlogical entertainment products have assumed permanent residency in the popular consciousness, and thus will always occupy at least some level of our perceived reality. This fictionalized/actualized dynamic will be examined more thoroughly in the conclusion of this book.

Whether or not they serve to fictionalize or actualize, what is clear is that movies of any genre inform our 'understanding' of the world around us. This was beautifully observed by the great British filmmaker Ken Russell, who said that "Hollywood fills the gaps in our knowledge of the world."[52] This is a profoundly true statement.

Hollywood as parasite

A great deal of Hollywood's UFO movie content has been informed directly by fact-based UFOlogical literature, events, and debate. In the chapters to follow, you will learn that Hollywood engages with UFO lore in parasitic fashion, with industry creatives latching onto and sucking-dry the rich veins of a ripe old subculture. This perspective contrasts with the popular assumption that the UFO subculture feeds on, and thrives as a result of images projected by the American entertainment industry (although this assumption is well-founded in certain cases).

With this in mind, *Silver Screen Saucers* also encourages the reader to ask: how has so much dense UFOlogical discourse – by its very nature fringe and subcultural – so successfully burrowed its way into Hollywood's populist narratives? Many in the UFO research community point to a "Hollywood UFO conspiracy" designed to acclimate us to an alien reality (and to subtly disinform us along the way). It's a scenario in which the US government exploits its close historical relationship with Hollywood by systematically seeding inside UFO information into entertainment media, slowly bringing us around to the truth of the phenomenon, or at least the truth as officialdom wishes us to perceive it. Others, meanwhile, suggest that Hollywood's UFO movies are merely the result of a natural cultural process driven by generic trends and stemming from a simple recognition among studio executives that, when it comes to the box-office, aliens sell like hotcakes. As we shall see, the truth of matter may lie somewhere in between both of these theories.

If you care about UFOs, you should care very much about UFO movies. Like it or not, they are the dominant cultural force shaping our perceptions of the phenomenon. A magical medium has distorted an underlying and mystifying truth. Cinema has moulded and simplified our expectations of how the phenomenon should manifest. And yet, at the same time, UFO movies have provided us with nuggets of truth – inspired as they are by a tangible conundrum sprung from our lived historical reality. The challenge is to separate the truth from the fiction, the fact from the fantasy. I have taken that challenge in this book with the certain knowledge that it cannot be met in full. The acceptance of the challenge alone is sufficient. To accept the challenge is to actively, rather than passively, engage with Hollywood's treatment of this multifaceted phenomenon. This is an essential task if ever we are to truly understand the particulars of our own UFO beliefs – beliefs which have been finely sculpted through both natural cultural process and deep political propaganda.

UFOs show no sign of leaving our skies, or our screens. They are here to stay. To read this book, then, is to anticipate your future and to understand that truth is often far stranger than the wildest Hollywood fiction.

CHAPTER TWO

A HOLLYWOOD UFO CONSPIRACY?

"Most Americans are content to accept Hollywood's message...
very few ever conduct any research to determine the truth."

– Paul Barry, former CIA Entertainment Liaison Officer

On 22 January 1958, the popular CBS television show *Armstrong Circle Theatre* presented an entire program dedicated to the subject of unidentified flying objects, titled, "UFO: Enigma of the Skies." Among the high-profile experts invited to speak on the show was retired US Navy Major Donald Keyhoe, Director of the National Investigations Committee on Aerial Phenomena (NICAP). Keyhoe was notable for his outspoken views on government secrecy surrounding the UFO phenomenon. Arguing against UFO reality on the program were astronomer and vehement UFO skeptic, Donald Menzel, and Air Force representative, Col. Spencer Whedon of the Air Technical Intelligence Center (ATIC). Their task should have been an easy one as the show's content had been scripted in advance by CBS in conjunction with the US Air Force (USAF), and all guests, especially Keyhoe, had been instructed to read their pre-approved material from a teleprompter.

When it came time for Keyhoe to speak, in frustration he veered from his script and stated to the nation, "And now I'm going to reveal something that has never been disclosed before..."[1] The rest of his announcement went unheard by television viewers. Unbeknownst to Keyhoe, his microphone had been cut by the station. He continued, "For the last six months, we have been working with a congressional committee investigating official secrecy about UFOs. If all the evidence we have given this committee is made public in open hearings, it will absolutely prove that the UFOs are real machines under intelligent control."[2]

After the show, CBS was inundated with calls and letters from viewers demanding to know why Keyhoe's audio had been cut, "Call it what you like," wrote one viewer, "but it appeared to be a very shocking display of censorship; and certainly offensive to the intelligence of the American public..."[3] Nine days later CBS admitted it had been subject to official censorship. In a letter to a disgruntled viewer dated 31 January 1958, CBS director of editing, Herbert A. Carlborg, stated:

> This program had been carefully cleared for security reasons. Therefore, it was the responsibility of this network to ensure performance in accordance with pre-determined security standards. Any indication that there would be a deviation might lead to statements that neither this network nor the individuals on the program were authorized to release.[4]

As will be shown in this chapter, the US government's historical efforts to manipulate UFO-themed media products extend considerably further than the Keyhoe incident and have affected the content of numerous film and TV products over a six-decade time span.

The US Department of Defense (DoD) has lent extensive cooperation to Hollywood for over sixty years in exchange for the right to edit scripts with the principal aim of encouraging the recruitment and retention of military personnel. However, in practice, the Pentagon's remit is more wide-ranging, as it routinely promotes its own, rather sanitized, version of US history, as with its removal of a key character in *Black Hawk Down* (2002) who in real life had been convicted of raping a twelve-year-old boy;[5] when it refused to cooperate on the 1998 movie *Counter Measures* (effectively shutting the production down) on the grounds that it did not want to remind the public of the Iran-Contra scandal;[6] or when it removed a joke about "losing Vietnam" in the James Bond film *Tomorrow Never Dies* (1997).[7]

Managing the Martians

When it comes to UFOs, the government's efforts at manipulating public perceptions are very well established. The prime example relates to the so-called 'Roswell Incident' of July 1947 when the Roswell Army Air Force (RAAF) hastily announced to the press its "capture" of a downed "flying saucer" on an isolated ranch in the New Mexico desert.[8] A few hours later, the RAAF changed its story to the effect that what had been recovered, in fact, was a common weather balloon.[9] The United States Air Force (USAF) was to change this story again in 1995 with the announcement that the "weather balloon" had been a top secret high-altitude spy balloon.[10] This story was then officially re-written in 1997 to account for a number of diminutive and seemingly non-human bodies numerous eyewitnesses claimed were recovered from the crash. The bodies, said the USAF, were human corpses, test dummies, or both.[11]

In light of the US military's persistent headache stemming from the UFO issue, it is hardly surprising that when filmmakers working on UFO-themed productions have sought cooperation from the Pentagon, the response typically has been dismissive: deny cooperation or else request script changes that delegitimize the study of the UFO phenomenon. This process of official delegitimization can be traced back to recommendations made in 1953 by the CIA-sponsored Robertson Panel – a group of leading scientists assembled by US government physicist, Howard Percy Robertson, for the task of reviewing the USAF's UFO files. The Robertson Panel concluded that UFOs did not pose a direct threat to national security. Still, the panel suggested that the USAF begin a "debunking" campaign employing the talents of psychiatrists, astronomers, and celebrities, with the goal of demystifying UFO reports.[12] Their formal recommendation was that, "The national security agencies take immediate steps to strip the Unidentified Flying Objects of the special status they have been given and the aura of mystery they have unfortunately acquired."[13]

The panel further stated that this should "be accomplished by mass media such as television [and] motion pictures..." making specific reference to Walt Disney.[14] The extent to which the Robertson Panel's recommendations were implemented is not entirely clear. However, even as late as 1966 the panel wielded a demonstrable influence over media representations of UFOs in the CBS TV broadcast of *UFOs: Friend, Foe, or Fantasy?* – an anti-UFO documentary narrated by Walter Cronkite. In a personal letter addressed to former Robertson Panel Secretary,

Frederick C. Durant, panel member, Dr. Thornton Page, confided to having "helped organize the documentary around the Robertson Panel conclusions,"[15] even though this was thirteen years after the panel had disbanded and despite the fact that he was personally sympathetic to the existence of flying saucers.

The mentality of the CIA-Robertson Panel was reflected in other productions during the 1950s, not least in the aforementioned Keyhoe CBS/USAF censorship case. Also notable is the 1956 docudrama, *Unidentified Flying Objects: The True Story of Flying Saucers*, which prompted the USAF to draw up contingency plans to counteract the anticipated fallout from the movie upon its release. The director of the USAF's official UFO investigations unit Project Blue Book, Captain George T. Gregory, was tasked with monitoring not only the movie's production process, but its public and critical reception. Believing the docudrama would stir up a "storm of public controversy," the USAF set about preparing a special case file that would debunk every saucer sighting examined and even went so far as to have three of its Blue Book officers provide "technical assistance" to the filmmakers in an effort to control content.[16]

Another case in this vein relates to a UFO-themed episode of the *Steve Canyon* TV show (1958–1959). Backed by Chesterfield Cigarettes and produced at Universal Studios with the full cooperation of the USAF, the NBC show chronicled the live-action exploits of Milton Caniff's famous comic strip character. The episode to which the USAF took objection, "Project UFO," saw Colonel Steve Canyon investigate a spate of flying saucer sightings reported to a local Air Force base. According to aviation historian, James H. Farmer, "This was an episode that the Air Force did not really want to be aired," because the UFO subject was "a hot potato."[17]

By the time the USAF had finished with the script, it was, according to Farmer, "pretty tame... compared to the earlier renditions."[18] In the episode as aired, the UFO sightings are attributed to a combination of hoax-induced hysteria and, in support of the USAF's original Roswell cover story, misidentifications of weather balloons. Producer, John Ellis, of the Milton Caniff Estate (which owns *Steve Canyon*) told me, "Every single page got re-written, and re-written, and re-written..."[19] David Haft, the show's producer, was more to the point in his recollection of the USAF's reaction when he submitted the first script draft for official approval, "Oh, oh, oh, oh! No, no, no, no!"[20] Haft also noted that the USAF had difficulty in deciding what was acceptable for broadcast.[21]

In one of the earliest drafts of "Project UFO," Steve Canyon speaks to his Commanding Officer, Colonel Jamison, in defense of a civilian UFO witness, "Why call him a jerk?" asks Canyon, "Seems to me like he acted like a pretty solid, clearheaded citizen..."[22] This dialogue was removed. Elsewhere in the draft, Canyon appears to be enthusiastic about flying saucers. At one point, when a fresh UFO report comes into the base from the local town, Canyon "Jumps to [his] feet, rushes to [the] door," and cries "This I gotta see!" before making "a hurried exit."[23] In the final scene as originally written, Canyon is actually seen opening a book on flying saucers, "and sits there quietly reading..."[24] This scene failed to make it into the final draft, and, in the version as aired, Canyon's excitement about UFOs is replaced with skepticism or plain indifference. An entire plot strand concerning the recovery and scientific analysis of what is initially suspected to be flying saucer debris (shades of Roswell) was also predictably removed. The draft included dialogue like, "That *thing* [flying saucer] dropped a small metal ball enclosing an electrical apparatus so intricate, so ingenious, nobody yet has been able to figure out its purpose," and, "the metal wouldn't respond to any of the standard tests." [25]

Despite the rewrites, the USAF insisted that the episode not be aired at all. "It got stuck on a shelf," Ellis explains in his *Steve Canyon* DVD commentary, "it was finished... but they held on until near the end of the series to air it."[26] Indeed, it was only through a last act of defiance on the part of the show's producers toward the end of its run in 1959 that the episode was screened at all.[27]

Government attitudes to UFO-themed film and TV productions were hostile even prior to the Robertson Panel's formation in 1953, as film historian Lawrence Suid observes: "The decision of whether the military should cooperate with a filmmaker depended not only on the way the military would be portrayed but also on whether the film differed from official Department of Defense positions on subjects like UFOs and alien life forms."[28]

The USAF did, however, take an interest in at least one UFO movie that had not even sought its cooperation. *The Flying Saucer* (1950) was America's very first UFO movie, and its director, Mikel Conrad, had claimed publicly while in production that he had managed to secure footage of a *real* flying saucer for use in his movie. In September 1949, Conrad told the *Ohio Journal Herald*, "I have scenes of the saucer landing, taking off, flying and doing tricks."[29] Shortly thereafter the director became the subject of a two-month official Air Force investigation.

Documents released under the Freedom of Information Act reveal that an agent of the Air Force Office of Special Investigations was dispatched not only to interrogate Conrad about his claims but also to attend the first private screening of his completed film. Unsurprisingly, Conrad's story was soon revealed as an elaborate marketing scam designed to promote what was, in reality, a tedious and uneventful movie.[30] The Conrad case is significant for its demonstration of the high degree of seriousness with which the USAF regarded the issue of media representations of the burgeoning UFO phenomenon.

That same year (1950) the USAF refused to cooperate with RKO pictures on *The Thing from Another World* (which was released in 1951). In a Pentagon meeting with the film's producer, Edward Lasker, USAF officers explained that they had just spent half-a-million-dollars proving that flying saucers did not exist and asked, "Why should we help you make a picture about one?" They emphasized that "the Air Force will not participate in any activity that could be interpreted as a perpetuation of the flying saucer hoax."[31] The "half-a-million-dollars" comment refers to the USAF's Project Grudge, an official UFO-debunking effort which ran throughout 1949, and which would reincarnate from 1952 to 1969 as Project Blue Book.[32]

The Day the Earth Stood Still (1951), which depicted a flying saucer landing in Washington DC, was similarly turned down by the USAF, although the Pentagon ultimately provided limited assistance through the National Guard, because, it said, in the event of an alien invasion, the Armed Services would indeed defend the nation.[33] In other words, although there were clear attempts throughout the 1950s to carefully monitor, and in some cases, impede the production of UFO-themed entertainment products, there was at least some flexibility built into the Pentagon's criteria for cooperating on such products.

Close encounters with the Pentagon

In 1969, the USAF closed Project Blue Book, its confused and half-hearted study of UFOs, concluding that sightings did not represent a threat to national security nor technological developments or principles beyond the range of modern scientific knowledge.[34]

Despite the closure of Blue Book, the government's negative attitude toward UFO movies and TV shows remained unchanged into the 1970s and beyond. In 1976, several branches of the government refused to cooperate on Steven Spielberg's UFO epic *Close Encounters of the Third Kind* (1977), the script for which drew heavily from factual UFO literature and which Spielberg had stated repeatedly was "science speculation," not science fiction.

Major Sidney Shaw of the National Guard Bureau in Washington wrote to Columbia Pictures:

> We have reviewed the script and believe it would be inappropriate for the Air Force or National Guard Bureau to support the production. In 1969 the USAF completed a study which concluded there is no evidence concerning the existence of UFOs. We have not been involved in UFOs since that study other than answering queries about the study. The proposed film leaves the distinct impression that UFOs, in fact, do exist. It also involves the government and military in a big cover up of the existence of UFOs. These two points are counter to Air Force and Department of Defense policy and make support to the production inappropriate.[35]

NASA also rejected the chance to cooperate on *Close Encounters*, even though the space agency had in the past been flexible over its willingness to cooperate with films that showed them in an unflattering light, including *Marooned* (1969) and even the NASA conspiracy movie *Capricorn One* (1977).[36] Not only did NASA refuse its cooperation to Spielberg, it even sought to convince the director not to make the film at all. In a 1978 interview for the journal *Cinema Papers*, Spielberg said:

> I really found my faith [in UFO reality] when I heard that the government was opposed to the film. If NASA took the time to write me a 20 page letter, then I knew there must be something happening. I had wanted cooperation from them, but when they read the script they got very angry and felt that it was a film that would be dangerous. I think they mainly wrote the letter because *Jaws* convinced so many people around the world that there were sharks in toilets and bathtubs, not just in the oceans and rivers. They were afraid the same kind of epidemic would happen with UFOs.[37]

An era of greater flexibility

By the 1980s it was at least possible for a film to mention UFOs without the DoD trying to stifle it, starting with the 1986 remake of *Invaders from Mars*, which was granted full cooperation from the DoD. This cooperation, however, was based on the fact that the film did not draw directly from established UFO mythology, that the traditional "flying saucer" motif received minimal screen time, and because the film presented positive images of the US military. Major Fred Peck of the Pentagon's Los Angeles Public Affairs Office helped the film's director, Tobe Hooper, visualise how Marines might actually react in the event of an invasion. Peck commented that "Marines have no qualms about killing Martians" – a line that made it into the film.[38] Peck also helped Hooper identify Marine reservists to constitute the cinematic leatherneck unit and recruited a retired public affairs officer, Captain Dale Dye, to prepare the extras.[39]

In the mid-1990s, in a brief return to its old ways, the DoD denied its cooperation to *Independence Day* (1996), although depictions of UFOs were not the Pentagon's only concern over the movie. In fact, Tom Mc-Collum of the Army Public Affairs Office in Los Angeles submitted a long list of technical changes to producer Dean Devlin. [40] Most notable among its list of recommended changes was the request that any government connection to Area 51 or to Roswell be eliminated from the film.[41] Major Nancy LaLuntas of the US Marines' Los Angeles Public Affairs Office stated explicitly that the Pentagon would not support a film that perpetuates the Roswell "myth" and added that the "DoD cannot hide info from [the] President (i.e. aliens and [a space]ship in custody)."[42]

In contrast to its disapproval of *Independence Day*, the DoD had no qualms about cooperating with Steven Spielberg on his 2005 remake of *War of the Worlds*. However, as was the case with the 1986 version of *Invaders from Mars*, Spielberg's movie did not draw in any readily identifiable way from modern UFO mythology as its narrative featured no government conspiracy, no UFO-related terminology (such as "Area 51"), no references to historical UFO events (such as Roswell), nor indeed, did it feature any UFOs in the conventional sense – only the 'tripods' of H. G. Wells' source material. So, while *War of the Worlds* projected to audiences a vivid *vérité* rendering of what a post-9/11 alien invasion might look like in reality, crucially for the Pentagon it also provided a recruitment-friendly depiction of the professionalism and sheer fire power with which the US military would respond to such an invasion. [43] Spielberg, it seemed, had learned from his 'close encounter' with the Pentagon some two decades prior and was now savvy to the fact that plotlines involving a pre-existing DoD cover-up of UFOs are strictly off-limits for filmmakers wishing to gain Pentagon support.

Two years later, in 2007, the DoD again saw fit to lend extensive support to Spielberg for his production of *Transformers*,[44] despite the film drawing extensively (albeit obliquely) from UFO mythology. Like *War of the Worlds*, however, although it dealt with the subject of aliens, *Transformers* was unlikely to have prompted a wave of flying saucer sightings as it contained no UFOs, per se, only giant transforming robots.

Robots in disguise

Directed by Michael Bay and produced by Steven Spielberg, *Transformers* was based on the popular Saturday-morning cartoon series of the same name (1984–1987), itself based on the 'must have' transforming robot toys of the 1980s, manufactured by Hasbro. While not about UFOs, per se, *Transformers* is loaded with UFOlogical references and, having grossed in excess of $700 million worldwide,[45] can be regarded as a significant contributor to the cinematic popularization of UFO-lore.

The film's main protagonist is Sam Witwicky (Shia LaBeouf), whose typical middle-class white American teenage life is thrown into turmoil when his fate becomes intertwined with that of a race of alien robots (the Transformers) who for centuries have waged a civil war on their home planet for possession of the "AllSpark" – a mystical artifact that gave rise to their species and which is capable of granting sentience to any electronic or mechanical object.

In an opening monologue by Optimus Prime, leader of the noble 'Autobots,' we learn that the AllSpark eventually was "lost to the far reaches of space" and that the warring robots scattered across the galaxy in an attempt to reclaim it. Megatron, leader of the evil 'Deceptacons,' succeeds in tracing the AllSpark to Earth, but crash-lands in the Arctic Circle before he can reclaim it. Succumbing to the sub-zero temperatures, Megatron lies dormant in an icy tomb until the late 19th Century when his body is discovered by a team of explorers led by Sam's great, great grandfather. Eventually, Megatron and the Allspark fall into the hands of the US government, where they remain in secret until the present day. Soon, both Autobots and Deceptacons arrive on Earth in pursuit of the AllSpark disguising themselves as human technology (cars, jets, helicopters, etc.) The ensuing 120 minutes see cities lain to waste as the allied Autobots and US military do battle with the Deceptacons.

The DoD had a deep-rooted involvement in the production process of *Transformers*. The USAF provided the director, Michael Bay, with billions-of-dollars' worth of state-of-the-art hardware for use in the movie, including the F-117 Nighthawk and, in its first Hollywood showcasing, the F-22 Raptor fighter. The DoD also granted Bay access to Holloman Air Force Base, [46] the highly sensitive location of an alleged real-life alien landing in 1971, a dramatic reconstruction of which was featured in the 1974 Pentagon-backed documentary *UFOs: Past Present and Future* (discussed later in this chapter).

The DoD saw *Transformers* as a perfect opportunity to bolster the image of the US military, which it achieved by exercising its considerable contractual power throughout the film's production. As such, the onscreen military is portrayed forcefully as a heroic and righteous institution comprised of decent men and women armed with the most sophisticated weaponry on Earth. Glittering PR from Hollywood, though, may not have been the sole motivating factor in the DoD's decision to grant the movie its coveted 'full cooperation.'

With numerous governments worldwide officially still engaged in the UFO debate, it is logical to assume that the Pentagon continues to monitor and, where possible, mould its media image in relation to the tricky issue of UFOs. In this sense, *Transformers* bears careful scrutiny. In one particularly self-serving scene, the US military is absolved of complicity in what we learn has been a decades-long cover-up of alien visitations. Blame for the conspiracy is instead placed at the doorstep of the extra-constitutional Sector 7 – a "special access division of the government" which has been concealing its "top secret" alien research since 1934 within "Special Access Projects." Crucially, the cover-up has been conducted without the knowledge or consent of the Secretary of Defense (played by Jon Voight), who is outraged when the truth is finally revealed to him, "And you didn't think the United States military might need to know that you're keeping a hostile alien robot frozen in the basement?"

The *Transformers* sequels, *Revenge of the Fallen* (2009)[47] and *Dark of the Moon* (2011),[48] also received extensive support from the DoD, and, in the case of the latter, NASA as well.

The DoD also threw its weight behind the alien invasion movie *Battle: Los Angeles* (2011), which received extensive cooperation from the US Marine Corps. In this case the filmmakers were provided with hardware and personnel for use onscreen and were granted access to military installations including Barksdale Air Force Base and Camp Pendleton Marine Corps Base.[49]

Central to the movie's sophisticated viral marketing campaign was a poster showing an authentic photograph of the real-life 'Battle of Los Angeles' of 1942 – one of the earliest and best documented UFO cases in modern history in which at least one saucer-shaped object hovered silently for several hours over Los Angeles on the night of February 24–25, drawing heavy artillery fire from the US Army, to no apparent effect.[50]

Despite its UFOlogical marketing campaign, *Battle: Los Angeles* contains no references whatsoever to the real-life case to which it owes its name, nor to any other aspect of UFO lore. As in most Pentagon-backed UFO movies, history is effectively re-written, giving the onscreen US military a fresh slate in the face of an alien invasion. When the ETs arrive, the Marines have no secret UFO documents or case files to refer to; no historical framework for understanding this new cosmic threat. The desired message seems to be, when it comes to UFOs, the Pentagon is as clueless as Joe Public. Still, the Marines make short work of their interstellar adversaries and naturally go to great lengths to ensure the safety of all civilians as LA crumbles around them. In one particularly subtle scene, a large billboard in the background reads, "SUPPORT OUR TROOPS!"

In the Navy

The following year saw the DoD combat ETs on the high seas as the US Navy leant its full support to *Battleship* – a big screen adaptation of the classic Hasbro board game, but with added aliens. *Battleship* was all about turning cinemagoers into sailors, and not since *Top Gun* (1986) had a movie been geared so brazenly toward naval recruitment. In a *Battleship* promotional featurette (also made with cooperation from the Navy), director Peter Berg said, "I have a good relationship with the Department of Defense and they know that I love soldiers and I respect the warrior spirit of any soldier... As a result, they've opened up their doors to us in fairly unprecedented ways."[51]

The fingerprints of Pentagon staffers can be found on almost every page of the movie's risible script. In one of the earlier scenes, the movie's main protagonist, Alex Hopper, tells a young boy curious about naval hardware, "battleships are great" but destroyers are "just awesome!" Throughout *Battleship's* run-time, the entire process of combat – from preparation of weaponry and selection of targets, to the devastation the Navy inflicts upon its enemy – is techno-fetishized by Berg's leering camera.

Further evidence of DoD script input can be seen in the immediate aftermath of the aliens' first strike when a sailor shrieks, "It's the North Koreans, I'm tellin' ya!" Russia and China are also considered as possible culprits – the Pentagon never missing an opportunity to paint a target on those countries it considers a threat to national security. Similar ground was trodden in *Transformers: Dark of the Moon*, in which the Human/Autobot alliance busies itself by dispatching black-ops military teams around the world to assist in solving human problems, with the world being represented onscreen by "the Middle-East," and "human problems" taking the form of an "illegal nuclear site" in Iran.

But the true enemy in *Battleship* is, of course, extraterrestrial in nature. And, in backing this movie, by officially shaping and approving its content, the DoD implicitly supports the message that potential extraterrestrial life poses a grave threat to US national security. To be clear, while aliens in Pentagon-backed movies undoubtedly *do* represent perceived terrestrial threats (North Korea, Iran, etc.), they are not merely cinematic allegories. As humanity now moves rapidly closer to answering the question "Are we alone in the universe?" hawkish eyes at the Pentagon no doubt view the notion of open alien contact with considerable suspicion and concern (justified or not) – just as shareholders in the defense industry surely view it with glee. Without a permanent threat to national security, America's multi-billion-dollar war machine is without purpose. From the perspective of the military-industrial-complex, providing support to Hollywood's UFO movies is as much about encouraging public fear of potential alien life as it is about drumming-up fear of human adversaries.

It should be noted that *Battleship's* director, Peter Berg, is fully aware of the reality of the UFO phenomenon, having co-starred in the 1993 movie, *Fire in the Sky*, which was based on the famous Travis Walton abduction experience of 1975 (see Chapter Five). Berg and his co-stars spent time with Walton during the shoot and heard the disturbing details of his unearthly encounter straight from Walton's mouth.[52] Despite Berg's knowledge of the UFO phenomenon, and in keeping with previous Pentagon-backed UFO movies, The US military as depicted in *Battleship* has no prior knowledge of ET visitation.

Demonstrably, then, the US government and military have acted to influence the content of UFO-themed entertainment media products since the earliest years of the phenomenon. For the most part, these actions have been in line with the CIA Robertson Panel's officially stated policy that UFOs are essentially non-existent and therefore should be debunked and demystified through media channels. Still, in recent years, the DoD has seen fit to lend its support to a small handful of UFO movies – notably those which downplay UFO conspiracy theories while emphasizing America's military prowess, thereby encouraging recruitment among cinemagoers. In the case of the *Transformers* franchise, the Pentagon provided support first and foremost for traditional military propaganda purposes, but its close involvement in the scriptwriting process here also seems to have been exploited to cover its own back in regard to historical UFO secrecy and to otherwise twist UFO lore in its favor.[53] The same can be said of *Battle: Los Angeles* and *Battleship*, both of which portrayed the US military as cartoonishly heroic and more than capable of defending Earth from an alien attack, despite the onscreen Pentagon's total lack of history with UFOs and extraterrestrial visitation.

Do such actions on the part of the US government constitute a "conspiracy"? Technically, no, as the interactions thus far described between the Pentagon, NASA, and Hollywood are entirely legal. The relationship between these institutions is a public one, albeit it seldom discussed by mainstream media. The DoD certainly cannot be accused of attempting to conceal its presence in Hollywood – its Entertainment Liaison Offices are located on Wilshire Boulevard, just a stone's throw from the heart of Tinseltown. It is there, on the 12th floor of the Oppenheimer Tower, that dedicated liaison teams from every branch of the US military – Army, Navy, Marine Corps, Air Force and Coast Guard – are immersed in a fast-flowing stream of Hollywood scripts, reading each one carefully and suggesting alterations as they see fit.[54]

~ THE HIDDEN HAND ~

So, what of the flipside of the coin? Is there any substance to the popular idea that the government has been using Hollywood to *encourage* us to believe in alien visitation through entertainment media? The short answer is yes, *some*. However, proof of a UFO acclimation agenda remains elusive as the entire theory rests on only a small handful of testimonies and cases.

The glittering robes of entertainment

The filmmaker and journalist, Linda Moulton Howe, claims to have been told by Air Force Intelligence officers in 1983 that the 1951 movie *The Day the Earth Stood Still*, which depicted an alien landing in Washington D.C., was "inspired by the CIA," and was "one of the first government tests of public reaction to such an event."[55]

At first glance, Howe's testimony would seem at odds with the fact that *The Day the Earth Stood Still* had been denied cooperation from the USAF, but it is well known that the intelligence community and the military do not always work in harmony. Moreover, UFO secrecy is heavily compartmentalized, with information being shared strictly on a 'need-to-know' basis. If the CIA was indeed testing public reaction to UFO reality through cinema in the early-1950s, it is entirely possible that the existence of such an operation was not shared with the USAF at that time (but that certain individuals within USAF intelligence might learn of it later).

If *The Day the Earth Stood Still* was really a CIA test of public reaction to open alien contact – possibly containing classified information about UFOs – then the Agency would have needed at least one trustworthy asset working on the production in a position of creative influence. With this in mind, it is notable that the screenwriter of *The Day the Earth Stood Still*, Edmund H. North, was a Major in the Army Signal Corps prior to being selected by 20th Century Fox to pen the script.[56] During his time in the Corps, North had been in charge of training and educational documentaries, and later established himself as a Hollywood scribe of patriotic war films including *Sink the Bismarck!* (1960) and *Submarine X-1* (1968), as well as *Patton* (1970), for which he received an Oscar – all of which raises the possibility that he maintained an official or quasi-official role in the government's cinematic propaganda campaigns throughout his career.

More notably, the man responsible for overseeing the production of *The Day the Earth Stood Still*, 20th Century Fox Production Chief, Darryl Zanuck, was himself in charge of an Army Signal Corps documentary unit during the Second World War[57] and was at the time of the movie's production a board member of the National Committee for Free Europe (NCFE), which was established by the CIA in 1949 ostensibly as a private anti-Soviet organization. As a star member of the NCFE, Zanuck was directly associated with the organization's executive committee, which included future CIA Director, Allen Dulles, and future US President, Dwight D. Eisenhower.[58] In 1951, when the *The Day the Earth Stood Still* was being written, produced, and released, the President of the NCFE was General Charles Douglas (C.D.) Jackson, who served as Deputy Chief of the Psychological Warfare Division of the Supreme Headquarters Allied Expeditionary Force (SHAEF) during WWII, and would later be appointed as special advisor to President Eisenhower on Psychological Warfare. He was, in the words of historian, Frances Stoner Saunders, "one of the most influential covert strategists in America."[59] Jackson referred to Darryl Zanuck as being amongst a group of Hollywood "friends," including Cecil B. DeMille, Jack Warner, and Walt Disney – those whom the government could rely upon "to insert in their scripts and in their action the right ideas with the proper subtlety."[60]

With the above in mind, and in light of what USAF intelligence officers allegedly asserted to Linda Moulton Howe about *The Day the Earth Stood Still* being a CIA test of public reaction to open alien contact, a memo from Darryl Zanuck to the movie's producer, Julian Blaustein, (also a veteran of the Army Signal Corps) and screenwriter, Edmund North, makes for fascinating reading. In the memo, dated 10 August 1950, Zanuck stresses that that every effort should be made to "compel the audience to completely *accept* [emphasis in original] this story as something that could possibly happen in the not too distant future."[61] Zanuck placed particular emphasis on the now iconic scene in which the alien Klaatu lands his flying saucer in Washington, D.C. before emerging to address the public. Zanuck advised Blaustein and North to "treat it as realistically as you possibly can,"[62] even suggesting that the scene play out documentary style, "You should suddenly hear radio programs being interrupted with startling flash announcements from Washington, New York, Los Angeles, etc. The whole nation is 'listening in.' This should be dramatized like the opening of a documentary film."[63] The audience must "'accept' our entire project,"[64] said Zanuck.

The script for *The Day the Earth Stood Still* was finally locked and approved by Darryl Zanuck on 21 February 1951. Virtually all of his script suggestions were followed. As a final thought on the movie in the context of propaganda and persuasion, the reader might find some significance in the following statement made by Zanuck in 1943 during his time in the Signal Corps: "If you have something worthwhile to say, dress it up in the glittering robes of entertainment and you will find a ready market... without entertainment, no propaganda film is worth a dime."[65]

Camouflage through limited disclosure

Other covert tests of public reaction to UFO reality apparently were made during the 1950s. While speaking at a conference for the Mutual UFO Network (MUFON) in 1979, the famed Oscar-winning Disney animator, Ward Kimball, claimed that the USAF had approached Walt Disney himself in the mid-1950s, requesting his cooperation on a documentary that would help acclimate the public to extraterrestrial reality. Kimball knew this because, as one of Disney's most trusted animators, he was directly involved in the project. In exchange for Disney's cooperation, said Kimball, the USAF would supply the animation giant with real UFO footage for exclusive use in his documentary. According to Kimball, Disney accepted the deal and began work immediately on the USAF project, which would not have been unusual considering Disney's established relationship with the US government: not only was Walt a "friend" of Eisenhower's chief propagandist C. D. Jackson in the early-mid-1950s, he also made around 80 animated propaganda shorts for the military during WWII.

While Disney waited patiently for the USAF to provide the UFO footage, his animators (Kimball among them) produced conceptual designs of what an alien might look like. However, the offer of the UFO footage was eventually withdrawn, provoking Kimball himself to challenge the official military liaison for the project – a USAF Colonel who told him that "there was indeed plenty of UFO footage, but that neither [Kimball], nor anyone else was going to get access to it."[66] Needless to say, the project was abandoned and forgotten by all but the few who had worked on it.

Indirect support for Kimball's claims was provided by Philip Corso, a retired Lieutenant Colonel and former Chief of the Pentagon's Foreign Technology desk. In his controversial 1997 book, *The Day After Roswell*, Corso claimed that the production of flying saucer movies was actively encouraged by government-led UFO study groups during the 1950s. The goal, claimed Corso, was to simultaneously fictionalize UFOs (through their association with fantastical Hollywood entertainment) and actualize them in the mind of the viewer, thereby acclimating cinemagoers to UFO reality and politically manipulating their perceptions of the phenomenon in the process. Corso referred to this strategy as "camouflage through limited disclosure." Corso said he and his colleagues never hid anything from anybody. "We just camouflaged it. It was always there [in documents, books, TV shows and movies], people just didn't know what to look for or recognise it for what it was when they found it. And they found it over and over again."[67]

Intriguing though they are, the testimonies of Howe, Kimball, and Corso are just that – testimonies. They are not supported by hard evidence. Still, other cases of official assistance on pro-UFO/alien movies are more substantial. For the 1982 blockbuster *ET: The Extra-Terrestrial*, for example, Producer, Kathleen Kennedy, and director, Steven Spielberg, brainstormed with NASA scientists on the likely official response to an alien's arrival. This collaboration shaped sections of the movie, including the scene where NASA personnel enter a sealed-off suburban home in search of E.T. The producers also asked NASA what sort of planet E.T. might call home. According to Kennedy, NASA suggested a "little green planet" populated by "little mushroom farmers." E.T.'s biology reflected this scenario, says Kennedy, as the now iconic alien "was closer to a plant than a biological human being."[68]

Cooperation in this case was likely offered as a low-level courtesy due to the fact that the film's representation of NASA was generally favorable – the professionalism and humanity of the space agency's personnel shining through even in the face an extraterrestrial bio-hazard – and because its story was concerned not so much with the UFO phenomenon as with the fantastical friendship between a boy and an alien. Despite NASA's assistance, it is notable that Spielberg was again denied technical support by the USAF, which clearly viewed *E.T.* as another *Close Encounters*. According to military film historian, Laurence Suid, "The Air Force refused to cooperate [on *E.T.*] because it says there is no such thing as flying saucers and so could not go against its policy."[69]

Strangely, the USAF had not adhered to this anti-UFO policy a decade prior to *E.T.* for the production of *UFOs: Past, Present and Future* (1974), a major documentary feature that gave very serious consideration to the extraterrestrial hypothesis and which stands today as the most significant case of government involvement in a UFO-themed production.

UFOs: Past, Present and Future

In 1972, filmmaker, Robert Emenegger, formerly Vice President and Creative Director at Grey Advertising, and his producing partner, Allan Sandler, were encouraged by the USAF to make a major documentary feature about the UFO phenomenon. Emenegger told me that his partner "had very strange connections" for a producer and that he thought Sandler "did things for the CIA, and maybe even the FBI... they all seemed to work together."[70] Emenegger himself was ideally suited to an assignment of this nature; as a student at UCLA in the mid-1950s his thesis examined "The Influence of Motion Pictures on Public Behavior," with the young Emenegger being especially interested in cinema "as an instrument of propaganda."[71] Additionally, Emenegger had spent a number of years working for the United States Information Agency (or USIA – a politically correct name given the government's long-running propaganda agency). During his time with the USIA, Emenegger developed a close professional relationship with its then Deputy Director of Motion Picture and Television, Bruce Herschensohn.[72]

In 1972, while Emenegger and Sandler were gearing up for the production of their USAF UFO documentary, Herschensohn left the USIA to serve full-time at the White House as an assistant to President Nixon. Emenegger had also performed duties for Nixon. In December 1968, the then President-elect wrote to Emenegger seeking his "active participation and assistance" in finding "exceptional individuals" worthy of appointment in his incoming administration. Nixon referred to Emenegger as "a leader" and "in a position to know and recommend... the best minds in America."[73]

Emenegger described to me how he was briefed on the UFO project at Norton Air Force Base in "a clean room used by the CIA... so there was no way anyone could eavesdrop on us."[74] In an offer similar to that made to Walt Disney some twenty years earlier, the USAF promised Emenegger real UFO footage, this time allegedly showing a UFO landing at Holloman Air Force Base in 1971 and the subsequent face-to-face meeting between alien visitors and delegates of the US government. Emenegger was skeptical but was assured by the USAF that the footage existed, and was genuine.

While he waited for the footage to materialize, Emenegger and his crew continued with their wider production research, for which they were given unprecedented access to DoD facilities, including the Pentagon. Emenegger was even granted time with high-ranking military officers apparently well-versed in UFO-related matters, among them Col. William Coleman, a former spokesman for Project Blue Book, and Col. George Weinbrenner, then head of Foreign Technology at Wright Patterson Air Force Base – the location where alien materials and bodies allegedly recovered from the 1947 Roswell crash are said to have been stored.

But who in the Air Force would sign off on such a controversial project? Emenegger put this question to Pentagon spokesman Col. Coleman, who informed him that "the Secretary of the Air Force gave us the order to cooperate."[75] Thus, in an unprecedented move, the Air Force, Army, and Navy gave their full backing to a UFO-themed production – so too did NASA, who provided Emenegger's research team with previously unreleased photographs of what appeared to be UFOs in space taken by Gemini astronauts. "We had carte blanche to go anywhere, ask any questions," Emenegger told me, "there were no restrictions put on us."[76] Emenegger even claims to have been shown "top secret" footage shot at Vandenberg Air Force Base which showed two UFOs "playfully running behind" a US missile.

After months of shooting, Emenegger's documentary was complete, save for one crucial ingredient – the much-hyped alien landing footage. At the eleventh hour, the USAF withdrew its permission for use of the material; the political climate had changed, it said, and was now deemed inappropriate due to the Watergate scandal which had recently broken. "I felt like we had egg on our face," Emenegger told me. "I felt cheated that we were not allowed to see this film. It was taken back to the Pentagon... I stupidly expected to have this footage, which would have been earth-shattering." Today, Emenegger seems as baffled by the whole affair as anyone, "Were we had? Were we being used?" he asks.[77]

Emenegger's Golden-Globe-nominated documentary, *UFOs: Past, Present and Future*, was finally released in 1974 and was ground-breaking in its extensive use of information provided by the DoD. In addition to the aforementioned photographs from NASA, it featured sit-down interviews with the former heads of Project Blue Book, and footage shot inside the Pentagon of Col. Coleman talking open-mindedly about the Extraterrestrial Hypothesis. In the absence of the landing footage, Emenegger was forced to include an animated reconstruction of the event as described to him by the USAF, complete with artistic renderings of the alleged aliens. The documentary presented the incident as "one that might happen in the future, or perhaps could have happened already."

But the promised landing footage wasn't entirely absent, at least not according to Emenegger. During the dramatic reconstruction of the alleged landing, the observant viewer can catch a few frames of what appears to be a genuine, self-luminescent Unidentified Flying Object descending slowly in the distance against the backdrop of Holloman's surrounding landscape. These frames, Emenegger claims, were taken from the original landing footage and authorised by the USAF during the editing stage for use in his completed documentary.

Echoes of Emenegger's deal with the DoD would resound decades later in the production of *Transformers* (2007) when director Michael Bay was granted the rare privilege of shooting scenes of his alien movie at the Pentagon. The DoD even threw open the gates to Holloman Air Force Base.

Although Emenegger's documentary was green-lit by the Secretary of the Air Force, the roots of the project likely lead back to Langley, Virginia, and to the CIA. Emenegger revealed to me that it was his production partner, the CIA-connected Allan Sandler, who brought the project to him in the first place; and let us not forget that Emenegger received his project briefing at Norton Air Force Base in a CIA "clean room." Furthermore, Emenegger told me that a "CIA courier" named Dick Beske shadowed him and his crew throughout his documentary's entire production process. Beske was "always hanging around us," said Emenegger, "observing."[78]

Richard 'Dick' Beske is today a member of the steering group for Veteran Intelligence Officers for Sanity (VIPS), an organization comprised of current and former officials of the United States Intelligence Community, including some from the Central Intelligence Agency (CIA), the U.S. State Department's Intelligence Bureau, and the Defense Intelligence Agency (DIA). VIPs was formed in January 2003 as a "coast-to-coast enterprise" to protest the use of faulty intelligence in the lead-up to the US-led invasion of Iraq.[79]

Race to... Cheyenne Mountain?

Perhaps the most surprising case of government involvement in a Hollywood UFO movie in recent years is that of *Race to Witch Mountain*, which seems to have received extensive support from the CIA, despite its plot drawing extensively from UFO mythology (with references both to Area 51 and Roswell) and its presentation of a sinister government UFO cover-up.

Working within the narrative constraints of the film's previous incarnation, *Escape to Witch Mountain* (1975), director, Andy Fickman, a self-described UFO enthusiast, took pride in infusing his remake with as many elements as possible drawn directly from UFO literature.[80]

Although the majority of the film's UFOlogical content came from Fickman, at least some of it seems to have been the result of CIA input.

In a highly unusual production arrangement, Fickman claims he and his crew were closely assisted by an active employee of the CIA whose advice extended to designing the alien writing seen in the UFO during the film's climactic scene. Fickman is unwilling to name the advisor, but claims he is a former Air Force Technical Intelligence Officer, that he had been "very active in Hollywood," and, that he "had a lot of connections in the computer world and [experience in] satellite imagery."[81] Fickman said of his CIA man:

> All of the on-camera alien language in terms of their spaceship and everything – that was all designed by him in the sense [of what] the mathematics of communication would be, so you know... there would be a similar mathematical equation that the government probably has if they were to ever come across an alien race. So a lot of the things we ended up using were things he was bringing to me... and the next thing you know, that's what I had on screen.[82]

The advisor also recommended that certain UFO-themed content be removed from the script, "There were things we got rid of in the script that he was just trying to follow logic [on] from a protocol standpoint," said Fickman, although the director would not elaborate on the nature of the changes made.[83]

Fickman further claims to have had an active Air force Colonel present on set throughout the shoot – again as a technical advisor. It was with this Colonel, along with the CIA advisor, that Fickman was afforded a visit to NORAD's sensitive Cheyenne Mountain facility in 2008, where the director claims his team spent twelve hours taking photographs and talking with on-duty military officers, including the heads of NORAD. "We wanted our *Witch Mountain* to resemble what NORAD and Cheyenne Mountain look like inside," he said, adding, "We took a thousand photos and then by the time they released us into the wilderness maybe we had three hundred that had been approved for us to somewhat copy [for production design purposes]."[84]

The CIA, for its part, claims to have had no involvement in *Race to Witch Mountain*. In an email to the author, CIA Office of Public Affairs media spokeswoman Paula Weiss said, "To the best of our collective knowledge in the media relations office, we did not provide any technical or other support to this production."[85]

Fickman was puzzled by the CIA's denial. Questioned by the author on whether or not his CIA man could have been a retired operative acting in a private capacity (as is the case with a number of CIA advisors in Hollywood) the director replied, "There's no way we would have had what we had, had he not been an active CIA employee..."[86] Fickman claims he relied heavily on the influence wielded by his CIA man: "Nothing happened at NORAD without him flashing his card and making his calls."[87]

Fickman believes it was due to the fact that his military and intelligence advisors were secured "through back door channels" that his production was granted such extraordinary access to the inner-workings of the national security apparatus, but he insists there was no hidden agenda behind the US government's uncharacteristic generosity: "All of a sudden I was in places that I don't know I would have been had I gone through normal channels. I don't think there was anything abnormal about what they were doing, I just think it was [that] phone calls were being made and doors were sort of opening."[88]

Could it be there really is a government agenda to acclimate us to UFO reality? If so, then, on the face of it, those behind this agenda would seem to have been working in direct opposition to the Pentagon, which clearly has worked hard over the years to keep UFOs out of the popular imagination and/or to distance itself from UFO conspiracy theories onscreen. But perhaps there has long been a separate, more sophisticated power group working through the national security apparatus, one whose Hollywood agenda transcends the polarized dynamic of 'debunk vs. acclimate'? Perhaps this power group has been behind such movies as the original *The Day the Earth Stood Still*, the aborted Kimball/Disney documentary of the 1950s, the Robert Emenegger documentary of the 1970s, and many others in between. The UFO subject has always been a divisive one, even within the corridors of power, and it would be a mistake to assume that all branches of the government and military see eye-to-eye on this thorny issue. If there is a 'hidden hand' tweaking and seeding Hollywood's UFO-themed products, it could well belong to a group or agency so secretive that its very existence is unknown to the public – a quasi-governmental/quasi-private entity accountable only to itself. Though many in the UFO research community consider it likely that such a group exists, it is at this point unnecessary for us to enter quite so deeply into speculative territory. For now, the agency that demands our attention is the CIA.

Lights, camera, covert action: the CIA in Hollywood

The Pentagon's activities in Tinseltown, although morally dubious and barely advertised, have at least occurred within the public domain. This much cannot be said of the CIA's dealings with Hollywood, which, until recently, went largely unacknowledged by the Agency. In 1996, the CIA announced with little fanfare the dry remit of its newly established Entertainment Liaison Office, headed by veteran operative Chase Brandon. As part of its new stance, the CIA would now openly collaborate on Hollywood productions, supposedly in a strictly "advisory" capacity, in order to encourage more favorable representations of the Agency onscreen, thereby boosting recruitment.[89]

The Agency's decision to work publicly with Hollywood was preceded by the 1991 "Task Force Report on Greater CIA Openness," compiled by CIA Director Robert Gates' newly appointed 'Openness Task Force,' which secretly debated, ironically, whether the Agency should be less secretive. Astonishingly, the now declassified report acknowledges that the CIA "has relationships with reporters from every major wire service, newspaper, news weekly, and television network in the nation," and the authors of the report note that this helped them "turn some 'intelligence failure' stories into 'intelligence success' stories, and has contributed to the accuracy of countless others." It goes on to reveal that the CIA has in the past "persuaded reporters to postpone, change, hold, or even scrap stories that could have adversely affected national security interests..."[90]

Movies and TV shows known to have 'benefitted' from CIA cooperation include *Patriot Games* (1992), *JAG* (1995-2005), *In the Company of Spies* (1999), *The Agency* (2001-2003), *Alias* (2001-2006), *The Sum of All Fears* (2002), *Bad Company* (2002), and *The Recruit* (2003), to name but a few.

The CBS TV series, *The Agency*, executive produced by Wolfgang Petersen (*Das Boot, Air Force One*) was co-written by ex-CIA agent and Marine Bazzel Baz, with additional ex-CIA agents working as consultants. The CIA gladly opened its doors to the production, facilitating both external and internal shots of its Langley headquarters as the camera gazed lovingly at the CIA seal. *The Agency* glorified the actions of US spooks as they fought predictable villains including the Russian military, Arab and German terrorists, Columbian drug dealers, and Iraqis. One episode even shows the CIA saving the life of Fidel Castro, which is particularly bizarre considering the CIA had in real-life made repeated attempts to assassinate the Cuban President. Promo's for the show traded on 9/11, which had occurred just prior to its premiere, with tag lines like "Now, more than ever, we need the CIA."[91]

The TV movie, *In the Company of Spies* (1999), starring Tom Berenger, depicted a retired CIA operative returning to duty to save captured Agency officers held by North Korea.[92] The CIA was so enthusiastic about this product that it hosted its presentation, cooperated during production, facilitated filming at Langley, and provided fifty off-duty officers as extras.[93]

Espionage novelist, Tom Clancy, has enjoyed an especially close relationship with the CIA. In 1984, Clancy was invited to Langley after writing *The Hunt for Red October*, which was later turned into the 1990 film. The Agency invited him again when he was working on *Patriot Games* (1992), and the movie adaptation was, in turn, granted access to Langley facilities. [94] In 2002, the big screen version of Clancy's *The Sum of All Fears* depicted the CIA as tracking down terrorists who detonate a nuclear weapon on US soil. For this production, CIA director George Tenet gave the filmmakers a personal tour of the Langley HQ, and the film's star, Ben Affleck, also consulted with Agency analysts, while Chase Brandon served as on-set advisor.[95] (It is also worth noting that Affleck's wife, Jennifer Garner, made an appearance in a CIA recruitment video in 2004 free of charge, so keen was the *Alias* star to scratch the back the of the Agency that had assisted in her rise to fame).[96]

Entertainment as stratagem

The CIA may even have used entertainment for psychological warfare purposes and to develop real-world scenarios, as Professor Tricia Jenkins heard in a series of sensational interviews for her book, *The CIA in Hollywood: How the Agency Shapes Film and Television*. Michael Frost Beckner, creator of the *The Agency* (2001–2003), told Jenkins that Chase Brandon phoned him to suggest a plotline for the TV series involving highly advanced biometric identification technology. When Beckner questioned Brandon on the story's realism, Brandon told him, "Put it in there, whether we have it or not. Terrorists watch TV too. It'll scare them." For another episode, Brandon suggested using a Predator drone outfitted with a Hellfire missile to kill a Pakistani general, asking Beckner to "see how it plays out, how you could make it work." One month after the show aired, the CIA assassinated a Pakistani general using Hellfire missiles from a Predator drone. "I'm not a big conspiracy theorist," says Beckner, "but there seems to have been a unique synergy there."[97]

Early screening

Although the CIA has been operating 'publicly' in Hollywood since the mid-1990s, the Agency's clandestine involvement in Tinseltown dates back considerably further. Letters penned in 1953 by an executive at Paramount Studios provide stunning insight into just how deeply the Agency was able to penetrate the film industry in the early days of the Cold War. The letters are significant for their revelation that the movie executive in question, Luigi Luraschi, Paramount Studios' head of domestic and foreign censorship, was simultaneously a CIA asset reporting to the government's Psychological Strategy Board (PSB). His identity was not discovered until five decades after the fact by British academic David Eldridge.[98] In letters to his CIA handler, Luraschi described how he had secured the agreement of several Hollywood casting directors to subtly plant "well dressed negroes" into films, including "a dignified negro butler" who has lines "indicating he is a free man" in *Sangaree* (1953), and in a golf club scene in the Dean Martin/Jerry Lewis vehicle *The Caddy* (1953). Luraschi also arranged for the removal of key scenes from the film *Arrowhead* (1953), which questioned America's treatment of Apache Indians, including a sequence where a tribe is forcibly shipped and tagged by the US Army.[99] Such changes were not part of a ham-fisted campaign to instil what we now call "political correctness" in the populace. Rather, they were specifically enacted to hamper the Soviets' ability to exploit the United States' poor record in race relations and served to create a peculiarly anodyne impression of America, which was, at that time, still mired in an era of racial segregation.

The Agency's silver screen meddlings date back further still. In 1950, the CIA, along with other secretive organizations like the Office of Policy Coordination (OPC), and aided by the PSB, bought the rights to and invested in the cartoon of George Orwell's Animal Farm (1954), which was given an anti-Soviet spin to satisfy its covert investors. Author Daniel Leab has pointed out that it took decades for the rumours about CIA involvement in *Animal Farm* to be properly documented; this, he observes, "speaks volumes about the ability of a government agency to keep its activities covert."[100]

In the shadows

The most authoritative book yet written on the subject of CIA and Hollywood is Professor Tricia Jenkins' aforementioned *The CIA in Hollywood: How the Agency Shapes Film and Television.* Jenkins spent many hours interviewing former and serving CIA officers about the Agency's role in the entertainment industry and devoted several years to her broader research into the topic. Despite this, Jenkins acknowledges that her book is far from comprehensive due to the inescapable fact that the CIA is, by its very nature, extremely secretive, stating, "The CIA is far from an open organization, and many who work for the Agency remained tight-lipped about even the most basic information."[101] Adding to the problem is that "the CIA rarely leaves a paper trail,"[102] which Jenkins attributes to the Agency's habit of communicating with theatrical agents "through phone conversations rather than through emails or letters," and to the fact that "many of its documents are exempt from Freedom of Information Act requests."[103] Jenkins also points out that the entertainment industry itself expresses little interest in attracting outside attention to its relationship with the CIA, noting that "those in Hollywood are often too busy, or simply unwilling, to speak with academic researchers about their collaborations with the government."[104]

Perhaps the biggest problem Jenkins faced in her research is that "the CIA's relationship with Hollywood involves 'deep politics,'"[105] so called because they involve activities which cannot currently be fully understood due to the covert influence of shadowy power players. As such, Jenkins is forthright in her admission that her book, despite its academic rigor, "cannot possibly claim to unveil all of the CIA's involvement in motion pictures..."[106] Jenkins states, "some of these collaborations may never be brought to light, while the exact nature of others will remain hidden."[107]

Making sense of it all

The CIA claims to wield far less influence in Hollywood than the DoD because it has less in the way of technological eye-candy to offer filmmakers. Unable to furnish productions with tanks, jets, or aircraft carriers, all the Agency can really offer in exchange for its recruitment-boosting Hollywood makeover is on-set advice and access to its Langley headquarters.

However, it is important to stress again that the CIA is a *covert* agency, and by necessity operates more in the shadows than in the harsh light of public scrutiny. In reality, the CIA's involvement in Hollywood is geared not so much toward recruitment and burnishing its own public image as it is to subtly manipulating public perceptions of hot-button national security issues and projecting a carefully constructed image of America and its perceived enemies. Today, the Agency achieves these goals both overtly, through its official Entertainment Liaison program, and covertly, by implanting itself into the film and TV-making process in an off-the-books capacity through "back door channels," as was the case with Disney's *Race to Witch Mountain* and Robert Emenegger's *UFOs: Past Present and Future*, as well as numerous genre pictures throughout the 1950s. Viewed in this context, the Agency's Entertainment Liaison Office is but the tip of a very large iceberg – little more than a public front for a much deeper program of entertainment-media manipulation. The question is, how deep?

A good way of judging is to look at the CIA's extensive infiltration of American news media, which began in an organized way in 1953 on the orders of CIA Director Allen Dulles.[108] It is now a matter of public record that the Agency succeeded in infiltrating and controlling the US news media during the Cold War and that this infiltration was complete as early as the mid-1970s. As was famously documented by Washington Post journalist Carl Bernstein, back in the 1950s the CIA ran a formal training program to teach its agents to be journalists in order that they could more effectively infiltrate print and broadcast media.[109] The CIA's efforts were so successful that between the early 1950s and mid-1970s over four-hundred American journalists carried out assignments for the Agency. Some were fully-fledged CIA operatives-turned-journalists, while others were existing media professionals who were added to the Agency's payroll or who acted merely out of a misguided sense of patriotism and/or for career favors. Organizations known to have cooperated with the CIA include the American Broadcasting Company (ABC), the National Broadcasting Company (NBC), the Associated Press (AP), United Press International (UPI), Reuters, Hearst Newspapers, ScrippsHoward, *Newsweek* magazine, the Mutual Broadcasting System (MBS), the *Miami Herald* and the old *Saturday Evening Post* and *New York HeraldTribune*.[110]

The CIA's reach into the news media extended even up to executive level. Media bosses who lent their cooperation to the Agency included William Paley of the Columbia Broadcasting System (CBS), Henry

Luce of Time Inc., Arthur Hays Sulzberger of the *New York Times*, Barry Bingham Sr. of the *Louisville CourierJournal*, and James Copley of the Copley News Service.[111]

It is worth reiterating that the CIA's infiltration of news media began in an organized way in 1953. It is no coincidence that this is the same year in which the Agency began covertly tampering with Hollywood movie scripts and financing (as revealed in the letters of CIA asset, Luigi Luraschi). Clearly, the CIA recognised with equal importance the role of news media and entertainment media in shaping public opinion.

It is my contention that the CIA infiltrated Hollywood as successfully (if not as extensively) as it did the US news media, and that today, as in the 1950s, the Agency has scores of assets scattered throughout the industry, at every 'choke-point' or 'gate' in the business, from Hollywood Readers (who vet scripts for studios), to script writers, script doctors (whose job it is to tweak or re-write other people's scripts), producers, directors, actors, and even studio heads and the directors of the parent companies themselves (some of whom have maintained direct ties to the arms industry – most damningly John Bryson of Disney/Boeing).[112] While some of these assets may be on the CIA's payroll, many would no doubt operate as they did during the Cold War, out of a sense of national pride and duty, or compelled quite simply by the allure of the CIA and the thrills and perks that only the secret state can offer.

The CIA, UFOs, and Hollywood

Quite how many movies were subverted by the Agency during the Cold War besides those already cited in this chapter is unknown, but if the CIA was taking time to covertly manipulate Hollywood's representations of race relations and colonial history, then we can be certain the Agency was also tweaking Hollywood's depictions of the UFO phenomenon during this period – UFOs were, after all, of far greater concern to the US national security apparatus in the early-to-mid-1950s than were simmering racial tensions. This is not to underplay the significance of the then burgeoning civil rights movement or the furrowed brows it caused in the corridors of power, but incidents of racial violence and equality marches were not occurring outside the gates of highly sensitive US defense establishments. UFOs, on the other hand, were regularly violating restricted military airspace at will and exhibiting a keen interest in America's nuclear capabilities, as the CIA's own declassified documents reveal.[113] The question, therefore, is not "why *would* the Agency have been interested in manipulating Hollywood's depictions of UFOs?" but "Why *wouldn't* it?"

Given the CIA Robertson Panel's formal recommendation in 1953 that UFO-themed media be targeted for manipulation, and in light of the Agency's documented covert involvement in other genre pictures during that very same year, it is logical to assume that, from 1953 onwards, the new UFO subgenre was also squarely in the sights of the CIA. Moreover, there is a strong possibility that the Agency had infiltrated Hollywood's UFO productions prior to the Robertson Panel's formation – beginning, perhaps, in 1951 with *The Day the Earth Stood Still* – especially since the Agency had by this time already bought the rights to Orwell's *Animal Farm* with an eye to spinning a movie adaptation in its favor. Clearly, the CIA knew full well the power of the silver screen.

Again, the exact number of UFO movies subjected to CIA manipulation during and after the Cold War is difficult to state with any degree of certainty due to the inevitable lack of a paper trail, though I do indulge in some educated guesswork in the chapters to follow, highlighting a number of productions I consider likely to have been tweaked by the Agency. As to *why* the CIA has attempted to shape UFO movie content, again, we can only hazard a guess, though we might consider whether the CIA's UFO-related activities in Hollywood were/are geared solely towards debunking and demystifying (as recommended by the Robertson Panel), or if the Agency's agenda was/is more complex and more concerned with subtle perception management than heavy-handed debunkery.

Although in its early years the CIA may well have followed the Robertson Panel's recommendation to the letter, using media to "debunk and demystify" UFOs, the Agency itself would soon have recognized this approach as illogical and unsustainable. It is impossible to disprove the existence of a phenomenon through media channels if the phenomenon persists in publicly and spectacularly manifesting itself (as has continued to happen in the United States and around the world). However, it is possible to *manage* how the public *perceives* the phenomenon. As such, the CIA has likely made concerted efforts over the years to manage popular perceptions of UFOs through big and small screen entertainment products in much the same way as the DoD has done (and hence the Pentagon's gradual shift in policy on lending its support to UFO movies: if you can't beat 'em, join 'em, and exert what influence you can from within). While there is an almost complete lack of official documentation to prove CIA involvement in Hollywood's UFO-related output, the idea is nonetheless strongly supported by a small handful of compelling testimonies, not to mention the clear-edged logic that if the CIA has covertly tampered with genre movies as diverse as Western, comedy, and historical melodrama, such efforts will undoubtedly have extended to the immensely popular genre of science-fiction, which has been dominated by UFO and alien movies since the 1950s. As the secret-keepers' understanding of the phenomenon has evolved with time, so too has the nature and purpose of their media manipulation – which may account in part for the apparent inconsistency in Hollywood's portrayals of alien agendas (malevolent one minute, benevolent the next).

The idea of a "Hollywood UFO Conspiracy," therefore, is not as clear-cut as many would like to believe. It is not so much about debunking or acclimating as it is about perception management, which encompasses disinformation and propaganda. That said, and as shown in this chapter, in the early years of the UFO phenomenon the DoD did make a number of successful attempts at outright UFO debunkery through film and television. However, the DoD and/or CIA (as well, perhaps, as more clandestine power groups), have, on occasion, involved themselves in entertainment products with the apparent goal of acclimating the public or testing its reaction to UFO reality. Regardless of the precise nature of the Hollywood UFO Conspiracy, it is clear that officialdom has long taken a keen interest in the industry's depictions of the UFO issue. Surely, this is strong incentive for us to do the same.

None of this is to suggest that our perceptions of UFOs and alien life have been shaped entirely by the government through film and television – far from it. Such instances of media manipulation are the exception, rather than the rule. By and large, our 'understanding' of these phenomena is the result of a natural cultural process – a process that owes more to the transference of memes and the cross-pollination of ideas between UFO literature and the minds of autonomous Hollywood creatives than it does to the clandestine activities of the US government.

The interlocking of Hollywood and the national security state is today as tight as ever. In 2008, the famed ex-CIA operative Robert Baer (whose life inspired the 2005 George Clooney thriller, *Syriana*) told me, "All these people that run studios, they go to Washington, they hang around with senators, they hang around with CIA directors, and everybody's onboard."[114] A sweeping statement, to be sure, and perhaps not intended to be taken literally; but there can be little doubt that the Agency will have gone to great lengths to ensure that all those it requires to be onboard, are. Cinema is, after all, too potent a medium to be left unexploited, too powerful a weapon to be left unchecked.

In his book, *The Power of Movies: How Screen and Mind Interact*, Professor Colin McGinn notes that "In the movie-watching experience we enter an altered state of consciousness, enthralling and irresistible."[115] And this, of course, makes cinema the perfect conduit for propaganda. When watching a film, says McGinn, "The critical faculties are reduced, the mind entering a state of dreamlike susceptibility and suggestibility – this is fertile ground for persuasion of one kind or another."[116]

A previous head of the CIA's Entertainment Liaison Office, Paul Barry, is on record as saying, "You cannot underestimate Hollywood's influence... most Americans are content to accept Hollywood's message... very few ever conduct any research to determine the truth."[117] In electing to read this book, you are among the "few" to whom Barry refers. You have chosen, through your own sense of intellectual inquiry, to determine for yourself the truth behind Hollywood's UFO depictions and to unravel the densely woven complexity of a tangible phenomenon that, through processes both cultural and political, has come to occupy a realm between fantasy and reality. With this in mind, let us now enter that realm together and begin the process of unravelling.

This chapter is an adaptation and extension of the article "A History of Government Management of UFO Perceptions through Film and Television" by Robbie Graham and Matthew Alford, which first appeared in issue 25 of the peer-reviewed journal of North American Studies, 49th Parallel (Universities of Birmingham and Nottingham), Spring, 2011.

CHAPTER THREE

DIE. DIE.

"We're aliens; that's what we do –
we come to planets, we destroy them, we move on."

— JAMARCUS (RICHARD AYOADE), *THE WATCH (2012)*

Extraterrestrials seek to conquer our planet and claim it as their
own. Their motivation stems either from desperation or despot-
ism: their own planet is dying or its people are suffering due to
a lack of essential resources, or else they have reached us as an inev-
itability in their cold quest for galactic empire. Whatever their justi-
fication for invasion, the aliens regard humanity as an obstruction to
be smashed, or as a pest to be squashed.

This is a generic silver screen scenario – Hollywood loves a good alien movie, and much more so if its aliens are evil. From *The Thing from
Another World* and *Invasion of the Body Snatchers*, to *They Live and Independence Day*, to *Battle: Los Angeles* and *Battleship*, overwhelmingly,
Hollywood's aliens have been malevolent creatures – sometimes monstrous, sometimes invisible and parasitic, but almost always invasive.

But just how plausible is the concept of an alien invasion of Earth,
and how realistic are Hollywood's depictions of how such an invasion
might unfold in light of what we know, or what we *think* we know, about
the UFO phenomenon? Moreover, what do scientists and the military

have to say about the possibility of an alien attack? Some of Hollywood's alien species favor conquest by stealth, others through sheer fire power. This chapter takes a look at the silver screen's most notable alien invasions, silent and invisible, explosive and spectacular, charting them chronologically and in parallel with real-world UFO occurrences.

~ UNITY THROUGH INVASION ~

Though it may come as a surprise to many, debates surrounding extraterrestrial invasion are not restricted to Hollywood and the UFO community. In recent years, mainstream science and even the US defense establishment have openly discussed 'falling skies' scenarios and what humanity might do to repel potential alien aggressors.

In April 2010, Professor Stephen Hawking made headlines by stating his firm belief that humanity should seek to avoid extraterrestrial contact: "If aliens ever visit us, I think the outcome would be much as when Christopher Columbus first landed in America, which didn't turn out very well for the American Indians." Hawking suggested that aliens "might exist in massive ships, having used up all the resources from their home planet" and would perhaps be "looking to conquer and colonize whatever planets they can reach."[1]

Two years later, in April 2012, Professor Paul Springer of the US Air Command and Staff College was granted special clearance by his employers at the Pentagon to discuss how the military would respond in the event of an alien invasion. Springer's comments were aired in a televised interview for Australia's Channel 9.

When asked by his interviewer exactly how an alien invasion might unfold, Springer replied:

> That really depends on why they are here in the first place. If they are here for the extraction of a specific resource, for example, they might just want to eliminate any resistance that might block them from their objective. If, on the other hand, their goal was actual occupation and conquest, then they would probably have to prioritize anything they perceive as a threat to their own dominance. So, they would probably start by wiping out as many communications networks as possible and eliminating as many weapons that might represent some form of threat either to them, or to the resources they are trying to extract.

Springer suggested that the aliens would likely be concerned about our nuclear weapons, but not necessarily for the reason we might expect: "They might very well want to counter every nuclear weapon, not because it represented a threat to *them*, but because it might destroy whatever they're here to collect."

Springer's comment about aliens wanting to neutralize our nuclear capabilities is especially interesting in light of the US government's own declassified files documenting persistent UFO activity over nuclear weapons storage facilities over a span of four decades. In many of these instances, UFOs were reported as tampering with the weapons themselves, activating and deactivating them with disquieting ease.

Springer was also asked by his interviewer, "Wouldn't it be a strange situation if humanity had to band together, fighting alongside Russia, or I guess, the Taliban?" He responded, "It would, but keep in mind that many of the greatest civilizations in human history have been formed, basically, to counter a common enemy. When you look at the great world powers of the globe today, you find a lot of them formed because of the fear of a common enemy."[2]

The nations of the world being brought together to thwart an alien aggressor is a notion that has been discussed publicly by influential individuals in the spheres of politics, science, and finance. Famously, in an address to the United Nations General Assembly in New York on 21 September 1987, President and former B-movie star Ronald Reagan said:

> In our obsession with antagonisms of the moment, we often forget how much unites all the members of humanity. Perhaps we need some outside, universal threat to make us recognize this common bond. I occasionally think how quickly our differences worldwide would vanish if we were facing an alien threat from outside of this world. And yet, I ask you, is not an alien force already among us?[3]

Referencing this statement in July 2012, theoretical physicist Professor Michio Kaku told CNN, "Ronald Reagan was probably right – if we are ever invaded by the Martians or some advanced civilization we *would* hunker down, we would get together to fight off the Martians."[4]

In August of the previous year, the Nobel prize-winning economist Professor Paul Krugman made headlines when, during a debate on CNN with Harvard economist Ken Rogoff, he stated that an alien invasion, whether real or staged by the United States government, would actually serve to stimulate the US economy thanks to the massively increased defense spending it would justify. Krugman said, "If we discovered that, you know, space aliens were planning to attack and we needed a massive buildup to counter the space alien threat and really inflation and budget deficits took secondary place to that, this slump would be over in 18 months."[5]

Krugman's statements elicited some interesting responses from other persons of influence, including SETI's Professor Seth Shostak, who told *The Huffington Post*:

> Any aliens that have the capability to come here and ruin our whole day by vaporizing Earth or terrorizing its hominid inhabitants, would be centuries – perhaps millennia – beyond our technical level. To spend effort preparing for such a lugubrious possibility would be like the Neanderthals organizing their society to defend themselves against the U.S. Air Force.

Shostak added, "That won't do them much good on the battlefield. But who's to say? Maybe it would improve the Neanderthal economy."[6]

These statements are notable, but the discourse on the possibility of alien invasion goes considerably beyond a handful of soundbites from public figures. Take, for example, the 2006 book *An Introduction to Planetary Defense: A Study of Modern Warfare Applied to Extra-Terrestrial Invasion*, which was written not by a tinfoil-hat-wearing conspiracy theorist, but by a group of space scientists and engineers who have spent years working for the likes of BAE Systems, NASA, and the US Department of Defense.

According to the authors, their book is "a starting point for developing defensive and offensive concepts in the event of an attack from advanced extraterrestrials," and is not an attempt to "refute, discuss, defend, or even enter into an argument about government conspiracies, UFO cover-ups, alien autopsies, or any other examples of the 'UFOlogy' genre."[7]

The book discusses the statistical probability of an ET invasion, the possible types of ETs that might invade our planet, their possible motives for invasion, the types of weapons they might use against us, and how exactly we might go about defending ourselves.

~ CLOSE ENCOUNTERS OF THE DISTURBING KIND ~

In light of such fear-mongering, it is worth asking, have UFOs and their alleged occupants ever exhibited an invasive or hostile intent? The short answer is, not really. At least, nothing to hang your hat on as a general statement of malevolence or a conscious desire to cause us harm. Indeed, as will be documented in Chapter Four, in a great many cases of reported human-alien contact the experiencer describes their close encounter/s as being at the very least benign, and often joyous and spiritually transcendental. That said, there are more than a few cases scattered across the decades that have sparked debate about whether or not the UFOnauts have our best interests at heart.

Foo Fighters were reported by military personnel in the theatre of war from the early-to-mid-1940s. Naturally, these reports were a cause of serious concern for governments, and details were collated and analyzed to determine if the mystery objects – seemingly physical craft under intelligent control – were the product of one or more terrestrial enemy nations (a theory that led nowhere). But, although Foo Fighters sometimes came perilously close to allied aircraft, none of these encounters could reasonably be interpreted as hostile. If anything, the Foo Fighters acted like benign observers, curious about our technology and our primitive in-species conflicts.[8]

It wasn't long, though, before the UFOs chalked up their first human fatality. On 7 January 1948, Captain Thomas Mantell, a 25 year old Kentucky Air National Guard Pilot, died while in pursuit of an Unidentified Flying Object. Mantell, who was honored with the Distinguished Flying Cross for his part in the Battle of Normandy, was one of four pilots ordered by the 156th Fighter Squadron to investigate UFO reports coming in to a number of military bases in Kentucky that afternoon, including Goldman Field at Fort Knox and Clinton County Army Airfield. The UFO was reported by military personnel as being up to 300ft in diameter, and white with a red border at the bottom.

The pilots, who were in radio communication with the control tower at Fort Knox, were ordered to approach the object, but it was now at a considerable altitude and appeared as little more than a dot in the sky. The pilots were then advised to break off direct pursuit and to level their altitude, a suggestion ignored by Mantell, who continued to climb in chase of the object. As Mantell got closer to the UFO, he told the control tower it looked "metallic," and was of "tremendous size." They would be some of his last words. It is thought that he blacked out soon after due to lack of oxygen. His plane spiralled to the ground, crashing on a farm south of Franklin, Kentucky. The cause of Mantell's crash as listed by the Air Force officially remains 'undetermined.'⁵

Little green men

Another disturbing UFO encounter occurred in 1955. On the evening of August 21, two families at a rural farmhouse near the towns of Kelly and Hopkinsville in Kentucky were besieged by small, non-human entities.

Around 7pm, Billy Ray Taylor went outside for a drink from the farm's water pump when he saw a bright disc-shaped object in the sky to the west. Excited, he rushed back inside to report his sighting, but his account was met with incredulity. An hour later the families began hearing unusual noises coming from outside, and the dog in the yard began barking loudly. This prompted Taylor and Elmer "Lucky" Sutton to grab their guns and investigate. Stepping outside, the two men observed a strange humanoid creature emerging from the trees nearby, which approached to within 20 feet of them. It was at this point that the men opened fire, one using a shotgun, the other using a .22 rifle. The men then heard a noise "like bullets being rattled about in a metal drum," and the creature, apparently unharmed, disappeared into the darkness. Before the men could give chase, they noticed another creature identical to the first perched on the roof of the farm. The men shot it, knocking it to the ground below. Again, their gunshots elicited a strange rattling noise, and the creature appeared unharmed.

As the night wore on, a total of seven family members would set eyes on the creatures, which repeatedly approached the house, peering in through windows almost playfully and scurrying about on the roof. They were shot at repeatedly, but never wounded. The witnesses described the creatures as two-and-a-half-feet tall, with silvery skin or clothing, large pointed ears, claw-like hands, and large yellow eyes. Their arms and legs were spindly, almost emaciated, and, perhaps most notably, they seemed to defy gravity as they were seen floating above the ground, propelling themselves with a distinctive hip-swaying action and steering with their arms.

Finally, at around 11pm, the terrified witnesses piled into their cars and fled to the Hopkinsville police station, whereupon twenty officers were dispatched to the farmhouse to investigate. Upon the officers' arrival the creatures had vanished, but evidence of a recent violent commotion was plain to see. The witnesses' account was corroborated in part by other individuals, including several local policemen and a state trooper who had been in the vicinity earlier that night and had seen strange lights in the sky and heard bizarre noises. The witnesses' neighbors also confirmed having heard multiple gunshots from the farm house on the night in question.

The local press reported on the incident the following day, referring to the creatures as "little men." By the time the national news media got hold of the story, the little men had become "little *green* men," despite the witnesses having described them as being silver.

The witnesses themselves neither sought nor gained money or fame from their testimonies, and all stuck to their story until the day they died. The local police, who believed the witnesses had experienced something truly extraordinary, labeled the case as "unexplained." Today, even UFO skeptics have few doubts about the sincerity of the witnesses, and the best earthly explanation yet offered for the Kentucky farm siege attributes it to the misidentification of meteors. The humanoid creatures, say the doubters, were angry owls.[10]

Sinister forces

In May 1962, legendary US Army General Douglas MacArthur made public statements about what he perceived to be a potential threat to Earth from extraterrestrials. During a speech to cadets of the US Military Academy at West Point, MacArthur said:

> We deal now, not with things of this world alone, but with the illimitable distances and as yet unfathomed mysteries of the universe... We speak in strange terms, of harnessing the cosmic energy... of ultimate conflict between a united human race and the sinister forces of some other planetary galaxy.[11]

MacArthur had made a similar statement to the Mayor of Naples, Achille Lauro, in 1955. In an October 7 meeting between the two men that took place in New York, General MacArthur told Lauro that the nations of Earth would one day be forced to "make a common front against attack by people from other planets."[12]

What inspired such comments from one of America's most celebrated military leaders may never be known for sure, but it seems reasonable to assume that an officer of MacArthur's stature and longevity would almost certainly have had at least *some* exposure to classified information pertaining to the UFO issue.

"It's not an aircraft"

Yet another aircraft would be lost in an apparent UFO encounter in 1978. On October 21, at 7:12 pm, 20-year-old Frederick Valentich and the Cessna 182L light aircraft he was piloting mysteriously vanished over Australia's Bass Strait.

Shortly prior to his disappearance Valentich had advised Melbourne air traffic control that he was being orbited by a large craft some 300 meters above him. Valentich said the craft was long, with a shiny metal surface and a green light on it. He then reported that the craft was approaching him from the Southwest. Moments later, the young pilot made what would be his final statement to air traffic control – or to anyone: "[the] strange aircraft is hovering on top of me again. It is hovering and it's not an aircraft." This was followed by 17 seconds of "metallic scraping sounds." No trace of Valentich or his aircraft was ever found. The cause of his disappearance remains undetermined.[13]

It is examples such as these that have long appealed to creatives in the entertainment industry: where there's the unknown, there's fear; where there's fear, there's drama; and where there's drama, there's money. Add spectacle to the drama and, potentially, there are *sacks* of money. It makes sense, then, that the inherently spectacular scenario of alien invasion continues to play out at the worldwide box-office.

~ THE SAUCERS LAND IN HOLLYWOOD ~

In 1947, an event occurred that would forever change Hollywood's relationship with all things extraterrestrial. Pilot Kenneth Arnold's June 24 sighting of nine unusual objects near Mount Rainier in Washington State sparked a media frenzy and opened the floodgates for hundreds of similar sightings in the coming months. Though not the first to report such things, Arnold's description of the objects' flight characteristics as being "like a saucer if you skip it across the water" inspired the press to dub the objects "flying saucers." The other frequently used term at the time was "flying disc." Witness descriptions of these phenomena varied in the fine detail – some discs had no protuberances whatsoever, being perfectly circular or ellipsoid, while many others were reported as being topped with a dome or cupola.

Following the Arnold sighting, "flying saucers" embedded themselves into the zeitgeist, and it wasn't long before Hollywood saw the dollar-potential of this new global hysteria. The first film to exploit the "flying saucer" term – Mikel Conrad's subtly titled (and Air Force-baiting) *The Flying Saucer* (1950) – was a shameless cash-in on the public's growing fascination with the saucer enigma. Curiously, however, the flying saucer of the title eventually proves to be a soviet secret weapon. Aliens didn't even get a look-in. Today, a UFO movie *sans* aliens would be a head-scratcher for audiences, UFOs and aliens now being synonymous in popular culture. But, in fact, the Earthly origin of Conrad's saucer was in keeping with public opinion during the fledgling years of the UFO phenomenon.

The first US poll of public UFO perceptions was released by Gallup on 15 August 1947. It revealed that the "flying saucer" term was familiar to 90% of respondents. However, in regard to the provenance of the saucers, the poll showed that, of those who were willing to provide an answer (33% had no opinion or refused to respond), the majority favored a mundane explanation. 29% said optical illusions, mirages or overactive imagination were to blame, 15% thought the saucers were a US secret weapon, 10% a hoax, 3% a "weather forecasting device," 1% believed they were of Soviet origin (presumably Conrad fell within this group), while 9% favored "other explanations," including fulfilment of Biblical prophecy, secret commercial aircraft, or phenomena related to atomic testing.[14]

Unfortunately for Conrad, by the time *The Flying Saucer* was released in 1950, the Extraterrestrial Hypothesis (ETH) had come firmly into favor among UFO believers, and his unimaginative movie failed to connect with audiences. Like many a real flying saucer, the film was seen by only a few people, and for a short time. But more UFO movies were to follow. They arrived in Tinseltown like an invading force, overwhelming industry output and capturing the imagination of an already saucer-saturated nation.

The Roswell 'Thing'

When the Roswell Army Air Force (RAAF) withdrew its announcement in 1947 of having captured a downed "flying saucer" in the deserts of New Mexico, claiming instead to have stumbled across a common weather balloon, a trusting public failed to bat an eyelid. If official-dom said it, then it must be true, such was the attitude of the time. Yet Roswell was not dead, only dormant, and some three decades later this sleeping giant would begin to stir.

In 1978, UFOlogists William Moore and Stanton Friedman con-ducted research that led them independently, and almost by chance, to a man of considerable interest, retired Air Force Officer, Major Jesse Marcel, who claimed direct knowledge of the recovery of truck-loads of material near Rowell, New Mexico, in early July of 1947. The mate-rial, said Marcel, was not of this world. In the years to follow, other researchers began pursuing the Roswell case, including, most notably, Donald Schmitt, Kevin Randle, and Thomas Carey. By the mid-1990s, their collective efforts had brought forth testimonies from scores of named individuals. Some were civilian witnesses, others were retired military officers formerly stationed at the RAAF. Some recalled hearing about and even handling strange, indestructible foil-like material from the wreckage, while others reported seeing a number of diminutive, non-human cadavers with disproportionately large heads and spindly bodies. Today, the number of testimonies supporting the unearthly na-ture of the Roswell incident stands at several hundred. Although some of these testimonies are slightly contradictory, the picture they paint, accurate or not, is one in which large quantities of debris, at least one partially intact craft, and between three and five alien beings (at least one of which was still alive) were recovered by military personnel and eventually were taken to, stored, and studied, at Wright Patterson Air Force Base in Dayton, Ohio.

Four years after the events that would eventually put the sleepy town of Roswell on the map, a film was released that had striking parallels with the Roswell narrative as we know it today. Howard Hawks' *The Thing from Another World* (1951) saw a US Air Force crew and a jour-nalist dispatched to a scientific outpost in the North Pole to investigate the wreckage of a crashed flying saucer. During their investigation, the Americans discover an alien body frozen in the ice nearby, which is then hauled back to their base. Inevitably, the frozen alien soon thaws-out and begins terrorizing its human captors.

The chief scientist at the research outpost, Dr. Carrington (Robert Cornthwaite), discovers that the 'Thing' is a form of plant life – a sort of intellectual vampiric carrot – and is impressed by its biological el-egance ("No pleasure, no pain... no emotion, no heart. Our superior in every way"). But while Carrington wants to protect and study the creature in the name of science, the Air Force wants to destroy it and keep it hushed-up. All the while, the tag-along journalist Scotty (Douglas Spencer) wants nothing more than to bring his "story of a lifetime" to the world's media.

Eventually, the eponymous Thing is killed by electrocution and incinerated. Its ultimate motivation for visiting our planet goes unspecified. Championing the notion of a free American press, the film ends with Scotty broadcasting a message and a warning to reporters:

> Here, at the top of the world, a handful of American soldiers and civilians met the first invasion from another planet... The flying saucer which landed here and its pilot have been destroyed, but not without causalities among our own meager forces... Everyone of you listening to my voice, tell the world, tell this to everybody wherever they are. Watch the skies. Everywhere. Keep looking. Keep watching the skies!

The parallels between *The Thing from Another World* and the Roswell incident have not gone unnoticed in the UFO community, or in Hollywood. Filmmaker Paul Davids, who wrote and produced the popular TV movie *Roswell* (1994), starring Kyle MacLachlan and Martin Sheen, notes:

> *The Thing* was the story of a flying saucer crash... all the themes of the Roswell Incident were there. The military covered it up. A newsman pleaded for disclosure. There was buried saucer wreckage. There was an alien body (that turned out to be still alive). There was secrecy. And, in the movie, there was danger.[15]

Davids wonders if the purpose of *The Thing* may have been to take a factual and highly sensitive event and to couch it in fiction, the goal being to ridicule the idea of saucer crashes by associating them with superficially outlandish sci-fi cinema, and/or to subtly drip-feed these realities into the popular consciousness. Hawks' movie was based on a science-fiction story called *Who Goes There?* by John W. Campbell Jr., "But there are thousands of science-fiction stories," says Davids, "and only a small fraction of them are produced as films. Was it a coincidence that a great producer put this tale to film just three years after [the Roswell incident]?"[16]

Intriguing as it is, the idea of a conspiracy behind *The Thing* would seem to be ruled out by the fact that the USAF had officially denied its cooperation to the filmmakers specifically on the grounds that their movie dealt with the thorny issue of flying saucers.

Still, this does not preclude the possibility that certain *individuals* may have acted independently of their colleagues at the Pentagon to influence Howard Hawks' distinctly Roswellian UFO movie. Such influence could, for example, have been exerted through Howard Hughes, the billionaire industrialist and defense contractor who, at the time of *The Thing*'s production, owned the movie's distributor, RKO, and had an intimate working relationship with the US Department of Defense. Indulging the conspiratorial reading of *The Thing*, perhaps in return for business favors down the line, Hollywood/defense mogul Howard Hughes allowed his lofty contacts at the Pentagon to tweak his movie's script in accordance with their own UFO-related goals ("I'll scratch your back, if you scratch mine.") In any case, and for whatever reason, the parallels between Roswell and *The Thing* are plain to see.

While the Thing of the 1951 movie was a hostile entity, there is no evidence to suggest that the Roswell beings – if real – came to us with mal-intent. If they had been part of a forward invasion force then, presumably, sometime during the 65 years since their crash-landing, we would have seen evidence of their plans in the form of charred cities across the globe. But perhaps this is over-simplifying the matter – our own history has shown that hostile agendas need not always manifest immediately or spectacularly.

Panic in the Capital

Following *The Thing*, 1951 saw the release of another iconic UFO movie: *The Day the Earth Stood Still*, a cautionary tale about the dangers of nuclear weaponry in which a flying saucer lands in Washington D.C. (see Chapter Four for a detailed discussion). Although the film's alien protagonist, Klaatu, essentially came in peace, his ultimate message for humanity was less comforting: "Your choice is simple. Join us and live in peace, or pursue your present course and face obliteration." Apparently, even friendly aliens were to be feared.

Life closely imitated art the following year when, between 12 and 27 July 1952, multiple UFOs were spotted on radar by numerous eye-witnesses over Washington D.C. The objects differed in appearance depending on the date of the sighting and the vantage point of the observer, but they were variously described as bright balls of light or disc-shaped objects that moved at high speeds and in a manner entirely unlike any conventional aircraft, sometimes stopping on a dime, making right-angle turns, and even vanishing into thin air. By the end of July, the sightings had whipped up a media frenzy, and the press reported, accurately, that USAF pilots had been placed on 24 hour nationwide alert against flying saucers and had received orders to shoot them down if they ignored orders to land. Alarmingly, at one point, some of the objects were seen to pass over the White House and the Capitol Building and President Truman himself put in a personal phone call to Project Blue Book head, Captain Edward Ruppelt, demanding an explanation for the flying saucer wave.

The D.C. sightings were the cause of such widespread panic that the US Air Force was compelled to publicly address the UFO issue in an attempt to quell growing fears of an alien invasion. On 29 July 1952, during the largest Pentagon press conference since World War II, Air Force Major Generals, John Samford and Roger Ramey, declared that the D.C. sightings were attributable to a combination of temperature inversions, and misidentified stars and meteors. Few were convinced by their explanation.[17]

Behind the scenes of the US national security apparatus those in the know were beginning to sweat, and, with the uncomfortably high-profile D.C. sightings as a catalyst, the CIA decided in 1953 to establish the Robertson Panel, which quietly but aggressively set about "debunking and demystifying" UFOs through cultural channels, including film and television.

Enter the Martians

That same year (1953), William Cameron Menzies directed *Invaders from Mars*, a fascinating addition to the burgeoning UFO subgenre. The movie opens with young David MacLean (Jimmy Hunt) witnessing a classic flying saucer from his bedroom window. It is self-luminescent and makes a high-pitched humming sound. Its shape is exactly like that reported and photographed by controversial contactee, Billy Meier, in his alleged experiences from the 1970s onwards (more on Meier in Chapter Four).

David watches as the saucer descends and disappears underground not too far from his home. He then alerts his parents, and his father, a scientist (played by Leif Erickson), goes outside to investigate. When

David's father returns the next morning, however, he behaves like an automaton and we see a strange red puncture mark on the back of his neck where an implant has been inserted. David soon realizes something is amiss as he begins to notice that many other people in his town are also behaving robotically.

The only people willing to believe David's seemingly crazy story are health-department physician, Dr. Pat Blake (Helena Carter), and local astronomer, Dr. Stuart Kelston (Arthur Franz), who conclude that David's flying saucer is the vanguard of a looming Martian invasion force. Soon the Pentagon is involved and the Army uncovers an alien plot to use mind-controlled human slaves to sabotage an atomic rocket project at a nearby government research plant. Invasion through infiltration.

The aliens themselves (referred to as "mu-tants") are humanoids with bald heads and large bulbous eyes (stock features of the now-archetypal Gray aliens described in countless abduction reports in the decades to follow, and variants of which were described by Roswell witnesses). Their leader, who controls them telepathically from within the confines of a small glass sphere, is essentially a tentacled torso with an oversized head. He is, we are told, "mankind developed to its ultimate intelligence."

Eventually, the Army pinpoints the exact location of the flying saucer underground and surrounds it with explosive charges, which, when detonated, force the saucer to the surface and back into the air where it is quickly destroyed by the Army's cannons.

Invaders from Mars bears close UFOlogical scrutiny, but one scene in particular cries out for analysis from a conspiratorial perspective. The scene in question sees the film's adult hero, the implausibly square-jawed astronomer, Dr. Kelston, declare the Martians' arrival as no surprise. He explains that the government has been studying the saucers for a number of years and is well aware that they are extraterrestrial in origin.

In the fashion of a public service announcement, Kelston goes on to describe various real-life cases catalogued by the Air Force's "Project Saucer" (the popular name for the USAF's real-life UFO investigations effort at the time, Project Sign), including the UFO-related death of Captain Thomas Mantell in 1948 and the "Lubbock Lights" (which refers to several incidents between August and September 1951 in which numerous residents of Lubbock, Texas, claimed to have witnessed a spectacular formation of lights passing silently overhead). Dr. Kelston illustrates his eight-minute lecture with genuine news-clippings and

UFO photographs, including a famous shot of the Lubbock Lights. "Life can, and does, exist on other planets," he intones, before displaying scale models of the multiple saucer types he says are known to exist by the Air Force.

This lengthy scene clearly was devoid of narrative function and it did not appear in the US theatrical cut of the film. The scene was shot some time after principal photography had wrapped, and it was too late for it to feature in the US cut, but someone, somewhere, for some reason, decided it should be inserted into the European version of the movie. From a filmmaking standpoint, the scene adds far more context than is necessary, stopping the movie dead in its tracks for over eight minutes. Without the scene, *Invaders from Mars* is 79 minutes in duration, short, but not at all unusual for sci-fi and horror B-movies of the time. Therefore, the idea that the extra scene was merely a filler to extend the movie to a more acceptable run-time holds little water. While the scene would have been cheap to produce, it would also have required a considerable amount of specialist research – a lot of effort to go to for no apparent reason.[18]

That the scene was scripted and shot at all, then raises questions about the possibility of subversive government involvement in the filmmaking process – a notion that cannot easily be dismissed in light of officialdom's historical efforts to manipulate the content of Hollywood's UFO movies. The *Invaders from Mars* scene may have been intended to fictionalize and debunk UFOs by injecting largely factual UFOlogical information into an otherwise outrageous and fantastical sci-fi narrative, as may have been the case with *The Thing from Another World* two years prior.

Another option to consider is that the government was not thinking merely in terms of actualization or fictionalization, but in terms of *vilification*. Just as the US propaganda machine (i.e. a complicit media) actively vilified the Nazis during WWII (not that they needed much vilifying), so too, post-war Hollywood was wielded by Washington as an essential psychological weapon in a parallel 'Cold War' against what it perceived to be, in the words of General Douglas MacArthur, "the sinister forces of some other planetary galaxy."

Just four months after Menzies' *Invaders from Mars*, Director Byron Haskin would further vilify our imagined Martian neighbors with his spectacular movie adaptation of H. G. Wells' classic novel *The War of the Worlds*, in which Martians from a dying civilization view our thriving planet with envious eyes and launch a full-scale invasion to claim it as their own, only to be defeated by the tiniest of foes – the human germ. The film's Martians were truly alien in their design, short stumpy creatures with no legs (only feet), and with one three-part eye embedded in the center of their torso. Their long arms end in long hands with spindly suction-cupped fingers. In step with the times, H. G. Wells' original tripod machines were replaced with saucer-like craft, although the novel's overly-convenient ending, in which the aliens suddenly drop dead en masse due to bacterial infection, remained intact. In reality, bacteria are the last thing that would foil an alien invasion of Earth. Any advanced civilizations interacting with our planet naturally would take every precaution to minimize or eliminate the risk of their becoming contaminated by our biosphere, either through a long process of physical acclimatization, or simply by wearing their equivalent of hazmat suits with a self-contained breathing apparatus.

"Observers"

By this point, audiences were leaving America's movie-houses with a clear thought in mind: aliens were a force to be feared. Not everyone bought into the fear-fest, however. One of the more enlightened perspectives on UFOs during this period came from the celebrated pioneer of rocketry, Professor Hermann Oberth. In an article for the *American Weekly* in October, 1954, Oberth wrote:

> It is my thesis that flying saucers are real and that they are space ships from another solar system. I think that they possibly are manned by intelligent observers who are members of a race that may have been investigating our earth for centuries. I think that they have been sent out to conduct systematic, long-range investigations, first of men, animals and vegetation, and more recently of atomic centers, armaments, and centers of armament production. They obviously have not come as invaders, but I believe their present mission may be one of scientific investigation.[19]

Although the UFO-related death of Thomas Mantell in 1948 had sparked debate about the potentially hostile nature of the UFO phenomenon, and despite occasional reports of close encounters of the troubling kind, on the whole, UFOs were more a source of fascination than terror throughout the 1950s. The freakish creatures that would frequent movie theatres throughout the decade only very occasionally ventured out into the real world (the Kentucky farm siege of 1955 being the most extreme of these occasions). Generally, beings described in UFO reports were less fantastical than those presented by Hollywood, and considerably less aggressive.

In 1954, the same year Hermann Oberth opined that UFOs were here on a mission of "scientific investigation," a global wave of UFO landings was occurring, with Western Europe and South America emerging as hotspots. In his study of this wave, computer scientist and now-legendary UFO researcher, Dr. Jacques Vallee, examined some 200 reports of landings or near-landings of UFOs, 42 of which involved descriptions of "pilots" who were witnessed either inside the UFO, or on the ground in close proximity to it. Of the 200 cases, 156 occurred in France, with the rest being spread across (but not limited to) counties such as Italy, Germany, Brazil, Venezuela, Spain, and Portugal. In the vast majority of these cases the UFOs were described as "discs" or as objects that were broadly disc-like in appearance. Many of the discs were reported as "spinning." Some of them had "portholes" around their rim, while others were topped with a dome. The discs were variously described as "silent," or as emitting a "whistling sound," or a "whirring sound."

The "flying saucer" term did not feature in any of Vallee's case studies – a fact he attributes to the UFOs exhibiting "an avoidance of population areas," meaning that the UFOs in the 1954 wave typically were witnessed in regions less immersed in popular culture than cosmopolitan areas. In other words, those who lived in back-water locales had restricted access to audio-visual and print media that would otherwise inform their perceptions of the burgeoning UFO phenomenon. Quite simply, the "flying saucer" term had yet to reach the ears of many rural folk by the mid-1950s.

Of the UFO occupants themselves, in sharp contrast to Hollywood's elaborate alien creations, Vallee noted that his case studies:

> Always involve beings which are near-human in appearance, sometimes absolutely human... these human operators are always said to be 'of European type' with few variations [even in non-European countries], and are never described as wearing respiratory devices [which would support the notion that any alien species visiting us are fully acclimatized to our biosphere and are not in the least bit concerned about Earth germs. Sorry, H. G. Wells].

A typical report from the 1954 wave came on December 9 from a farmer in Linha da Vista in Brazil, who observed on his land three men and a "machine" (a landed craft) which was enveloped in a haze. Two of the men were outside of the craft inspecting their surroundings, while the third was visible inside it. The craft made a noise "like a sewing machine."

Shocked at the sight before him, the farmer dropped his pitchfork. One of the men then approached, picked it up, examined it, and handed it back to the farmer. The two beings on the ground then joined the third in their craft, motioning the farmer not to come too close. The craft then took off. The beings in this case wore "brown coveralls, ending with shoes which had no heels." They were "of average height, had broad shoulders, long hair, very white skin and slanted eyes." Hardly the stuff of Hollywood nightmares.

In most of the cases Vallee studied the UFO occupants seemed to be engaged in "sampling," and actively avoided direct contact with their human observers, usually departing the scene soon after being sighted. Despite the non-hostility of the majority of the UFO occupants in the 1954 wave, many of the witnesses "showed signs of extreme terror," in some cases fainting "either during the experience or immediately afterwards." In six cases examined by Vallee, witnesses actually required medical attention as a result of their experience. Non-hostility, then, does not necessarily equate to a pleasant experience for all involved.[20]

It is notable that human-looking extraterrestrials piloting flying saucers would show up the following year in the 1955 film *This Island Earth* (see Chapter Four), but this would be a rare silver screen appearance for their type – Hollywood now, as then, expressing little interest in attractive space beings.

Body-snatchers and soul-eaters

In 1956 came *Invasion of the Body Snatchers*, in which alien invaders replace humans with 'pod people' – duplicates superficially identical to the original victim, but which are utterly devoid of individuality or emotion. Film critics have since interpreted *Invasion of the Body Snatchers*, as well as many other sci-fi movies of the Cold War era, as political allegory.

Discussing the idea of allegory in alien invasion movies of the 1950s, film writer Peter Biskind notes that "critics of popular culture have always been quick to point out that the Other is always other than itself, which is to say, the pods and blobs are "symbols" standing for something else." Because the Other in films of this period frequently was linked to radiation (as in *Them!* (1954)), or to mind control and loss of identity (as in *Invaders from Mars* (1953)), it has been customary in film studies to equate aliens with the dangers associated with atomic power or communism. But Biskind argues that critics often give Cold War sci-fi movies too much credit and that many of them were not political allegories at all, but literal reflections of cultural preoccupations. For the preferred reading of many of these films, says Biskind, "all we have to do is look at what's before our very eyes."[21] When asked how to account for the tremendous appeal in the 1950s of the science fiction genre (dominated at the time by the UFO movie), actor Billy Gray (who played the character of Bobby Benson in the original *The Day the Earth Stood Still*) was unequivocal: "It correlated with reports of UFOs. At the time it was just rampant – every other person had seen something mysterious in the sky. I think that's what made science fiction popular at this time."[22]

Invasion of the Body Snatchers would be memorably remade in 1978 by Philip Kaufman with Donald Sutherland in the lead role, before being lamentably 're-booted' by Oliver Hirschbiegel in 2007 as the Nicole Kidman vehicle, *The Invasion*. Body-snatching aliens have appeared in many other Hollywood narratives, including, most notably, *Life Force* (1985), *The Hunted* (1988), *The Faculty* (1998), *Dark Skies* (1996-97), *Invasion* (2005), and *The Host* (2013), based on the Stephanie Meyer book in which alien entities called "Souls" silently conquer Earth by occupying the bodies of its inhabitants.

The central concept of all these body-snatcher narratives, that the human will (and even the soul) can be invisibly hijacked by a malevolent alien power, is one that has become increasingly popular in recent years within the most paranoid factions of the UFO-conspiracy community. British TV-sports-presenter-turned-conspiracy-icon, David Icke, has been chiefly responsible for the popularization of the idea that many of our world leaders secretly are lizard-people from another dimension. Icke's massively popular books and lectures posit that the world as we know it is in fact a hologram designed and maintained by a race of inter-dimensional reptilian beings, known to ancient Mesopotamian cultures as the 'Anunnaki,' who feed not only on human flesh, but on the suffering of the human soul. According to Icke, many prominent figures of the global elite are descended from reptilian bloodlines and are working in secret to enslave humanity. In his development of these theories throughout the 1990s, Icke borrowed notably from Ancient Astronaut writer Zecharia Sitchin, who first made the theoretical connection between the Anunnaki and extraterrestrials in his 1976 book *The 12th Planet.*

But while Icke's premise may have come from Sitchin, the finer details of his elaborate conspiratorial tapestry seem at least partially indebted to Hollywood entertainment. Some sixteen years prior to Icke's first book on the 'reptoid' agenda (*The Biggest Secret*: 1999), the television mini-series *V* (1983–1984) was spinning its own compelling yarn about flesh-eating reptilian aliens who disguise themselves as humans and exert their influence on our society and politics. The 2009 'rebooting' of *V* explored similar themes to the original, but this time, ironically, seemed to owe more to Icke's by-now fully developed reptilian lore, with the show's alien 'Visitors' craving not only human flesh, but the human soul itself.

Keyhoe vs. Hollywood

One of the most significant productions of the 1950s to deal with alien invasion was *Earth vs. the Flying Saucers* (1956), which was very loosely based on Donald Keyhoe's 1953 non-fiction book *Flying Saucers from Outer Space*. In the movie, the last of a dying species of aliens arrive on Earth seeking a new home. Although the aliens request a meeting with world leaders to discuss their desires for occupation, the US military, with the help of one America's top scientists (played by Hugh Marlowe), formulates a plan of attack involving the use of sonar canons mounted on trucks to be fired at the aliens' flying saucers (the sonar supposedly interfering with their propulsion and navigation systems and disabling their force fields). Conspiracy writer Kenn Thomas has noted that this fictional battle strategy seems to have been directly inspired by real-life UFOlogical events which occurred just one year prior to the release of *Earth vs. the Flying Saucers* when the legendary scientist, Wilhelm Reich, claimed to have used his "cloudbuster" invention to attack UFOs (which he believed were hostile) by sucking the energy out of them.

Reich's cloudbuster was an atmospheric device constructed from two rows of 15-foot aluminium pipes mounted on trucks and connected to cables that were inserted into water. Its appearance and functionality were strikingly similar to that of the sonar cannons in *Earth vs. the Flying Saucers*. Reich believed that his cloudbusters served to unblock cosmic 'orgone' energy in the atmosphere, which he said would be beneficial to human health. Apparently, Reich also found them handy for shooting down alien spacecraft in what he described as a "full-scale interplanetary battle" in Tucson Arizona in 1955.[23]

The production history of *Earth vs. the Flying Saucers* is intriguing. In 1955, Donald Keyhoe, then a jagged thorn in the side of the US government's UFO secret-keepers, was approached by a group of Hollywood producers seeking to buy the rights to his aforementioned non-fiction book. The producers told Keyhoe their film was to be a serious documentary about UFOs. Although initially suspicious, Keyhoe eventually went along with the deal. Big mistake. Upon its completion in 1956, the "documentary" turned out to be the schlock sci-fi B-movie of our discussion. Keyhoe was outraged and demanded that his name be removed from the film's credits, to no avail. Someone, it seemed, had it in for this outspoken advocate for government transparency on UFOs (likely the same "someone" who, two years later, censored Keyhoe's statement on live TV that flying saucers were "real machines under intelligent control").[24]

Keyhoe's book, despite its pulpy title, was a serious examination of UFOs that drew extensively from the USAF's own investigations into the phenomenon. The movie that the book inspired, however, was an outlandish affair, depicting scientists and the military as fighting-off ridiculous rubber-suited aliens with plans to occupy the Earth. This deviation into kitsch fantasy is especially frustrating because the film also retained a considerable amount of fact-based UFOlogical detail from Keyhoe's source material. The film's saucers, for example, designed by Ray Harryhausen with a stationary central dome and a rotating outer-rim with slotted vanes, were based exactly on real-life descriptions collated by Keyhoe. Harryhausen also sought advice on his saucer design from UFO 'contactee' George Adamski (whose controversial accounts are detailed in Chapter Four). The shrill sound emitted by the movie's saucers also has been a common feature in UFO close encounter reports from the 1940s to present day, with witnesses often associating high-pitch whirring, humming, or hissing sounds with UFOs.

Particularly interesting is a scene in which Foo Fighters make a casual appearance. The scene in question sees heroic scientist Russell Marvin (Hugh Marlowe), his wife Carol (Joan Taylor), and the latter's father, General Hanley (Morris Ankrum), having a family lunch while discussing their work on Project Skyhook – an American space program that launches research satellites into orbit. Suddenly, two glowing balls of light appear above their house, hovering silently. "Look! What are those lights?" asks the General. "They're what the pilots call 'Foo lights,'" Carol replies, "there have been so many around the project the last couple of days we all just take them for granted." This is an unmistakable reference not only to Foo Fighters, but also to the many anomalous fireballs reported by military personnel around sensitive government facilities in the late-1940s which resulted in Project Twinkle, a two year study program at Holloman Air Force Base tasked with solving the mystery.[25]

Earth vs. the Flying Saucers even has echoes of Roswell in the form of its alien invaders, not as they appear in their cumbersome spacesuits, but in their true form underneath. When the protagonists remove the space-suit from one of the dead aliens, the being bears an uncanny likeness to the Roswell beings as described by firsthand witnesses from 1947, but these testimonies would not come to light until more than twenty years after the release of *Earth vs. the Flying Saucers*. How do we account for this apparent cinematic prescience? Were the Roswell witnesses influenced after the fact by Hollywood, or was Hollywood influenced by intelligence operatives with knowledge of the Roswell Incident?

A sharp contrast

In 1956, while millions of cinemagoers were watching *Earth vs. the Flying Saucers*, far fewer were reading a then newly-released book about flying saucers written by retired USAF Captain, Edward J. Ruppelt, who, from 1951 to 1953 served as head of Project Blue Book. Today, Ruppelt's book, *The Report on Unidentified Flying Objects*, is considered one of the most important ever written on the UFO topic, not least of all for its popularization of the "UFO" acronym, which, for its clinical ring, was favored by the USAF over "flying saucer," a term that had become synonymous in the public mind with alien visitation.

Ruppelt's book left the reader with little doubt that Unidentified Flying Objects, despite their apparent non-hostility, continued to be a source of deep concern and puzzlement to the United States Air Force, and it even revealed the existence and mandate of the now infamous CIA Robertson Panel. Perhaps the most jaw-dropping revelation in

Ruppelt's book was that, in 1948, the USAF's Project Sign (the forerunner to Blue Book) had concluded in its top secret "Estimate of the Situation" that the flying saucer phenomenon was "interplanetary" in nature.[26]

But while the government continued to treat the UFO phenomenon with the utmost seriousness, the vast majority of Hollywood filmmakers took the opposite approach (which, perhaps not by chance, worked out nicely for the government). The back end of the 1950s saw the release of numerous ultra-low-budget alien invasion movies, most notable among which were *The Blob* (1958), a charming teen flick in which a rampaging meteorite excretion is finally defeated by being frozen and dumped in the Arctic, and *Plan 9 from Outer Space* (1959), Ed Wood's gloriously nonsensical film in which aliens resurrect Earth's dead as "ghouls" in a bizarre attempt to stop humanity developing a doomsday weapon that would destroy the universe.

Also ludicrous was *Invasion of the Saucer Men* (1957), which saw teenagers do battle with anti-social spacemen. The movie is gleefully outlandish, especially so when a dead alien's hand detaches itself, grows an eye, and runs amok. But, as with other invasion movies of the 1950s, the influence of real-life UFO encounter reports is evident. The movie drew considerable inspiration from the famous Hopkinsville Kentucky case of 1955, in which impish creatures are said to have terrorized a farming family for several nights. In *Invasion of the Saucer Men* the aliens are aggressive little creatures with green skin who get their kicks by violently harassing the residents of a rural American town. In one scene, the heroine of the piece (played by Gloria Castillo) even refers to one of the aliens as "a little green man," just as the press had (erroneously) used the "little green men" term when reporting on the Hopkinsville case.

~ TIMES (AND UFO MOVIES) THEY ARE A-CHANGIN' ~

Fascination with the saucers (by now more commonly referred to as 'UFOs,' thanks to Edward Ruppelt) was diminished slightly during the 1960s and 1970s. Public interest in UFOs, though still considerable, was eclipsed by more overt socio-political issues: civil rights, free love, Vietnam, women's lib, political assassinations... this revolution, of sorts, paved a sprawling road to the future and left many cultural artifacts from previous decades, including flying saucers, strewn along the wayside. This was despite the fact that the 1960s witnessed some of the most important and high-profile events in the history of UFOlogy, including the apparent alien abduction of Betty and Barney Hill in 1961 (the first such event of its kind to be widely publicised), and, in 1964, the close encounter between Police Sergeant Lonnie Zamora and what appeared to be a landed UFO and its humanoid occupants in Socorro, New Mexico.[27] The decade also boasted a major American UFO wave, beginning in 1964 and peaking in 1966, during which literally thousands of UFO sightings were reported by seemingly reliable observers.

One of the most impressive UFO encounters from the late-1960s occurred not in the United States, but in neighboring Canada, and resulted in serious injury for the unfortunate witness. On 20 May 1967, while prospecting for quartz near Falcon Lake in Manitoba, Stefan Michalak observed two glowing cigar-shaped objects descending, one of which landed around 160 feet away from him. Michalak estimated the craft to be 35 feet in diameter and 12 feet in height and said it made hissing and whirring noises. He watched the craft for half an hour before a door opened in its side; Michelak could now hear human-like voices coming from within. Assuming it was a classified military test flight gone awry, Michelak, keeping his distance, attempted to communicate with the voices in a number of different languages, but received no response. He cautiously glimpsed inside the door, but was unable to see any sign of life. Suddenly, the craft spun round on its axis and Michelak was now faced with a grid-like exhaust vent, which expelled an extremely hot burst of gas onto his chest, knocking him to the floor and setting his shirt alight. Luckily, he was able to pat out the flames, and the craft flew away as he did so.

Soon after his encounter, Michalak began to suffer from sickness and a pounding headache. Later that day he was treated in hospital for a first degree burn covering his chest. It was shaped like a grid. In the weeks and months that followed, Michalak suffered from a variety of health problems including hair-loss, lack of appetite, weight loss, swelling, and fainting spells. After being examined by a total of 27 doctors, all of whom were at a loss to explain Michelak's symptoms, Dr. Horace Dudley, a former chief of the Radio-Isotope Laboratory at the US Naval Hospital in New York, reached the tentative conclusion that Michelak's symptoms presented "a classical picture of severe whole body [exposure to] radiation with X or gamma rays." Dr. Dudley estimated that the patient had "received in the order of 100–200 roentgens," and noted that "it is very fortunate that this dose of radiation only lasted a very short time or he would certainly have received a lethal dose."[28]

UFOs on the box

As UFO events unfolded throughout the 1960s, sci-fi TV shows continued to develop the alien invasion narrative. ABC's *The Invaders* (1967–1968) depicted beings from a dying world who have taken on human form in order to infiltrate our society and ultimately destroy Mankind. The series was superficially inspired by the real UFO phenomenon, as evidenced in the design of the aliens' flying saucers, which was based closely on the testimonies of Rex Heflin and George Adamski.

Heflin, a highway traffic engineer, snapped three impressive pictures in August 1965 while working near the Santa Ana freeway in California. They showed a metallic, flat-hat-shaped object glinting in the sunlight as it hovered at close range above the road. Heflin said the object departed at high speed, leaving a ring of smoke in its place (also photographed). The veteran UFO investigator Richard H. Hall described Heflin's case as "a highly credible, thoroughly investigated case that meets all the criteria for significant evidence of a real, structured, craftlike UFO."[29]

Adamski's photos, which are now derided within the UFO community, also left their mark on *The Invaders'* saucers. Numerous photographs taken by Adamski from the early 1950s through to the mid-1960s show a bell-shaped craft with three semi-spherical protuberances equally spaced under its rounded flange. The saucer design in *The Invaders* featured the flat top from the Heflin case, combined with the lower bell shape of the Adamski case. It even had semi-spherical protuberances on its undercarriage, but while Adamski's craft had three, the TV show's had five.

The other two sci-fi TV shows of note in the 1960s were *The Twilight Zone* (1959–1964) and *The Outer Limits* (1963–1965) – anthology series featuring many episodes that drew from UFOlogical literature and debate. A memorable episode from *The Twilight Zone*, 'To Serve Man' (broadcast in March 1962), saw a race of seemingly benevolent nine-foot-tall aliens land on Earth and solve humanity's most pressing problems, including hunger, energy, and the threat of nuclear war. Before long, Earthlings are volunteering to visit their alien saviors' home planet, unaware that they are offering themselves up as ingredients in an alien cookbook, titled... 'To Serve Man.'

In 'Chameleon,' an April 1964 episode of *The Outer Limits*, a flying saucer lands in a remote part of the United States and destroys a military patrol sent to investigate. Fearing that the aliens are planning a nuclear attack, the government calls on Mace, a loose-cannon CIA operative, to infiltrate the ship and save the day. Once inside, however, and having undergone genetic modification to blend in with the aliens, Mace begins to question not only his allegiance but his own human nature.

Despite TV breathing new life into the 'dastardly alien' meme throughout the 1960s, scientific UFOlogy remained level-headed about possible extraterrestrial agendas. In July of 1968, during Congressional hearings on the UFO issue before the House committee on Science and Astronautics, one of America's leading atmospheric physicists, Professor James McDonald, echoed the conclusions of Professor Herman Oberth and Dr. Jacques Vallee: "My own present opinion, based on two years of careful study, is that UFOs are probably extraterrestrial devices engaged in something that might very tentatively be termed 'surveillance.'"[30] During the same Congressional hearing, McDonald also suggested that the great North-East-American power blackout of 9 November 1965 may have been the result of UFO activity: "It is puzzling that the pulse of current that tripped the relay on the Ontario Hydro Commission Plant has never been identified," said McDonald. "Just how a UFO could trigger such an outage on a large network is however not clear. But this is a disturbing series of coincidences that I think warrants much more attention than they have so far received."[31] The idea of aliens causing mass power outages and feeding off Earth's electricity was explored in forgettable fashion in the 2011 movie *The Darkest Hour.*

Threat assessment

Just as TV was beginning to fully embrace UFOs, movie studios were turning their backs on them. Simplistic narratives about flying saucers and space blobs suddenly had become passé as a new generation of cinemagoers were opting for more socially-progressive, highbrow science-fiction fare such as *Planet of the Apes* and *2001: A Space Odyssey* (both 1968). Old-school fare such as *Moon Pilot* (1962), *First Men in the Moon, Robinson Crusoe on Mars* (both 1964), and *Bamboo Saucer* (1968) seemed curiously out of place in America's rapidly expanding sociocultural landscape.

By the end of the 1960s it appeared that Hollywood's alien invaders had packed their bags and left America's movie houses for good. In 1971, though, they made a notable return to the silver screen, albeit in microbial form. Adapted from Michael Crichton's novel, *The Andromeda Strain* relied upon methodical procedure and clinical detail as opposed to more traditional, action-based thrills to engage audiences, and its portrayal of an uncontrollable extraterrestrial virus was inspired by serious scientific debate of the time. It had been two years since Neil Armstrong had taken his giant leap for mankind, and the Apollo program was now well under way. Within this new astronomical context, genuine public fears existed concerning the possibility of an ET virus accidentally finding its way to earth via a lunar module.

In 1967, four years prior to the release of *The Andromeda Strain*, the United States, Britain, and Russia had signed an agreement covering "outer-space activities," which took into consideration concerns regarding "harmful contamination" and "adverse changes" to "the environment of the Earth resulting from the introduction of extraterrestrial matter."[32] *The Andromeda Strain* tapped these concerns to great effect, and the film proved top draw for terrified audiences everywhere.

Although officialdom was still open-minded about the possibility of 'invasion' by microbial "extraterrestrial matter" during the late 1960s, the threat posed by UFOs was officially declared to be non-existent. In 1969, the USAF breathed a long sigh of relief as it finally closed Project Blue Book on the grounds that:

1. No UFO reported, investigated, and evaluated by the Air Force was ever an indication of threat to our national security;
2. There was no evidence submitted to or discovered by the Air Force that sightings categorized as "unidentified" represented technological developments or principles beyond the range of modern scientific knowledge; and
3. There was no evidence indicating that sightings categorized as "unidentified" were extraterrestrial vehicles.[33]

By publicly washing its hands of the UFO issue, the US government had effectively ended its official accountability on all matters pertaining to unexplained aerial intrusions, and the subject was now dead. Except that it wasn't...

Regardless of the closure of Blue Book, and despite the absence at the time of any notable alien visitation films to fuel imaginations, Americans continued to report UFOs to civilian organizations throughout the 1970s. While some of these encounters were deeply traumatic for the witnesses involved (as in the Travis Walton abduction case of 1975, which is discussed in detail in Chapter Five), the UFO occupants rarely, if ever, exhibited clear signs of hostility towards humans. Animals, however, weren't so lucky.

Beginning in 1967 in Colorado and sweeping rapidly across the South-Western United States throughout the 1970s, the seemingly UFO-related phenomenon of 'animal mutilations' baffled ranchers, scientists, and law enforcement. Many hundreds of ranchers were discovering their cattle dead, having had specific organs removed from their bodies with surgical precision. The mutilations were always bloodless and exhibited no physical evidence of human involvement (such as footprints or tyre tracks). There was also no evidence of animal predation. In most cases, other animals seemed to be spooked by the mutilated carcases and gave them a wide berth. Disturbingly, a great many of the mutilation cases were directly preceded or followed by sightings in the same location of mysterious lights in the sky.[34] In Hollywood, studio scribes were slow to catch on, and, to this day, only handful of Hollywood products have explored the animal mutilation phenomenon, the most notable of which being the 1980 movie *Endangered Species*.[35]

~ PARANOIA AND SECRECY ~

The 1980s was a transformative decade for UFOlogy as it saw the publication of numerous game-changing books on the UFO issue: *The Roswell Incident* (1980), by Charles Berlitz and William Moore, re-interpreted the Roswell cover-up as an alien event of unrivalled significance; while *Clear Intent* (1984), by Lawrence Fawcett and Barry Greenwood, and *Above Top Secret* (1987), by Timothy Good, presented proof of a much broader, decades-long campaign of UFO secrecy and compelling evidence that a cover-up was still in effect. Good's book, an international best-seller, also shone a light on Majestic 12 (or MJ-12), an alleged top secret UFO working group formed under President Truman in response to the Roswell Incident.

It was in this decade, also, that the now iconic image of the alien 'Gray' began to bore its way into popular consciousness thanks in large part to Whitley Strieber's phenomenally successful 1987 book *Communion*, which documented the author's intense and ongoing interactions with otherworldly visitors. The book's hypnotic cover image of an expressionless non-human face with black, almond-shaped eyes provided the blueprint for numerous Hollywood alien designs in the years to follow. *Communion* would be adapted for the big screen in 1989 (see Chapter Five).

1989 was also the year that the term "Area 51" began to pass lips outside of the UFO community. It was in this year that Robert ("Bob") Lazar first captured the attention of international news media. Lazar, a physicist whose story is examined in Chapter Seven, claimed to have worked at a super-secret military installation in the remote Nevada desert where he was tasked by Naval Intelligence with studying a captured flying saucer, which Lazar said was just one of several stored at the base.

Despite UFOlogy's emerging obsession with the cloak-and-dagger during the 1980s, the decade saw a dramatic change in Hollywood's depictions of alien visitation from the monstrous to the angelic. This was thanks to the surprise success of Steven Spielberg's *E.T.: The Extraterrestrial* (1982), which destroyed all box-office competition and became the most successful movie of all time. Other filmmakers were quick to cash in on the idea of benevolent alien contact, resulting in the likes of *Starman* (1984), *Cocoon* (1985), *Fight of the Navigator* (1986), *Batteries Not Included* (1987) and *The Abyss* (1989).

Not all of Hollywood's '80s aliens came in peace, however. UFOlogy's shift in focus from the dry documenting of sightings in the 1950s, 1960s, and 1970s, to the more speculative investigation of subjects like alien abduction, secret UFO bases, and clandestine UFO control groups, gave the UFO field something approaching sex appeal. Certainly it seemed sexier than ever to Hollywood screenwriters, who by now were beginning to incorporate this 'dark side' of UFOlogy into their narratives.

Though not directly inspired by any particular UFOlogical event, John Carpenter's *They Live* (1988) captured lightning in a bottle for the increasingly paranoid UFO-conspiracy community as it tapped into, and arguably helped shape, prevailing ideas about extraterrestrials colluding with human elites – ideas that had already been effectively sown into pop-culture through the *V* television series (1983–1984), which itself was partially indebted to the work of Ancient Astronaut theorist Zecharia Sitchin.

"Snatched"

Based on Ray Nelson's 1963 short story *Eight O'clock in the Morning*, *They Live* depicted a blue collar drifter (played by Roddy Piper) who finds a pair of sunglasses that allow him to see the stark reality of corporate America where shops are covered with subliminal signs that say "SUBMIT," "STAY ASLEEP," and "DO NOT QUESTION AUTHORITY." The world is being secretly run in this Orwellian fashion by malevolent, skeletal-faced aliens who are allied with the US establishment – the human elite having been promised tickets off-planet when Doomsday arrives.

Carpenter pulled no punches in describing his film's politics, "I looked at the country and thought we were in really deep trouble. This seems like fascism to me, the rise of the fundamentalist right and the kind of mind control they're putting out, the kind of presidency Reagan has had. We haven't got a chance."[36]

Unfortunately for Carpenter, his film's searing political vision may have been a key contributing factor to its undoing at the box-office. *They Live* was pulled just two weeks after its 4 November 1988 release date. While Carpenter blamed audiences who "don't want to be enlightened," co-star Keith David had a more conspiratorial take on the film's failure: "not that anybody's being paranoid," said the actor, "but it was interesting that *They Live* was number one at the box office... and suddenly you couldn't see it anywhere – it was, like, snatched."[37]

They Live opened at number one at the US box office and easily made its $4 million investment back over its first weekend. By the second weekend, it had dropped to fourth place but still made $2.7 million. It also received good reviews, with the notable exception of the two newspapers at the very center of power, the *New York Times*[38] and the *Washington Post*.[39] It's easy to see why Keith David was suspicious of higher level involvement. As part of the film's marketing campaign, the distributor, Universal Pictures, published an advert that showed a skeletal alien standing behind a podium in suit and tie, with a mop of hair strangely similar to that of the Vice President-elect of the United States – the much maligned Dan Quayle. The advert was headlined, "I know human beings. Human beings are friends of mine. You sir, are no human being!"

Regardless of the circumstances of *They Live*'s abrupt termination, it is clear that it was way out in the blue yonder politically, leaving it exposed and defenseless.

The truth is out there

As the 1990s slipped into gear, Hollywood (as well as American television) began to draw more extensively from the rapidly expanding UFO subculture. Beginning in the late 1980s and continuing throughout the 1990s, UFOlogy took a sharp turn towards the sinister as diabolical and long-festering conspiracy theories rose to the fore. Using the fledgling Internet as their canvas, researchers began to paint a picture in which malevolent aliens from dying worlds had taken a keen interest in our own, and, for their own purposes, were harvesting our livestock and tampering with our fragile reproductive systems.

This was the stuff of great television, as Chris Carter knew when he created *The X Files* in 1993. For nine years Carter's ingenious show served to crystallize the entire UFO enigma and its related mysteries in the minds of the millions who watched it, capturing the collective imagination in the process and pushing UFO-lore into living-rooms around the world. In this sense, it could be argued that cinema was beginning to take a back seat to television insofar as its ability to shape public perception of the UFO phenomenon was concerned. But cinema rose to TV's challenge, and the production slates of Hollywood studios were heaving with UFO-related movies throughout the 1990s. Almost all of these movies adopted overwhelmingly negative perspectives on potential alien life. *Fire in the Sky* (1993), based on the famous Travis Walton abduction case of 1975, played fast and loose with historical testimony and subjected cinemagoers to what remains the most disturbing UFO abduction sequence ever committed to film; *Stargate* (1994) depicted nuclear warfare between the US military and a despotic alien god; Species (1995) explored the idea of the alien as a sexual predator (with predictably gooey results); *The Arrival* (1996) re-heated the 'aliens among us' stew for the David Icke generation; *Mars Attacks* (1996) spoofed the whole UFO subgenre as Martians wiped out almost the entirety of the world's population; and the *Astronaut's Wife* (1999) saw Johnny Depp's alien-possessed astronaut impregnate his increasingly suspicious wife (Charlize Theron) with freaky twins in a film that tries but fails to recapture the creeping dread of *Rosemary's Baby* (1968).

Hollywood awakens a giant

In 1993, responding to the concerns of his constituents, Congressman Steven Schiff of New Mexico made inquiries at the Pentagon and several government archives seeking information on the Roswell Incident. The unusually brusque, evasive, and unprofessional responses he received convinced Schiff he was being stonewalled and that indeed the government did have something to hide regarding Roswell.

In an unprecedented move, Schiff urged the General Accounting Office (the investigative arm of Congress) to look into possible improprieties related to Roswell. After an 18 month investigation the GAO concluded, astonishingly, that many records of government activity in Roswell during the summer of 1947 had been illegally destroyed. In the absence of these records Schiff's investigation came to a standstill.[40] The Congressman died in 1998 after a short fight with an aggressive form of squamous-cell skin cancer. He was 51. He did, however, live long enough to see the Roswell Incident brought to popular attention through both film and television.

Based on the book *UFO Crash at Roswell*, by Kevin Randle and Donald Schmitt, the 1994 Showtime movie *Roswell* was the first entertainment product ever to present the details of the Roswell Incident as a stand-alone narrative. Two years later, in 1996, the TV series *Dark Skies* (discussed in-depth in Chapter Seven) also incorporated details from the Roswell story into its plot. The permanent embedding of Roswell into the popular consciousness was assured that same year when, despite disapproval from the Pentagon, it featured in one of the most iconic movies of the decade. At $75 million, Roland Emmerich's *Independence Day* was one the most expensive films of the 1990s, and, with a worldwide box-office gross of some $800 million, it was also one of the most successful.[41] A reinvention of the alien invasion movies of old, the film's plot linked the beings allegedly recovered from the Roswell Incident to Area 51, alien abductions, and the near-eradication of humanity.

In the movie a mammoth alien mothership in Earth orbit deploys dozens of city-sized flying saucers over the major cities of the world, causing mass panic in most quarters and feverish celebration in others. Both reactions are ultimately pointless, however, as soon after their arrival, the saucers obliterate their chosen cities using directed-energy weapons. With millions killed in the attacks, Earth's only hope is a team lead by US President, Thomas Whitmore (Bill Pullman), brilliant but misunderstood scientist, David Levinson (Jeff Goldblum), and top gun fighter pilot, Captain Steven Hiller (Will Smith).

Hiller manages to shoot down a small alien attack ship and drags its half-dead pilot across the Nevada desert to Area 51, where President Whitmore and his staff are now holed-up along with a small group of socially inept scientists, led by Dr. Brackish Okun (Brent Spiner). The President is shocked to learn that the aliens are not new to our planet, and that the US military secretly recovered one of their spacecraft along with its deceased pilot in Roswell in 1947. Craft and body were studied and stored at Area 51.

While being examined at the base, Dale's captive alien regains consciousness, grabs hold of Dr. Okun and psychically manipulates his vocal chords in order to converse with President Whitmore. "Can there be a peace between us?" asks the leader of the free world. "No peace," replies the alien (which, facially, bears a strong resemblance to the classic alien Gray). "What do you want us to do?" demands the President. The response leaves no room for negotiation, "Die. Die."

The alien then launches a psychic attack on President Whitmore, causing him to collapse. After the alien is shot to death by military personnel, the President tells his companions: "I saw its thoughts. I saw what they're planning to do. They're like locusts. They're moving from planet to planet... their whole civilization. After they've consumed every natural resource they move on... and we're next." His proposed solution? "Let's nuke the bastards."

Nuking duly ensues, but proves utterly ineffective against the aliens' force fields. Fortunately, however, ace scientist David Levinson manages to hack into the aliens' computer mainframe and plant a virus that disables the force fields on all of their saucers worldwide. The US president then coordinates militaries from around the world to launch an all-out attack on the now defenseless alien invaders. Meanwhile, having successfully docked with the mothership in orbit using the craft recovered from Roswell, Hiller and Levinson plant a nuke and fly back down to Earth. When the nuke detonates, the mothership is destroyed and the saucers that remain in other countries are soon taken out by national militaries.

Among *Independence Day*'s millions of fans is President Bill Clinton, who referred to the movie publicly on five occasions. "I loved it... and I was glad we won," Clinton told Tom Brokaw during a 15 July 1996 interview for MSNBC. When asked by Brokaw if he thought America could actually win a war against extraterrestrials, Clinton replied, "Yes,

I think we'd fight them off. We find a way to win. That's what America does – we'd find a way to win if it happened."

Like President Reagan before him, Clinton then took the opportunity to discuss the possibility of alien invasion in the context of a united world: "The good thing about *Independence Day*," the President enthused, "is there's an ultimate lesson for that – for the problems right here on Earth. We whipped that [alien] problem by working together with all these countries. And all of a sudden the differences we had with them seemed so small once we realized there were threats that went beyond our borders...That's the lesson I wish people would take away from *Independence Day*."[42]

Alien terrorists

Hollywood was slow to catch onto the crop circle craze. The often spectacular formations (most common in the South West of England) had been making international headlines for over two decades by the time director M. Night Shyamalan made Hollywood's first and, to date, only crop circle blockbuster. *Signs* (2002) was the industry's first major UFO film since the events of 9/11 and its fear-based narrative situated the alien threat directly within the American family home.

Inspired by speculation in the UFO community in the 1980s that crop formations were alien navigation coordinates, *Signs* presents them as the foreshadower of a worldwide extraterrestrial invasion. Fortunately for humanity, the aliens have a natural weakness – water. With one of the most illogical plot devices in cinematic memory, Shyamalan chose to present water-intolerant aliens as invading Earth, a planet seventy percent saturated with H_2O. Naturally, their invasion never really gets off the ground.

Signs was a box-office smash, grossing $408 million against its $71 million budget.[43] But the master of the modern UFO movie, Steven Spielberg (with a little help from star Tom Cruise), would top Shyamalan's success three years later with his 2005 cinematic updating of H. G. Wells' classic *War of the Worlds* story, which grossed an impressive $607 million against its huge $132 million budget. Although Spielberg's movie features no 'UFOs' in the conventional sense (due in part to his source material having been written 49 years prior to the birth of the modern UFO phenomenon), the director, a self-described "UFOlogist," did add some UFOlogical flourishes. The film's aliens, for example, have large glassy black eyes and yawning craniums, and, from their shoulders-up, at least, bear a striking resemblance to the archetypal alien Gray.

Appropriately, in a nod to sound science, Spielberg chose to dispense with all things Martian by removing from his adaptation all references to the Red Planet, opting instead to leave the aliens' origin to the imagination of the viewer. Presumably their roots are extra-solar – numerous NASA missions over the decades having thrown cold water on the idea that Mars might be teeming with sentient life.

The tagline for Spielberg's film, "They're already here," is a reference to the fact that the aliens strike not from above, but from below, having buried themselves beneath our feet in a time long forgotten. "They've been planning this for a million years," says Tim Robbins' cracked survivalist, Ogilvy, "They defeated the greatest power in the world in a couple of days. Walked right over us... this is not a war any more than there's a war between men and maggots. This is an extermination."

Having been backed by the US Department of Defense, Spielberg's film gives considerable screen time to the military, despite it being essentially helpless in the face of an overwhelmingly superior foe. It is only when the Tripods' impenetrable force fields are rendered ineffective by Earthly bacteria that US troops are able to inflict any damage on them whatsoever.

The most terrifying scenes in *War of the Worlds* are entirely alien-free – it is the human-on-human violence that draws the most horrified gasps. As panic grips the world, humanity's basest survivalist instinct kicks in. Within hours, it's every man for himself as widespread looting, car-jacking, and general criminality sweeps the streets, and it is in these moments that Spielberg's film is arguably at its most realistic, such behaviour being tragically inevitable when a society fractures through external force.

Like the 1953 original, Spielberg's *War of the Worlds* tapped into what Susan Sontag referred to as the "imagination of disaster," fear of "the cataclysmic destruction of civilization, [and] mayhem of an unimaginably higher order than we had ever seen before."[44] Spielberg stated to the press that his film's distinctive imagery was intentionally reminiscent of that seen in New York as the Twin Towers fell, and, with dialogue like "is it terrorists?" during the first wave of the aliens' sneak-attack, the parallels are far from subtle.

Monsters, aliens, and slave children

In 2009, DreamWorks Animation's *Monsters vs. Aliens* successfully lampooned 1950s B-movies, presenting heroic monsters squaring-off against an alien invasion force. Commanding an army of clones, the diabolical Gallaxhar (voiced by Rainn Wilson), has come to earth seeking quantonium, an extremely rare and powerful material that has recently arrived on our planet by way of a meteorite. Upon obtaining this precious natural resource, Gallaxhar uses it to power a machine that creates an army of clones in his own image. As he prepares for invasion, Gallaxhar announces:

> Humans of Earth, I come in peace. You need not fear me, I mean you no harm. However, it is important to note that most of you will not survive the next 24 hours. The few of you that do survive will be enslaved and experimented upon. You should, in no way, take any of this personally. It's just business. So to recap, I come in peace, I mean you no harm, and you all will die. Gallaxhar out.

As Gallaxhar's ship arrives in the skies of San Francisco, a TV news reporter (voiced by Ed Helms) announces, "Once again, a UFO has landed in America – the only country UFOs ever seem to land in," both acknowledging and propagating the meme that UFOs are a uniquely American obsession, which, of course, could not be further from the truth. The film also features a 'first contact' scene based entirely on previous cinematic depictions of such an event, paying homage in particular to the ending of Spielberg's *Close Encounters of the Third Kind* (1977). But while in Spielberg's film government scientists commune with their angelic visitors through a now iconic five-tone musical greeting, in *Monsters vs. Aliens* the idiot President (voiced by Stephen Colbert) welcomes the alien craft with an enthusiastic keyboard rendition of the *Beverly Hills Cop* theme. Gallaxhar is not impressed, and the first strike of his planned clone invasion is soon underway. It doesn't last long, however, as the alien tyrant is soon defeated by a rag-tag team of government-owned monsters who infiltrate Gallaxhar's ship and activate its self-destruct sequence.

After the success of his *War of the Worlds* remake in 2005, Spielberg returned to the alien invasion subgenre in 2011 as Executive Producer of the TNT TV series *Falling Skies*. The series tells the story of the aftermath of a world-wide alien invasion by green-skinned six-legged creatures known as 'Skitters,' a species that uses robotic bipedal attack droids to fight the last dregs of human resistance. The Skitters, who themselves are answerable to an overlord species, have wiped out over 90% of the human population, neutralized the world's power grid, and are systematically rounding-up children between the ages of eight and eighteen and forcing them into slavery through the influence of bio-mechanical obedience devices inserted into their spines.

Fact and fantasy... and alien penises

The 2010 alien invasion film *Skyline* incorporated real alien-related news stories into its marketing campaign. The trailer for the film begins with bold text against a cosmic backdrop, reading: "On 28 August 2009, NASA sent a message into space farther than we ever thought possible in an effort to reach extraterrestrial life." This is true. On the date specified, the Australian government, through its "Hello from Earth" science initiative, and with the help of NASA, sent some 26,000 carefully vetted messages from the public to the extra-solar Earth-like planet Gliese 581d in a single transmission.[45] This proactive approach to alien contact, known as METI (Messaging Extraterrestrial Intelligence), differs from the traditional passive approach favored by SETI (Search for Extraterrestrial Intelligence), which devotes its efforts simply to listening for any potential incoming alien signals.

The METI approach is controversial for the reason that some scientists consider it unwise to knowingly alert our presence in the galaxy to any potentially technologically superior civilizations. The reader will recall Professor Stephen Hawking's fear of resource-starved aliens existing in "massive ships... looking to conquer and colonize whatever planets they can reach."[46]

In a bid to blur fact and fantasy for viral marketing purposes, *Skyline* made use of Hawking's comments in its trailer, which featured well known American newsreaders (including Dan Rather) citing Hawking on the potential dangers of extraterrestrial contact. The trailer then cuts to panoramic views of an American city being obliterated by dozens of the "massive ships" to which Hawking had referred. Against a black screen, and again referring to the professor's warning, bold text then reads: "Maybe we should have listened."

The blurring of fact and fantasy was also central to the marketing campaign for the alien invasion movie *Battle: Los Angeles* (2011), the posters for which made prominent use of a real photograph of the saucer-shaped UFO which hovered silently for several hours off the coast of LA on the night of February 24–25, 1942, drawing heavy artillery fire from the US Army. These events made national headlines and became known as 'The Battle of Los Angeles.'

In the movie, which is set in present day and inexplicably makes no spoken reference to the real historical event that inspired it, aliens launch a full-scale invasion of major cities worldwide. The invaders are tall, featureless biomechanical humanoids whose guns are a living part of their anatomy. A news report speculates that they are seeking Earth's water as a fuel source, noting that ocean levels have dropped by several feet since their arrival.

For a species with interstellar travel capabilities, the aliens in *Battle: Los Angeles* have come to Earth with a remarkably primitive attack strategy, using remote-controlled drones to wage a US-military-style 'shock and awe' offensive. When the US Marines identify the drones' central command module, they shoot it with a bazooka, disabling the entire alien drone fleet. Thank goodness for bazookas.

The real-life 'Battle of Los Angeles' of 1942 was rather less dramatic than that depicted by Hollywood, although it did result in at least six civilian deaths by way of shrapnel wounds, falling debris, and even terror-induced heart attacks. The origin of the flying object remains unexplained to this day.

A more light-hearted approach to alien invasion came in 2012 with *The Watch*, in which alien scouts from a looming invasion force infiltrate an American suburb by stealing and wearing the skin of its residents. The only thing standing in their way is the local neighborhood watch group, led by Ben Stiller. In their true form, the aliens are hideous reptilian creatures who can be killed only by having their penis ripped off or shot off. As for their motivation for invasion, the character of Jamarcus (Richard Ayoade), who is revealed to be an alien infiltrator in Stiller's group, declares, nonchalantly, "We're aliens, that's what we do – we come to planets, we destroy them, we move on."

Maritime mayhem

For decades, UFOs having been sighted above and below oceans and lakes around the world. In UFOlogy, these objects are known as 'USOs': Unidentified Submerged Objects. In July 2009 the Russian Navy declassified some of its records of encounters with UFOs and USOs. The records, which date back to soviet times, were compiled by a special group headed by deputy Navy commander Admiral Nikolay Smirnov.

According to Vladimir Azhazha, a former navy officer and Russian UFO researcher who reviewed the files upon their release, "Fifty percent of UFO encounters are connected with oceans. Fifteen more with lakes. So UFOs tend to stick to the water."

A notable case from the Russian files involved a nuclear submarine on a combat mission in the Pacific Ocean. The crew reported being pursued by six unknown objects which out-maneuvered their own vessel. Eventually, the mysterious objects took to the surface and flew away.

Recalling his own USO experiences, retired submarine commander Rear Admiral Yury Beketov was quoted as saying:

> On several occasions the [submarine's] instruments gave readings of material objects moving at incredible speed. Calculations showed speeds of about 230 knots, of 400 kph... It was like the objects defied the laws of physics. There's only one explanation: the creatures who built them far surpass us in development.[47]

Three years after the release of the Russian Navy's UFO files, *Battleship* docked in cinemas. Though not the first movie to deal with aliens at sea (*The Abyss*, discussed in the following chapter, beat it to the punch by more than two decades), *Battleship* is certainly the dumbest to date. The opening moments of the movie are set in 2005 when NASA transmits a signal to a nearby star system, referred to only as "Gliese," in the hope of contacting intelligent extraterrestrial life.

So far, so factual... almost. As previously discussed in the context of *Skyline*, the Australian government and NASA did indeed transmit a signal to the extra solar planet Gliese 581d in an effort to establish contact (though this signal was sent in 2009 as opposed to 2005). As in the trailer for *Skyline*, Stephen Hawking's warning about ET contact is also referred to in one of the opening scenes of *Battleship*. As NASA prepares to transmit its signal to the Gliese system, a wise-cracking scientist comments that "it's going to be like Columbus and the Indians – only we're the Indians." But the signal is sent anyway and NASA gives itself a hearty pat on the back.

Cut to 2012: a fleet of five alien ships decides to answer the signal NASA sent out seven years prior. Their objective is to forcibly acquire Earth's abundant natural resources. One spaceship crashes in Hong

Kong, while four others settle in Hawaiian waters. The Navy then sends out US destroyers Sampson and John Paul Jones to investigate and maritime mayhem ensues within the confines of a large force field erected by the aliens. The force field is intended to protect the alien craft from human attack, but, unfortunately for the hapless ETs, actually seals the Navy's destroyers inside it along with the Japanese vessel, Myōkō. The Sampson and Myōkō are obliterated by the aliens, but the John Paul Jones, at the hands of its heroic Tactical Officer, Lieutenant Alex Hopper (Taylor Kitsch), goes on to save the world.

Surprisingly, in addition to cooperation from the Department of Defense, *Battleship* also received support from The Science & Entertainment Exchange. Established in 2008, "The Exchange" is a program of the National Academy of Sciences (NAS) that, according to its website, "connects entertainment industry professionals with top scientists and engineers to create a synergy between accurate science and engaging storylines in both film and TV programming." The goal of The Exchange is "to use the vehicle of popular entertainment media to deliver sometimes subtle, but nevertheless powerful, messages about science." Unfortunately, in *Battleship*, the NAS failed to achieve its goal of creating a synergy between accurate science and engaging storylines.[48]

Witness, for example, the movie's aliens, a species that, despite having mastered interstellar travel, is still reliant upon 21st Century explosives (only marginally more advanced than our own) and cumbersome flying 'machine-bombs' to wage war. So, while in real-life the US military has in its arsenal weaponized laser technologies, in *Battleship*, the superior alien invaders do not.

We learn very little about the aliens themselves, which are bipedal beings with human-like faces, bald heads, and coarse goatee beards. They wear full body armour and helmets. As regards natural weaknesses, we are told the aliens are "sensitive to sunlight," but this potentially interesting narrative device is quickly thrown to the wayside as the Navy soon realizes the aliens are even more sensitive to its hulking guns, just as the ill-prepared aliens in *Battle: Los Angeles* were sensitive to the Marines' bazookas. If hostile aliens really do decide to invade one day, we can only hope they're as technologically and strategically inept as the Pentagon's Entertainment Liaison Office imagines them to be.

Conclusion

The primary goal of this chapter has been to chart the invasive actions of Hollywood's aliens over the decades, assessing their plausibility in relation to real-life scientific debate and UFOlogical occurrences. Clearly, the behaviour of Hollywood's alien invaders has altered little since the earliest entries into the UFO subgenre. While the aliens' motivations seem plausible enough (invasion for essential resources or for expansion of empire), their warfare strategies often strain believability to breaking point, as do Hollywood's depictions of humanity's ability to effectively repel our interplanetary aggressors.

If aliens should ever decide to invade Earth for its natural resources (water, minerals, human DNA, etc.), it seems unlikely in the extreme that they would opt for the scorched earth approach depicted in the likes of *War of the Worlds* and *Independence Day*. Actually, it seems improbable that the aliens would launch air strikes at all, let alone anything as messy as the ground invasions seen in *Falling Skies* and *Battle: Los Angeles*. Any tactics that would provoke a military response from Earth's leaders would probably result in damage to the very resources the aliens are seeking to acquire, especially if weapons of mass destruction are used by either side.

Even if the aliens' goal is simply to eradicate humanity, direct engagement with our military forces would almost certainly be entirely unnecessary. Many real-life UFO reports describe objects penetrating restricted airspace around some of the world's most sensitive military installations, appearing and disappearing in the blink of an eye, coming and going with impunity and showing little concern for our ability to interfere with their activities. These objects can pierce our atmosphere and our oceans with equal ease. Some of the objects even seem immune to our artillery, as in the real Battle of Los Angeles of 1942. In the Hopkinsville case of 1955 the aliens themselves were reported as being impervious to gunshots at point blank range. And this is to say nothing of the alleged psychic abilities ascribed to many UFO occupants in countless close encounter and abduction reports (discussed in the chapters to follow). Many UFO movies depict aliens using psychic force to harm or control those around them (as in *Invaders from Mars* and *Independence Day*, for example) – but could UFO occupants use such abilities on a mass scale? If so, our psychically puny species would be conquered within a matter of hours, or instantly, even.

Possible psychic abilities aside, advanced ETs might very well have psychotronic and psychotropic weapons with which to attack the mind, and even weapons that target specific parts of the body, both external and internal – eyes, ears, legs, even the heart or brain – causing targets to fall down dead en masse, and all without inflicting so much as a scratch on the skin. There would be no resistance from their enemies, and minimal effort on their own part. For Hollywood's purposes, however, such scenarios are utterly lacking in spectacle and drama.

Invasion by stealth could also be an effective strategy – alien infiltration of our society as depicted in numerous big and small screen productions, from *Invasion of the Body Snatchers* to *The Host*. Although the idea of an alien enemy seeking to invisibly exert control over our thinking and behaviour may seem particularly far-fetched, it's a strategy that's been employed for decades by intelligence agencies around the world. The CIA, for example, spent millions of dollars during the Cold War attempting to unlock the secrets of the mind. From the 1950s through to the 1970s, as part of its illegal MK-Ultra program, the CIA sought to manipulate people's mental states and alter their brain functions through the administration of LSD and the use of hypnosis, sensory deprivation, isolation, verbal and sexual abuse, and other forms of torture. One of the aims was to create programmable spies and assassins for both foreign and domestic use.[49] From the 1970s through the 1990s, as part of its controversial Stargate Project, the Agency poured millions of dollars into the research of psychic phenomena for espionage and military applications. Under Stargate, military personnel were trained in 'remote reviewing,' the ability to psychically 'see' events, locations, and information across an unlimited distance. Attempts were even made to psychically influence the thoughts and behavior of specific enemy combatants.[50] It is not implausible to think that aliens might adopt similar strategies.

Forget all the Hollywood movies

Do UFOs mean us harm? Can we expect an invasion any time soon? One school of thought within the UFO community holds that if our alien visitors truly are hostile then their mal-intent would have manifested long ago, certainly before our species developed nuclear, biological, chemical, and laser weapons, as well as other technologies that might effectively help repel an alien invasion. Moreover, this same school of thought notes that the behavior of UFOs and their occupants reflects a scientific and anthropological interest in Earth and its inhabitants, with UFOs consistently being reported over areas of technological and environmental significance, such as major nuclear and electrical facilities, deep lakes and active volcanoes, and frequently in locales where large-scale natural disasters have recently occurred, or are about to occur. In all such cases, benign curiosity rather than aggressive hostility is the overriding characteristic.

It is also a commonly held belief among UFO researchers that any extraterrestrials visiting us naturally will be peaceful owing to the hundreds, thousands, or even millions of years of evolution they would boast in comparison to Homo sapiens. If they have travelled to us from another star system, it goes without saying that their level of technological advancement far exceeds our own. Many mainstream scientists, including Professor Michio Kaku, are confident that any extraterrestrial civilization capable of interstellar travel will, as an evolutionary necessity, long since have overcome its primitive warlike tendencies. "They will have had thousands of years to work out their internal problems of racism, fundamentalism, sectarianism," Kaku told CNN in July of 2012, "so I think they probably will be friendly."

And besides, says Kaku, even if they are hostile, they would have little reason to bring their hostility to our neck of the woods: "There are lots of uninhabited planets with resources on them; so, if they can reach the Earth, they can reach other planets that are uninhabited, so for the most part I think they're going to leave us alone."[51]

Still, some scientists, including Stephen Hawking, are less optimistic about the inherent benevolence of advanced ET civilizations, and some UFO researchers caution that advanced technology does not necessarily go hand-in-hand with moral and ethical enlightenment. In a theoretical time travel experiment, authors Richard Dolan and Bryce Zabel send a small group of 21st century humans back to medieval Europe where they meet with philosophers and scholars of the time. Upon seeing our iPhones, laptops and Bluetooth devices, the medieval folk quickly conclude that, in order to have reached such a wondrously advanced stage of technology, modern-day humans must have solved all of their social and political problems, else how could they have survived despite their awesome power? "Having advanced science and technology does not indicate superior ethics or spiritual evolution," say the authors.[52]

If the UFO occupants do harbour plans for invasion, it seems fair to say that their tactics and technology would make any resistance on our part entirely futile. *"If* they are hostile," warns Michio Kaku, "it would be like Bambi meeting Godzilla if we ever had to fight them... we would present no military challenge to such an advanced civilization... We would be a pushover for them. Forget all the Hollywood movies."[53]

Thankfully, if nearly seventy years of witness reports are anything to go by, our otherworldly visitors are rather less fearsome than Hollywood would have us believe. Indeed, from time-to-time, even Tinseltown can't help but succumb to the wondrous possibilities of peaceful alien contact.

CHAPTER FOUR

WE COME IN PEACE

"You're an interesting species, an interesting mix.
You're capable of such beautiful dreams,
and such horrible nightmares."

— ALIEN INTELLIGENCE (DAVID MORSE), *CONTACT* (1997)

This chapter charts Hollywood's imaginings of peaceful contact, scenarios in which aliens visit our planet or communicate with our species in a spirit of goodwill, or at least with non-hostile intent. In parallel, it chronicles real-world accounts of contact with benign or benevolent UFO occupants, highlighting commonalities or disparities between UFOlogical 'fact' and Hollywood fantasy.

Although Hollywood projected a fearsome alien image throughout the 1950s and beyond, the picture being painted by UFO researchers and witnesses was somewhat reassuring. Reports of close encounters during the early years of the phenomenon were characterized by spiritually enlightened beings consistently voicing their concerns for the wellbeing of humanity.

~ DELIGHTFUL ENCOUNTERS ~

The 'contactee' movement as it is understood today took root in the early-1950s with the stories of George Adamski, whose claimed interactions with attractive, human-looking 'space brothers' (and sisters) would come to define the American UFO subculture of the era.

Adamski was born in Poland on 17 April 1891. A self-styled New Age sage, his first claimed encounter with an extraterrestrial was detailed in his 1953 book *Flying Saucers Have Landed*, which he co-authored with British writer Desmond Leslie. According to Adamski, on 20 November 1952, he and six of his friends/followers drove out to Desert Center near the California-Arizona border. At their remote destination, shortly after 12 noon, the group watched as "a gigantic cigar-shaped silvery ship" cut a silent path through the blue sky above.

"Someone take me down the road, quick!" Adamski yelled, "That ship has come looking for me and I don't want to keep them waiting!" He was obliged by two of his friends, who drove him to a more isolated location a half-mile further out into the desert. Adamski then instructed the two to go back and join the others and to watch for anything that might take place.

Soon thereafter, a "beautiful small craft" arrived on the scene and landed about half a mile from Adamski's position. Looking in the same direction, he noticed a man standing about a quarter of a mile away, motioning for him to approach. Adamski moved cautiously to within arm's length of the mysterious stranger, who he described as being about five-feet six-inches in height, approximately 28 years old, with gray-green eyes, slightly aslant at the corners. His forehead was extremely high by normal human standards, as were his cheek bones, and his complexion was tanned with no sign at all of facial stubble. He wore a one-piece, shiny chocolate-brown outfit, devoid of fasteners. His sandy-colored hair was long, reaching to his shoulders. This description immediately calls to mind the Brazil close encounter case of 1954, detailed in the previous chapter, in which a stunned farmer described a saucer occupant wearing "brown coveralls," and who was "of average height, had broad shoulders, long hair... and slanted eyes."

Back to Adamski. Although, for all intents and purposes, the man looked human, Adamski was in no doubt that he was in the presence of an alien being. "The beauty of his form surpassed anything I had ever seen," wrote Adamski in his 1953 book, "and the pleasantness of his face freed me of all thought of my personal self. I felt like a little child in the presence of one with great wisdom and much love."

Through a combination of spoken English, sign language and telepathy, a conversation ensued between Adamski and the stranger. His name was Orthon, and he and his people were deeply concerned about our use of atomic weapons and their impact not only on Earth but beyond our planet's atmosphere. Orthon told Adamski that he was from Venus(!), and that his people travel to Earth in giant carrier ships, with their smaller craft, flying saucers, being launched from the larger ones.

Adamski asked Orthon many questions, including one about death, enquiring if they die as humans die:

> He [Orthon] pointed to his body and nodded in the affirmative that bodies do die. But, pointing to his head, which I assumed to mean his mind, or intelligence, he shook his head in negation; this does not die. And with a motion of his hand, he gave me the impression that this, the intelligence, goes on evolving.

This was one of the earliest references in the literature linking alien visitors with spiritual concepts. Throughout the ensuing decades, countless more individuals would go on to claim their own encounters with beings espousing spiritual notions, and, as we shall see, the religious connotations of alien contact have not gone unnoticed in Hollywood.

Adamski and the scout craft

As they stood in the desert, Orthon indicated for Adamski to follow him toward his landed craft, which the latter described as being "shaped more like a heavy glass bell than a saucer." It was "translucent and of exquisite color," although Adamski could not see through it. "I definitely do not believe this was a ship made of glass such as we know it. It was a specially processed metal..." This was one of the first descriptions by a UFO witness of "translucent" metals being utilized by unearthly beings. Today they are a common feature in contactee and abductee testimonies.

Adamski asked if he could take a ride in the craft, but his request was politely declined. Thus transpired George Adamski's first claimed meeting with a being from another world. He stood and watched as the scout craft ascended silently before it departed at speed. Later, the six witnesses would each sign an affidavit swearing to the reality of the events. It read as follows:

> I, the undersigned, do solemnly state that I have read the account herein of the personal contact between George Adamski and a man from another world, brought here in his flying saucer, 'Scout' ship, and that I was party to, and witness to the event as herein described.

If Adamski's first claimed encounter were not hard enough to swallow, his stories to come would test the belief even of his most devoted supporters: trips into space aboard a mothership, orbits of the moon, even whistle-stop tours of Venus and Saturn. Such claims were dismissed by Adamski's longtime friend and co-worker Lou Zinsstag as falling under the banner of "personal mental experience." Today, few would dispute that Adamski was prone to showmanship, embellishment, and outright fantasy in the telling of his claimed encounters, and yet, evidence exists which, if looked at dispassionately, casts at least *some* of his claims in a more believable light.

Proof?

Adamski took numerous photographs showing what appear to be flying saucers; a handful are interesting, most strain credulity. In any case, for the determined hoaxer, convincingly fabricating images is an easy enough task when those images are still. Moving images, on the other hand, are a different kettle of fish, and Adamski had reels of film, shot between the early-1950s and mid-1960s, showing what appear to be saucer-like craft in motion. Some of Adamski's footage is impressive, and faking it would have been very difficult if not impossible for anyone, including Hollywood's top special effects experts of the era.

During the afternoon of 27 February 1965, just two months before his death, Adamski, in the presence of four other witnesses, including his longtime friend Madeline Rodeffer, shot remarkable close-range footage of a classic bell-shaped flying saucer (precisely matching his earlier description of Orthon's Scoutcraft) outside Rodeffer's home in Silver Spring, Maryland. The 8mm, black and white film shows the object performing maneuvers over Rodeffer's front yard, retracting and lowering one of three spherical pods on its undercarriage. Rodeffer told UFO researcher Timothy Good in 1967:

It looked blackish-brown or grayish-brown at times, but when it came in close it looked greenish and bluish, and it looked like aluminum: it depended on which way it was tilting. Then at one point it actually stood absolutely still between the bottom of the steps and the driveway.

After a short while the craft disappeared vertically. Rodeffer told Good that she could make out human-like figures at the portholes, but that details were obscured.

The footage was later analyzed by optical physicist William T. Sherwood, formerly a senior project development officer for the Eastman-Kodak Company in Rochester, New York. Sherwood opined that the film was genuine insomuch as it showed a real, three-dimensional object, apparently performing aerial maneuvers. No strings or other evidence of photographic trickery were identifiable. Furthermore, the object captured on film, far from being a small model, was approximately 27 feet in diameter. The most curious aspect of the footage is what can only be described as a distortion effect, seemingly caused by what Sherwood referred to as a 'forcefield' surrounding the object. In several frames of the film, the flange of the saucer visibly droops, as if liquid metal, before returning to its original shape. Sherwood and Good speculate that this is an optical illusion caused by a powerful gravitational field. The distortion effect described must be seen to be appreciated; certainly, this writer has seen nothing of its like in any science-fiction movie of the period. Indeed, it is more comparable to the modern morphing effects pioneered in the mid-late-1980s in movies like *The Abyss* (1989) shortly prior to the CGI revolution sparked by *Terminator 2: Judgment Day* (1991). How Adamski could have created this morphing effect in 1965 using an 8mm home movie camera has never been accounted for by any of his detractors.

In his book *Alien Base*, Timothy Good concludes of Adamski that, although some of his claims were "exaggerated" and "preposterous," many of his reported encounters were fundamentally true, albeit "embellished both by Adamski and by friends and supporters to the extent that they later assumed mythical qualities." Good suggests that Adamski's claims are ripe for re-evaluation, "lest, in throwing out the proverbial baby with the bathwater, potentially important data may be lost to analysis."[1]

Adamski was not the only one claiming personal interactions with benevolent extraterrestrials during the Cold War. Other well-known contactees who described encounters strikingly similar to Adamski's include George Van Tassel,[2] Truman Bethurum,[3] Howard Menger,[4] Paul Villa,[5] and Eduard "Billy" Meier,[6] to name but a few. All of these individuals claimed liaisons with extraterrestrials who not only expressed peace and love in their messages, but who emanated it from their very being. Invariably, these aliens were human-like in appearance, attractive, often with long, light-coloured hair (blonde, white, or sandy), pale skin, and fine facial features. They ranged in height from around five to seven feet. For their passing resemblance to the people of Scandinavia, this alien type would come to be known collectively in UFO literature as the 'Nordic.'

It is important to note that not all reported encounters with friendly space folk fall into the contactee category. Most do not. While contactee cases involve a witness experiencing multiple encounters over several years or even decades, the majority of benevolent alien contact accounts describe unexpected encounters, fleeting in nature and never to be repeated.

"Very nice chaps"

An altogether pleasant encounter with human-looking spacemen is said to have occurred in early May 1940, near Townsend in Montana. While working at his gold-mining claim, Udo Wartena, aged 37, witnessed the landing of an unusual craft measuring at least 100 feet in diameter and around 35 feet in height. From within came a man with "snow white hair" who Wartena described as "extremely good looking, with perfect, almost translucent skin, and [who] appeared to be very youthful and strong." The man informed Wartena that it was not his people's usual policy to allow themselves to be seen. A brief conversation ensued before Wartena was invited onboard the craft, wherein he was introduced to another man closely resembling the first, albeit slightly older in appearance (they stated their ages at around 600 and 900 respectively). When asked about their origin, the men told Wartena only that they were from "a distant planet." As to their agenda on Earth, "We mingle with you people, gather information, leave instructions, or give help where needed." This was Wartena's first and only encounter with the beings, in whose presence he felt "love, or comfort," and who he described as "just like us, and very nice chaps."[7]

A fleeting greeting

> On a summer's afternoon, in either 1948 or 1949, my mother, Brenda, was walking with our dog and myself in the area we called simply 'The Field' at the back of our housing estate... in what was then the outskirts of Chippenham in Wiltshire [England]. Whilst there, she saw an unusual, occupied aircraft...

So began a handwritten letter addressed to this author; tidy and succinct, it documented a mother and daughter's close encounter with a peculiar flying object, piloted by apparently non-human beings. Many years later, the daughter, Karen, a mere toddler at the time of the incident, solicited from her mother, Brenda, a detailed description of what they had both witnessed that day, making a written record of her response. Brenda had no trouble in recalling the details:

> We were walking through 'The Field' when this aircraft came out of nowhere and stopped nearby. There were two beings inside, sat facing one another. The aircraft was like a boat with a see-though cover. The two beings inside were neat and compact; they were dressed in grey and had helmets with a sort of crest on top. They were looking towards us, then one of them raised a hand as if he were waving. Then the aircraft just went.

Through further conversation with her mother, Karen was able to establish that:

> There was no accompanying sound or scent with the aircraft; that it was in view for no more than three minutes; it was about nine feet long, and stopped approximately fifteen yards away at bungalow-roof height; there were no trains on the track nearby at the time; and that the area was otherwise deserted.

Their dog, incidentally, "was interested in the aircraft, but was not alarmed."

Regarding her nondescript recounting of the object's departure, beyond stating that "it just went," Brenda had difficulty expressing the character of its movement. "She said that it didn't exactly vanish instantly, it just 'went' very rapidly," Karen related.[8]

Speaking with her by telephone, I found Karen to be charming and genuine, an intelligent and well-spoken woman whose bewilderment at the event described was evident nearly sixty years on. What, then, to make of her story?

It was obvious that Karen had no prior interest in UFOs, and no UFOlogical knowledge of which to speak, and at no time had she or her mother sought to publicize their experience. Indeed, the witnesses' names as written here – 'Brenda' and 'Karen' – are pseudonyms, a reflection of Karen's continuing desire for anonymity (their real names and backgrounds are known to me).

During our telephone conversation, Karen told me that her mother had always been a 'no nonsense' sort of lady, and had been reluctant to speculate about the precise nature of the 'aircraft,' or about the possible origin of its occupants. Sadly, Brenda passed away a few years ago, but despite her apparent nonchalance at what she and her daughter had witnessed, she had always acknowledged the high-strangeness of the event. "She said that she realized that what she was seeing was 'something very different,'" Karen wrote in her letter, "but she wasn't alarmed or afraid. She felt the beings were friendly."⁹

The above reported encounters are just a small handful of such documented in UFO literature and they are included here if only to demonstrate that, by the time Hollywood entered the UFO scene in the early 1950s, cases of peaceful alien contact were already a global (albeit not widely reported) phenomenon. The movies that were to follow along these lines, from *The Day the Earth Stood Still*, to *Close Encounters of the Third Kind*, and *The Abyss*, were, in essence, examples of art imitating life, rather than vice versa; although, in certain cases, specific details from the movies undoubtedly have influenced UFO reports.

~ TO HOLLYWOOD, WITH LOVE ~

A warning and an ultimatum

The first UFO movie to feature a human-looking extraterrestrial came in 1951 with *The Day the Earth Stood Still*, in which the enlightened alien Klaatu and his indestructible robot Gort land their flying saucer in Washington D.C. Their mission: to warn of the dangers atomic weaponry poses not only to humanity, but to the denizens of other worlds in the universe. This, of course, was the very same message

George Adamski claimed to have received from Orthon the following year in 1952.

The movie opens with Klaatu's flying saucer being tracked on radar at high altitude before it lands on the President's Park Ellipse in the nation's Capital. Not quite the White House lawn, but close enough, and hence the popular question: "Why don't aliens just land on the White House Lawn?" The response that most immediately springs to mind is that aliens are unlikely to model their diplomatic strategies on Hollywood entertainment.

No sooner has Klaatu's craft touched down than it is encircled by US soldiers with itchy trigger fingers. As he steps out of his craft, Klaatu announces: "We have come to visit you in peace and with good will." But the military doesn't buy it, and, when Klaatu reaches into his flight-suit and produces a peculiar-looking device, a jittery soldier presumes it to be a weapon and opens fire on the poor alien, wounding him and destroying the object he was holding. In response to this act of aggression, Gort, Klaatu's humanoid robot, emits a powerful beam from his visor which he uses to systematically disintegrate all military hardware on the scene, much to the horror of the military and civilian onlookers. Gort continues his defensive actions until Klaatu utters the phrase: "Gort! Deglet, ovrosco!" at which point the robot ceases its attack and returns to its formerly placid state. Klaatu then explains to the military that the destroyed object was intended as a gift for the US President – a viewing device through which he could have glimpsed the wonders of life on other planets.

After Klaatu is taken into custody, the military attempts to unlock the secrets of his craft (which is still parked just a stone's throw from the White House). But these efforts prove futile as the metal skin of the alien saucer is utterly impregnable, withstanding cutting torches and even diamond drills. Soon enough, Klaatu escapes from his captivity and decides to lodge at a boarding house under an alias, "Mr. Carpenter." It is at the boarding house that Klaatu befriends Helen Benson (Patricia Neal), a World War II widow, and her son Bobby (Billy Gray), both of whom initially are oblivious to his extraterrestrial nature.

When Klaatu asks Bobby who is the greatest person on Earth, the young science fanatic tells him it's the leading American scientist professor Jacob Barnhardt (Sam Jaffe), who happens to live in D.C. This leads to a meeting between Klaatu and Barnhardt in which the former tells the latter that the people of the other planets are deeply concerned about our recent development of atomic power and its destructive potential both on Earth and on other planets.

Klaatu tells Barnhardt that if his anti-nuke message goes unheeded, "planet Earth will be eliminated." This prompts the professor to arrange a meeting of scientists at Klaatu's ship; however, in order that the scientists take Klaatu seriously, Barnhardt suggests that the alien first give a demonstration of his power. Thus, Klaatu arranges for a thirty-minute worldwide power blackout, effectively bringing planet Earth to a standstill.

When the blackout ends and the military finally catch up with Klaatu, he is shot and fatally wounded. Gort takes Klaatu's corpse back to the saucer where Helen (now fully aware of Klaatu's otherworldly nature) watches as the alien is brought back from the dead through the use of advanced technology. Klaatu's revival is only temporary, however, as even *his* science cannot truly conquer death; this power, he tells Helen, is reserved solely for the "Almighty Spirit."

In the film's closing scene, Klaatu steps out of his saucer and addresses the scientists that Barnhardt has assembled at the scene in what is today regarded as one of the silver screen's most memorable speeches:

> I am leaving soon, and you will forgive me if I speak bluntly. The universe grows smaller every day, and the threat of aggression by any group, anywhere, can no longer be tolerated. There must be security for all, or no one is secure... It is no concern of ours how you run your own planet, but if you threaten to extend your violence, this Earth of yours will be reduced to a burned-out cinder. Your choice is simple: join us and live in peace, or pursue your present course and face obliteration. We shall be waiting for your answer. The decision rests with you.

UFO acclimation?

In chapter two of this book it was suggested that officialdom may have played a role in the production of *The Day the Earth Stood Still*. Further circumstantial evidence for government collusion in the movie comes from Paul Davids, the writer/producer of the 1994 Showtime TV movie, *Roswell*. According to Davids, *The Day the Earth Stood Still* director, Robert Wise, was a firm believer in ET visitation and his belief was based on information provided to him by possible government insiders. "He [Wise] met with me in his office in Beverly Hills,"

Davids told me during a 2013 interview. "He told me he absolutely did believe that the saucers were real and that some of them were extraterrestrial. He believed it not because he had seen one, but because of all the information that had come to him while he was making *The Day the Earth Stood Still.*" Wise told Davids that scientists and engineers from Washington had taken him aside during filming and talked to him about UFOs. "What they told him convinced him that the government took this really seriously," said Davids, "that some of these craft were visitors from space."[10]

UFO technology

Precisely what these scientists and engineers from Washington told Wise about UFOs is unknown, but it is fair to say that *The Day the Earth Stood Still* boasts a remarkable degree of UFOlogical verisimilitude. In earlier movies, UFOs were clunky-looking contraptions, as with *The Flying Saucer* of 1950, in which the eponymous craft is little more than a circular plane on wheels. The sleek, domed saucer shape typically described in witness reports and in government documentation since 1947 was not realized onscreen until 1951 in *The Day the Earth Stood Still.* More notably, the subtle, uniform glow given off by Wise's saucer calls to mind the appearance of ionized air – a common effect recalled by UFO witnesses around the world and which some speculate is the product of electromagnetic propulsion systems.

Klaatu's concern about our use of nuclear weapons actually has precedent in official government documentation (classified at the time) describing UFO incursions into restricted airspace over US nuclear bases. Another real-life parallel in the movie is the impenetrable metal of Klaatu's craft, in which we see shades of Roswell. Numerous first and second hand witnesses have testified that debris recovered from the Roswell crash in July of 1947 was uncuttable, untearable, unburnable and undentable – essentially indestructible. Additionally, the shrill sound emitted by Klaatu's flying saucer also has been a common feature in UFO close encounter reports from the 1940s to present day, with witnesses associating high-pitch whirring, humming, or hissing sounds with UFOs.

The appearance and glow of Klaatu's saucer, its impenetrable metal skin and the high-pitched noise it emits, and Klaatu exhibiting an interest in our nuclear capabilities. Is it possible that such details could have been slipped in at the behest of the CIA during the screenwriting phase through the Agency's high-level asset Darryl Zanuck by way of his fellow Army Signal Corps propagandists, screenwriter Edmund North, and Producer Julian Blaustein? If so, were these details fine-tuned during the filming stage by on-set advice from Wise's Washington scientists? Due to the CIA's longstanding unwritten motto, "Nothing on paper," it is unlikely that we will ever know for sure.

Aliens among us

One of the most interesting details in *The Day the Earth Stood Still* is that the alien Klaatu is entirely human in appearance. Here again we find clear UFOlogical parallels. In the mid-1960s, the North Atlantic Treaty Organization (NATO) conducted a Cosmic Top Secret Study of the UFO problem titled The Assessment, a kind of NATO version of the USAF's 1948 'Estimate of the Situation.' But while the USAF study merely concluded that some UFOs were likely "interplanetary" in origin, The Assessment went many steps further. This, at least, is according to the testimony of Robert Dean, a retired US Army Command Sergeant Major who was assigned to NATO's SHAPE headquarters in Brussels during the mid-1960s. Dean is now a grandfatherly figure in the UFO community whose words are taken by many with a pinch of salt. Dean claims that, while stationed at SHAPE in 1964, he had limited access to The Assessment, and its conclusions were shocking. Dean asserts that "part of the study stated that [NATO] had come to the conclusion that we had four different civilizations – cultures, intelligences – that were present here on Earth and that were visiting us and interacting with us." Particularly interesting, says Dean, was that one of the alien groups was identical in appearance to humans; or, rather, we were identical to *them*. This was of grave concern to NATO leadership.

Delivering a public lecture at the Civic Theater in Leeds, England, in 1994, Dean stated that some of the human-looking ETs were so similar to us that "they could sit next to you in an airplane or in a restaurant in a coat and tie or a dress and you would never know. They could be sitting next to you in a theater like this." Dean noted that "this was a matter of great concern to the admirals and generals at SHAPE Headquarters in Paris. Some of the discussions which went on in the War Room were kind of frightening and some of them were rather amusing. One officer said: 'My God, man, do you realize that these [aliens] could be walking up and down the corridors of SHAPE Headquarters and we wouldn't even know who the hell they were?'"[11]

In *The Day the Earth Stood Still*, Klaatu effortlessly infiltrates human society, walking among us unnoticed, casually but keenly observing our curious ways. This idea also puts us in mind of the aforementioned case of May 1940, in which alien beings allegedly told Udo Wartena: "we mingle with you people, gather information, leave instructions, or give help where needed."

Klaatu as Christ

The only aspect of *The Day the Earth Stood Still* that dates it UFOlog-ically and reminds us of its firm roots in Hays-code-era Hollywood is its subtle allusions to Christianity. Klaatu's reference to "The Almighty Spirit" is a clear nod to God and was intended by the film's writers to be understood in a Christian context. It is no accident, for example, that Klaatu is given the alias of "Carpenter," Christ's worldly occupa-tion as described in scripture. Nor is it coincidence that Klaatu, a man with otherworldly powers who preaches peace to the masses, is killed only to be resurrected before rising into the sky (in a flying saucer). But the film's Christian allegory is ironic, given that, in many contact cas-es, UFO occupants have alluded to a divine power in secular and dis-tinctly non-Christian terms, speaking of God not as a supreme (male) 'being,' but instead espousing the notion of a universal life force or all-pervasive cosmic energy.

"For us, what you call God is a form of absolute energy," the Argen-tinean contactee Orlando Jorge Ferraudi claimed he was told by a hu-man-like UFO occupant in August 1956, "and as to death, it is only a change in molecular structure, a change of state."[12] In an alleged UFO contact case from Campitello in Italy, in July 1968, a human-like being with slightly feline features told car salesman Walter Marino Rizzi that "God is everywhere; in us, plants, stones, grass, and nature, everything that exists," and added that when his own people die of natural causes, it is as a result of "exhaustion of cosmic energy."[13] In these terms, alien faith would seem to have more in common with the Eastern philoso-phies of Taoism and Buddhism than with Christianity.

Legacy

In 1995, *The Day the Earth Stood Still* was selected for preservation in the United States National Film Registry as being "culturally, historically, or aesthetically significant."[14] Certainly its influence cannot be understated. This was not an obscure B-movie catering solely to frisky teens at the drive-in; this was a major motion picture event, a high quality studio product that had the enthusiastic backing of one of the most influential figures in Hollywood (Darryl Zanuck) and that was seen by millions of cinemagoers the world over. One of those cinemagoers was Ronald Reagan. Himself no stranger to the movie business, Reagan starred in numerous B-movies between the late-1930s and mid-1960s. He was also an avid movie-watcher, and no motion picture struck quite such a chord with the future Commander in Chief as *The Day the Earth Stood Still*.

Famously, in his address to the United Nations General Assembly on 21 September, 1987, President Ronald Reagan wondered aloud "how quickly our differences worldwide would vanish if we were facing an alien threat from outside of this world."[15] It is a matter of public record that Reagan was himself a UFO witness,[16] but his "alien threat" statement to the UN, which he would repeat publicly on multiple occasions throughout his Presidency, may have been directly inspired by *The Day the Earth Stood Still*. According to Presidential UFO researcher Grant Cameron, "World peace and aliens were never far from Reagan's mind. He used to walk around the White House asking people if they had seen the movie *The Day the Earth Stood Still*, uttering the phrase 'Klaatu barada nikto.'" Just as the character of Helen had uttered the alien phrase in the nick of time and saved the world, Reagan planned to do the same. Cameron even posits the notion that Reagan's fascination with *The Day the Earth Stood Still* may actually have led to the end of the Cold War: "In 1989, inspired by Klaatu's words, 'There must be security for all, or no one is secure,' Reagan stood at the Berlin Wall and asked his friend Gorbachev to 'tear down this wall.' Gorbachev removed the wall which separated the two Germanys, and there has been peace between the West and the Eastern bloc countries ever since."[17]

Reagan is not the only President to have been inspired by *The Day the Earth Stood Still*. On 21 March 2012, while in Maljamar, New Mexico, President Barack Obama paraphrased Klaatu's immortal line: "We have come to visit you in peace and with good will." Addressing a crowd of reporters, Obama declared: "It was a wonderful trip... we landed in Roswell. I announced to people when I landed that 'I come in peace.'"[18] It was a cheap tactic to elicit some laughs and to associate a real, historical UFO incident with Hollywood fiction. Perhaps someone should have pointed out to the President that *The Day the Earth Stood Still* was a poor choice in this regard, standing, as it does, as one of the most believable UFO movies in history.

Friendly cycloptic gelatinous blobs

Released in 1953, *It Came from Outer Space* was one of the first movies of its genre to exploit the newly developed 3D process, and popcorn flew in the aisles during its opening sequence as an asteroid-like UFO hurtled 'out' of the cinema screen and into the laps of terrified cinemagoers. But the aliens here, despite their monstrous exteriors, were not hostile at all, just misunderstood.

In the movie, a flying saucer crashes near the sleepy town of Sand Rock, Arizona. Most of the unsuspecting locals assume it to have been a meteorite, but, after a number of the townsfolk go missing and later reappear acting dazed and distant, local authorities begin to suspect an alien invasion. Not all is as it appears, though. It transpires that the aliens are benign entities whose saucer crashed on Earth due to a technical malfunction. In order for them to repair their ship and be on their way home they must first procure the necessary parts. But this requires blending in with the locals – not an easy task when your natural form is that of a cycloptic gelatinous blob. Fortunately, these aliens are shape-shifters, though they require 'blueprints' for their transformation if they are to replicate the human form, and hence the missing townsfolk. When the aliens are unable to believably mimic human behavior, suspicions are raised and an angry mob marches on the stranded saucer. It is only through the heroic efforts of a local amateur astronomer, John Putnam (Richard Carlson), that the aliens manage to escape. Putnam seals them off in an abandoned mine to protect them from the advancing mob as they finish repairing their ship. The aliens leave our planet in the nick of time, albeit having suffered two casualties at the hands of fearful Earthlings. All the human abductees are released by the aliens before their departure.

Here, then, is another early UFO movie in which UFOlogical detail is identifiable: a saucer crash (echoing Roswell), aliens abducting humans (in a foreshadowing of the countless abduction reports in the decades to follow), even the idea of UFOnauts as shape-shifters, as popularized in the conspiracy community by David Icke over four decades later. Although some readers may be inclined to attribute such detail to the subtle handiwork of the CIA, the government collusion angle here seems less plausible than with other movies of the era. The movie's screenplay was penned by Harry Essex, but the source material was provided by Ray Bradbury, a man who openly loathed anyone with a belief in flying saucers or alien visitation. Indeed, *Roswell* writer/producer Paul Davids has described Bradbury, the legendary author of *The Martian Chronicles*, as "an arch skeptic."

Davids was sat next to Bradbury at a luncheon when famed monster maker Ray Harryhausen got his star on Hollywood Boulevard. Both Rays had agreed to help Davids in the production of his documentary that was to become the 2006 Saturn Award-winning *The Sci-Fi Boys*, but Bradbury was displeased to learn of Davids' involvement in another movie. Davids described his 'close encounter' with Bradbury as follows:

> "When he heard that I had made *Roswell* he started yelling at me! He started attacking me! Saying 'what are you doing making a piece of fiction like that and trying to pass it off as something that's true?' I was so taken aback. I said 'Mr Bradbury, with all due respect, have you heard what the witnesses really said? Do you *know* the case?' He said, 'I don't have to now the case – *I know it didn't happen!*' And I said, 'Mr Bradbury, can I ask why you're so sure?' He said, 'Because I'm Ray Bradbury! They would have told ME! You think this would have happened and they wouldn't have told ME!? You're crazy!'"

Davids ascribes Bradbury's dismissal of the Roswell crash and UFO reality to "pride and ego."[19]

"Among friends"

1954 saw the publication of an influential book in the burgeoning contactee literature. The *White Sands Incident*, written by rocket test technician Daniel Fry, was a first-person account of the author's claimed encounter with an extraterrestrial people whose roots trace back to ancient mythological civilizations on Earth, specifically, Atlantis and Lemuria.

Though published in 1954, Fry's book describes events he claims occurred on 4 July 1949 (although, suspiciously, he later changed the year to 1950). According to Fry, on the night in question, an object shaped like an "oblate spheroid," 30 feet wide by 16 feet high, landed in front of him in the New Mexico desert. Fry approached the object and cautiously laid a hand on its metallic skin. It was then that he heard a loud disembodied male voice, "Better not touch the hull, pal, it's still hot!" Fry leapt backwards in shock as the voice continued with a chuckle; "Take it easy, pal, you're among friends." Through the conversation that ensued, Fry discovered that the voice belonged to a human-like alien being (whose name he would later learn was 'Ah-Lahn,' or 'Alan' for short) who was operating the remote-controlled craft from a mothership some 900 miles above the Earth. Fry claims to have been invited aboard the smaller, remotely-piloted craft and flown to New York City and back within 30 minutes, the wondrous sights below him miraculously being made visible by technology that renders metal translucent. According to Fry, a projector-like device shone a beam down onto the door through which he had entered the craft; "and under its influence the door became totally transparent," wrote Fry. "It was as though I were looking through the finest type of plate glass or Lucite window."

Following publication of his book Fry became a cult leader, preaching his cosmic teachings to all who would listen. He lectured widely and gave hundreds of TV and radio interviews before his death in 1992 at the age of 84.[20]

In 1986, 32 years after the publication of Fry's book, Walt Disney Pictures released *Flight of the Navigator*, an endearing family adventure that exhibited clear parallels with the Fry case. Directed by Randal Kleiser of *Grease* fame, the film follows the adventures of 12-year-old David Freeman, who mysteriously vanishes one evening while walking in the woods only to reappear eight years later not having aged a day. Meanwhile, an alien spacecraft is discovered nearby, which NASA believes may explain David's disappearance. By accessing complex technical data mysteriously uploaded into the boy's subconscious mind from an alien source, NASA learns that David has, in fact, spent the last eight years on a planet called Phaelon, some 560 light years away.

The film recalls Daniel Fry's testimony with its talking, artificially-controlled UFO, nicknamed 'Max' (voiced by Paul 'Pee Wee Herman' Reubens), treating its awestruck human passenger to a whistle-stop tour of the United States, the sights below being made visible to David, as they were to Fry, by a translucent metal door. As with 'Alan' in the Fry case, Max in *Navigator* even uses colloquial language, prompting David to declare, "You sound just like a human!"

Nordics, off-screen and on

In addition to the publication of Fry's book, 1954 saw a particularly vivid report of a close encounter with two human-like saucer occupants in rural England. At 4.45pm on the afternoon of 21 October, Jessie Roestenburg and her two young sons witnessed a UFO hovering directly over their roof while outside their farmhouse in Ranton, Staffordshire. Roestenburg described it as "a massive disc, bright silver and shaped like a Mexican hat." It made a loud hissing sound, she told the Staffordshire Newsletter, "like when a blacksmith puts hot iron into water, but much louder." Roestenburg further described the object as having "a dome, like glass," within which were "two beings," looking directly down at her and her sons. "They were the most beautiful people I have seen," she continued, "but they were not human. Their foreheads were large in proportion to the rest of their faces and they had long golden hair. I could only see them from the chest upwards, and they were wearing what looked like vivid blue polo-neck jumpers and what looked like fish bowls on their heads."

Presumably the beings were friendly, for Roestenburg related that she experienced no tension at all as she gazed upon their faces, noting, "I felt a sense of peace I have never felt since." The object then proceeded to circle the cottage before departing vertically at great speed. The incident was widely reported by the local media at the time, and Roestenburg's sons confirmed her account. She later suffered from symptoms her doctors speculated may have been caused by radiation poisoning. "For a while, I was in a terrible mess, but gradually I got better." Despite being subjected to intense ridicule by understandably incredulous locals, Roestenburg stuck to her story until the day she died.[21]

Aliens closely resembling the Nordics would reappear the following year, this time in the 1955 movie *This Island Earth*, a lavish Technicolor space opera based on the 1952 novel of the same name by Mormon writer Raymond F. Jones (the Mormon link to UFOs is discussed in detail in Chapter Six).

In the movie, a race of human-looking extraterrestrials with white hair and high foreheads called Metalunans have come to Earth to recruit our best scientists to help defend their home-world in a war against the evil Zagons, referred to throughout as "Mutants," ridiculous-looking creatures with huge exposed brains and claws for hands who shuffle about like zombies.

The seemingly-friendly Metalunans have ulterior motives, however. They abduct scientists Dr. Cal Meacham (Rex Reason) and Dr. Ruth Adams (Faith Domergue) and take them back to their home-world, where the Metalunans reveal their plan to relocate their dying civilization to Earth – a plan that will call for invasion. These aliens are hostile to us, but their hostility is borne of desperate necessity (the survival of their species) rather than innate malevolence. Indeed, the Metalunans are partially redeemed through the actions of the alien Exeter (played by Jeff Morrow), who sees the immorality of his people's strategy and decides to set Cal and Ruth free, ultimately saving their lives at the cost of his own. The planned invasion of Earth is thwarted when the planet Metaluna self-destructs. *This Island Earth* was a commercial and critical success upon its release and is today considered one of the best science fiction movies of the 1950s.

The movie abounds with UFOlogical themes and imagery. The Metalunans, with their white hair and high foreheads, are virtually identical to the Nordics of contactee lore, and their mode of interstellar transport is a classic flying saucer. Furthermore, and as noted by Paul Meehan in his book *Saucer Movies*, "this was the first film to depict the secret infiltration of our society by a superior alien civilization [Klaatu, four years prior, had been a lone infiltrator]."[22]

Fly me to the moon

While *This Island Earth* had shown humans assisting aliens in their scientific endeavors, Disney's live-action comedy *Moon Pilot* (1962) depicted the reverse. The movie follows astronaut Capt. Richmond Talbot as he prepares to make the first manned flight around the moon. The mission is classified top secret, requiring Talbot to be kept under close and constant observation by NASA, the CIA, and the FBI.

When Talbot is approached by a mysterious and attractive "foreign" woman, the government immediately suspects her to be a spy. Calling herself 'Lyrae,' the woman has a disquieting amount of knowledge about the US space program and warns Talbot about possible technical faults in his spacecraft, offering to remedy them with a special formula. We soon learn that Lyrae is a friendly extraterrestrial from the planet Beta Lyrae (Beta Lyrae, incidentally, is a real binary star system in the constellation of Lyra, approximately 960 light-years from Earth). Inevitably, Talbot falls for the cosmic beauty and decides to give his government tails the slip in order to spend some quality time with her. The movie ends with Talbot in his rocket launching successfully into lunar orbit with Lyrae onboard as a stowaway, the two lovebirds singing a kitsch ballad about Beta Lyrae as the credits roll.

Moon Pilot is notable most obviously for its depiction of an attractive human-looking alien who wouldn't seem out of place in any classic contactee story, but it also boasts a few other points of interest. Lyrae can read minds, an ability commonly attributed to aliens in both contactee and abductee accounts. At one point in the movie, she even manifests a psychic projection of a little boy, who we are told is actually her and Talbot's future offspring, an early allusion to alien-human interbreeding and hybrid children.

Curiously, the movie received limited co-operation from the US Air Force,[23] despite the USAF's almost unbroken track record up to this point of denying assistance to UFO-themed productions (although, technically, no 'UFOs' are featured in the film). The FBI, on the other hand was less sympathetic to the production. Upon seeing the movie's portrayal of FBI agents as buffoons, J. Edgar Hoover himself reportedly put in an angry phone call to Walt Disney. But Hoover's concerns about the film likely went deeper than its comical depiction of FBI field agents, as Paul Meehan observes: "Hoover's interest in the UFO phenomenon is well documented, and one presumes that he was concerned with the public image of the FBI in connection with the investigation of UFOs."[24]

"Ungraspable intelligence"

The mid-1960s was a time of intense UFO activity worldwide, particularly in the United States, and the wave of 1964–1966 helped inspire the popular UFO-themed TV show *The Invaders* (1967–1968). Meanwhile, UFO depictions on the big screen were strangely few and far between, although UFOlogical themes continued to manifest subtly in movie narratives.

In 1968 cinemagoers were by turns wowed, infuriated, and perplexed by Stanley Kubrick's masterpiece *2001: Space Odyssey*, which was part-inspired by Arthur C. Clarke's short story, *The Sentinel*. The movie is notable here for its musings on a benign cosmic super-intelligence dispassionately jump-starting human evolution.

In their extensive research for the film, Kubrick and Clarke approached famed astronomer Carl Sagan for his opinion on what might constitute a realistic depiction of an extraterrestrial intelligence. Sagan advised against using actors in alien suits on the grounds that alien life forms would almost certainly bear no resemblance to human beings, although countless real-life reports of UFO occupants fly in the face of this idea (Sagan, it should be noted, was fiercely skeptical of the UFO phenomenon). Kubrick followed Sagan's advice, choosing simply to *suggest*, rather than explicitly depict, an alien intelligence. It was a wise decision on the director's part, one that added to his film's profound sense of mystery and wonder. During a 1968 interview for *Playboy* magazine, Kubrick hinted at the true nature of his movie's aliens, suggesting that they had evolved over millions of years from biological beings to "immortal machine entities," and then into "beings of pure energy and spirit [with] limitless capabilities and ungraspable intelligence."[25] Still, despite being the most successful alien-themed movie in the history of cinema at the time (and the most successful sci-fi movie, period), *2001* had no discernible UFO-logical impact upon its release and failed to spark any UFO waves. In fact, UFO sightings declined in 1968 and into 1969, the year the USAF said goodbye to Blue Book.[26]

ETH vs. IDH

In the same year the USAF had declared the death of the UFO, Dr. Jacques Vallee declared the death, or at least the gross inadequacy, of the Extraterrestrial Hypothesis. In the early years of his research Vallee had been a champion of the ETH, however, as time went on, the scientist grew incredulous at the nature of many UFO contact cases. Although he remained convinced of UFO reality and of the overall authenticity of UFO occupant reports, Vallee's theories about UFO origins had begun to evolve.

In his 1969 book *Passport to Magonia*, Vallee argued that the ETH was too simplistic to account for many aspects of UFO phenomena which seemed too bizarre to be merely extraterrestrial. Sure enough, innumerable UFO reports across the decades have included characteristics that are hard to reconcile with the idea of simple alien visitation. UFO and alien encounters have been reported as having occurred on astral levels and in conjunction with paranormal and even cryptozoological phenomena, from ghosts to Bigfoot. The ETH has always ignored these characteristics.

Thus Vallee laid out the interdimensional hypothesis (IDH), which posited that the intelligences behind the UFO phenomenon exist beyond space-time and can flit in and out of our reality at will, assuming a multitude of forms, from the faeries, goblins, and incubi of ages past, to the UFOs and aliens of modern times. Their interactions with humanity are perhaps designed to test us, trick us, and to encourage us to question the nature of our own reality. This theory was also championed around the same time by American parapsychologist and UFOlogist John Keel, whose 1975 book *The Mothman Prophecies* linked UFOs to a variety of disturbing supernatural phenomena. The book was chillingly adapted for the big screen in 2002 with Richard Gere in the lead role, although UFOs barely feature.

Vallee's alternative to the ETH was not well-received by the mainstream UFO research community, which preferred a more 'nuts and bolts,' less mystical line of enquiry. However, if indeed UFOs are extraterrestrial spacecraft, researchers are no closer to proving it today than they were in 1969. The IDH, although arguably more holistic and sophisticated than the ETH, is no less problematic as it is, by its very nature, impossible to test. After all, how does one go about verifying the objective existence of an omnipresent intelligence which for millennia has been responsible for quietly shaping our perceptions of ourselves and our universe? Today, as ever, the phenomenon persists while the UFO theorists squabble in vain.

From the Pleiades to The X-Files

In the mid-1970s a new contactee came to the fore in Eduard "Billy" Meier. A one-armed Swiss, Meier claimed to have been in contact with Nordic extraterrestrials since 1942, but it was not until early 1975 that his contacts intensified. According to Meier, it was at this point in his life that he entered into regular face-to-face and psychic communication with 'Semjase' and 'Ptaah,' beings from the Pleiades star cluster, located approximately 440 light years from Earth in the constellation of Taurus. Meier says his alien friends tasked him with spreading the word to all those who would listen about crucial issues in our world, including environment, spirituality, and the dangers of organized religion.

Meier is best-known for his crystal clear daylight photos of what appear to be flying saucers hovering majestically over the Swiss countryside. He also shot video footage showing saucer-like objects in motion and vanishing into thin air. Superficially, some (though certainly not all) of Meier's photographic evidence is impressive, especially so since it comfortably predated our age of computer software and digital trickery. This is not to suggest that Meier's photos and videos could not have been faked; indeed, some of them have been convincingly exposed as hoaxes. Still, his elaborate stories of alien contact continue to influence thinking in certain corners of the UFO community. In any case, like most of the contactees before him, Meier today resides on UFOlogy's garbage heap, with barely a handful of researchers willing to support his contact claims, and fewer still, the authenticity of his photographic evidence.[27]

Meier is notable in the context of film and television for the fact that his most iconic saucer photo, shot on 18 March 1975, would be used some two decades later in the immensely popular TV series *The X-Files* (1993–2002). It appeared in the show in poster form, prominently and permanently adorning the wall of Agent Fox Mulder's basement office. It was inevitable that Mulder's poster, emblazoned with the words "I want to believe," should find its way into video and music stores worldwide, and, in turn, onto the bedroom walls of countless 'X-philes.'

More intriguingly, a saucer almost identical to Meier's was featured in the 1953 movie *Invaders from Mars*, which is discussed in the previous chapter in the context of possible CIA involvement. Did the Agency seed the movie with a real saucer design it secretly knew to exist, or did a Swiss fraudster simply base his own saucer design on a piece of Hollywood fiction? Take your pick.

In the same year Billy Meier was allegedly talking with Nordic aliens and shooting home movies of their craft, Disney released its own movie about the Nordics, albeit absent any explicit use of the "Nordic" term. *Escape to Witch Mountain* (1975) saw two blond-haired children slowly uncovering the truth about their extraterrestrial origins. The children, Tony and Tia (played by Ike Eisenmann and Kim Richards), are possessed of telekinetic and telepathic abilities respectively. *Escape to Witch Mountain* spawned two sequels, one in 1978 which rode the box-office UFO wave caused by Spielberg's *Close Encounters* the year prior, and another in 1982, five months ahead of Spielberg's all-conquering *E.T.: The Extraterrestrial*.

The Spielberg effect

More so than any other filmmaker, Steven Spielberg has moulded our perceptions of otherworldly visitors. His films teem with iconic imagery seared into the minds of millions: a mothership's miraculous ascension at Devils Tower; a boy and his fugitive friend from the stars cycling in silhouette across the face of the moon. Even Spielberg's less memorable alien offerings, *War of the Worlds* (2005) and *Indiana Jones and the Kingdom of the Crystal Skull* (2008), have enjoyed enormous success at the worldwide box-office, raking in some $1.3 billion between them.[28]

Although he has donned his director's cap for just four alien-themed movies, Spielberg's role as a producer has long seen him neck-deep in entertainment of the extraterrestrial kind. His credits to date include *Batteries Not Included* (1987), the *Men in Black* franchise (1997–2012), the alien abduction mini-series *Taken* (2002), the *Transformers* franchise (2007 –), the alien invasion series *Falling Skies* (2011–2015), the 'Sci-fi-Western' *Cowboys and Aliens* (2011), and *Super 8* (2011). That Spielberg continues to make movies about life elsewhere is owed not simply to good business sense, but is due in large part to his own childhood fascination with UFOs, a fascination that would intensify into his late-twenties and culminate in his cathartic production of *Close Encounters of the Third Kind* (1977).

Close Encounters was a miracle of a movie. It imparted to the viewer a message of universal hope, revealing to cinemagoers that aliens were not *necessarily* a force to be feared. According to Spielberg's vision, aliens were simply misunderstood and are not our maleficent destructors but our gloriously beneficent friends. Here was the work of an unashamed idealist, its director's childlike sense of wonder infusing its every frame.

The film's plot, such as it is, follows line worker Roy Neary (Richard Dreyfuss), a Spielbergian everyman with a thirst for adventure who is trapped in a joyless marriage with bratty kids in middle-American suburbia. Roy's life is turned upside down one night after a close encounter with a UFO convinces him that we are not alone in the universe. This experience prompts Roy to embark upon an obsessive and isolating quest for the truth behind the UFO enigma and ultimately leads him to Devils Tower in Wyoming where he meets angelic extraterrestrial beings with whom he blissfully takes his leave of our humdrum planet.

Close Encounters is notable for being the first film ever to feature the archetypal 'Gray' alien. While shades of the Gray are identifiable in film and TV products dating back to the 1950s (and notably in the 1975 TV movie *The UFO Incident*, discussed in the following chapter), *Close Encounters* marked the Grays' first fully crystallized appearance onscreen, with trademark spindly bodies, small stature, oversized heads and eyes, and otherwise featureless faces. Many commentators have used this fact to suggest that it was the deep cultural penetration of Spielberg's iconic movie, *not* real-life occurrences, that lead witnesses to claim personal encounters with the diminutive Grays. However, the man who designed the aliens for *Close Encounters*, famed production designer Joe Alves, deflates this theory. When I interviewed Alves in 2013 he told me he had based his alien designs on descriptions he'd received directly from witnesses. "I had called a lot of people when trying to design the aliens to see if people had actually seen anything," said Alves, "and I talked to a lot of legitimate people... who described to me very simplistic creatures with large eyes and small mouths, no nose."

Based on what he heard during his research, Alves began conceptualizing the alien beings. "The descriptions I heard were of these big-eyed things with small mouths and no nose, long fingers, that kind of thing. So I made some sketches and I also made a couple of clay models." Spielberg was pleased with Alves' designs: "Steven said 'I like these simple little childlike beings. That's what I want.'"[29] It was soon after that Spielberg made the decision to have little girls wear the alien costumes in order to imbue the cosmic entities with a sense of innocence and grace.

Spielberg's film is rich in UFOlogical detail beyond the appearance of its aliens, from its depiction of silent but spectacular UFO manoeuvres, UFOs interfering with electrical grids and car engines, government secrecy and disinformation surrounding the subject, and even alien abduction (around a decade before such stories began to permeate the literature). The movie achieved its extraordinary UFOlogical realism thanks in large part to the advice of legendary UFO investigator Professor J. Allen Hynek. It was Hynek's classification system for UFO sightings that gave Spielberg's movie its unusual title (a 'Close Encounter of the Third Kind' referring to any sighting of a UFO within 500 feet of the witness during which UFO occupants are also observed), and Spielberg appointed the man himself as his official UFO advisor on the movie.

Close Encounters also owes a debt to the pioneering UFO research of Hynek's most famous protégé, Dr. Jacques Vallee. Indeed, one of the movies main characters, the Frenchman Claude Lacombe (Francois

Truffaut), was partly inspired by Vallee himself. Spielberg consulted briefly with Vallee during the movie's production and the scientist
attempted to sway the director in favor of a more exotic explanation
for the UFO phenomenon. Spielberg's movie should explore the Inter-
dimensional Hypothesis, Vallee insisted. "When I met Steven Spielberg, I argued with him that the subject was even more interesting if
it wasn't extraterrestrials," said Vallee, "if it was real, physical, but not
ET." Spielberg wasn't convinced, however, telling Vallee; "You're probably right, but that's not what the public is expecting; this is Hollywood
and I want to give people something that's close to what they expect."[30]

For years, *Close Encounters* has been the subject of fervent speculation in the UFO conspiracy community, with even some of the most
level-headed of researchers inclined to believe it was part of an official
UFO acclimation campaign. Such speculation can be traced back to
the production of the movie itself. On 23 July 1976, after a hard day's
shoot, around forty of the *Close Encounters* cast and crew (including
stars Richard Dreyfuss and Melinda Dillon) gathered in the sticky
night air of Mobile, Alabama, to hear a lecture on UFOs delivered by
Hynek (who had been flown in for a brief cameo in the film's closing
scenes). It was shortly after this lecture that the co-star of the movie,
Bob Balaban (who plays the character of translator David Laughlin),
spoke of an intriguing rumour that had been circulating during the
production – "a rumour," said the actor, "that the film is part of the
necessary training that the human race must go through in order to
accept an actual landing, and is being secretly sponsored by a government UFO agency."[31] I asked *Close Encounters* production designer Joe
Alves if he had heard any such rumours during the shoot and if there
was any substance to them. "There were a lot of rumours," he replied
ambiguously, before changing the subject.[32]

In 1977, after the production had wrapped, Spielberg told *Sight and
Sound* magazine what had inspired him to make a film that dealt seriously with the UFO issue. "I realized that just about every fifth person I talked to had looked up at the sky at some point in their lives and
seen something that was not easy to explain," said the director, "and
then I began meeting people who had had close encounters... where
undeniably something quite phenomenal was happening right before
their eyes. It was this direct contact – the interviews – that got me interested in making the movie."[33]

Spielberg's interest in UFOs even extended to a belief in an official cover-up. "I wouldn't put it past this government that a cosmic

Watergate has been underway for the last 25 years," Spielberg remarked during a *Close Encounters* promotional interview in 1977, "eventually they might want to tell us something about what they've discovered over the decades." During the same interview, the director spoke with relish of "rumours" that President Carter was due to make "some unsettling disclosures" about UFOs later that year. Needless to say, no such disclosures were forthcoming.[34]

But was Spielberg dropping a hint? Was *Close Encounters* really part of a government-sponsored UFO indoctrination program, an effort to educate the public about the reality of an alien presence? We may never know for sure, although comments made more recently by another Hollywood professional make for intriguing reading in the context of this discussion. In February of 2011, thirty-four years after the release of *Close Encounters*, I spoke with Andrew Thomas, a writer/director/producer who worked on Spielberg's UFO epic in 1976 as head of 'special marketing.' Eighteen months before the film was scheduled to premiere, at the behest of the film's studio, Columbia Pictures, Thomas worked with a major planetarium to create a dazzling twenty-minute show for the American public. He described it to me as follows:

> You sit down and a UFO shoots across the planetarium dome and then the audience is trained on how to figure out whether that was a meteor, a comet, or actually an extraterrestrial. We managed to bus-in tens-of thousands of kids from all around the country on the pretence of seeing an educational planetarium show, but what they really got was a sophisticated message to explain to them that extraterrestrials and UFOs are real and what an encounter of the first, second, and third kind actually meant.

At first glance, this testimony would seem to lend weight to the indoctrination rumours, but Thomas himself has a different take on why Columbia Pictures adopted such an unusual and deceptive marketing strategy; "They were concerned that the title 'Close Encounters of the Third Kind' sounded suspiciously like a pornographic movie, because no one had any reference to what that vocabulary meant." Thomas says his job was simply to introduce the 'close encounter' terminology into the vernacular, "so when the film opened-up everyone would know what was being discussed, and there wouldn't be any question."[35]

There were further indications of secrecy and deception relating to *Close Encounters* shortly after the movie was released. It is curious, for example, that the Carter Presidential Library contains no record of the film-loving President ever having viewed *Close Encounters* while in office. However, in a 1977 Canadian TV interview conducted directly after the movie's theatrical release, Spielberg said matter-of-factly that Carter had viewed the movie "Last Saturday." Spielberg remarked, "We haven't heard the direct feedback," but added, "We hear he [Carter] liked it quite a bit."[36] The following March, *The Phoenix Gazette* cited *Close Encounters* as "Jimmy Carter's favorite movie," noting that "The President has seen the movie many times."[37] This is not the only discrepancy over the official record concerning Carter and Spielberg. Officially, Spielberg never set foot in the Carter White House and had never met the President, and yet a solitary photocopy of a photograph discovered in the Carter Presidential Library proves that the two men did meet. The photo shows Carter and Spielberg engaged in conversation and is signed: "To Steven Spielberg, [from] Jimmy Carter." An accompanying White House stationary note signed by White House Social Secretary Gretchen Poston and addressed to Spielberg reads: "The President thought you would enjoy receiving the enclosed photograph."[38]

This apparent secrecy almost certainly resulted from a desire among Carter's staff to keep the Administration from being further publicly associated with flying saucers. Famously, Carter had his own UFO sighting in 1969 in Leary, Georgia, witnessing a bright white round object that approached his position before stopping and then receding into the distance. Carter was with twelve other people at the time, all of whom witnessed the strange phenomenon.[39] Needless to say, a UFO-spotting President viewing the ultimate UFO movie at the White House and having get-togethers with its alien-obsessed director would have been a PR nightmare.

By far the most outlandish of the conspiracy theories surrounding *Close Encounters* relates to 'Project Serpo' – an alleged human/alien exchange program between US military personnel and a race of extraterrestrials from the Zeta Reticuli star system. The story goes that, in July of 1965, twelve astronauts were taken to the planet Serpo aboard an alien spaceship and remained there for thirteen years. In exchange, the aliens left one of their own in the custody of the US government. This story didn't emerge until 2005 in the form of a string of anonymous emails that were sent to selected UFO researchers, including Project Camelot/Avalon's Bill Ryan, who created a website dedicated to the "leaks."[40]

The Serpo story led some in the conspiracy community to speculate that *Close Encounters* was partly inspired by the alleged alien-human exchange program of 1965, which assumes that Spielberg himself was privy to inside information on the UFO issue. In the movie's final scenes, a taller alien (this one not designed by Alves but by effects expert Carlo Rambaldi) is seen to exit the mothership and communicate with the character of Claude Lacombe via a series of hand gestures. Immediately before this we see twelve scientists clad in jumpsuits preparing to board the mothership and take permanent leave of planet Earth. Roy Neary joins the group as its thirteenth member.

Again, it is important to note that the Serpo story, which has not a shred of evidence to support it, did not emerge until 2005, twenty-eight years after the release of *Close Encounters*. The logical assumption, then, would be that the former inspired the latter, rather than vice versa.

Whether or not there is any truth to the conspiracy theories surrounding *Close Encounters*, Spielberg's movie remains hugely significant for the fact that it played a central role in Hollywood's mid-to-late-1970s economic revival – its $338 million worldwide box-office gross forced aging studio executives to recognize America's vast and largely un-catered-for youth market and to adapt their output accordingly.[41] Two other alien-themed movies of the period also played a key role in this industrial paradigm shift: *Star Wars* (1977) and *Superman* (1978). Together, these three films about the wonders of the universe acted as adrenalin, shot straight into the heart of a dying industry (though many critics would argue, perhaps justifiably, that this adrenalin acted as poison in the long-term, stifling creativity and individuality in Hollywood). Spielberg's film also reignited public curiosity about UFOs as an enduring enigma, and its release closely coincided with the thirtieth anniversary of the Roswell Incident. Just one year later, Jesse Marcel would spill the beans on his firsthand experiences of that event, opening the floodgates for hundreds more closely-corresponding Roswell testimonies.

It had taken the better part of thirty years, but Hollywood's aliens had made the transition from invaders to saviors. Remarkably, this transition was affected almost single-handedly by a wunderkind director with a vision. With Vietnam and Watergate still fresh in the mind, *Close Encounters* came as a reassuring hug for America towards the end of a decade of disillusionment, and, for the next few years, Spielberg's movie would redefine Hollywood's working relationship with aliens.

~ SAVIORS FROM THE STARS ~

For Hollywood, the 1980s was gargantuan – a decade of blockbusters and movie merchandise, of sequels and trilogies, and of action, adventure, and science fiction thrills. Thanks to the huge success of Steven Spielberg's *Close Encounters*, cynical studio bigwigs had by now cottoned-on to the public's enduring fascination with UFOs and extraterrestrials and had accepted that aliens needn't *always* come as invaders; benevolent beings could generate big bucks too. And so, Hollywood's new sci-fi blueprint was drawn in the image of the alien savior, of intergalactic missionaries and humanity's ultimate cosmic salvation. It was perhaps inevitable that the most significant film of the decade to work from this blueprint would spring from the very imagination that conceived it. Spielberg's *E.T. The Extraterrestrial* (1982) was an instant global phenomenon and reduced millions of hardened cinemagoers to tears with its tender tale of a lonely boy and his stranded alien botanist buddy.

E.T.'s plot is as simple as they come: a friendly and physically vulnerable alien bestowed with powers of healing, telekinesis, and mental telepathy becomes stranded in suburban America only to be 'adopted' by a lonely boy named Elliott (Henry Thomas). They become the best of friends, connected by a deep psychic and spiritual bond. Meanwhile, government agents are in hot pursuit of E.T., intent on subjecting him to medical experimentation. At one point, E.T. actually dies at the hands of his government captors, but he returns to life in Christ-like fashion. Eventually, he is reunited with his own people and returns to his home planet, but not before assuring Elliott that the bond they share will span the stars forever.

Few would have believed prior to its release that a modest film about a little alien could become the biggest film in the history of cinema, but that's exactly what happened, and it would remain at the peak of the box-office heap for eleven years until Spielberg's own *Jurassic Park* finally toppled it in 1993. As Elliott bids an emotional farewell to his Christ-like friend, he tells him: "I'll believe in you all my life, every day." It was a sentiment many Americans seemed to share. When asked in a 1982 Gallup Poll 'Do you believe life exists on other planets?' 50% of men and 43% of women answered in the affirmative.[42] The poll was taken one month before the nationwide release of Spielberg's film. It would have been interesting to have seen the figures for one month after.

Bizarrely, *E.T.* was very nearly a nightmarish horror movie. In 2011, Spielberg told *Entertainment Weekly*: "It [*E.T.*] was going to be called *Night Skies*, based on a piece of UFO mythology... where a farm family reported little spindly aliens attacking their farm...This farm family basically huddled together for survival... It's a story that's well-known in the world of UFOlogy, and we based our script on that story."[43] Spielberg was, of course, referring to the Kelly-Hopkinsville farm siege of 1955. The director even went so far as to hire legendary effects designer Rick Baker (*An American Werewolf in London*: 1981) to bring the impish Hopkinsville aliens to life for the big screen. It was only when Harrison Ford's then-girlfriend Melissa Mathison came onboard to rewrite the screenplay that the movie became the one that audiences know and love today.

Romancing the alien

As the decade approached its mid-point, UFOs were beginning to arrive in Hollywood *en masse*, planting their landing gear firmly into pop-culture. 1984 saw the release of John Carpenter's *Starman*, an *E.T.* wannabe starring Jeff Bridges as the eponymous alien who crash-lands on Earth, finding himself stranded. Romance ensues as fate brings him to an attractive but lonely widow and the pair set off on a cross-country adventure to a site designated by Starman's people for his heart-rending return to the stars. Inoffensive, but ultimately uninspired, Carpenter's film sought to capitalize on the popularity of the emerging image of the alien as savior, and, fittingly, his Starman performs all manner of 'miracles' during his time on earth, including seeding his infertile lover with a star child (who, we are told, will be a "teacher"), and twice bringing the dead back to life (though he stops just short of turning water into wine).

UFOlogical themes are identifiable in the movie. For example, Starman's spacecraft is recovered by the US military, and his star child with Jenny brings to mind the stories of hybridization that would proliferate in UFO literature toward the end of the 1980s, throughout the 1990s, and beyond. It is important to note, though, that real-life stories of human-alien interbreeding comfortably pre-dated *Starman*, most notably in the case of Antonio Villas Boas, who in 1957 claimed to have had intercourse with a human-like alien woman aboard a landed UFO near São Francisco de Sales in Brazil. When the deed was done, the alien smiled at Boas, rubbed her belly and gestured upwards: the child would live among the stars, Boas assumed.

The producers of *Starman* requested no support from any branch of the government. Unsurprising, since, as military historian Lawrence Suid notes, "the Pentagon would undoubtedly have looked unfavorably on a request for assistance because of [the negative] portrayal of the military leadership and of the alien spaceship as a flying saucer."[44] Suid is correct in essence, although *Starman*'s spaceship is not a flying saucer, per se, but rather a flying, highly-reflective sphere. The work of *Close Encounters* production designer Joe Alves, the *Starman* UFO was intended to break the flying saucer mould, which Alves felt was at risk of becoming stale. "It was a more simplistic design," Alves told me of his *Starman* craft, "it was a counter thing to *Close Encounters*."[45]

Several months prior to the release of *Starman*, a 1984 reader survey for the American *Psychology* magazine posed the question 'Do you believe in UFOs?' its implication being that UFOs are extraterrestrial in origin. 50% of respondents said yes,[46] a strong indication of America's growing conviction that we were not alone in the universe. The closing ceremony for the Olympic games in Los Angeles that year was a testament not only to how deeply UFOs and aliens had become engrained in the American psyche, but to the extent to which they had become inseparable from cinema. The highlight of the event was the staged landing of a giant flying saucer and the subsequent emergence from within of a space alien (friendly, of course) who then officially declared the games closed. In an awesome spectacle clearly inspired by the final scenes of *Close Encounters*, the Olympic saucer communicated with the awestruck crowd below through a series of elaborate lightshows, the orchestral music swelled to a crescendo, and the UFO descended to rapturous applause. It was a sight both bizarre and magnificent to behold.[47]

The healing touch

1984 saw the release of *The Brother from Another Planet*, a low-budget, independent social commentary piece from director John Sayles. In the movie, a UFO crashes near Ellis Island Immigration Center and its human-looking, black-skinned occupant emerges dazed and confused into the strange and unwelcoming landscape of 1980s New York City – just another lost soul trying to find his way in the world. We soon learn that The Brother has ESP abilities and, by touching any given object, he can 'hear' its history. He also has healing powers like so many other screen aliens of the 1980s. Healing powers have also been attributed to alien visitors in a number of contactee accounts. Take Jose Benedito Bogea, for example, a bespectacled Brazilian chicken farmer, who, after being rendered unconscious by a close encounter with a UFO near San Luis in July 1977, awoke the next morning to find that he had 20/20 vision and thus no further use for his glasses. Bogea would later recall being taken to an expansive alien environment populated by men and women "all looking very much alike; about 30 years old, five feet tall, slender, and nearly all dressed in grey and brown clothes..." Most of the people were "light skinned," said Bogea, and "the women were pretty and had long blond hair." Bogea further noted that the people seemed to be talking to each other, but he could hear no words. Presumably mental telepathy was at play.[48]

Another fascinating case involving health benefits for a contactee is that of Paul Mayo, who now resides in Worcestershire, England. Mayo shared his story with me in 2010, and it is published here for the first time. Growing up in the 1950s and '60s, Mayo was afflicted by numerous physical ailments stemming first from his prolonged exposure as a young boy to thick mould concealed behind the walls of his bedroom, and later from organophosphate poisoning caused by a farming accident which saw him immersed in sheep dip. All throughout his youth Mayo suffered constant headaches and, by the ache of 22, he had developed chronic bronchitis. His doctor at the time told him bluntly that he may not live past the age of 30, such was the dire condition of his immune and respiratory systems. Then, on a Saturday morning in November 1978, at the age of 29, Mayo had an experience that transformed him both mentally and physically. He was sat on the edge of his bed, dressing himself for the day ahead. His wife was downstairs making breakfast. It was around 7am. They had risen early as they had planned to drive into town that morning to do some grocery shopping. As Mayo sat there in his bedroom pulling on his socks the door began to open slowly and he was puzzled to see a "man" poke his head around the door. The man, who was five foot six in height and ordinary in appearance, entered the room silently and raised his palm in a waving gesture. It was at this point that Mayo realized he could not move. He was paralyzed where he sat at the edge of his bed. The stranger now began to "dissolve" before his eyes, leaving only an intricate outline of his nerves and blood vessels, which shone brilliantly, "like a million fibres of light."

Suddenly Mayo felt himself leaning backwards on his bed. The action was involuntary. His peripheral vision could now detect other men, as many as four, positioned either side of him; they were dressed in "tight-fitting silver clothes." The last thing Mayo can consciously recall about this experience was being "ejected" from his bed and literally "floated through" his bedroom wall. Approximately three hours later, at around 10.15am, Mayo found himself back on his bed. He was so exhausted that he fell into a deep sleep for around an hour. When he awoke it was after 11am. He went downstairs to see his wife, who seemed not remotely curious as to why it had apparently taken her husband four hours to dress himself. Mayo asked her why she had not come upstairs to check on him, they had, after all, planned to go out earlier that morning for their grocery shopping. Mayo's wife seemed confused; the thought to check in on her husband had literally never once occurred to her in those past four hours. She had eaten breakfast without him. His had gone to waste. They both agreed that this was most peculiar and Mayo's wife was at a loss to explain her behaviour that morning. Mayo thought it best not to tell his wife of his experience for the time being; he was unsure even how to articulate it. One thing, however, was immediately clear to Mayo following his experience, for the first time since he could remember, he felt fit and healthy. In fact, he was "bouncing like a ball" for the remainder of the day. His many physical ailments, including his chronic bronchitis, seemed to have been cured. When Mayo saw his General Practitioner a few days later he was declared to be in perfect health, which the doctor said was nothing short of "miraculous." Mayo's experience also affected his diet as he thereafter found it completely impossible to ingest any kind of meat product. Mayo found that if he attempted to eat meat he would be prevented from doing so. The very act of bringing the meat to his mouth would make him feel instantly nauseous. It wasn't until several years later that he discovered he could eat fish again, albeit only in small portions. Today Mayo is able to include meat in his diet, although only top-quality organic produce, and only in modest servings. Mayo, now in his late-sixties, remains in excellent health, having suffered nothing more severe than a couple of minor head colds in all the years since his described experience.[49]

Further parallels

The next three years in Tinseltown would see a flurry of 'friendly alien' movies released in close succession. In June of 1985 came Ron Howard's *Cocoon*, in which, yet again, enlightened aliens arrived as saviors, this time to a group of senior citizens in a Florida retirement community. The movie's ETs are vaguely similar to the Grays in appearance, although they glow with an angelic radiance. Biblical themes are evoked when the beings grant their elderly friends eternal life and whisk them up to the heavens to an existence among their celestial peoples. Ancient Astronaut theory is hinted at in a subplot suggesting Atlantis was founded by extraterrestrials – a notion espoused by contactees such as Daniel Fry and Billy Meier in preceding decades. Both of these men alleged that certain alien races have their roots in the lost civilizations of Earth, and that their resemblance to us, or rather us to them, is no coincidence. *Cocoon*'s producers sought assistance from the USAF, but were denied, according to Lawrence Suid, "because the film portrayed the service unrealistically and posited the existence of UFOs, which ran contrary to Air Force policy."

With July came Joe Dante's *Explorers*, an underrated, highly imaginative children's film about the adventures of three young boys (played by Ethan Hawke, River Phoenix, and Jason Presson) and their attempts to make contact with aliens after receiving a schematic for an anti-gravity device via their dreams. The trio use the schematic to build a small spacecraft and make a fantastic voyage to the stars where their alien friends await them.

The UFO literature is replete with examples of contactees and abductees claiming to have received information from alien intelligences via remote mental download, images and information seemingly projected into the mind as if from nowhere. The British contactee Paul Mayo claims to have had an extraordinary boost in knowledge following his aforementioned experience in 1978. Specifically, he found he had an aptitude for science, despite having no qualifications in the subject and no prior understanding of it. Mayo's newfound scientific knowledge was such that he would go on to work for several years as a high school physics teacher.

This 'downloading' theme would feature again in 1986 in Disney's *Flight of the Navigator*, which sees a young boy's brain 'implanted' with complex data from an alien source and which is later downloaded by NASA scientists. In other respects previously mentioned, the film also recalls the story of 1950s contactee Daniel Fry. Additionally, it touches on the theme of alien abduction, including the phenomenon of 'missing time' (in this case eight years). *Flight of the Navigator* features a secret UFO retrieval (although no crash), and scenes of the spacecraft parked in a secret government hangar which anticipate the stories of Area 51 that would emerge three years later. Despite instigating a cover-up and taking a boy away from his family for experimentation, NASA ultimately comes off as an essentially harmless organization, much as it did in Spielberg's *E.T.*

Paul Mayo considers *Flight of the Navigator* to be the most "accurate" UFO-themed movie he has ever seen. It should be noted that while Mayo's 1978 encounter was his first of the otherworldly kind, it was not his last. He claims to have had further experiences with different alien species (all of whom were benevolent) in the early 1980s and again in the early '90s. All of these encounters were experienced in 'real-time' and were consciously recalled. In short, Mayo claims to have been onboard spacecraft on multiple occasions and that some of the beings he encountered expressed to him a grave concern for the future of our planet. "Whenever *Flight of the Navigator* comes on the TV I have to watch it," Mayo told me. "I'm not a person to watch any film twice, but when that comes on I'm riveted. A lot of the things in it are the things I encountered myself." When I asked for details, Mayo drew particular attention to the *Navigator* UFO being extremely similar to craft he claims to have been inside. He was especially struck by the sparse but functional interior of the *Navigator* UFO. The spacecraft Mayo claims to have experienced were essentially a series of empty rooms, and yet he had a clear sense that they were highly functional and that their technological apparatus was ingeniously concealed from view, as is the case in the Disney movie.[51]

The following year, Steven Spielberg executive-produced *Batteries Not Included* (1987). Here, the aliens came in the form of tiny, living (and procreating) flying saucers that devote themselves to bettering the troubled lives of the tenants of a rundown New York apartment block, with typically heart-warming results.

Perhaps the most serious alien savior film of the decade came in 1989 with the release of James Cameron's aquatic Cold War epic, *The Abyss*. The film follows the blue-collar crew of a submersible oil rig in its fateful discovery of Unidentified Submerged Objects (USOs) and a Non-Terrestrial Intelligence located in the depths of a cavernous trench. Back on dry land, as the Cold War approaches boiling point, the aliens (or N.T.I.s as they are referred to in Cameron's script) reveal their presence in spectacular fashion and deliver, à la *The Day the Earth Stood Still*, a message and an ultimatum to our warlike people, the gist of which is, 'grow up and live in peace or we'll destroy you all.' Unsurprisingly, humanity complies.

Researcher Ivan T. Sanderson explored the UFO-USO connection in his 1970 book *Invisible Residents: The Reality of Underwater UFOs*, and its influence on Cameron's movie is plain to see. Throughout the 1990s, UFO researchers would document numerous USO encounters involving militaries worldwide, as well as persistent rumours that a number of undersea alien bases were dotted around the globe.

"Friends, playmates, brothers, and lovers"

The sudden influx of heart-warming UFO movies in the 1980s prompted cinema theorist Vivian Sobchack to observe that aliens had become "our friends, playmates, brothers, and lovers." In her 1987 book *Screening Space*, Sobchack noted that "in quite a transformation of earlier generic representations, most of the new SF films do not represent alien-ness as inherently hostile and Other." [52] This was true enough, though the genre was not without its fair share of malevolent ETs either. John Carpenter's *The Thing* (1982) was a deeply unsettling throwback to the paranoid invasion flicks of the 1950s. However, despite being arguably the best movie of Carpenter's career thus far, it tanked at the box-office. Released hot on the heels of the warm and fuzzy *E.T.*, critics and audiences alike were repelled by the horrific imagery of Carpenter's ice cold creation, and its failure was regarded within the industry as a death knell for the 'alien invader' archetype of old. Three years later, director Tobe Hooper felt Carpenter's pain when his 1985 'space vampires' movie, *Life Force*, suffered a spectacular defeat in a head-to-head box-office battle with Ron Howard's *Cocoon*. [53]

The invaders would continue to rear their ugly heads, albeit sporadically, throughout the remainder of the decade. James Cameron's 1986 sci-fi-action sequel, *Aliens*, filled seats (and pants) around the world with its intense and gritty rendering of humanity's first organized battle against the terrifying Xenamorph species of Ridley Scott's original *Alien* outing, and its muscular, techno-fetishistic approach to extraterrestrial combat would act as a major influence on the 1987 Schwarzenegger vehicle *Predator*. Three months after the release of the latter, in September 1987, President Ronald Reagan would politicize earth's potential alien threat in his afore-mentioned speech at the UN. One might wonder if the ex-B-movie star's personal obsession with a space-based missile defense system (fittingly referred to as 'Star Wars') was fuelled in part by his own extraterrestrial concerns so frequently articulated. Within the Reagan Administration, space increasingly was being discussed as a potentially hostile arena – a notion that would re-emerge post-9/11 and assume tangible form in the Bush Administration's large-scale militarization of the final frontier. The films of the 1990s and beyond would serve to reinforce the political perception of space as a US National Security concern.

Aykroyd and Travolta feel the love

Hollywood maintained at least some appetite for positive ET inter-actions throughout the 1990s. In the 1993 comedy *Coneheads*, based on the *Saturday Night Live* sketches, Dan Aykroyd's awkward alien Beldar Conehead is tasked by his leaders on the planet Remulak with scouting out Earth in preparation for their invasion. Beldar's mission goes awry when his ship is tracked on radar and shot down by the USAF. Beldar and his family escape and gradually assimilate them-selves into American society, despite their obviously alien ways and appearance. As time goes on, the Coneheads learn to love our world and its people, and the family orchestrate events which ultimately avert the alien invasion. Aykroyd was no stranger to alien movies at the time, having already starred in the 1988 comedy *My Stepmother Is an Alien*, which saw a gorgeous blonde from beyond the stars (Kim Basinger) arrive on Earth in her flying saucer in order to save her people from a death ray accidentally fired at their planet by Aykroyd's widower scientist Steven Mills. In real-life, Aykroyd has always been vocal about his belief in UFOs and alien visitation and is a proud life-time member of the Mutual UFO Network (MUFON), the world's largest civilian UFO research organization. In 2005, Aykroyd was the subject of a documentary feature called *Dan Aykroyd: Unplugged on UFOs*, in which the star sits for 80 minutes and talks passionately about every aspect of the subject.[54]

A UFO for positive change

In 1996, the same year *Independence Day* obliterated the White House and all box-office competition, *Phenomenon* looked at the positive impact of an otherworldly experience. Directed by Mike Nichols (*The Graduate*), the movie follows George Malley (John Travolta), a simple small town guy whose life is turned upside down one night by a chance encounter with an unidentifiable light in the sky which blasts him with a beam that leads to a doubling in his I.Q. and his development of telekinetic powers.

George uses his newfound abilities to better the lives of those around him and to make his town eco-friendly through the utilization of non-polluting energy. The exact nature of the UFO George encounters goes unspecified. Perhaps it is extraterrestrial, perhaps it is something less tangible. Calling to mind Vallee's IDH theory, the 'phenomenon' here blinks out of our reality as quickly as it blinks in, leaving the individual experiencer to interpret its true nature, and, in turn, his own true purpose in our world. *Phenomenon* was a box-office hit, bringing in $152 million against its modest $32 million budget.[55]

"I can't prove it"

Robert Zemeckis' *Contact* (1997), based on the novel by Carl Sagan, was the last big-budget Hollywood production of the 1990s to show that benevolent aliens could indeed rake in the cash from satisfied cinemagoers. An introspective film calling to mind the likes of *Close Encounters* and even *2001: A Space Odyssey*, *Contact* is a spectacular sci-fi that milked every penny of its $90 million budget to gross in excess of $166 million worldwide.[56]

In the movie, SETI scientist Ellie Arroway (Jodie Foster), whose character is inspired by real-life former SETI director Jill Tarter, discovers an alien signal beamed from Vega, a star in the constellation of Lyra, some 25 light years from Earth. Her discovery and its subsequent public disclosure by President Clinton constitutes proof that we are not alone in the universe and captures the imagination of the entire planet, sparking fervent scientific, political, and religious debate. Soon, Ellie and her team realize the signal is actually a complex schematic for a transport pod designed to carry one person to a destination unknown. That destination, it transpires, is Vega itself, and is to be reached via multiple wormholes. Naturally, it is Ellie who takes the cosmic voyage, and, at the end of her epic journey, she finds herself in an elaborate simulacrum of a childhood memory: a warm beach in Pensacola, Florida. It is here that she speaks face-to-face with an alien intelligence which has assumed the form of her long dead father: "We thought this might make things easier for you," he says, smiling gently. No little green or Gray men for Ellie, then; no flying saucers, no motherships or gleaming alien cityscapes, only a mirage of Earthly forms created for her personal comfort. "You're an interesting species, an interesting mix," he tells her. "You're capable of such beautiful dreams, and such horrible nightmares. You feel so lost, so cut off, so alone, only you're not. See, in all our searching, the only thing we've found that makes the emptiness bearable, is each other." She longs to learn more before being sent home, but is told: "This was just a first step. In time you'll take another... this is the way it's been done for billions of years. Small moves, Ellie, small moves." And so an individual is selected for contact and provided with philosophical nuggets but zero physical evidence of her alien encounter before being left to tell her story to whomsoever will listen. Ellie, it seems, has much in common with the contactees of UFO lore.

Back on Earth, during a government inquiry into her claims, Ellie is reminded by a panel member that she has "no evidence, no record, no artifacts. Only a story that, to put it mildly, strains credibility." Ellie is asked, "Why don't you simply withdraw your testimony, and concede that this 'journey to the center of the galaxy,' in fact, never took place?" She responds:

> Because I can't. I... had an experience... I can't prove it, I can't even explain it, but everything that I know as a human being, everything that I am tells me that it was real! I was given something wonderful, something that changed me forever... A vision of the universe, that tells us, undeniably, how tiny, and insignificant and how rare and precious we all are! A vision that tells us that we belong to something that is greater than ourselves, that we are *not*, that none of us, are alone! I wish I could share that. I wish that everyone, if only for one moment, could feel that awe, and humility, and hope. But... That continues to be my wish.

Ellie is visibly frustrated. She has experienced direct contact with an alien intelligence, but she has done so in a manner that flies in the face of our preconceived notions (a saucer on the White House lawn, for example, a notion, which ironically, was borne of cinema), and thus her claims are dismissed by official culture.

As Ellie leaves her hearing, the hardheaded atheist realizes that her contact experience was, in essence, a spiritual awakening not so different from those claimed by religious disciples. Indeed, the throngs of worshippers who greet her outside with placards hailing her discovery of "the new world" confirm her new status as a religious icon. Like many a contactee, Ellie has attracted followers with her stories of otherworldly communion. Certain elements of society see fit to believe her, while most do not. Either way her story is out there.

Carl Sagan was a UFO skeptic, but it is perhaps worth noting that the screenwriter for *Contact*, James V. Hart, is a believer in alien visitation.[57] Not that this seems to have had much bearing on the film. Any UFOlogical readings we might ascribe to *Contact* the movie are also identifiable in the book. Intentionally or not, the idea of 'missing time' features prominently as Ellie assumes her hyperspatial voyage has lasted hours or even days, when to the eyes of outside observers her transport pod travelled nowhere at all. It is implied that her experience occurred in the space between spaces. Certainly it was beyond her limited comprehension and of those she would seek to convince of its actuality – something UFO witnesses can relate to.

Contact and Clinton

One final UFOlogical note on *Contact*: when in the movie President Clinton announces the discovery of the alien signal, the Clinton we see and hear is the *real* Clinton, which is to say his image and words have not been manipulated by the filmmakers, as could so easily have been done through digital trickery. The President says, in part:

> If this discovery is confirmed, it will surely be one of the most stunning insights into our universe that science has ever uncovered. Its implications are as far reaching and awe inspiring as can be imagined. Even as it promises answers to some of our oldest questions, it poses still others even more fundamental. We will continue to listen closely to what it has to say as we continue the search for answers and for knowledge that is as old as humanity itself but essential to our people's future...

These words, although actually spoken by Clinton, were presented out of context in the movie. While in the scene in question it certainly sounds like Clinton is delivering a cautious disclosure of contact with an alien intelligence, in reality his comments were delivered in August 1996 and referred to the *possible* discovery of fossilized microbial life in a Martian meteorite. Director Robert Zemeckis simply lifted this part of Clinton's speech and used it to heighten the believability of his fictional movie. It was a decision that landed the director in hot water with the White House, which issued a complaint to the film's producers citing unauthorized use of the President's image.[58] In truth, Clinton was probably delighted to be seen on the big screen announcing alien contact. By his own public admission, the Democratic President was, and is, fascinated by the idea not only of extraterrestrial life, but of UFO visitation; he has even spoken publicly of his frustration at being stonewalled on the issue. At a speech in Belfast in 1995, the President made a point of bringing up the famous Roswell Incident of 1947: "If the United States Air Force did recover alien bodies, they didn't tell me about it either, and I want to know."[59] He was even more direct in a question and answer session following a speech in Hong Kong in 2005. When asked about Roswell, the President replied:

> I did attempt to find out if there were any secret government documents that revealed things. If there were, they were concealed from me too. And, if there were, well I wouldn't be the first American President that underlings have lied to, or that career bureaucrats have waited out. But there may be some career person sitting around somewhere, hiding these dark secrets, even from elected presidents. But if so, they successfully eluded me.[60]

UFO movies featuring friendly aliens were thin on the ground as the new millennium dawned. The comedy *What Planet Are You From?* (2000) starring Gary Shandling and Annette Benning featured a number of UFOlogical flourishes, with a direct mention of Roswell and dialogue like: "It's always a flock of geese or a weather balloon," in reference to the mundane explanations typically offered by officialdom for UFO sightings. In another scene, Shandling's human-looking alien is asked: "How come you don't have a head like a pear with bug eyes?" the description of the Gray by now having assumed iconic status through innumerable abduction accounts and their depiction onscreen. Shandling's alien replies: "There's a lot of aliens. We're not the only ones.

Those guys with the big heads scare me. I wouldn't want to bump into one of them. I hear they perform those anal probes. How primitive is *that* technology!" The movie also places great emphasis on the aliens' desire to interbreed with us and, crucially, to study us in the hope of rediscovering their own emotions that were lost to them aeons ago. This exact theme has long been at the core of abductee testimonies.

Apocalyptic Nordics

Yet more human-looking aliens, this time of the old-school Nordic variety, would show up in real-life in 2009 in the immediate vicinity of a spectacular crop formation that appeared near Silbury Hill in England on July 5. In his write-up of the alleged encounter, UK UFO investigator Andrew Russell described receiving a phone call from one of his contacts in the Wiltshire Police constabulary. According to Russell;

> The contact, who doesn't want to be named, was driving past Silbury Hill early Monday morning (6th July 2009) when he saw three figures in the formation there. At first he thought they were forensic officers as they were dressed in white coveralls. He stopped his car and approached the field. The figures were all over 6ft and had blond hair. They seemed to be inspecting the crop. When he got to the edge of the field he heard what he believed to be a sound not dissimilar to static electricity... He felt the hair on his arms and back of his neck raise up. He shouted to the figures who at first ignored him, not glancing at him. When he tried to enter the field they looked up and began running.

The police officer told Russell the beings ran at a superhuman velocity, so fast that the officer became scared: "I'm no slouch but they were moving so fast," he related. "I looked away for a second and when I looked back they were gone." The crackling noise was still audible, however, and the officer began to feel uneasy and decided to head back to his car. "For the rest of the day I had a pounding headache I couldn't shift," he claimed.

In the days following his experience the officer inexplicably acquired an awareness that the beings he saw were clones of one another and shared a hive mind. Despite their interest in the crop circle, they were not responsible for creating it, he explained. "He doesn't know where this information came from," says Russell, "and these concepts and thoughts are outside his usual frame of reference."[60] Again, an information download is implied.

The crop circle the beings were said to be inspecting was 350 feet in diameter and took the form of a quetzal feathered crown once worn by Mayan kings. *The Telegraph* referred to it as an "apocalypse crop circle" and quoted researcher Karen Alexander as saying:

> It appears to be a warning about the world coming to an end when the [Mayan] calendar does. For the ancient Maya, reaching the end of a cycle was a momentous event, so we are taking this crop circle very seriously as an indicator of a possibly huge event in 2012.[61]

In March 2009, four months before a police officer reported seeing Nordics inspecting an apocalyptic crop circle in England, the Nordics were on apocalypse watch at the box-office. The Nicolas Cage movie *Knowing* delivered a story of extraterrestrial visitation and intervention in human destiny in which our planet is all but wiped out by a giant solar flare and the few survivors are selected by an alien race to be transported to another world for a second human genesis (complete with a garden of Eden and an 'Adam' and an 'Eve'). The movie's aliens are tall platinum-haired men with stern expressions whose agenda is unknown until they finally reveal their true form as angelic winged light beings who whisk Earth's chosen ones up to the heavens as the apocalypse unfolds. Original as this plot may seem for Hollywood, in fact, as ever, it was based heavily upon pre-existing UFOlogical/New Age literature and debates. For decades, contactees and abductees have claimed that, in the event that humanity were facing the threat of immediate extinction, extraterrestrials would intervene. Take, for example, the Italian journalist and contactee Bruno Ghibaudi, who claimed to have spoken face-to-face with human-looking spacemen in the summer of 1961. The beings were here to help us, he said, and to prevent a global catastrophe if it became unavoidable. Ghibaudi stressed that, although the aliens were technologically and ethically our superiors by thousands of years, they are not gods. "They are men," he said, "so we must not rely on them to get us out of our difficulties... even their efforts and their concern might not always suffice to avert disaster if something went wrong or some accident nullified their plans to avert the worst."[62]

"UFO 101"

The Nordics were back the following month in Disney's remake of its own 1975 family adventure *Escape to Witch Mountain.* The 2009 incarnation, *Race to Witch Mountain,* received close but unofficial cooperation from the CIA and NORAD (as documented in Chapter Two) and is one of the most significant UFO films of the new millennium. The Nordics in the new movie, teenagers Seth and Sara, crash their spaceship 150 miles outside of Las Vegas (in real life Area 51 is approximately 150 miles north-west of Las Vegas), whereupon the wreckage is seized by Project Moon Dust, a black ops Defense Department unit led by Henry Burke (Ciarán Hinds). Burke and his Men in Black soon begin their ruthless search for the alien pilots who have fled the scene and are seeking the guidance of Jack Bruno (Dwayne Johnson), a tough but warm-hearted taxi driver, and Dr. Alex Friedman (Carla Gugino), a brilliant scientist who controversially believes in UFOs and alien visitation.

The aliens reveal to Bruno and Friedman that their own world is dying and that their military is intent on invading and occupying our planet. This idea is unpopular with the majority of their people, however, and Seth and Sara have been sent to Earth by their parents in order to retrieve data from ongoing alien experiments which will provide a peaceful alternative to invasion. To save both worlds, Seth and Sara must retrieve their spaceship from Witch Mountain, a secret government installation in California, and return home.

The film's director Andy Fickman is a self-confessed UFO 'buff' born and raised in Roswell, New Mexico, who took pride in infusing his remake with as many elements as possible drawn directly from UFO literature. In a 2010 interview, Fickman explained to me that the majority of the film's UFO-related content had been shaped by him from the outset and that he had personally schooled his cast, including Johnson and Gugino, in UFO history: "I would spend time with my actors literally just going through 'UFO 101 – we'd watch every DVD that was out there, every documentary; I would give them book, upon book, upon book."

Fickman further noted that:

> In UFO mythology – in terms of literature, in terms of research – there begins to become a language; people in the UFO movement would easily speak of Roswell and have very clear ideas of what that

means, what an 'EBE' means [EBE is an abbreviation used in the controversial MJ-12 documents discussed in Chapter Seven, meaning 'Extraterrestrial Biological Entity'] all of this terminology we were kind of slipping in... even the wormhole theory of travel and how someone could visit us from so many light years away – that was all stuff that we were repositioning for our own mythology and storytelling, but all based on previous research.

Such minute attention to detail was a bid on Fickman's part to "engage the UFO community." In a scene in which the characters attend a Las Vegas UFO convention, the director went so far as to populate the set with real UFO researchers and enthusiasts: "Almost every extra in there was someone from the UFO community," said Fickman; among these people most notably, and visibly, are Whitley Strieber (whose 1987 book *Communion* played a huge role in popularizing debates surrounding alien abductions), Dr. Roger Leir (a medical doctor famous for specializing in the removal of alleged alien implants from abductees) and William Birnes (Editor of *UFO Magazine*). Fickman also confirmed to me that the character of Dr. Alex Friedman was partly inspired by famed UFOlogist Stanton Friedman, and that the name of another character in the movie 'Pope' was a reference to Nick Pope, a former head of the UK government's official UFO desk.[63]

Although Fickman recognizes that his film is first and foremost an entertainment product, he remains hopeful that it may also hold some educational value with regard to UFOs and that it might encourage wider acceptance of the fundamental reality of the phenomenon. Ironically, though, by grounding his 'science-fiction' film so deeply in UFOlogical literature and by incorporating so many references to documented UFOlogical theories and events, the director arguably has further muddied the waters on a subject he hopes one day will be treated seriously by mainstream science and culture.

I am... not as bad as I look

Nordic aliens were back again two years later in the teen sci-fi *I am Number Four* (2011), based on the novel by Pittacus Lore. The film was produced by Michael Bay (director of the *Transformers* franchise) and released through Disney's Touchstone Pictures. The plot follows the adventures of John Smith (Alex Pettyfer), a ludicrously good-looking alien from the planet Lorien. John was sent to Earth as a child with eight others of his kind in order to escape an invasion of their planet by the evil Mogadorians, a monstrous and sadistic alien race. He now wants nothing more than to blend in with the humans, although his sudden development of extraordinary powers in his teen years makes this increasingly difficult, and it is not long before he draws the attention of his alien enemies.

That same year saw a truly monstrous alien wreak havoc on the big screen in *Super 8*, J.J. Abrams' affectionate homage to the Spielbergian sci-fi-adventure fare of the 1970s and 1980s which effortlessly evoked the childlike wonder of *E.T.* and *Close Encounters*. The movie features a huge, multi-limbed alien trashing a small American town after it escapes from a train en route to Area 51. Refreshingly, the alien turns out to be peaceful at heart, but its mistreatment at the hands of the US government has caused it to become vengeful and destructive. It takes the compassionate eyes of a child to convince the alien that not all humans are poisoned with mal-intent. Also released in 2011 was *Paul*, a densely UFOlogical comedy about a crude but friendly Gray alien (the eponymous Paul) who befriends two English sci-fi geeks on an American road trip. This movie is discussed further in Chapter Seven.

Conclusion

This chapter has looked at movies in which aliens visit our planet with benevolent, or at least benign intent, who seek to learn from, teach, or even save the human race. Regardless of their appearance, these aliens typically are bestowed with Christ-like powers, and allusions to Jesus and Christian scripture are common features. In short, friendly ET contact, when it occurs on the silver screen, is often depicted as a religious or magical experience, and this mirrors the sentiment of many real-life contactee testimonies. Hollywood's contactee narratives also share much in common with those of UFO literature in their fine details, as both have featured Nordics or other beings who exhibit a spiritual interest in humanity, who walk among us unnoticed by the masses, who are possessed of wondrous abilities (including healing and telepathy), and who are deeply concerned about our nuclear weapons and the survival of our species.

Unsurprisingly, Hollywood's peaceful alien narratives have, at times, borrowed liberally from UFO literature and debate, often subtly, but sometimes very blatantly, as with *Close Encounters* and *Race to Witch Mountain*, both of which made prominent use of UFOlogical imagery and terminology, and which even featured famous UFOlogists in cameo roles.

The favored strategy of Hollywood's friendly aliens traditionally has been to select a limited number of individuals for contact and to maintain relations with them in a discreet manner so as to go unnoticed in human society while having a positive impact on those around them (see, for example, *Cocoon* and *Batteries Not Included*). Only in extreme circumstances do celluloid aliens reveal their presence on a large scale through grand public gestures, as was the case in *The Day the Earth Stood Still* and *The Abyss*. This discreet contact strategy is remarkably similar to that described in UFO literature. But is it realistic?

When addressing the possibility of benign alien visitation, certain scientists speculate that the majority of advanced space-faring civilizations would abide by a strict policy of non-interference. In this context, scientists have cited the 'Prime Directive' of the fictional United Federation of Planets in the *Star Trek* TV series. The Prime Directive prohibits members of the Federation from interfering directly or overtly with the internal development of alien civilizations, especially technologically primitive ones, such as ours is today.

The Prime Directive makes sense. When studying 'undiscovered' cultures on Earth, modern anthropologists have sought to keep their distance and to strictly limit face-to-face interactions. Sometimes, though, direct contact is unavoidable. It is in these cases that a tribesperson might return home to report an encounter with strange men who descended from the sky (in a plane or helicopter), who wore curious clothes, and who made use of unfathomable technology (such as mobile phones or iPads). The tribesperson's story is accepted by some and rejected by others, but the myth of the visitors spreads throughout his culture.

So, Hollywood is well grounded in its assumption that alien intelligences, should they decide to interact with us, would probably do so in a decidedly low key fashion so as to avoid rupturing our existing, and rather myopic, universal paradigm. In this sense, science also loosely supports the overarching contactee narrative, in which UFO occupants interact with us according to their own Prime Directives. The beings in contactee lore select individuals from around the world for limited but sometimes ongoing communication exchanges. They voice their concerns for our planet and our species, imparting philosophical and spiritual wisdom and occasionally wowing us with 'miracles' performed through advanced psychic or technological means. They also express a reluctance to involve themselves overtly and on a large scale in our affairs for worry of societal fracture, as contactee Bruno Ghibaudi explained in 1963:

> There are cosmic laws which prevent the more evolved races from interfering, beyond certain limits, in the evolution and development of the more backward races. For every race must be the maker of its own progress, paying the price for it with its sacrifices, its failures, and its victories...[64]

The aliens of contactee lore often wish to impart to humanity what they deem to be important messages, but they prefer the 'pebble in a pond' approach, whereby information is conveyed to certain individuals whose resulting testimonies will ripple out gradually across society. There is a certain logic to it, one could argue. Rather than contacting high-profile scientists and politicians whose public statements might be accepted at face value and result in acute societal shock, the aliens choose everyday folk, some of whom, like George Adamski, have personality traits that disallow for immediate and widespread acceptance of their claims, i.e. eccentricity and a propensity for embellishment and fantasism. The result is that only folk-culture is willing to consider the core truth of the contactees' claims. As ever, though, folk-culture bleeds into pop-culture, and thus is facilitated a gradually increasing awareness and acceptance not only of the idea that we are not alone in the universe, but of the spiritual philosophy espoused by the UFO occupants.

An obvious question worthy of contemplation is, if all contactees are fantasists, then why are their descriptions of UFO occupants not vastly more creative? Why limit a fraudulent description to the dull parameters of our own human form when limitless anatomical variations are accessible to the boundless imagination? This, in turn, raises another question, how *do* we account for the human-like appearance of the aliens described by contactees? Science traditionally has told us that the anatomy of alien life will be radically different to our own, unrecognizable in every way. But this is not necessarily so.

In "The Chase," an episode of *Star Trek: The Next Generation* which aired in 1993, it is proposed that an ancient alien species seeded worlds across the galaxy with life that would evolve into sentient beings in their own human-like image. Speaking in the form of a recorded holographic image, one of these ancient aliens explains to Captain Jean Luc Picard and his Klingon, Cardassian, and Romulan company:

> Our scientists seeded the primordial oceans of many worlds where life was in its infancy. The seed codes directed your evolution toward a physical form resembling ours – this body you see before you, which is of course shaped as yours is shaped. For you are the end result... You are a monument, not to our greatness, but to our existence...

This calls to mind the scientific theory of panspermia, which posits that Earth life did not evolve on Earth at all, but instead came here from elsewhere in the galaxy in microbial form.

In 2010, Cambridge University Professor of Paleontology Simon Conway Morris told a conference on alien life that extraterrestrials are likely to closely resemble human beings. "It is difficult to imagine evolution in alien planets operating in any manner other than Darwinian," *The Telegraph* quoted Morris as saying. "In the end, the number of options is remarkably restrictive. I don't think an alien will be a blob. If aliens are out there, they should have evolved just like us... In short [alien life] is likely to be very similar to us."[65]

According to Bruno Ghibaudi, the human form is "universal throughout the cosmos... and yet the idea of this has generally been rejected by Earthmen as impossible, no doubt because, as almost always, the truth is too simple to be accepted."[66]

Perhaps the most obvious question raised by this chapter is, did Hollywood's peaceful alien contact movies give rise to the contactee stories, or did the contactee stories give rise to the movies? Frankly, it is very difficult to determine precisely what influenced what, and when. The two have danced together intimately in such a way that confidently identifying where one begins and the other ends is a nigh on impossible task. George Adamski's descriptions of human-like aliens with generous foreheads and a dislike of nuclear weapons came three years prior to the movie that thrust their spitting image into popular culture (*This Island Earth*), but one year *after* the human-like, nuke-intolerant Klaatu had graced our screens in *The Day the Earth Stood Still*. Jessie Roestenburg's claimed encounter with Nordic beings in rural England in 1954 anticipated *This Island Earth* by a year, and there are numerous other Nordic accounts pre-dating not only *This Island Earth* but also *The Day the Earth Stood Still*.

The movies discussed in this chapter, for all their silly flourishes, are probably more realistic in essence than any of Hollywood's outings into evil alien territory. This can be stated based on the fact that leading space scientists are today confident that the vast majority of advanced alien species in our universe will be non-hostile. Former SETI director Jill Tarter (the real-life Ellie Arroway from *Contact*) has opined that alien invasion movies are nothing more than a reflection of our own fears: "Often the aliens of science fiction say more about us than they do about themselves," she remarked on the SETI website in 2012. "While Stephen Hawking warned that alien life might try to conquer or colonize Earth, I respectfully disagree. If aliens were able to visit Earth that would mean they would have technological capabilities sophisticated enough not to need slaves, food, or other planets. If aliens were to come here it would be simply to explore." Tarter added: "Considering the age of the universe, we probably wouldn't be their first extraterrestrial encounter, either. We should look at movies like *Men in Black III*, *Prometheus* and *Battleship* as great entertainment and metaphors for our own fears, but we should not consider them harbingers of alien visitation."[67]

Although this chapter has examined a fair number of movies in which extraterrestrials extend to us a peaceful hand, Hollywood's friendly aliens are still vastly outnumbered by its invasive ones. Why is this so? Why does the entertainment industry remain reluctant to positively depict the scenario of alien visitation? Perhaps it is because altruistic aliens seem inherently less dramatic, and therefore less profitable. Also, from a screenwriting perspective, it is arguably more challenging to explore the positive implications of alien contact than the negative – explosions are easier to pen than a profound socio-political or spiritual debate.

Perhaps in the years to come Hollywood will be more inclined to shake ET's hand than to blow it off with a bazooka and a one-liner. But as long as Hollywood continues to draw inspiration from UFO literature there will be no shortage of creepy alien imagery on our screens, and here we refer specifically to the iconography of the Close Encounter of the Fourth Kind – alien abduction.

1. Production designer Joe Alves (center-left in flares) in one of his sets during the production of Steven Spielberg's *Close Encounters of the Third Kind*. Alves also designed the movie's aliens based on real-life accounts of alien encounters. *Courtesy of Joe Alves.*

2. Conceptual artwork for *Close Encounters of the Third Kind* by illustrator George Jensen. *Courtesy of Joe Alves.*

3. Conceptual artwork for *Close Encounters of the Third Kind* by illustrator George Jensen. *Courtesy of Joe Alves.*

4. Construction of the *Close Encounters* mothership. *Courtesy of Joe Alves.*

5. Construction of the *Close Encounters* 'Big Set' – the site in the movie of the aliens' open contact with the US government and contactee Roy Neary (Richard Dreyfus). *Courtesy of Joe Alves.*

CBS ENTERTAINMENT

FINAL SHOOTING SCRIPT

INTRUDERS

BY

Tracy Torme'

Part Two   No. 12/16/91

Rev. 12/31/91 (blue)   ENTIRE SCRIPT

6. The title page of the shooting script for *Intruders*, written by Tracy Torme, dated December 1991. Harvard psychiatrist Dr John Mack worked as a consultant on the project. His handwritten notes fill the page. One note reads: "How will they <u>sound</u> the communication?" This is a query about how the reported telepathic abilities of the Grays would be conveyed onscreen. Another reads: "<u>Ruthless</u> eyes too strong." Mack is here taking issue with Torme's negative characterization of the aliens' hypnotic stare, expressing a desire that the Grays not be depicted as malevolent or consciously hostile. *Courtesy of John E. Mack Archives LLC.*

7. Experiencer Steven Jones.
Courtesy of Steven Jones.

8. Abductee Bret Oldham.
Courtesy of Bret Oldham.

9. Experiencer Brigitte Barclay. *Courtesy of Brigitte Barclay.*

10. Experiencer Christopher Bledsoe Sr. *Courtesy of Christopher Bledsoe Sr.*

11. Experiencer Peter Faust. *Courtesy of Peter Faust.*

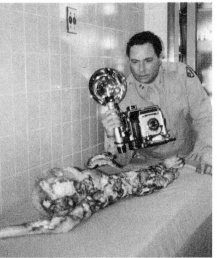

12. Paul Davids, writer/producer of the Showtime TV movie *Roswell*, pictured during the shoot in 1994. *Courtesy of Paul Davids.*

13. Paul Davids playing a cameo role in his *Roswell* movie, pictured photographing a dead alien from the crash. *Courtesy of Paul Davids.*

14. Paul Davids with Martin Sheen and Kyle MacLachlan during the *Roswell* shoot. *Courtesy of Paul Davids.*

15. Paul Davids at home in his office with the star of his *Roswell* movie. *Courtesy of Paul Davids.*

16. Speakers at the 1995 Disney UFO conference in Orlando, Florida. Left to right: Russ Estes, Vicki Ecker, Yvonne Smith, Don Ecker, George Knapp, Kevin Randle, Zecharia Sitchin. *Courtesy of Don Ecker.*

17. More Disney conference speakers: Left to right: Don Ecker (standing) Jesse Marcel Jr., Don Schmidt, Bruce Cornet, William Bramley, Budd Hopkins, Barry Taff, Clifford Stone, Stanley McDaniel. *Courtesy of Don Ecker.*

18. The 'Mousker' presented to Don Ecker by Disney for his organization of the two-week UFO conference at Disney World. Its plaque reads: "To Don Ecker, UFO, Thanks from the Publicity Staff, Walt Disney World Resort, 'UFO Summit' – 1995." *Courtesy of Don Ecker.*

19. The cover page of Bryce Zabel and Brent Friedman's pitch for their *Dark Skies* TV show, dated 8 Feb, 1995. This particular pitch was addressed to ABC Productions, but the show was ultimately accepted by NBC. The design of the pitch was based on the infamous MJ-12 documents, which were 'leaked' to selected individuals beginning in the early-1980s. MJ-12 also featured as a major plot device in the show. *Courtesy of Bryce Zabel.*

January 2, 1995

Bryce and Brent,

The truth must be told. You have been chosen as instruments to achieve this objective.

The truth, however, must <u>not</u> be represented as truth. Too many people who are needed in the struggle will die.

The cover of <u>fiction</u> must be used to present this truth. Those who fear the light will not want to bring attention to you by allowing your death.

This is the only way.

Do not be afraid.

The fight for Humanity demands your courage.

John Loengard

DARK SKIES

20. The letter written by Bryce Zabel and Brent Friedman, addressed to themselves from their own fictional *Dark Skies* protagonist, John Loengard. The letter informs the producers they have been chosen to help reveal the truth about UFOs in the guise of fiction. Zabel and Friedman would later be approached in real life by mysterious men who claimed to have chosen them for this very same purpose. *Courtesy of Bryce Zabel.*

21. Bryce Zabel and Brent Friedman in Washington D.C. during the production of the *Dark Skies* pilot, November, 1995. *Courtesy of Bryce Zabel.*

22. Left to right: Brent Friedman, director Tobey Hooper (front), who also directed alien movie *Life Force* (1985) and the *Invaders from Mars* remake (1986), Joseph Stern, and Bryce Zabel. Shooting *Dark Skies* in Washington D.C. in 1995. *Courtesy of Bryce Zabel.*

23. Bryce Zabel and wife, Jackie, with *Dark Skies* star Eric Close, who played the character of John Loengard. Pictured at the *Dark Skies* wrap party, 21 September, 1996. It was as this event that Zabel and his production partner Brent Friedman were approached by a man (and later men) claiming to be from Naval Intelligence. *Courtesy of Bryce Zabel.*

24. Bryce Zabel's UFOlogically-inspired ID badge for the *Dark Skies* wrap party. *Courtesy of Bryce Zabel.*

25. A much-visited UFO-themed road sign on Nevada's Highway 375, otherwise officially known as 'The Extraterrestrial Highway' in celebration of the nearby Area 51. Thousands of tourists flock to the surrounding area each year. This is what UFO Disclosure looks like in the age of hyperreality. *Photo by and courtesy of Shepherd Johnson.*

CHAPTER FIVE

BREAKING THROUGH

"You expect answers so quickly! We don't even know all the
questions yet!"

– Dr. Janet Duffey (Frances Sternhagen), *Communion* (1989)

Here we examine alien-abduction-themed entertainment
products – movies and TV shows in which extraterrestrials
spirit-away humans and subject them to traumatic medical
experimentation. Agendas relating to genetics, cross-species breed-
ing, and invasion are implied. Rarely are the aliens' actions depicted
as beneficial to the abductee or to humanity at large. As we shall see,
Hollywood's imaginings of these experiences represent a murky and
sometimes grotesquely distorted reflection of the phenomenon as reported in reality.

This chapter presents the core abduction research theories and a
select few abduction cases spanning the late-1950s to the mid-1980s.
These cases have been chosen for their clear illustration of features and
themes common to abduction accounts across the decades, and for
the ample context they provide for the film and TV analyses to follow,
which bring us up to present day. It should be stressed that, although
the presentation of abduction cases here stops in the 1980s, the cases in reality do not. The phenomenon persists, as demonstrated in the

second half of this chapter, which is dedicated to exclusive interviews with some of today's most notable abductees. It is then we hand-over to the experiencers themselves as they share with the reader their unique perspectives on Hollywood's engagement with the mystifying phenomenon that has so profoundly affected their lives.

Disturbing accounts of trauma inflicted on individuals by otherworldly entities puncturing the membrane of our reality are nothing new. Global folk traditions brim with tales of men, women, and children being lured into strange realms by mysterious forces. Legends of incubi and sucubi in particular invite comparisons to modern day abduction accounts. These entities would appear as if from nowhere at night in the dwellings of women and men respectively, temporarily paralyzing them whilst having their sexual way. Half-breed children were sometimes said to have been borne of these unholy unions, just as many modern day experiencers speak of alien-human hybrids.[1]

Modern abduction research

Throughout the 1970s, a number of UFO researchers, Coral and Jim Lorenzen, Dr Leo Sprinkle, and Raymond Fowler, among others, began to uncover half-hidden memories in certain UFO witnesses who had experienced periods of missing time. With the assistance of professional hypnotists, these researchers recovered accounts of capture and examination by alien entities.[2]

It was during the late-1970s that New York artist Budd Hopkins began to specialize in abduction research, working extensively with hypnotists to extract memories of otherworldly encounters in hundreds of men and women from all walks of life. Hopkins' work here lead to his first book, *Missing Time* (1981), which, as UFO historian Jerome Clark notes, introduced several ideas that would become central to the abduction research field:

> (1) that abductions are not random events; (2) that they occur periodically over an abductee's life, starting in early childhood; (3) that the abductors subject their victims to intrusive physical procedures (such as the insertion or removal of small devices thought

to be monitoring or tracking mechanisms); (4) that the abductors, typically small Gray-skinned humanoids, treat their captives with cold indifference on the whole; (5) that the purpose of abductions may have to do with alien interest in human genetics; and (6) abduction experiences may have happened to tens of thousands of Americans whose encounters have never been revealed.[3]

Hopkins was at the forefront of abduction research throughout the 1980s, and his work had an immeasurable impact on the UFO community. By 1985, around 300 cases of abduction had been documented in the literature, with an additional 500 being added over the next six years. A 1992 Roper Poll indicated that as many as 3.7 million Americans exhibited symptoms of abduction, and many UFO researchers now considered the phenomenon to be epidemic.[4]

1992 also saw the publication of Dr. David Jacobs' *Secret Life*, in which the history professor-turned-UFO-researcher postulated that abductions were not merely a part of the UFO phenomenon, but were central to it, and that the aliens' reported genetic experiments on abductees were not just another component of these experiences, but were at their core. Jacobs concurred with Hopkins that an alien-human hybridization effort was underway, only Jacobs' slant was more alarmist – the aliens' ultimate goal, he would later conclude, was global domination.[5]

Another key development occurred in 1992 – an abduction study conference held at MIT at which all the key figures were present, including, most notably, Pulitzer Prize-winning Harvard psychiatrist Dr. John Mack.[6] It was following this conference that the word 'abductee' began to be replaced with 'experiencer,' a term favored by Mack and his patients for its less victimizing and more participatory implications. Mack, who initially thought abductions were a form of psychosis, soon came to the conclusion that the phenomenon was real insomuch as his patients, who came from all walks of life and whose honesty was not in doubt, were of unquestionably sound mind. Like Hopkins and Jacobs, Mack was also impressed by the physical evidence of abduction, although the physicality of the experiences was of less concern to the psychiatrist. Mack was fascinated by the psychological and spiritual aspects of abductions and suggested that a purely mental experience shouldn't necessarily be considered less 'real' than a physical one. Mack would repeatedly urge that Western science and culture broaden its parameters for what constitutes 'reality.'

1994 saw the publication of Mack's hugely influential book *Abduction: Human Encounters with Aliens*,[7] in which he suggested that the abduction phenomenon was representative of a higher consciousness attempting to 'break through' into our own collective consciousness using a subtle and age-old approach. The phenomenon was benign, if not benevolent, said Mack, despite the initial trauma it often inflicts on individuals. Mack believed these experiences to be "an outreach program from the cosmos to the consciously impaired."[8]

Mack's book, along with his considerable charisma and academic stature, was principally responsible for bringing the experiencer phenomenon to widespread attention in the mid-1990s beyond the realms of UFOlogy and science-fiction. Around the time of his book's publication Mack appeared on the Oprah Winfrey show in an episode dedicated entirely to alien abduction. Oprah was skeptical but open-minded, and Mack and a select few of his patients were given considerable time to share their views and testimonies. It made for powerful and convincing viewing.[9]

By this point, abduction accounts fitting clear and repeating patterns had intensified to the extent that they constituted a whole new category of UFO experience: Close Encounters of the Fourth Kind. The 'CE4' term initially described literal physical abduction by alien entities, but in 1998 Dr. Jacques Vallee recommended in the *Journal of Scientific Exploration* that the category also include "cases when witnesses experienced a transformation of their sense of reality," in order that more ambiguous though perhaps no less significant UFO experiences not go unscrutinized.[10]

~ ABDUCTION AS ENTERTAINMENT ~

One of the earliest Hollywood products to contain details now identifiable as common to abduction accounts was the 1953 movie *Invaders from Mars* (discussed in Chapter Three from a conspiratorial perspective). The Martian leader in the movie is a diminutive being with a distinctly oversized cranium and powers of telepathy and mind-control – classic characteristics of alien Grays as described by experiencers. Even the Grays' hypnotic black eyes are present in the movie's alien drone soldiers, who wear tight-fitting one-piece suits (also a typical detail in abduction reports).

Alien implants serve as a major plot device. Following his sighting of a flying saucer the night before, our child protagonist, David, notices a red puncture mark at the base of his father's skull. We later learn that the big-eyed drone soldiers have been implanting townsfolk with these devices in order to control them from afar in much the same manner as modern experiencers report.

The movie ends bizarrely with David suddenly back in his bed, as in the opening sequence. He then runs into his parents' bedroom, confused and frightened. They reassure him he was merely suffering night terrors. After returning to his own bed, David looks through his window once again and witnesses the very same flying saucer of his dream, descending slowly, exactly as it had in his sleep-state. The film ends here. Is the child still unconscious, trapped in a recurring nightmare, or was his bad dream a premonition of this now real event?

This 'was it all a dream?' ending brings to mind many abduction accounts to follow, in which the experiencer, during or immediately after a period of sleep, is initially unsure if the vivid alien encounter they have experienced was real or merely a hypnogogic hallucination. This kind of experience did not come to widespread attention until the 1980s, some three decades after the release of *Invaders from Mars*.

Two years later, in 1955, *This Island Earth* depicted Earth scientists being abducted by Nordic aliens. Abduction lore was barely embryonic at the time, and yet, not only was the act of alien abduction depicted, but fine details central to today's abduction narratives are also identifiable, as Paul Meehan observes:

> The two scientists are abducted by extraterrestrials from a dying world that desperately needs "new blood" from Earth. It is not stated, but nonetheless suggested, that Cal and Ruth will mate to produce offspring for their abductors. This theme was to emerge frequently in later abduction reports.[11]

How do we account for such specific abduction-related details in movies from the 1950s? A CIA strategy to test public reaction to the troubling 'truth' of alien contact, or to sow the seeds of fear? Perhaps it's a case of our timeless collective unconscious being channeled through the creative writing process, with focused screenwriters unknowingly anticipating a future UFOlogical development, or tapping into an existing albeit as yet unreported one? Maybe the writers of these movies were themselves abductees and were drawing from their own firsthand experiences. The most obvious explanation for the skeptical researcher is that the abduction phenomenon is a product purely of audience-culture, early UFO movies fueling the fantasies of psychologically imbalanced individuals. As is typical of UFO studies, there are no solid conclusions to be drawn at present, although the idea of abduction as pop-cultural product, entirely hallucinatory in nature, is sorely lacking. This much can be stated confidently based on the fact that numerous abduction accounts feature multiple individuals abducted together and sharing a collective experience. In countless cases physical evidence is detectable, including scoop marks and other scars on the body. In some cases, remarkable, almost miraculous, health benefits have been linked to abduction experiences. Skeptics also often fall back on sleep paralysis and hypnagogia as a catch-all explanation for the phenomenon. While this theory has considerable merit in certain cases, it again falls short for its inapplicability to the many accounts in which the experiencer is taken while wide-awake and engaged in activities such as driving, walking, or fishing, for example, again often while in the presence of independent witnesses (who also are taken).

The 1957 case of Brazilian farmer Antonio Villas Boas, mentioned in the previous chapter, was the first abduction experience on record. While not a perfect match for modern accounts, it did bear a number of hallmarks, including capture by alien entities and sexual activity resulting in hybridization. Boas never sought fame or profit from his testimony but endured inevitable ridicule. His case was not publicized until seven years after the fact because UFO researchers suppressed it, believing its sexual component would damage the case and, in turn, the UFO research field. Boas went on to become a lawyer and stuck to his story until the day he died in 1991.[12]

The Hills

The first case on record more typical of the Fourth Kind experiences we know today was that of Betty and Barney Hill, a middle-aged interracial married couple, who encountered a UFO on the night of 19 September 1961 while driving on a rural road in New Hampshire. It is, by now, the most documented abduction case in history. In essence it involved both husband and wife witnessing a UFO in the night sky, which soon positioned itself low above the road they were driving on.

Barney stepped out of the car with his binoculars to get a better look at the object, which he and Betty could now clearly see was a disc-shaped craft, and was disturbed at the sight of up to eleven humanoid figures staring back at him through its windows.

Recognizing that the beings were not human, Barney jumped back in the car and became hysterical. "They're going to capture us!" he screamed at his wife. Before they could drive away, the Hills entered an altered state of consciousness in which they became docile and it was at this point that they could hear strange beeping or buzzing sounds, which seemed to vibrate through their car. When the sequence of noises ended and then repeated, the Hills found they had traveled close to 35 miles south of their last position but had almost no recollection of where the time had gone. They would return home with full conscious memory of all events leading up to those described above, but with only hazy recall of their missing time.

Two days later, Betty reported their encounter, absent of some of its more 'unusual' details, to Pease Air Force Base, and, true to form, the USAF informed the Hills they had probably misidentified the planet Jupiter.

Eventually the Hills underwent regression hypnosis with Dr. Benjamin Simon, a respected Boston psychiatrist and neurologist. Over the following six months, Dr. Simon was able to recover the two hours of missing time from the Hills' ordeal. In recorded hypnosis sessions (which make for extremely disturbing listening) the couple spoke of being taken aboard the craft, wherein they were both medically examined by their captors before being returned to their vehicle.

The beings were described as approximately five feet tall, with large heads, extremely large slanted eyes, small nose and mouth, and gray skin. Significantly, Betty recalled being shown a 'star map' as an indication of the beings' stellar origins. She later drew the map from memory and eventually an amateur astronomer, Marjorie Fish, claimed to have identified the system as Zeta Reticuli, belonging to the constellation of Reticulum, some 39 light-years from Earth (though her interpretation has been disputed). The Hills' story did not become widely known until 1966, five years after the fact, when it was published as the best-selling book *The Interrupted Journey*, by John G. Fuller.[13]

Today, the Hills' abduction case is considered one of the strongest in the literature, but it will always have its fierce critics. How, for example, do we account for the close parallels between the alien experiences depicted in the 1953 movie *Invaders from Mars* and those described eight years later by Betty and Barney Hill? The movie featured beings vaguely resembling those described by the Hills, and could, like those in the Hill case, exert mind-control over humans. Skeptics have also noted that an alien with wrap-around eyes not too dissimilar to those in the Hill case was featured in an episode of the *Outer Limits* TV show just twelve days before the Hills' first hypnosis session, although the Hills claimed no knowledge of *The Outer Limits or Invaders from Mars*, and there was no evidence to suggest the couple were fans of science-fiction more broadly.[14]

Still, the critics argue, surely these and similar entertainment products preceding the Hill case prove their experience was a product of audience culture? In response, most UFO researchers would hold that abductions were almost certainly occurring long before the release of *Invaders from Mars* in 1953 and were likely ongoing throughout the 1950s. The Hills' account, it could be argued, was simply the first abduction experience to seriously capture the attention of the press and public at large, due in no small part to the couple's controversial interracial marriage, and because such a stealthy and private phenomenon naturally will take some measure of time to force its way into the sphere of popular debate.

Only a small handful of abduction accounts were reported in the years following the publication of the Hill case, most notable among which were the Herbert Schirmer case of December 1967, in which a Nebraska police sergeant encountered a UFO hovering above a road and later recalled being abducted by and communicating with its humanoid occupants;[15] and the Pascagoula Mississippi case of October 1973, in which two men, Calvin Parker and Charles Hickson, claimed to have been abducted one evening while out fishing on the Pascagoula River. The men described being physically accosted by three distinctly non-human entities which floated them in a powerless state back to their saucer-shaped craft which was hovering over the river. A medical examination ensued before the men were returned to their boat in a state of shock.[16]

Creative power

A most peculiar production was broadcast in 1974 as an ABC Movie of the Week. *The Stranger Within* starred Barbra Eden as a suburban housewife with a vasectomized husband who finds herself inexplicably pregnant. As the narrative unfolds the wife's behavior grows increasingly bizarre. Her husband and her doctor eventually reach the radical conclusion that she has been abducted and impregnated by aliens, and that her memory of these events has been erased. The film plays out as a serious psychological drama, free of the cheap sensationalizm it could so easily have embraced.

The author Mike Clelland provides insightful analysis of the movie in his essay 'The Stranger Within and the Predictive Power of the Creative Process.' Clelland writes: "What is terribly bizarre is that this movie seems to have predicted so much of what has now become well documented within the UFO abduction research field – accounts of women who are mysteriously pregnant, seemingly after an abduction by aliens." Clelland draws particular attention to the film's climax, in which Barbra Eden's character "gives birth to what seems to be some sort of super-enhanced (or god-like) child. This parallels the accounts of hybrid children and their unwitting abductee mothers meeting onboard a craft and communicating through telepathy."

Clelland further observes a list of plot points in this obscure little movie which anticipate with eerie precision what are now considered to be key characteristics of the abduction phenomenon:

~ A pregnancy without any sexual source.
~ A female abductee with gynecological problems.
~ The urge to research and study scientific topics.
~ Hypnosis as a tool for recovering memories of the abduction experience.
~ An abductee channeling an alien being.
~ Telepathic communication.
~ A sense of longing for an alien world.
~ Experiencing a dramatic healing.
~ Marks on the body that can't be explained, only to heal rapidly without scarring.
~ Lower than normal body temperature.
~ An abductee with Rh blood factor.
~ Sensitivity to sound.
~ Craving salt.

The Stranger Within was scripted by famed writer Richard Matheson, based closely on his own 1953 short story *Trespass*. "How did Matheson write something that so closely predicted what would unfold decades later?" Clelland asks. "One thought is that he might have been an abductee, and he was simply using his own experiences, either remembered or buried, when he wrote the story." Clelland dismisses this idea, though, "because he [Matheson] had a massive output of work, and little else [of his] seems to match these ideas."

Clelland instead suggests that a far stranger force could be at work in this case. He writes:

> "I am convinced that there is a very real power in the creative process, and when abandoning (or disciplining) oneself to this kind of artistic inspiration, something mysterious can unfold. The artist can somehow tap into deeper truths. The work-a-day routine of sitting in front of a typewriter (or canvas, or drawing board) can be seen as a ritual act, very much like the forgotten alchemist who sits before his candle. Matheson must have been on fire during those early years writing for pulp magazines, and something weirdly predictive seems to have been manifested in his tight little story."[17]

The power of the creative process to anticipate and manifest realities has been explored extensively by Jeffrey J. Kripal, J. Newton Rayzor Chair of Philosophy and Religious Thought at Rice University in Texas. In his book *Mutants and Mystics*, Kripal asserts that: "There is something fundamentally mystical about writing... words, stories, and symbols can *become real*."[18] Kripal means this literally, not figuratively. It is through the creative process, he says, that: "The imagination can become empowered to make contact with what appears to be a real spiritual world or, at the very least, an entirely different order of mind."[19]

Kripal has suggested that abductions and other 'impossible' phenomena are more usefully examined within the context of the "imaginal," a "superpowered version of the human imagination,"[20] rather than as absolute ontological truths to be proved or disproved by skeptics or believers. Millions of people have experiences that current science tells us are impossible, but which are nonetheless vividly real for the experiencer. This demands our serious engagement, says Kripal, and the imaginal provides an effective framework through which to engage.

The UFO Incident

In 1975, the Hill abduction story became even more famous when it was adapted for television as a feature-length movie starring Estelle Pasrons and James Earl Jones as Betty and Barney. With a teleplay based directly on Dr. Simon's taped hypnosis sessions with the couple, *The UFO Incident* was remarkably faithful to the Hills' actual account of capture by gray-skinned saucer occupants in September of 1961. Another film, the little-known Italian production *Eyes Behind the Stars*, had touched on the theme of abduction three years prior in 1972, but *The UFO Incident* was the first direct treatment of a real-life case and the first to bring together many of the now common themes and motifs of abduction experiences, including medical examination, missing time, and hypnosis. The movie's aliens, although smallish with large eyes and bald heads, are of normal proportion (perhaps a little on the stocky side) and are not strikingly similar to Grays as they would later be realized onscreen in Spielberg's *Close Encounters* as decidedly smaller, more spindly beings with significantly larger heads, and larger, blacker eyes.

The UFO Incident is certainly one of Hollywood's best treatments of a true-life abduction experience. It works first and foremost as a powerful human drama propelled by the obvious commitment of Parsons and Jones in excellent central performances as the Hills. Despite its fantastical subject matter, the film remains sober throughout.

Five days gone

Not only did 1975 see Hollywood's first direct treatment of a real-life abduction case, it also saw what stands today as one of the most compelling, and surely one of the most famous, accounts of alien abduction on record.

On 5 November 1975, 22 year old logger, Travis Walton of Snowflake, Arizona, vanished without a trace for no less than five days after appearing to have been abducted by a flying saucer. The events leading up to his apparent abduction were witnessed directly by the six other men on his logging crew: his close friend Mike Rogers (who headed the crew), Ken Peterson, John Goulette, Steve Pierce, Allen Dalis and Dwayne Smith – all residents of Snowflake.

Driving home from a hard day's work in the forest, the crew, all huddled in the same truck, noticed an intense yellowish light coming from behind a hill. As they drove closer they were awestruck by the sight of a large golden disc hovering low over a clearing in the trees. They estimated the craft to be around 8 feet high and 20 feet in diameter.

As Rogers stopped the truck for a closer look, Walton jumped out of the vehicle in excitement and ran toward the disc. His co-workers screamed at him to return, but it was too late. As Walton stood directly beneath the craft it began to wobble and emit a sound like a turbine. The loggers then watched in horror as a blue-green light beam struck Walton square in the chest, lifting him a foot off the ground and hurling him some 10 feet through the air. He hit the earth with a thud, lifeless, or so it seemed. In sheer terror, Mike Rogers hit the gas and fled the scene along with the rest of the crew.

The next five days saw a swirling storm of confusion, anger, and allegations descend on the sleepy town of Snowflake. The loggers, having reported to police that their friend had been taken by a UFO, immediately were considered suspects in Walton's disappearance and possible murder.

On 10 November, the remaining logging crew were subjected to polygraph examinations administered by Arizona Department of Public Safety employee Cy Gilson. The men were asked a number of questions with the aim of establishing if they had harmed or killed Travis, and if they had indeed witnessed a UFO. With the exception of Allen Dalis, who was uncooperative, all men were judged to be truthful in their assertions that they had caused no harm to Walton and that they had indeed seen a UFO on the night in question. Gilson's official report stated in part: "These polygraph examinations prove that these five men did see some object they believed to be a UFO, and that Travis Walton was not injured or murdered by any of these men on that Wednesday." Based on the tests, local Sherriff Marlin Gillespie accepted the UFO story, announcing: "There's no doubt they're telling the truth." Of Dalis' failed test, Jerome Clark writes: "Dalis was a man with much to hide: a criminal past and… a criminal future. He had behaved with hostility all through the polygraph process, as if fearing secrets he had every reason not to wish revealed would accidentally come to light." In any case, Sherriff Gillespie essentially disregarded Dalis' test in the context of the others, saying: "I feel sure that all six of them saw a UFO."

Later that night, Walton returned. He was found in a telephone box some three miles outside of Snowflake, huddled and shivering. He had five days' growth of beard and was visibly malnourished. As he was taken back to Snowflake he began babbling about strange creatures with large eyes. He assumed he'd been gone just a couple of hours and was stunned into prolonged silence when he was told five days had passed.

His return to Snowflake brought only more chaos and confusion to the town, the minutia of which have been exhaustively documented in numerous books and TV programs. "Nearly lost in the complicated human saga that the Walton episode quickly became was Travis' account of what he claimed happened to him during his disappearance," notes Jerome Clark, urging that the details of Walton's experience itself not be forgotten. Walton could recall only around two hours of his ordeal, but, unlike most abductees, he could do so consciously, without the aid of hypnosis.

In essence Walton's story is as follows:

An indeterminate amount of time after being struck by the light beam, Walton awoke on a table in a hospital-like room, his body aching and his head pounding. As his vision cleared he was startled at the sight of three non-human beings standing next to him. He described them as "shorter than five feet," with "very large, bald heads, no hair." Walton said they "looked like foetuses. They had no eyebrows, no eyelashes," but that they had "enormous eyes – almost all brown, without much white in them." Their mouths, ears, and noses, were "real small," said Walton. Essentially, he was describing archetypal alien Grays, albeit around a decade before accounts of these beings would become central to abduction research.

Unlike in most abduction accounts, Walton had full control of his mind and body – something which seemed to shock the aliens when their captor stood up and shoved one of them backwards and yelled at them aggressively. Walton was expecting a struggle, but the beings instead stood back and raised their hands in a gesture for him to 'cease.' They then hurriedly left the room. It was the last Walton would see of them.

When the beings had left, Walton exited the room via a hallway, which led him to a sparse spherical room with a high-backed chair at its center. Walton sat in the chair, and as he did so the room was filled with stars, almost like a planetarium display. Using a lever on the chair, Walton found he could rotate the position of the stars around him, but he thought better of meddling further. As he stood to leave the room he was surprised to see a man standing in the doorway, who he described as tall, Caucasian, and muscular, with sandy blond hair long enough to cover his ears, and bright hazel eyes. The man wore a transparent bubble helmet and a bright blue coverall suit with a black band around the waist. He motioned for Travis to follow him, offering only a "tolerant grin" in response to Walton's flurry of questions. The man escorted Walton out of the craft whereupon the two stepped into a room of tremendous proportions that Walton assumed was some sort of airlock or hangar, inside which were a number of saucer craft. The man then led him to another room where he saw more humans, two men and a woman, who bore a strong family resemblance to the helmeted man (these other three did not wear helmets). When Walton began asking them questions they forcibly but politely restrained him on a table and covered his mouth with what he said looked like a wireless breathing apparatus. Before he could fight back, he was out cold.

Walton awoke on a road near the phone box where he was found later that night. His physical ordeal had ended, but his emotional torment was just beginning. The next few years would see him in the media spotlight, defending his story against all comers. Walton was judged to have failed a polygraph test taken soon after his return, but he later took two additional tests, both of which he passed. He stands by his story to this day, but his case remains a divisive one.

One of the many skeptical arguments against the Walton case was that it was reported only a few weeks after the NBC broadcast of *The UFO Incident* – the TV adaptation of the Hill abduction story. The implication is that Walton drew details from the TV movie to fuel his own UFO fantasy. This idea holds no water for Jerome Clark: "Travis insisted neither he nor any other witness had seen the show [movie]," he writes of the case. "In any event, there is not much similarity between the Hills' story and Walton's. There is, moreover, not a great deal of similarity between Walton's and any other abduction narrative that would have been known to him from the UFO literature as of November 1975."

Clark concludes of this baffling case:

> In the end how one views the Walton controversy depends on how one feels about UFOs in general and alien-abduction claims in particular. If one believes it is possible that UFOs exist as piloted extraterrestrial vehicles, one can accept that Travis Walton boarded a spacecraft and interacted with its occupants. If one believes such things are not possible, one has little choice but to insist that a heretofore-undetected hoax scheme underlies the claim... Nearly all of the available evidence would lead one to the conclusion that Walton, his family, and the

logging crew are not hoaxers. If there is compelling evidence to the contrary, it has yet to emerge.[21]

Two years after the Walton controversy UFOs would serve as the inspiration behind one of history's most iconic motion pictures – Spielberg's *Close Encounters of the Third Kind* (1977). The movie's Gray aliens, which were based on descriptions gathered by production designer Joe Alves from his own primary research, are revealed to be benevolent and angelic, despite earlier abducting people and tearing apart families. Their actions never entirely make sense to us; their methods are mysterious and their agenda unknown, but in the final scenes their spiritual warmth shines through.

Owls and UFOs

To those with no interest in either, owls and UFOs might seem like chalk and cheese, but these 'phenomena,' one assumed to belong exclusively to our world, the other thought to originate elsewhere, often go hand-in-hand.

It has long been theorized in the UFO research community that the sighting of an owl or owls shortly prior to, during, or immediately after a UFO close encounter is a strong indication of a repressed abduction experience, with the image of the owl acting as a screen memory for the traumatized abductee. The logic here is that the large, penetrating (and sometimes glassy black) eyes of an owl closely resemble those of the alien Gray. Owls, like UFOs, can also be silent and invisible.

In his essay 'Owls and the UFO Abductee,' Mike Clelland considers the possible psychological function of owl imagery so common in abduction reports, but ultimately he ascribes it a more profound and mystical meaning, suggesting that the owl in these circumstances may be "part of a shamanic initiation," a wake-up call from the universe itself for those who suspect but refuse to acknowledge their lifetime of hidden experiences with intelligences beyond the realm of everyday perception.[22]

Communion

Owl imagery has been used prominently in a number of UFO movies dealing explicitly with abduction. One of the earliest films linking owls to abduction was *Communion* (1989), based on the non-fiction book by now legendary experiencer Whitley Strieber, which to date has sold more than two million copies worldwide and which acted as a catalyst for thousands more men and women to recognize and deal with their own similar experiences. The movie starred Christopher Walken in a compellingly manic performance as Strieber, and Lindsay Crouse as his wife Anne (also a strong, naturalistic performance).

The book is primarily focused on an experience which occurred 26 December 1985, when Strieber was, for lack of a better word, 'abducted' from his cabin in upstate New York while on a short break with his family and some close friends (incidentally, the male friend is played by Andreas Katsulas, who a few years later would go on to star in the sci-fi series *Babylon 5*, which featured multiple species of Gray aliens).

Strieber had almost no conscious recollection of what had happened to him. He wrote in his book: "I awoke the morning of the twenty-seventh very much as usual, but grappling with a distinct sense of unease and a very improbable but intense memory of seeing a barn owl staring at me through the window sometime during the night." Strieber felt increasingly uneasy as the day wore on, as did his friends, who had been frightened by an intense white light which had inexplicably flooded the cabin on the night in question. "I wanted desperately to believe in that owl," continued Strieber. "I told my wife about it. She was polite, but commented about the absence of tracks [in the snow]. I really very much wanted to convince her of it, though. Even more, I wanted to convince myself."[23] The significance of the owl was transferred from page to screen in a scene in the movie where, following the events described, Strieber (Walken) asks his wife and friends repeatedly if they'd seen an owl the previous night. They had not.

In the months that follow, Strieber begins to suffer an untraceable emotional and psychological toll. Eventually he agrees to be hypnotically regressed by psychiatrist Janet Duffey (played by Frances Sternhagen), and it is through these sessions that the bizarre events of that night come back to confront him – events involving small, spindly, beings with oversized oval heads and large hypnotic black eyes. Other beings are encountered too – hooded dwarf-like creatures with blue skin with whom Strieber clowns around at one point, dancing with them and high-fiving them. There's even a robot.

The events make no sense to the viewer on a narrative level, just as they made no sense to Strieber. His memories have the feel of a surreal nightmare. They are symbolic impressions only. Time and space are meaningless. His communications with the entities are nonsensical. Despite the fear they invoke in him, Strieber eventually realizes his abductors are not hostile, although certainly they are tricksters, concealing their true nature while peeling back the layers of his own. Crucially, in both book and film, Strieber draws no conclusions about the origin of what he terms "the Visitors." The extraterrestrial hypothesis is considered, but is far from satisfactory.

Communion was the first Hollywood entertainment product to engage thoughtfully with the more surreal aspects of the abduction phenomenon. With a screenplay penned by Strieber himself, the film captures the tonal essence of his book, if not its deeply layered psychological and metaphysical complexity. It's a flawed film, but it dares to show abduction for the baffling, hallucinatory, deeply troubling, intellectually challenging, and spiritually transformative phenomenon it is, or that it can be. "You expect answers so quickly," Strieber's psychiatrist remarks to him at one point in the movie, "we don't even know all the questions yet!"

The film depicts Strieber attending an abductee support group in the city in a nod to the then current work of Budd Hopkins and a number of other researchers. Still in denial, Strieber reluctantly listens to the group's individual stories of otherworldly abduction. He's extremely disturbed by what he hears, and so are we. This is a film, which, for the most part, is rooted firmly in our own mundane world. The thought of non-human intelligences breaking through into this reality from a strange realm is psychologically jarring, both for Strieber and for the viewer.

As real life does not conform to genre, so *Communion* comes in many shades: sci-fi, horror, family drama, but above all else it's an existential story. Its failure at the box-office should have come as no surprise. Although he wrote the screenplay, Strieber did not always see eye-to-eye with director Philippe Mora (an old friend of his), and he was famously dissatisfied with the end product. Strieber recently commented that no Hollywood movie to date, including his own, has believably simulated the true nature of the abduction experience. "Nothing does and nothing *can*," he told Catherine Austin Fitts on his Dreamland radio show.

"The reason is you're not in 'this' reality... you're between worlds. And some of the physics of where you are is different from 'this' physics. You're in a different level of reality of *yourself*."24

Communion remains an important film, not only for its ambition, but for further popularizing the image of the now archetypal Gray alien – an image which first came to prominence on the cover of Strieber's own bestselling book two years prior and would later feature on the movie's VHS cover, staring hypnotically into the eyes of millions of creeped-out customers in video rental stores worldwide. "That image of that iconic Gray alien is forever seared into the consciousness of our pop-culture," observes Mike Clelland. "It is as instantly recognized as Ronald McDonald or Santa Claus."25

Intruders

The other key abduction book of 1987 was Budd Hopkins' *Intruders: The Incredible Visitations at Copley Woods*, which investigated the claims of a number of abductees, but was more specifically concerned with the case of Debbie Jordan-Kauble (known in the book as "Kathie Davis"). Jordan-Kauble described having been abducted from her parents' home in June of 1983 and being taken aboard an egg-shaped craft which had landed outside. She claimed to have been impregnated by her alien captors, who later removed the fetus and eventually introduced her to her human-alien hybrid child. Jordan-Kauble was dissatisfied with the treatment of her case in Hopkins' book and later went on to write her own, more detailed account, not only of her 1983 abduction, but of other related experiences throughout her life. As to the nature and origin of these experiences, Jordan mused:

> I have had so many different types of experience with so many different aspects of this field that I am somewhat mixed as to what I think they are and where they come from. I have seen the hard evidence that debunkers claim does not exist. I have also experienced the psychological and physical effects, as well as the spiritual awakening of a close encounter. I am also smart enough to realize how powerful the human mind can be when faced with something that it cannot comprehend. All I have ever been able to do was report what I saw and let everyone else sort it all out.26

Hopkins' *Intruders* book would later be very loosely adapted for television by Tracy Tormé (son of legendary jazz singer and musician Mel Tormé). The 1992 mini-series *Intruders* was concerned less with the Jordan-Kauble story and more with the broader abduction phenomenon as it was then understood by the leading researchers in the field, namely Hopkins and Mack.

In the mini-series a psychiatrist, Dr. Chase, investigates the abductions of two seemingly unconnected women from different American states and in the process immerses himself in broader research into the UFO phenomenon. Eventually he and a local UFOlogist start a therapy group where abductees can collectively attempt to make sense of their traumatic experiences. Richard Crenner's psychiatrist character was modelled on both Hopkins and Mack. Crenner wears an oversized woollen fisherman's sweater throughout, clearly inspired by Hopkins' trademark garment. The actor drew greater influence from Mack, spending time with the Harvard psychiatrist in order to study his mannerisms.[27]

Intruders remains significant for its thoughtful and sympathetic treatment of the abduction phenomenon, and for grounding itself convincingly in a normal world occasionally intruded upon by a profound and sometimes terrifying non-human intelligence. It explored many themes and motifs common to abduction accounts, including intrusive examinations, alien impregnation, hybrid children, screen memories, and hypnotic regression.

1993 saw another influential contribution from Tracy Tormé in his screenplay for *Fire in the Sky* – Hollywood's take on the famous Travis Walton case. Featuring solid performances from D.B. Sweeney as Travis and Robert Patrick as Mike Rogers, it was a reasonably faithful accounting of the Walton experience – that is until the last act, which notoriously distorted Walton's encounter out of all recognition. The Nordic beings described by Travis and their walkabout with him in a spaceport were nowhere to be seen in the movie. Walton's skittish Grays were replaced with frightful goblin-like beings who literally drag the logger like a sack of spuds through their pestilent, rotting spaceship – all dank tunnels and dripping embryonic sacks – before gluing him to a table with a suffocating membrane and subjecting him to graphic torture with a thick needle to the eyeball. It is a horrific sequence, so powerful as to almost erase all memory of the events that precede it. This marked the point in time when alien abduction truly entered the horror genre. The film would go on to influence abduction-themed fright-fests such as *Altered, The Fourth Kind, Dark Skies, Alien Abduction*, and, specifically, the 2014 movie *Extraterrestrial*, to name but a few.

The UFO community was outraged by *Fire in the Sky*, and all fingers were pointed at Tracy Tormé. In a 2014 interview with the author, Tormé explained his writing process for both *Intruders* and *Fire in the Sky*, the cultural climate in which they were written, and the circumstances which led to the latter being so creatively distorted.

Tormé had been attempting to get an abduction movie off the ground long before *Intruders*. "I optioned Budd Hopkins' first book, *Missing Time*, and spent three long years trying to get it launched in Hollywood," Tormé told me of his initial effort. "At that time people didn't take abductions very seriously and it seemed like a very odd subject to launch for a multi-million dollar movie. This was in the early-to-mid 1980s."

Tormé had developed a close relationship with Hopkins during his research for the *Missing Time* movie and was an admirer of his work. "I felt he was a very good person, a very good thinker," the screenwriter said of Hopkins. "He'd invite me to witness regression hypnosis sessions that he was conducting with abductees. I was hearing these stories that sounded so much like science-fiction, so unbelievable, but what Hopkins was uncovering were these clear patterns in abductions… pattern, after pattern, after pattern." Tormé was also struck by the artistic renderings of the abductors shown to him by Hopkins:

> He had a great collection of different drawings of the beings made by various abductees, and it was amazing how similar they were to each other. This was at a time when no one knew about so-called Grays. This is back in the early 1980s when if you asked a hundred people what an alien was, you get a hundred different answers.

As time passed, the initially undecided screenwriter became a believer in the reality of the phenomenon:

> The more of Hopkins' sessions I observed, and the more abductees I met, I became 98 percent convinced that this stuff was real. I couldn't say 100 percent, because I hadn't seen anything with my own eyes. But I'd just met too many people who were very sincere and who did not want their names in the newspaper, who did not want to be

a part of UFO phenomena. They were victims in a lot of ways. They were damaged people; damaged by the experience. They expressed to me how they really didn't like that they were never asked to go along with this [the abduction experience]; that this would happen to them if they liked it or not. They were very disturbed by that, and that made a big mark on me.

A *Missing Time* movie had yet to come to fruition by the early 1990s, but by that point Hopkins' 1987 book *Intruders* was already in the process of being adapted for the small screen as a CBS mini-series. Tormé, then a staff writer and creative consultant on *Star Trek the Next Generation*, was approached to pen the teleplay.

Tormé met with the producers and learned that both Hopkins and John Mack were to be consultants on the mini-series. "That sat well with me," he recalled, "so I wrote it very, very quickly. It was shot quickly, and soon after that it was on CBS." Tormé added that, although he respected Mack, he did not share his perspective on the abduction phenomenon: "I did not agree with a lot of his theories," Tormé stressed to me. "He believed that this is all being done for the benefit of mankind, and they are our kind of our saviors and our brothers, and that if the experiencer can really think clearly and take some time he would come to realize that this was all good and that they're here to help us and save us from destruction and all that. I just didn't see it. I do not believe that they are intentionally hostile, but they seem to be lacking in emotions and they don't treat human beings with the respect that they deserve."

Intruders was broadcast by CBS through 17–19 May 1992 and was generally well received by TV critics. Despite its success, the mini-series would have a detrimental effect on Tormé's next project...

Fire in the Sky

Tormé had successfully explored the abduction phenomenon through television, but now he wanted to do so through cinema. His *Missing Time* movie was dead in the water, which he now attributes to its source material's lack of one stand-out case that could captivate audiences: "That's when I shifted my focus to Travis Walton." Tormé reached out to Walton in 1985:

When I first met him over the phone, it was ten years almost to the day since the incident had happened. I told him that I had a lot of respect for his story and I really wanted to make a movie, but first I wanted to investigate the story more and see how I felt about it. Travis was very, very reticent. He felt like no one had really treated him fairly in the past. Especially people from Hollywood. So he was not inclined to do this.

Tormé agreed that they should meet in Snowflake, Arizona, so that screenwriter and experiencer could get better acquainted. Tormé recalled:

> I spent three days with Travis. I went up to the site where it happened and I took him and Mike Rogers with me and had them re-enact the incident. They had not been back to the site in nearly ten years at this point, and they were both extremely haunted to be up there again. It's a very lonely place and it had changed hardly at all. There was even a wood pile on the ground that had been there ten years ago when they were there.

Tormé returned to Snowflake at least six times over the next six years: "I just tried to learn more and more about the case every time I went. I got to know Travis and Mike very well. All the ideas for *Fire in the Sky* really formulated out of those trips." Selling the script to studios, however, was an uphill struggle for Tormé:

> On several occasions I thought we'd found a buyer, then I would have to go back to Travis and tell him the sad news 'no, they're not going forward.' The studios at the time found the subject of abductions strange and unbelievable, and really, ultimately, not satisfying. If the aliens had come here and invaded the Earth and blown up the cities or something they might have been more open to making the movie.

Tormé emphasizes that abduction movies in general were a hard sell in the late-1980s-early-1990s:

> At that time there was not a lot of interest in this subject. People wonder why it was such a struggle to get *Fire in the Sky* made and to get *Missing Time* made. But the public really did not know about the abduction phenomenon. They weren't following it, they weren't reading about it. It had not broken through in a big way in the mass media. I

really believe these two projects [*Fire* and *Intruders*] were part of the process of people becoming aware of how these things allegedly work.

When eventually Paramount Studios bought Tormé's script, it had been six-and-a-half years since the screenwriter had first approached Travis Walton. The dream would now become a reality. But the reality would be compromised...

Script changes

"The original script was, I would say, close to one-hundred-percent accurate to Travis' memory of the events," Tormé told me:

> I literally used his memory of waking up on the table and then everything that happened to him up to the point that he's put back on the highway. I followed his story to the tee. I felt an obligation to these guys to tell the story in the truest way that I could. And I thoroughly believed him by this point, too. I had come to the conclusion that the case was real, and that he was not a liar, that's for sure. So I originally wrote exactly what he said.

One day, Tormé received a phone call in his office at Paramount Studios:

> It was a panicked Paramount executive who just happened to have seen *Intruders* on TV the night before. He was unbelievably put-off and worried because he'd seen little gray men with big eyes standing over a table doing experiments on someone, therefore it'd 'been done before,' therefore he had no interest in doing the Walton movie and was going to kill the project if I didn't come up with something else.

Tormé was shell-shocked. "They were serious," he stressed, "they were firm on it. They were going to shut the project down and not make it. We were going to have to start back at square one." Tormé had no other option but to re-write the abduction sequence: "I got together with the director and with Travis and we devised the fictional sequence that is seen in the movie."

Tormé did at least attempt to maintain the essence of the encounter:

I insisted that if we're going to fictionalize this, lets at least mirror his real occurrence. So one example would be, when Travis said he'd had trouble breathing when he came to in the strange environment, we put a scene in where they put a mask over his face. That's an example of the type of thing we tried to do. Yes, we were creating something wholly fictional, but we were going to try to maintain somewhat the feel and integrity of the terrifying experience that he had. So we tried our best to write a scary, disturbing sequence. But it was entirely fictional. I knew very early on that a lot of UFO people were going to be very upset about this.[28]

Despite its divisive ending, Tormé is proud of *Fire in the Sky*, first and foremost on its undeniable strength as a human drama. The movie made back its budget, but little more. It received mixed reviews from the critics, although, ironically, the legendary Roger Ebert praised the film's final sequence for its believability, writing: "The scenes inside the craft are really very good. They convincingly depict a reality I haven't seen in the movies before, and for once I did believe that I was seeing something truly alien, and not just a set decorator's daydreams." However, Ebert was left deflated as the credits rolled, adding: "The movie ends on an inconclusive and frustrating note."[29] Film critic James Berardinelli described *Fire in the Sky* as a "muddled-up mess," saying "It can't make up its mind whether it wants to be horror, drama, or science-fiction. As a result, it ends up being ineffective as any of the three."[30]

These criticisms, essentially describing the movie as a mishmash of genres with an inconclusive ending, in fact speak to its overall authenticity as an abduction story. As mentioned previously, the phenomenon, as experienced in reality, does not comfortably lend itself to any one genre, encompassing as it does an array of complex facets straddling drama, sci-fi, fantasy, horror, and others besides. Walton's real-life experience had no satisfactory resolution, and neither did the film. In this sense, 'true' abduction movies arguably will always struggle to make sizable dents at the box-office. Extreme 'Hollywoodization' is deemed essential to bringing these stories successfully to a mass audience.

The X-Files

Fire in the Sky made a mark on popular perceptions of the abduction phenomenon in 1993, but it was a different entertainment product that year that really captured the public's imagination. *The X-Files* ran from 1993 to 2002 and devoted many compelling hours to the exploration of UFOlogical ideas, not least of all abduction, which served as the focus of the very first episode and was a running theme throughout all nine seasons. *The X-Files* brought sharp focus to the phenomenon as reported by experiencers, and its authenticity was no fluke. Series creator Chris Carter and his co-writers were well versed in UFO literature, and even spent time with John Mack and his patients in an effort to enhance the realism of the show's many pivotal abduction scenes.[31]

Like UFOs, the series was itself a global phenomenon. Mulder and Scully became cultural icons whose names were synonymous with all things unexplained, particularly UFOs, and the show's classic slogan – "The Truth Is Out There" – was instantly adopted by the UFO community. The show's influence continues to be felt more than a decade after it ended. At the time of writing a new series of the *X-Files* is scheduled for early 2016.

Babylon 5

In 1994 the TV space opera *Babylon 5* gave sci-fi fans a rich, harder-edged alternative to *Star Trek*, albeit on a slimmer budget. The show, which ran until 1998, featured an array of alien species, including three different variants of the archetypal Gray, which by now had firmly embedded itself into pop-culture. The Vree, with oversized craniums and large black eyes, feature memorably in an episode in which a human attempts to sue one of the beings for personal damages, claiming the alien's ancestor had abducted his own great-grandfather. Another Gray variant in *Babylon 5* are the Zeners – Gray-skinned humanoid scientists with black eyes and long fingers. The Zeners are known for abducting other species and installing implants in them. Finally, and most notable, is a species of Gray called the Streib, whose name is inspired by Whitley Streiber and who also abduct and perform experiments on other lifeforms.

Taken

The new millennium began promisingly for abduction-themed products with Steven Spielberg's *Taken*, an epic ten-part mini-series for the

Sci-Fi Channel. Set between 1944 and 2002, the series spans five decades and four generations and centers on the lives of three families:
the Crawfords, who are intimately involved in the Roswell cover-up
and who serve as architects of UFO secrecy throughout; the Keys,
who suffer cross-generational abduction by the Grays; and the Clark-
es, whose alien-human DNA represents the emotional bridge between
the aliens and humanity.

The series is explicitly UFOlogical, exploring almost every facet of
the phenomenon from Foo Fighters and UFO crash/retrievals, to cattle mutilations, crop circles, and, naturally, alien abduction, which is
here given unusually thoughtful treatment thanks to the series' largely
faithful interpretation of many real-life testimonies. The third episode,
"High Hopes," which is set in the early 1960s, features a clear reference to the Hill abduction case when a government UFO investigator
examines a photo of an interracial married couple who claim to have
been abducted by aliens.

As in real-life reports, the Grays in the series are physically frail
but highly psychic, and their technology is an extension of their own
minds, appearing to us as nothing short of magic. They are capable of
inducing utterly realistic hallucinations in abductees, manipulating
their perceptions of what is happening to them. Screen memories are
implanted in those taken, as is described in the literature.

Hybridization is at the core of the series' overarching narrative. The
aliens' goal is to hybridize themselves with humans in an attempt to
recover their own long-lost emotions and moral compass. Many real-life experiencers have come to believe that while their abductions
can be traumatic, their abductors do not act with malice. This is reflected in *Taken* as the aliens here have no concept of good or evil, and
are oblivious to the emotional trauma they inflict in their ongoing efforts to bring themselves closer to humanity.

With a budget of $40 million,[32] *Taken* was, at the time of its pro-
duction, one of the most expensive TV shows ever made. The gamble
paid off as it was hugely popular with audiences and well received by
critics, winning the 2002 Emmy Award for Outstanding Mini-series.
Most of Hollywood's abduction-themed products to follow have failed
to reach *Taken's* high bar in terms either of UFOlogical authenticity
or human drama.

The Fourth Kind

A trend has emerged in Hollywood for filmmakers to actively seek to dissolve the boundaries between UFO fact and fantasy through the utilization of vérité techniques and wilfully deceptive viral marketing campaigns. Take *The Fourth Kind* (2009) for example, which was purported by Universal studios to be a true story "based on actual case studies" from the files of Dr. Abigail Tyler, a psychologist who had collected disturbing testimonies from the town of Nome, Alaska, where numerous residents allegedly had vanished since the 1960s. Universal presented archive news clippings online from various Alaskan newspapers, painting a picture of a town historically plagued by UFO sightings and apparent alien abductions.

The movie draws extensively from UFOlogy, featuring a psychologist (à la John Mack) interviewing numerous people whose lives have been turned upside down by mysterious nocturnal disturbances. In a knowing reference to the owl in abduction lore, each of the experiencers report seeing the bird immediately prior to and during their traumas. The owl is later revealed to be a screen memory enforced by the aliens, who here are almost demonic in nature as they physically possess and speak through the bodies of their victims in a dark and twisted tongue, which we are told is Sumerian – a clear reference to the Anunnaki of Ancient Astronaut lore. Invasive experimentation is depicted, including procedures on the female reproductive system, but the aliens' ultimate agenda is left a mystery.

The Fourth Kind was presented as a docudrama featuring "real" footage capturing the events in Nome alongside dramatic reconstructions with Hollywood actors. In the opening scene, actress Milla Jovovich, looking directly into the camera, tells the audience: I'm actress Milla Jovovich and I will be portraying Dr. Abigail Tyler... every scene in this movie is supported by archive footage." At various points throughout the film, the 'dramatic reconstructions' and 'real events' are presented simultaneously in split-screen in order that the viewer can clearly distinguish between the two. Naturally, though, none of it is real. The "real" footage was fabricated in its entirety, so too were all of the Alaskan news clippings used by Universal in its marketing campaign. Dr. Abigail Tyler never existed, neither did anyone else portrayed in the film. When this elaborate Hollywood sham was revealed, Universal was served with a lawsuit from the Alaska Press Club, to whom the studio agreed to pay $20,000 for undermining the credibility of the various papers whose names had been exploited by the studio.[33] The film went on to make a respectable $49 million from its $10 million investment.[34]

Dark Skies

The abduction phenomenon was firmly back in horror territory in 2013 with the movie *Dark Skies* – not to be confused with Bryce Zabel's unrelated *Dark Skies* TV show from the 1990s, from which the movie brazenly took its title.

The movie follows the plight of the Barretts, a suburban family who have been 'marked' by evil Grays for nocturnal terrorization and abduction. Husband and wife Daniel and Lacey (Josh Hamilton and Keri Russell) slowly come to accept that the insidious events plaguing their lives have no earthly explanation and in desperation turn to local UFOlogist and abductee Edwin Pollard (J.K. Simmons) for answers.

Dark Skies is formulaic and predictable, but upon close viewing it demonstrates some understanding of the abduction phenomenon as reported, or at least of its key characteristics. As is standard, some of these characteristics are distorted for horrific effect. One scene in particular makes acute use of abduction research. When Daniel and Lacy visit Pollard at his cluttered apartment he tells them he no longer resists his abductors. "I don't fight them anymore. The Grays. That's what they're called." The couple seem confused. "There are three generally accepted kinds of aliens," Pollard tells them, "the Grays, the Insectoids, and the Reptilians, but nine times out of ten what people report seeing are the Grays."

Addressing the Grays' possible motives, Pollard echoes statements made by numerous experiencers and researchers: "This is beyond our comprehension. What answer would a lab rat understand from a scientist in a white coat putting electrodes in its brain giving it cancer?" Pollard informs Daniel and Lacey that they "probably already have implants. That's how they control you." The couple appear distressed. "The Grays hide what they do," he continues, echoing the stated belief of many researchers in the UFO field. Calling to mind the work of implant-removal expert Dr. Roger Leir, Pollard says the Grays "disguise the implants as something perfectly normal. Most people don't even know they have them." The abductee can attempt to resist the Grays, to make their job a difficult one, says Pollard, but typically such efforts are futile: "The presence of the Grays is now a fact of life – like death and taxes."

The behaviour of the Grays in *Dark Skies* is not too far wide of the mark UFOlogically. At times they behave like poltergeists, invisibly raiding the family's fridge, stealing family photos from their frames, and, in a scene seemingly paying homage to the *Poltergeist* movie (1982), elaborately stacking household items in the kitchen. The effect is to bemuse and to frighten. Although exaggerated, these scenes are significant in that numerous abductees have reported paranormal occurrences in conjunction with their experiences – specifically poltergeist phenomena and so-called 'shadow people.' These latter phenomena are depicted in *Dark Skies* in scenes where CCTV captures blurry images of shadow-like figures silently infiltrating the family's home at night, looming at the children's bedsides. In this respect the movie is faithful to abduction literature, which describes Grays and other entities effortlessly gaining access to abductees in any given environment – windows, doors, even brick walls are no obstacle for intelligences who consistently demonstrate almost supernatural abilities.

Dark Skies features UFOlogical flourishes from start to finish, suggesting a reasonable level of research on the part of writer/director Scott Stewart. Paintings of owls hang prominently in a child's bedroom, family members experience missing time, disorientation, nose bleeds; they discover implants in their bodies and unexplainable marks on their skin, including bruises and even geometric shapes, as has so often been reported in real life cases.

Dark Skies received poor to middling reviews from critics, but went on to gross a very respectable $27 million against its very modest $3.5 million budget.[35]

Under the Skin

The following year marked the first time in long time that a film engaged with the experiencer phenomenon at an intellectual level, beyond genre tropes, beyond dialogue, even. It was able to do so as it was produced outside of the Hollywood system; outside of America altogether. In *Under the Skin*, a UK production, a beautiful woman (Scarlett Johansson) seduces random men off the street and lures them to their doom. But she is not human, only playing at it. Something cold and otherworldly moves beneath her skin. The precise nature of her mission on Earth is never specified and, like most everything else in this striking and challenging film, is left open to viewer interpretation.

Based on the novel by Michel Faber, *Under the Skin* divided critical opinion, with some commentators dismissing it as pointless and impenetrable, and others hailing it as a masterpiece. Certainly it is unique; a bizarre clash of Kubrickian precision and a gritty naturalism more identifiable with British realist cinema. The plot plays second fiddle to disturbingly beautiful imagery, which evokes themes of urban alienation, isolation, sexual identity, humanity, and compassion.

This is also a film about alien abduction, and, intentionally or not, the abduction scenarios it depicts are remarkably similar in certain respects to those reported in real-life experiencer accounts, despite the absence of little Gray aliens or flying saucers (although lights in the sky do feature early on).

Johansson, a succubus of sorts, lures her men into various dilapidated buildings wherein they submit entirely to her desire. Upon entering these seemingly normal urban spaces and shedding their clothes, the men find themselves in a distinctly alien environment and submerged in a strange dense liquid. Abductees often have reported moving inexplicably and seamlessly from an earthly environment to an alien one. In the film, Johansson's alien leads her men into what appear to be earthly structures, but which inside are surely alien spacecraft, or an alien dimension of some sort. In one abduction scene, a man with a neurofibromatosis disfigurement (Adam Pearson) remarks to his naked seducer: "I'm dreaming." Given his situation and surroundings, certainly he has no reason to believe otherwise. Many abductees have described their experiences as being dreamlike, and yet clearly distinct from a dream.

The aliens here are hostile insomuch as they abduct humans and, but for one exception, never return them. The abductees' fate is a grisly one, never fully explained in the movie but made clear in Faber's source material (clue: they're a delicacy). But labelling the aliens in *Under the Skin* as 'hostile' seems redundant given their harsh terrestrial surroundings and the, at times, predatory nature of the humans we meet. We see our world (specifically Glasgow in Scotland) exclusively through alien eyes, and it's a scary place indeed. Eventually we begin to empathize with Johansson's alien as she suffers an identity crisis and the world around her begins to suffocate both her and us. The ending is devastating as the hunter becomes the hunted and the final reveal of 'what's under that skin' is realized through jaw-dropping, photorealistic CGI.

Alien Abduction

Abduction movies regressed into mindless horror again in 2014 with the imaginatively titled *Alien Abduction,* a found footage flick which received limited theatrical distribution following a Video on Demand release. The events of the movie are documented by an autistic eleven-year-old-boy (played by Riley Polanski), who, along with his family, is attacked and abducted by Grays while on a camping trip in the Brown Mountains of North Carolina – a region known in real life for its folklore relating to mysterious lights in the sky.

The film's Director Matty Beckerman told *Open Minds UFO Radio* that the production had made a believer out of him. "I went into it very skeptically," he explained to journalist Alejandro Rojas, "and then after interviewing [local] people and really talking to them... I converted into someone who really believes and who studies it," adding "I've interviewed [people] directly who talk about being abducted, who talk about Gray aliens."

Beckerman further explained: "For over 800 years there have been these mysterious lights that appear and disappear around Western North Carolina. And it's real. I've seen the lights myself, I've taken pictures of them. There are all these abduction stories that have happened right around that area."[36]

Seeking to blur UFO fact and fantasy, the movie opens with text informing us that what follows is "actual leaked footage from the US Air Force." We then see shaky-cam shots filmed inside the alien spacecraft of people being tortured. Screams fill the thick, putrid air. As in *Fire in the Sky,* and in sharp contrast to experiencer testimonies, the alien environment here is dungeon-like.

A title card then reads: "For centuries, people have been disappearing on and around the Brown Mountain, North Carolina. Locals believe the disappearances are directly linked with sightings of THE BROWN MOUNTAIN LIGHTS."

This is followed by faked footage of 'real' news reports documenting the sightings. As with *The Fourth Kind,* the goal here is dissolve the boundaries between fantasy and reality. Another title card then reads:

> In the 1952 the United States Air Force established PROJECT BLUE BOOK. It had two goals.
>
> 1. To determine if UFOs were a threat to national security.
> 2. To scientifically analyse UFO related data.

This much is true, at least. But the next title card is pure fantasy, most obviously for the reason that Blue Book shut down in 1969:

> Project Blue Book Case #4499 – October 2011: The Brown Mountain Abductions. 27 people went missing after hundreds of eyewitnesses claim to have seen the lights. The camcorder of autistic 11 year old Riley Morris was recovered in a nearby field... Riley and his family went missing while canoeing on Brown Mountain, North Carolina.

The narrative then begins proper, as Riley's camera footage reveals to us the events that befell him and his family, which play out almost like a stalk-and-slash story. A substantial chunk of the action takes place in a tunnel on a lonely road, wherein the family stumble across dozens of abandoned cars, their drivers and passengers apparently having been abducted en masse. The method of abduction is a violent and messy one, requiring the abductee to be directly within the clawing grasp of a Gray, or clearly within a tractor beam. The aliens here seem far away from thinking, reasoning beings. They are brutal monsters whose methods are crude and dirty.

When all family members have been killed or abducted, including Riley (whose camera continues to film aboard the spaceship before being jettisoned back down to earth by a snarling Gray), the footage is retrieved by Project Blue Book personnel. A card reads: "All footage property of the U.S. Air Force: Project Blue Book Case #4499."

Extraterrestrial

Sadistic abductors returned to the big screen later that same year in *Extraterrestrial* (2014). In a well-worn horror setup, a group of young friends gather for a good time at a secluded cabin in the woods. It's not zombies or demons who spoil their fun, though, but tall Grays, who have crashed their flying saucer nearby. The movie plays out as 'teens vs. aliens' with a heavy debt to UFOlogy. *Fire in the Sky*, in particular, served as a strong influence. The opening scene is a clear homage to the phone box scene in *Fire* where a traumatized, animal-like Travis Walton desperately calls for help following his abduction. *Extraterrestrial* even features a scene which mirrors almost shot-for-shot the famous scene in the Walton movie where Travis steps out of the car and gazes awestruck at the craft above, only to be 'zapped' by a beam of light before being taken. The interior of the spaceship in *Extraterrestrial* is very much like that in the Walton movie – organic, dank, and gooey. If these allusions weren't subtle enough, the name of one the characters in *Extraterrestrial*, Michael Ironside's gruff woodsman, is Travis.

Beyond its homages to *Fire in the Sky*, *Extraterrestrial* references other UFOlogical facets and events. It opens with a montage of real UFO footage and photographs in the same fashion as *Race to Witch Mountain*. The plot features animal mutilations and a crashed UFO with wreckage "like tinfoil," a description used by Roswell witnesses. There is even a Project Moon Dust-style crash/retrieval team, whose government bosses have maintained a treaty with the aliens since 1947. The treaty, we are told, is "a basic simple agreement with one cardinal rule: do not engage." Essentially, then, the government has been turning a blind-eye to the aliens' human experimentations for almost seven decades – an idea lifted directly from the UFO conspiracy community, as we shall see in the following chapter. The experiments in *Extraterrestrial* are restricted mainly to lethal anal probings with large metal drills. The aliens here are monsters, nothing more. How such violent creatures survived long enough as a species to develop interstellar or transdimensional travel is, unsurprisingly, never considered.

~ THE HARSHEST CRITICS ~

By this point the reader should have a clear understanding of the nature of Hollywood's historical engagement with the abduction phenomenon. That said, considerable value has yet to be added by the experiencers themselves, through their own personal engagement with Hollywood's abduction-themed products. Presented over the pages that follow are abridged transcripts of interviews conducted by the author with five individuals whose cases have received considerable attention in the UFO research field. These interviews are focused not on the fine details of their cases (which have by now been thoroughly documented elsewhere), but rather on their experiences of watching movies and TV shows popularly labelled as 'science-fiction,' but which, for them, are often closer to fact.

Much of what these individuals have experienced is subjective and wide open to interpretation, although parts of each of their contact stories are indirectly and/or directly supported by independent witnesses. What is beyond doubt to all those who have spoken with these experiencers one-to-one, myself included, is that they each are telling the truth as *they* see it. In other words, they clearly have experienced *something* considerably beyond the norm, not once, but multiple times throughout their lives, and they seem distinctly disinclined to embellish or to deceive in the telling of their stories. They are driven by a powerful desire to make sense of the impossible events that have shaped their lives and to understand one question in particular: "Why me?"

None of the following experiencers would consider themselves film experts, but all have watched at least a few of the big and small screen entertainment products discussed throughout this book and have kindly shared with me their unique perspectives on Hollywood's treatment of the abduction/experiencer phenomenon, and how, for them, the viewing of these movies and TV shows is anything but a passive and escapist activity.

STEVEN JONES
Interview conducted 11/04/2015

Steven Jones' 2010 book *An Invitation to the Dance* documents his life-time of experiences with what he considers to be extraterrestrial intelligences. He has worked with both Budd Hopkins and John Mack. Some of his experiences were recovered through hypnosis while others occurred in real-time and were recalled consciously. Steven's accounts involve the archetypal Grays, as well the Nordics and other alien variants.

For many years Steven felt confused and powerless, but as the nature of his experiences slowly began to evolve, he came to think of himself as an empowered participator in these events, no longer an abductee, but an experiencer. After almost 50 years of trying to comprehend the nature and purpose of his experiences, Steven cautiously began to share them with the public in an effort to raise awareness of a broader reality. His book was the first step, and public lectures followed in the UK and US. In 2013 he starred as a co-host of the Discovery Channel's *Uncovering Aliens* TV documentary show, which examined UFO experiences across America.[37]

RG: I'm interested in your personal views on Hollywood's historical engagement with the UFO subject, and, specifically, how movies and TV shows have depicted the experiencer phenomenon, for better or for worse. What are your general thoughts here?

I suppose my strongest feeling towards the majority of these movies is disappointment. That there is a basic truth underlying the phenomenon, but as soon as Hollywood gets hold of it, the truth very soon goes out the window. And what extraterrestrial contact truly means to the human race is never investigated.

RG: Do abduction-themed film and TV products provoke in you a visceral reaction, or are they so 'alien' to your own experiences that you can watch them with cool detachment?

My contact has been a patchwork of emotions. The people, the beings, I have been in contact with, I don't think it was their intention at any point to scare me or hurt me. But, because certain elements of my contact were leaps of faith in the dark, I experienced this primal fear that we human beings have. When you're taken from your home in the middle of the night and in the next instance you're in another place, and there are beings there that are not human-looking, and things are being done to you that are intrusive, this creates a fear element. However, as I've investigated my experiences over the last ten-to-fifteen years, I've understood that it was *me* who brought the fear element. It was my fear of the unknown. So when I watch a movie now that depicts something of this nature, I watch it with excitement, but then there are buttons that are pressed in the viewing that tune me back in to when I used to feel frightened about it. So it's a mixture of feelings.

RG: To what extent are your own experiences reflected in Hollywood's UFO-themed products?

SJ: It's very limited. There are certain elements of *Fire in the Sky* that I think are good, but then there are certain aspects of it that are so wrong in so many ways. The interior of the craft is shown as dirty and organic, and that's not an accurate depiction. *Close Encounters of the Third Kind* was a brilliant movie. I think it depicted a truth and Spielberg was allowed to run with it, with no real outside manipulation. When it came to Spielberg's *Taken*, I was really excited at the idea that he was going to be focused on my experience, not *my* experience per se, obviously, but on the experience of being taken specifically. But I was so disappointed with *Taken* because the subject matter was always on the periphery of the production. The series just revolved around people's stories that were not necessarily related to the abduction subject as advertised.

RG: As a child, did you actively seek out UFO-themed media in the hope of finding answers?

SJ: I used to watch *Lost in Space* like it was a religious experience. But I wasn't watching it consciously thinking 'I'm having contact, and I'm watching this to make sense of my experiences,' because during my childhood there was an element of my contact that remained a secret from my conscious self. But in answer to your question, no, I didn't consciously seek-out anything. Later on in my life when I became actively interested in UFO phenomena I would step back from any book or movie that dealt with abduction specifically. When

I got to the part in a book, or magazine, or movie about abduction, I couldn't get past it quick enough. It was too disturbing. But that was before everything rose to the surface. That was before I consciously, emotionally, spiritually, intellectually, totally embraced and accepted what I was – that I was an experiencer, and that I no longer needed to hide or suppress that part of me.

RG: The *Communion* movie encompassed horror, sci-fi, marital and existential drama, and surreal comedy. Would you like to see more filmmakers engage with the experiencer phenomenon in its full spectrum of weirdness?

SJ: Whitley Strieber's story of *Communion* is his story. It's not my story. It's not anybody else's story. It's only his story. So, the elements you just mentioned that were depicted in that film could be very confusing for other people; they could be confusing to other experiencers, or just to Joe Public watching a movie. They might think 'this is really stupid. This is a silly film.' The humorous aspects of it where the ETs start dancing – Joe Public is going to watch that and say 'well, Whitley Strieber's a nutcase and the whole subject matter is stupid.' So you've got to be very careful how individual personal experiences are depicted onscreen.

RG: Are you saying Strieber should have censored himself in order to make his story more digestible for a mainstream audience?

SJ: Yes, absolutely. Just because it happened doesn't mean it has to be told in the story. There are aspects of my story that I have never told because they would influence the perception of my experience in a negative way, based on how I responded to it at the time. Like you said, the experiencer phenomenon is a very, very complex story, and it's multi-layered. A movie writer probably has only 120 minutes in which to tell a story.

RG: What would you consider to be the most truthful and considered cinematic or televisual depiction of the experience phenomenon to date?

SJ: I suppose it's *Close Encounters*, really. It stands on its own. But it's almost forty years old now, and I don't see anything else touching it, which is a major disappointment. The only other great ET contact film is the original *The Day the Earth Stood Still*. To me, *Independence Day* is the film furthest from the mark where depictions of ET contact are concerned. In my experience, the only beings that we should be scared of are human beings. The things humans do to each other on this planet is the real scare story. Why is it that in the majority of these stories ETs are depicted as ugly, horrible, monsters? Whether they know it or not, the writers of these stories are holding up a mirror to the human race.

BRET OLDHAM
Interview conducted 12/04/2015

Bret Oldham is the author of *Children of the Greys*, a biographical accounting of his life as an abductee (he does not consider himself an experiencer): "You have to call it what it is," he told me. "You're not going voluntarily. It's all against your will." From mind control experiments, sexual interludes, healings, unexplainable scars, hybrids, and even a multiple witness abduction he experienced, Bret's candid book was written as catharsis. Although he feels he has grown considerably as a person as a by-product of his experiences, he insists that the personal growth of abductees is not a conscious objective of the abductors, whom he considers to be cold and indifferent to human emotion, although not necessarily hostile or malevolent. Bret also emphasizes the paranormal connection to UFO encounters, which he can attest to through extensive personal experience.

Bret informed me that his experiences are ongoing: "They haven't stopped. I think that, as far as the Grays go, once they find someone with the genetic make-up they're looking for, that's it. It is less frequent, though, which is something that I'm really happy about."

Today, Bret and his wife Gina are paranormal investigators whose research encompasses ghosts, UFOs, and cryptozoology. They have featured in numerous magazine and newspaper articles, as well as on radio and TV shows in the USA, New Zealand, and Europe.[38]

RG: Describe to me your state of mind when watching abduction-themed film and TV products.

BO: Toward my late-teens and into my early twenties, before I was fully aware of my past experiences, whenever I'd see a movie or TV show dealing with this topic it would elicit a sort of sinking feeling in me. If there was a scene of a child being taken it would really affect me. Or sometimes the camera would be placed as if the beings are looking over you on a table... even to this day I don't want to look into their eyes. It's just repulsive. It's hard to describe. So when I see scenes like that it still affects me, because I know that's actually pretty accurate. It's also very bright like they show in a lot of movies. Not to the point where you can't see the other stuff around the room, but their light is much different to ours.

After I became aware of my experiences I tried to read some of the literature – Budd Hopkins, John Mack – but I just could not get through it. Too close to home. But with films, I found I could watch them with a certain level of detachment, because it was 'Hollywood,' you know? I recognized that they were taking liberties with the facts, so I found I could relate to some of the material but that I could remain sort of detached from it because I knew it was sci-fi. It felt a little bit safer because of that, although I still find some of it disturbing.

RG: What would you consider to be the most and least truthful cinematic or televisual depictions of the experiencer phenomenon, and why?

BO: The series that Spielberg did – *Taken* – there was a lot of stuff in that that I thought was pretty accurate. The *Communion* film also was good. The psychological aspects of those were engaging. But I really don't think anyone has nailed it yet in Hollywood. The only film I can think of that came close was the *UFO Incident* [the Hill abduction movie], because they didn't go too sci-fi with it. But a lot of the recent stuff, especially *The Fourth Kind*, I didn't care for at all. There was one that we recently watched where a family was out driving and end up in this tunnel [Bret is here referring to the 2014 movie *Alien Abduction*]. It was almost comical, because what they leave out is the mental capabilities of the Grays. These guys can do anything that they want, because when you control somebody's mind, you control everything. So when the characters in the movie fight back by shooting the aliens it's absurd. Hollywood wants action, but in reality these beings don't have to exhibit any kind of violence to achieve their goals. Whatever they want to do with us as a species, they can do.

Signs was also stupid when it showed the aliens coming after them and the characters are able to get away and hide. We're not! You know, that's something the public may not be able to handle, but we're *not* able to get away. That alone should be scary enough for a movie without throwing all of the action stuff in with it. It's a reality that people probably don't want to deal with, but we're at the mercy of these beings. Any species that's that advanced is just something that we're not prepared for.

That's why films like *War of the Worlds* and *Independence Day* are just ridiculous, because in reality their technology is so far superior to ours. Technology isn't even necessary for them to control us. You can take one Gray and stand him up to an army. It wouldn't make any difference, because he can control the thoughts of those in front of him and have people shoot each other, or make everyone think they're suffocating, or even create the illusion that there are a million more Grays standing behind him. But none of those scenarios makes for a very entertaining movie. Hollywood prefers to shoot at everything.

RG: The complexities of the abduction phenomenon seem to be filtered out through genre filmmaking. Would you like to see Hollywood explore these phenomena beyond the tropes of horror cinema?

BO: The abduction phenomenon really is horror. But it's horror beyond the experiences themselves. What Hollywood usually depicts is the event itself – the screaming and all that. And that's real, but they don't go into the long-term aspects of it. They don't go into what it's like to live your life on a daily basis with these events hanging over you; to go to bed at night not knowing 'is this the night?' and the feeling of helplessness that you have, and will they even bring you back, what are they going to do this time, and will it hurt, and can I take it? This feeling of 'I have to survive, I have to survive.' Are they going to take my family? You live your life on the edge. Hollywood rarely goes into all of that. The human interest side of it.

The other major thing Hollywood is missing out on is the dimensional aspect of it. I recently watched *Interstellar* and I found it very interesting that they explored this dimensional aspect. In one of my experiences I witnessed an actual portal open up on my bedroom wall. I could see through it. It was an oval shape. There were three Grays standing at the side of my bed and I could look through this portal, and it had this white misty stuff around the edges, but through it there was a texture change, and I could actually see into another craft, and another Gray stood inside. I was trying to scream because I didn't want them to take my wife. I was trying to scream the word "no," and I couldn't. I couldn't get it out. Anyway, in an instant I was on the craft then I could speak again and the word came out. So they took me that fast – within the space of a one-syllable word. Hollywood rarely shows that kind of stuff.

Hollywood also ignores the paranormal aspects of these phenomena. During my childhood I had a lot of extreme paranormal events happen, and I was scared all the time. I didn't understand what was happening. Since then I've talked to a lot of people who've had similar experiences. Especially people who've had multiple abductions – they come back with some degree of enhanced psychic awareness, and I believe it's a result of having been taken through dimensional portals. It changes our vibrational frequency, our energy, and we then vibrate closer to the spirit world. The spirits reach out to us, sensing that our vibrations are closer to theirs. I think that's why so many abductees also have paranormal experiences.

RG: Do film and TV have a role to play in educating people about this phenomenon?

BO: Well, unfortunately, society as a whole seems to get its education from those outlets, because people are often too lazy to actually do some research and find the facts for themselves. It's easier just to sit down in front of the television or a movie screen and have it spoon-fed to you. But also I think Hollywood is conditioning us psychologically for when the reality of this phenomenon is finally revealed. Although I don't really buy into the idea of a 'Disclosure event.' Disclosure is happening all around us, all the time, if you just pay attention. But I don't see the government ever coming clean on this issue, so I think they're using the media to prepare us more subtly, and they're eliciting fear as they do so.

BRIGITTE BARCLAY
Interview conducted 14/04/2015

Brigitte Barclay is one of the UK's most high-profile UFO experiencers with memories of 'impossible' events dating back to her early childhood. She would later work with both Budd Hopkins and John Mack. While in her early-20s, prior to becoming known publicly as an experiencer, Brigitte had a short-lived career as a glamor model in the UK and the US, appearing in newspapers and magazines such as *The Sun*, *Playboy*, and *Penthouse*. Skeptics and debunkers have, on occasion, attempted to use her past against her as a form of ill-judged character assassination, but Brigitte has no regrets: "My past has made me the person I am today. We all started out somewhere – some beginnings are just more interesting or gossip-worthy than others."

Following her glamor career, Brigitte became a make-up artist in LA, and it was there in 1993 that she and a friend had a daylight close encounter with a saucer-shaped craft hovering low over the 405 freeway. This event served as a catalyst for Brigitte, prompting her to fully acknowledge the many strange experiences of her past, and, through hypnosis sessions to follow, she would recover memories of multiple interactions over multiple decades with non-human intelligences. Brigitte has since appeared on a variety of TV shows and documentaries for the likes of the BBC, the History Channel, SyFy, National Geographic and others.[39]

RG: Film and TV products such as *Communion*, *Fire in the Sky*, *Taken*, *The Fourth Kind*, etc., I'm interested in your subjective experience of watching these 'entertainment' products.

BB: I think experiencers watch these movies with different eyes to everyone else. We're watching with our brain slightly detached, whizzing around somewhere else, thinking about our own experiences and how what we're watching differs or not from what we've experienced, analyzing specific details. We're probably the best critics of these movies in that sense. Sometimes I gasp for breath because some of the images are so true, but I do feel sort of detached in some ways because I'm also thinking 'oh, no, no, that's wrong... it didn't happen to *me* like that.'

In *Fire in the Sky* I hold my breath when Travis Walton gets out of the car and is staring up in awe at this craft above him, because I totally get that. Because nothing else around you matters at that point. I know that.

I remember watching *The X-Files* for the first time. I had had my encounter in February 1993 out in Los Angeles. A couple of months later I came back to England, and I think *The X-Files* started in September [it did: 10 September 1993]. Anyway I remember seeing an advert for it on TV when I was back in England, and I just stopped in my tracks. When I watched the first episode I was like little Carol Anne from *Poltergeist* when she sat in front of the TV. I remember sitting right next to the TV, legs crossed, on the floor, and I watched the first abduction scene, and I just cried.

Looking back, though, I can't honestly say that I've had a bad experience. I've had beings next to me insert a needle into my spine, but despite this I've never been afraid. I know that might sound crazy, because if you speak to certain other experiencers they describe their own encounters as absolutely awful. Extremely traumatic. Maybe something in me is desensitized to the fear because I don't know any different. I don't know. But I do get feelings when I watch these films; there's a nervous feeling, a build-up feeling, almost butterflies. These movies never scare me, though, because I've never feared my own experiences.

RG: To what extent during your childhood did you expose yourself to UFO-themed entertainment products?

BB: I rarely watched TV as a child because we were very much an outdoor family, and most of my memories of childhood are of being outside playing. Certainly there were no UFO or alien-themed films or TV shows that I can recall watching as a child. None that stick in my mind anyway. I can barely even recall the experience of watching *ET: The Extraterrestrial* as a twelve-year-old. The only thing I remember from that was that my mum cried when we were at the cinema. But the film itself didn't really leave an impression on me.

RG: What would you consider to be the most truthful and considered cinematic or televisual depiction of the experiencer phenomenon to date, and why?

BB: This weekend I watched *Close Encounters* with my partner. That film brings in family life; it shows the phenomenon ultimately as being about people. It features aliens, but it's really about people. It shows these intelligences bypassing the government and communicating directly with everyday people.

I also very much enjoyed *Intruders*. It affected me. Usually the moments when films affect me most are purely visual, when there are no words, when there's just a knowing. In *Intruders*, where the character is looking at the eggs in the frying pan, they're just staring at her... and we know they're the alien eyes.

Also, Spielberg's *Taken* was phenomenal. That I really did like. I like that it explored screen memories, because screen memories play a big part in my own experiences.

RG: Would you like to see filmmakers engage with the experiencer phenomenon in its full spectrum of weirdness?

BB: Of course. Without a shadow of a doubt. A lot of the newer films get it wrong. I would say that more independent movies need to be made on this subject, but I think it requires a spiritual approach to understand it.

The recent film *Extraterrestrial*, although I enjoyed it, is stupid in the sense that it shows these aliens as trying to kill, kill, kill some people in a cabin, attacking them like in a war film, chasing them and trying to grab them. That really does piss me off, because they're shown as being quite primitive and clumsy. But I've seen craft go through walls and I've seen beings materialize in front of me, so the reality is very far from how Hollywood imagines.

So I think someone should make a proper alien movie, because there really isn't one that presents all the facts. The amount of money from Hollywood going into these films is crazy, and they've still not got it right. A truthful UFO movie would have to feature all the really weird stuff, including the paranormal experiences that go along with the encounters. I used to have lots of paranormal experiences. Growing up I used to see ghosts very, very clearly. I used to see them as clearly as I'm seeing my coffee now or my newspaper in front of me, and they would come in various forms.

On the whole I'd like to see less terrifying depictions of UFO experiences. Hollywood's UFO depictions are almost all negative. There isn't anything really right now that projects it in a positive light.

CHRISTOPHER BLEDSOE SR.
Interview conducted 19/04/2015

Chris Bledsoe was born in Fayetteville, North Carolina, where he was raised a fundamentalist Christian. A highly respected member of his community, Chris was the owner of an award-winning, multi-million-dollar construction business for which he was nominated as Businessman of the Year in 2003 by the National Republican Congressional Committee and invited to President George Bush's inauguration. His life changed forever on 8 January 2007, when, during a fishing excursion with his son and three friends/colleagues near his home in Fayetteville, Chris had a spectacular UFO sighting which resulted in several hours of missing time and, later that same night, a conscious, face-to-face encounter with a non-human entity. Chris' friends also had dramatic UFO and entity sightings that night, and his son, Chris Jr., also witnessed humanoid entities. These events and others to follow for Chris and his family are vastly more complex than this short introduction can hope to convey, but his case, which is intense and ongoing, has been thoroughly investigated and is arguably one of the most compelling UFO contact accounts of modern times. Chris has struggled for a long time to reconcile what he saw that night with his fundamentalist Christian beliefs. Although, interestingly, the story he tells has strong religious overtones. This could be down to his own preferred interpretation of unfathomable events, or perhaps it is a result of the intelligences involved tailoring their manifestations and messages to the perceiver's existing framework of belief. In any case, Chris is unquestionably sincere in his recounting of the events that shattered his reality and eventually rebuilt it anew.

Chris' case was the focus of a lengthy MUFON investigation which was documented in an episode of the TV series *UFOs over Earth*. A major Hollywood studio has since expressed an interest in bringing Chris' story to the screen.[40]

RG: What are your general thoughts on how Hollywood engages with the experiencer phenomenon?

CB: Before I was an experiencer I never thought about it. I was generally like everybody else – if you'd mentioned the word alien or UFO I'd think of monsters. Bad guys. But it seems almost every depiction of these phenomena has been negative. My experience wasn't negative;

in fact, it was quite the opposite. I reported them as angels. That's what I told MUFON right away: 'they're angels.' They asked me what that means. To me it means something divine. Other than that I can't tell you, but Hollywood has portrayed it all as being negative. Maybe it's because fear sells. Maybe people don't want to buy happiness and positivity, they'd rather buy fear. I don't know.

RG: How do you feel when you watch UFO and abduction-themed entertainment products?

CB: Before my experience I saw very few UFO movies or TV shows. I'd seen films like *Alien* and more traditional movies about outer space. But since my experience I've watched everything I could put my hands on. And when I watch this stuff, well, it's like nails on a chalkboard. When I see it I immediately want to shout out 'That's not the way it is! That's not the way it was for me!'

RG: To what extent are your own experiences reflected in these products?

CB: Very little. The *Dark Skies* movie, *Falling Skies*, *Fire in the Sky*, all these other shows that come out are about the end of the world, apocalyptic stuff. Since my original experience I have watched every movie I can find, and very little if any of what's out there lines up with what my experience was. What's out there is mostly negative and is unrelatable to me in its general message. But some of these movies depict telepathic communication, and that I can relate to. The beings on TV and in movies –the little Gray guys – they're a bit different. In my experience they're blue-eyed and more human-like, and they glow.

RG: Hollywood depicts UFOs and related phenomena almost exclusively as extraterrestrial in nature. How does this gel with your own experiences?

CB: These beings told me that they work for creation. That's what they told me – that they work for creation. They said 'we are what you would call angels from the Bible.' It's not about space beings or aliens. Maybe they're there. I'm sure the whole universe is permeated with people. Just full. But what I experienced is *here*. It's always been here. It's always watching after us. It's nothing new. It's just that this generation is being awakened.

The first five years after my experience was hell. I was so confused and I lost my faith in the Bible and in my church because, being a fundamentalist all my life, I couldn't compute how this could be part of the church or part of God in any way. But since 2012, when I started to tell what I experienced, everything has gotten better. For my whole family. Life in general. I still get ridiculed, but I don't care anymore. I feel sorry for those people. Because these beings are real.

RG: Is it even possible to make a truthful and accurate movie on this subject?

CB: I would say yes, you can make it truthful as far as my experience goes, but I can't answer for everyone else.

RG: So there is no one film that can ever accurately reflect the experiencer phenomenon as a whole? It's more of an individual thing?

CB: Yes, I would say that.

RG: Why does Hollywood focus so much on the negative aspects of these phenomena?

CB: I'll give you two ideas. 1. It sells better – fear. People would rather go and see monsters and blood and guts. Or, 2. Maybe there's some sort of deception going on where authorities don't want us to think that these beings are the angels from the Bible or anything near the Bible because it might prove God is real.

RG: Is it possible that the beings described by the contactees of the '50s and '60s were the same ones you interact with, only in a different form?

CB: I think they're probably the same ones. I think they can take on different forms to different people.

PETER FAUST
Interview conducted 16/04/2015

Peter Faust came to prominence as an abductee/experiencer in the mid-1990s following the publication of John Mack's famous book *Abduction: Human Encounters with Aliens*, which devoted an entire chapter to his story. Peter was one of Mack's early patients and appeared alongside the Harvard psychiatrist in the aforementioned episode of *Oprah*.

Peter's story was also central to the award-winning 2003 documentary *Touched*, which looked sensitively at how the abduction phenomenon can impact the personal lives of experiencers.

Peter's experiences trace back to his youth, and his first conscious recollection of them came in 1988 at the age of 33. John Mack would later invite Peter to participate in his group therapy sessions, and it was through these, and also through hypnosis, that he began to find the missing pieces of his puzzle.

Earlier in his life Peter had worked as a chef and later went into hotel management with his wife (to whom he is still married) in the Caribbean. As of 2015, Peter Faust, M.Ac. has been practicing the Healing Arts for over 20 years, and has maintained his private practice since 1993. Peter is today a licensed Acupuncturist, Herbalist, Energy Healer, and Family Constellation Facilitator.

I asked Peter if his experiences are ongoing. He replied that, although their physical component has ceased, the effect of his experiences, both physical and mental, continues to be felt in his daily life. In this sense, he said, his experience is ongoing and will likely never end. When I asked him if he misses his direct interactions with otherworldly intelligences, he told me:

> When you come back from that experience and go back into ordinary reality, trying to pay the mortgage and the bills and plan for retirement, you know, just back into human existence, there's a gap there. You've reached a state of bliss, you've had contact with the divine, or whatever you want to call it, and thereafter there's always a part of you that thinks 'those are my people, those are my tribe, that's my real home,' and there's a sense of longing for that, because you've had that taste of it. So in that regard I miss it. But I don't focus on it because I have to live in this world. I think that's what's hard for many people who've had the contact experience.[41]

RG: UFOs and Hollywood – what are your immediate thoughts?

PF: It seems to me that Hollywood has a history of sensationalizing the phenomenon and consistently presenting it as traumatic – that the beings are malevolent, and that there's a threat of invasion.

RG: What's your emotional state while watching abduction-themed entertainment products? Do they provoke in you a visceral reaction, or are you able to view them with detachment?

PF: They absolutely elicit a visceral reaction in me of the initial trauma and the disbelief that I felt at the time. It has been very difficult for me to watch these films without being triggered, so I avoid most of them, although I have seen a few over the years. The last one I saw was *The Fourth Kind* (2009).

Aside from trauma, the other reaction I have is 'This is not the whole story.' It's disheartening that Hollywood leaves its exploration of the phenomenon at the level of trauma, invasion, and abuse, and that it hasn't moved into the next level, which I personally have experienced, where these intelligences are trying to break through our consciousness and have a communion with us, a conversation with us, and are trying to impart a message to us.

RG: To what extent are your own experiences reflected in these products?

PF: I would say the initial aspects – the sense of 'this can't be happening,' 'am I going crazy?', 'who do I trust, who do I tell?' The obsessional aspect of it – *Close Encounters of the Third Kind* captured that well. The complete shattering of one's belief system and a feeling of alienation, of going crazy, of losing your mind, and the effect that it has on your family and loved ones.

RG: After becoming aware of your experiences in adulthood did you find yourself drawn to UFO-themed entertainment media in the hope of finding answers?

PF: When I first went to Dr. Mack with my experiences in my 30s, he immediately said to me 'Please don't read any material or watch any films on this subject, and don't talk to anybody else, so that our regression hypnosis sessions are not tainted by an overlay of what you've read or seen in the media.' So I did not look at any of these films or read anything on this topic until 1995 or 1996 after John's book had come out.

RG: Are there any film or TV depictions of the experiencer phenomenon you've found to be particularly truthful or authentic?

PF: I would say that there isn't one film that I can remember that depicts all of it, although I would say there are elements in all these movies that reflect *parts* of the experience. Certainly *Close Encounters of the Third Kind* reflected the obsessional tone of it. *Communion* reflected another tone, and I would say that *Taken* reflected the feeling and importance of the individual recognizing their experiences and then finding others who have experienced the same. In that show there was a recognition among the characters that they were not alone in their experiences, that they were not isolated, that they were part of a collective experience, whereas in *Communion* it was more isolated to the individual.

Another movie, *Knowing*, was good in the sense that it depicted a consciousness trying to reach us and show us that there are worrying events occurring that they're aware of, and they're trying to connect with us. It shows an individual following the threads and coming to the point where he has actual contact with these beings.

RG: What facets of the experiencer phenomenon would you like to see filmmakers explore more in the future?

PF: What I would love to see Hollywood explore more is the arc of one person, or several people's lives, who seem to not be connected, and who individually go through the process of horror and disbelief and then move through that to acceptance, then moving to a more mutual contact with the beings to discover their true intent. I don't want to see any more straight horror films on this subject. I think the general public is ready for a film that depicts people waking up, having the experience, following the experience, people no longer traumatized by the experience, and then moving toward something larger and more profound. A movie more along the lines of *Contact*. That film took it to the next level. None of the existing films show the transformation that happens for the individual. I think the subject as a whole is challenging Hollywood to explore the next arc of this ongoing story, which is 'how will the collective consciousness of humanity respond to this larger reality?' So in this sense, *Contact*, *Knowing*, and even *Interstellar* are the only films I can think of which depict a higher intelligence trying to communicate a message to us that's to our benefit, but their methods of communication are mysterious and sometimes scary. *Contact* and *Interstellar* actually show us going out into space to meet these higher intelligences, whereas in the 1950s movies, the aliens came to us. But now we're starting to have the technology to be able to go *out there* and meet them, and Hollywood is starting to depict that – that we can decipher their communication, we can decipher that they're trying to connect with us, and that they're actually trying to help us.

RG: What do you feel is the overall cultural effect of UFO-themed movies?

PF: It's been a slow process of disclosure over sixty years using the mediums of our time, the mediums of communication, which are film and television. And I think ultimately humanity is being prepared for contact.

RG: Is this disclosure a planned political strategy, or is it a natural cultural process whereby we're all subconsciously raising our own awareness of the phenomenon?

PF: Yes, it's cultural. If we take a step back and put conspiracy theories to one side, I fundamentally believe that there is a collective form of preparation going on through mass media; we're preparing ourselves for the possibility of contact. The media in any of its forms, from the town crier, to the newspaper, to the radio, to film and television, to the Internet, has always been a way for consciousness to expand; for humanity to broaden its view.

RG: So you feel that Hollywood does have a part to play in this process of awakening and acceptance? That Hollywood

wields enough power as a medium to influence what people will think and ultimately do?

PF: Absolutely, because all the seeds of our imagination are planted through film and television at this point in our history, and through the media more broadly. And if the seeds are 'don't react with terror,' 'don't react with fear,' 'don't react with a SWAT team' then we'll be more predisposed to that.

Conclusion

While the true nature of the abduction phenomenon remains elusive, Hollywood continues to depict it almost exclusively as extraterrestrial (with occasional demonic overtones), and as almost wholly negative. In the late-1980s and early-1990s a handful of Hollywood creatives attempted to engage literally with the full complexities of phenomenon as reported by experiencers. Genre-defying products such as *Communion* and *Intruders* were some of the first serious and respectful treatments of real-life abductee testimonies. They were also some of the last. When in 1993 *Fire in the Sky* was tweaked and distorted at the behest of jittery studio executives, the potential of abduction movies to horrify was made explicitly clear and the movie would serve to influence numerous future entries into the UFO subgenre. The continuing success of horrific abduction narratives over the years has essentially squeezed out more subtle cinematic examinations of the experiencer phenomenon, leaving viewers with bland and generic products which nonetheless serve as the dominant cultural force shaping popular perceptions of this multifaceted mystery.

Perhaps the most obvious effect of abduction-themed products has been the deep embedding of the now iconic alien image into our cultural landscape. Descriptions of what we now call Grays were surfacing in abduction accounts reported to Budd Hopkins and other researchers in the 1970s, and Travis Walton had described such entities as early as 1975. The first fully crystalized cinematic image of the Grays was thrust upon us in Spielberg's proudly UFOlogical *Close Encounters* in 1977, but it wasn't until the late 1980s that those big black eyes began to penetrate the popular consciousness. Whitley Strieber's 1987 *Communion* book was key to this, as was its movie adaptation two years later. Then followed *Intruders*, *The X-Files*, *Babylon 5*, *Dark Skies*, and others. By the late-1990s the image of the Gray had supplanted almost all other pre-existing cultural imaginings of what an alien might look like.

Tracy Tormé has marvelled at the speed of this process, telling me: "The way that the image of the Grays has since become known in society is incredible. They've seeped into television commercials and all aspects of society, and they're now part of Americana. The image is now worldwide."

Tens-of-thousands of individuals the world over continue to report physical and/or mental interactions with otherworldly intelligences. Regardless of one's personal perspective on the abduction/experiencer phenomenon, it is clear that, but for a few exceptions, Hollywood's treatment of the subject has been crude and simplistic. All five experiencers interviewed in this chapter agreed that the entertainment industry must move beyond the genre trappings of sci-fi and horror, past even the explicitly 'alien,' and focus instead on the 'human' and on the frequently reported psychologically and spiritually transformative aspects of these experiences at individual and collective levels. Surely a movie along these lines would be more interesting than yet more 'found-footage' of motiveless monsters anally probing families at random.

Is Hollywood up to the challenge?

CHAPTER SIX

WHEN GODS WALKED AMONG US

"They lived a long time ago. Perhaps they're part fable, perhaps they're part fantasy..."

– ROD SERLING, *THE TWILIGHT ZONE* (1963)

T his chapter takes a look at movies in which extraterrestrials visit our planet in its distant past, or at least prior to the post-1947 UFO era, and interact with its primitive inhabitants, influencing our beliefs, our technology, even our evolution. Herein the reader will learn how the emergence of Ancient Astronaut (AA) theory in the late-1960s and early-1970s – particularly the work of Erich von Däniken – correlated with an increased emphasis on related themes in film and TV narratives, which in turn served to push AA theory from the fringes of UFOlogy to the forefront of popular culture.

~ ROOTS OF A THEORY ~

The pages of ancient history are filled with references to celestial phenomena wondrous and terrifying that lend themselves to UFOlogical interpretation. In 1347 BC in the Nile Valley of Egypt, Pharaoh Akhenaten witnessed "a shining disc" descend from the morning sky, which proceeded to speak to him, instructing that he build a new capital for Egypt.[1] In 593 BC in Chaldea, Iraq, the Prophet Ezekiel observed a bizarre contraption in the sky above. He described non-human entities or "living creatures" and a flying "wheel," which many in the UFO field have come to interpret as a classic flying saucer. Ezekiel wrote: "The appearance of the wheels and their workings was, as it were, a wheel in the middle of a wheel." Even the object's manoeuvrings bring to mind the gravity-defying capabilities described in modern UFO reports: "When they moved, they went toward any one of four directions; they did not turn aside when they went."[2] Ezekiel, perhaps an early abductee, goes on to tell how the objects and beings lifted him up and away.[3]

Ancient Indian literature bristles with accounts of technologically advanced flying machines or "vimanas." These craft are described in the Sanskrit epics the Mahabharata and Ramayana as military machines capable of inflicting great death and destruction across the world. Author Peter Brookesmith observes that "vimanas bear some resemblance to UFOs. Some are small, single-seater craft; others are enormous. Some, in a manner that are recalled in accounts of UFOs by abductees, have a remarkable capacity to seem infinitely spacious inside, while showing only modest exterior proportions." Brookesmith also notes that one account in the Mahabharata, of the kidnapping of King Duryodhana by a demonic female entity, "exactly parallels the modern accounts of abductions by aliens, even down to hints of genetic manipulation."[4]

The rise of Ancient Astronauts

The development of AA theory as it is understood today can be attributed primarily to one man, Erich von Däniken, a Swiss former hotel manager whose 1968 non-fiction book *Chariots of the Gods?* presented an alternate history of human civilization. Von Däniken suggested that numerous historical wonders, from the Giza Pyramids, to the Nazca Lines, to Stonehenge, were not constructed by man alone, but with the guidance and technology of advanced extraterrestrial beings whom the ancients worshipped as gods. In his book, von Däniken interpreted ancient artwork from multiple cultures as depicting the aliens themselves, as well as their advanced technology. The book also reinterpreted religious texts as evidence of early human encounters with aliens. Crucially, the book presented these existing ideas in a straight-forward, easily digestible form. The result was a worldwide bestseller.

Perhaps the second most influential AA author to follow in von Däniken's footsteps was Zecharia Sitchin, a Soviet-born American who interpreted Mesopotamian cuneiform scripts as evidence that the Sumerian civilization, and humanity itself, was the product of alien bio-engineering. In his 1976 book *The 12th Planet* and its sequels,[6] Sitchin theorized the existence of a hidden planet beyond Neptune called Nibiru that passes through our solar system every 3,600 years. According to Sitchin, Nibiru was home to highly advanced human-like aliens whom the Sumerians called the Anunnaki and who arrived on Earth's African continent some 450,000 years ago in search of gold and other minerals. In Sitchin's narrative, alien genes were eventually crossed with those of Homo erectus resulting in Homo sapiens – a slave species created to mine gold for their alien masters.

Together, von Däniken and Sitchin dominated the AA literature market throughout the 1970s. By the 1980s, popular interest in AAs had waned significantly, perhaps due to fierce and unrelenting criticism from the scientific community, which equated AA theory with New Age belief systems. But the 1990s saw a resurgence of public fascination in ancient archaeological mysteries with books such as the bestselling *Fingerprints of the Gods* (1995) and *Keeper of Genesis* (1996) by Graham Hancock and Robert Bauval.

Like von Däniken and others of his ilk, these newer authors also presented an alternate history of human civilization, only this time aliens were removed from the equation. Humans were smart enough and old enough as a species, and planetary cycles tumultuous enough, to have allowed for the rise and fall of numerous lost, highly advanced civilizations throughout history, it was argued. Aliens were superfluous, then, although certainly not removed from ancient mysteries altogether.

Before von Däniken

Although modern fascination with ancient extraterrestrial influence typically is traced to von Däniken's *Chariots of the Gods?*, in fact, ideas surrounding ancient astronauts can be found in literature dating back well over a century. In his 1898 book *Edison's Conquest of Mars* (a work of science fiction), Garrett B. Serviss imagined Martians as having built the great wonders of ancient Egypt. In his 1919 non-fiction work *The Book of the Damned*, Charles Fort speculated that extraterrestrials may have been monitoring and interacting with us for millennia in much the same manner as farmers tend to cattle. Additionally, author and Ancient Astronaut scholar Jason Colavito notes the influence of science fiction literature of the 1920s and 1930s: "especially the work of H.P. Lovecraft, which used Theosophy and Charles Fort's ideas and combined those into what is a recognizable ancient astronaut theory."

Theosophy (meaning literally "God's wisdom") is a religio-philosophic doctrine tracing back to the founding of the Theosophical Society in 1875 and is concerned with unlocking the secrets of divinity in order to understand the true nature of Man's relationship to the broader universe. Colavito points out that Theosophers literalized existing ideas of Earthly interactions with heavenly bodies and peoples, "so that what was once semi-supernatural – angels and souls – gradually became more closely associated with flesh and blood extraterrestrials." Significantly, the early Theosophers not only believed in existence of alien intelligences, but that these intelligences had been influencing humanity for eons.

Theosophical ideas were later read by H. P. Lovecraft, who consciously incorporated them into his fiction work, specifically into what would come to be known as his Cthulhu Mythos, as Colavito observes: "Lovecraft's fictional alien gods came to Earth millions to thousands of years ago; they built great cities, they invented religion, they were the actual creators of human beings." Lovecraft's stories were particularly influential, says Colavito, because they in turn served as inspiration for the highly influential 1960 non-fiction book *The Morning of the Magicians*, by Jacques Bergier and Louis Pauwels:

> In it, they presented the themes found in Lovecraft as nonfiction, speculating about such alternative history touchstones as the 'true' origin of the Egyptian pyramids, ancient maps that appear to have been drawn from outer space, advanced technology incongruously placed in the ancient past, and the other staples of later ancient astronaut theories.

Crucially, Colavito points out that *The Morning of the Magicians* directly influenced Erich von Däniken:

> If you did a close textual analysis of the material in *Chariots of the Gods?* to *Morning of the Magicians* you would find that there is a very close similarity bordering on direct copying. A lot of the material in *Morning of the Magicians* shows up in slightly altered form in *Chariots of the Gods?*

Indeed, von Däniken even references *The Morning of the Magicians* in *Chariots'* bibliography.[7]

With the above timeline in mind, then, a picture begins to emerge of quasi-religious concepts informing fictional narratives, which in turn served to inform the bedrock literature of the 'factual' AA field.

~ ANCIENT ASTRONAUTS ONSCREEN ~

Aliens in the Garden of Eden

Before Erich von Däniken became a household name, ideas of pre-visitation and alien-based religion were being explored on the small screen in *The Twilight Zone*. In an episode titled "Probe 7, Over and Out," which aired 29 November 1963, an astronaut, Colonel Cook, crash lands on an alien planet similar to his own in atmospheric and gravitational conditions. Soon after his crash, Cook learns that his own world has succumbed to nuclear Armageddon. Return is not an option.

While exploring his new surroundings, Cook meets a woman from another species who has crash-landed on the same planet while fleeing her own dying world. Her name is Norda. Together, Cook and Norda head with hope toward a "garden" area rich in fruits and vegetation, but not before fully introducing themselves to one another. Cook reveals his first name to be "Adam," while Norda gives her last name as "Eve." They name their new world after Eve's word for soil: "Irth," pronounced by Adam as "Earth." The episode ends soon after Eve offers Adam a "seppla" – an apple she picks from a tree. As ever, Rod Serling provides the closing narration:

> Do you know these people? Names familiar, are they? They lived a long time ago. Perhaps they're part fable, perhaps they're part fantasy. And perhaps the place they're walking to now is not really called 'Eden.' We offer it only as a presumption. This has been the Twilight Zone.

Martian ancestry

Four years later, in 1967, a year ahead von Däniken's *Chariots of the Gods?*, Britain's Hammer Studios released *Quatermass and the Pit*, a feature film based on a BBC TV serial of the same name that was broadcast live in December 1958 and January 1959. The plot concerns the discovery below the streets of central London of an ancient Martian spacecraft and its deceased pilots. Our hero, Professor Quatermass, declares the craft and aliens (whose horned visage invites comparisons with the Devil) to be around five million years old. Furthermore, suggests the professor, the Martians played a key role in shaping human evolution and intelligence. Quatermass deduces that historical reports of paranormal occurrences in the area are related to the ancient concealed presence of the Martian craft, which itself is intelligent and possessed of a power to violently influence the minds of those in its proximity.

Quatermass theorizes that the Martians came here because their own world was dying. When Earth proved inhospitable to their species, they decided to plant Martian memories deep in the subconscious of primitive Earthlings, thereby preserving some vestige of their own civilization and jumpstarting intelligence on Earth in the process. Ideas surrounding ancient Martian civilizations and their links to those on Earth have been explored by a number of filmmakers over the decades and have even found their way into conspiracy lore as woven by Richard Hoagland, for example, a big name in the UFO community who contends that advanced civilizations once existed (and may still exist) on our Moon, Mars, and on other planets in our solar system, and that NASA and other agencies of officialdom have long been engaged in a cover-up of these facts.[8]

Kubrick engages

In 1968, while *Chariots of the Gods?* was flying off the shelves, director Stanley Kubrick was flirting with Ancient Astronauts in his seminal movie *2001: A Space Odyssey*, the plot for which concerns the discovery of ancient extraterrestrial artifacts and the notion that mankind is the product of a prehistoric alien experiment.

The film eschews traditional narrative structure and is largely dialogue-free, conveying its sweeping themes through a harmonious marriage of Kubrick's astonishing mise-en-scène and stirring classical music. Essentially, *2001* is an evolutionary tale. It begins in humanity's distant past when a tribe of early hominids is shocked by the sudden appearance of a glassy black monolith in their immediate territory. Through processes unknown, the monolith jumpstarts human evolution, eventually leading mankind into the final frontier of space. In the year 2001, astronauts discover another monolith on the moon, buried fifteen meters below the surface of the Tycho crater. It is estimated to have been there for four million years. The monolith sends out a signal to the intelligences that placed it there that humankind has now reached a turning point in its evolution, having broken the bonds of Earth.

Now begins a voyage to Jupiter, to where the moon monolith has been beaming a mysterious signal. It is en route to Jupiter that an existential battle plays out between man (astronaut Dave Bowman, played by Keir Dullea) and machine (the spaceship's artificially intelligent computer, the HAL 9000, voiced by Douglas Rain). Man wins, just, and proceeds to Jupiter orbit, where he encounters yet another monolith; this one pulls him into a vortex that transports him across the universe to a realm beyond the laws of time and space. Here, in a controlled environment, Bowman lives a lifetime in a series of moments, the lab experiment of some unseen higher intelligence. His last sight before death is yet another looming monolith. Bowman (representing mankind) is then reborn as a Starchild – a foetal being in an orb of light, gazing down from space with cosmic wisdom at precious planet Earth.

It is well known that Stanley Kubrick and Arthur C. Clarke had a joint 'UFO' sighting three years prior to the release of their epic movie. The event is described by Paul Meehan in his book *Saucer Movies:*

> One night in 1965 Clarke and Kubrick were kicking some screenplay ideas around when they went outside on the balcony for a break. Gazing up into the night sky, they spied a UFO-like light moving slowly, high in the heavens. Clarke could not explain the light with his knowledge of astronomy, so the two duly filed a UFO report. After checking with some of his contacts at the local observatory, Clarke was able to ascertain that they had witnessed a transit of the satellite Echo 1.

The object was terrestrial in construct, then, but the sighting impacted Kubrick nonetheless, as Meehan observes:

> He developed an anxiety that extraterrestrial contact would occur before *2001* was released, thereby invalidating his film. Accordingly, he approached Lloyds of London hoping to insure *2001* against the possibility of ET contact, but dropped the idea when the proposed cost proved astronomical.[9]

In 1968, the year of his movie's release, Kubrick sat for an interview with *Playboy* magazine, in which he revealed his active interest in UFOs. The director spoke of Project Blue Book and the Condon Committee that ultimately ended the USAF's UFO investigations. Kubrick told *Playboy* that he was "really fascinated" by UFOs and that the phenomenon was worthy of rigorous scientific investigation.[10]

2001 is also of note for anticipating theoretical research avenues of the 21st Century. In 2011, renowned astrobiologist Professor Paul Davies and his associate Robert Wagner of Arizona State University published a paper in the journal *Acta Astronautica*, titled 'Searching for Alien Artifacts on the Moon.' In it the authors suggest that our moon should be scoured for ancient traces of intelligent extraterrestrials, arguing that images of the lunar surface and other information collected by scientists could hold clues as yet unnoticed by casual eyes – a detailed computerized search of existing lunar imagery may yield startling discoveries. The authors note that: "Although there is only a tiny probability that alien technology would have left traces on the moon in the form of an artifact or surface modification of lunar features, this location has the virtue of being close, and of preserving traces for an immense duration."

In what seems like a case of life seeking to imitate art, Davies and Wagner suggest that an alien civilization may even have left a message on our moon intentionally, perhaps contained within a capsule at a lunar landmark, patiently awaiting discovery. In this context the authors suggest we direct our attention toward the Tycho crater, the same location of the moon monolith in *2001*. The authors further postulate that alien messages could be buried beneath the lunar rock and fitted with transmitters that could penetrate the surface, again, just as we saw in Kubrick's classic movie.[11]

Today, *2001: A Space Odyssey* is considered by many to be the greatest science fiction film of all time; certainly it remains one of the most ambitious and stylistically influential. *2001* and its famously reclusive director have since become tightly woven into conspiracy lore, with a number of researchers convinced that Kubrick used special effects techniques pioneered in his 1968 movie to help NASA fake the moon landings the following year. Author and filmmaker Jay Weidner even suggests that Kubrick's 1980 horror classic *The Shining* is best read as a confessional on the part of its director. Weidner sees the movie's mise-en-scène as being laced with subtle hints that the historic Apollo 11 mission was a ruse. These elaborate theories are explored in detail in the feature documentary *Room 237* (2012).[12]

From the tabloids to the dinner table

Public fascination with Ancient Astronaut theories continued to grow throughout the 1970s. Books on the subject played their part, especially those of von Däniken and Sitchin, as did film and television. Documentaries were particularly influential. The German documentary *Chariots of the Gods* (1970) was a big screen exploration of von Däniken's work, taking the viewer on a speculative tour of ancient sites around the world. Its tagline read: "Did Spacemen Visit Earth in Ancient Times? Now We Have Proof!" Three years later an edited version of the same documentary would become the pilot episode of the hugely popular American TV series *In Search of...*, narrated by Rod Serling. *In Search of Ancient Astronauts* (1973) was, notes Jason Colavito, "broadcast to the entire nation and seen by more than a third of all American television viewers. It is also the most viewed Ancient Astronaut documentary ever." The impact of the Serling documentary and others that followed it during the same decade cannot be understated, says Colavito: "It was almost entirely due to the 1970s documentaries that the Ancient Astronaut theory went from a fringe thing you read in the back pages of pulp magazines and tabloids, to something that was being discussed around the dinner table and on the street corner."[13]

AA theory was more popular than ever by the middle of the decade, and Hollywood producers continued to cash in. 1975 saw the release of two AA-inspired titles: the feature documentary *The Outer Space Connection* suggested aliens had visited Earth in ancient times and may return at a future date, while the low-budget adventure *Search for the Gods* saw a fresh-faced Kurt Russell on the hunt for a medallion that would prove extraterrestrials were busy on our planet in its prehistoric past. Russell would pursue Ancient Aliens again almost twenty years later in the blockbusting *Stargate* (1994).

Yet another von Däniken title received the documentary treatment when his 1976 book *Miracles of the Gods* became William Shatner's *Mysteries of the Gods* (1976), fronted by Captain Kirk himself. Shatner opens the documentary with a statement to-camera:

> As Captain Kirk, and with the rest of the crew of the USS Enterprise, we made many wondrous voyages into the future; into the vastness of space. But that was *fiction*. I'd like to take you along another kind of voyage. This is based on *reality* – the real world we live in...

Here then we have 'factual' ideas sprung from the "real world," presented to us by a sci-fi icon in the context of the fictional universe from which he has become inseparable.[14]

An AA conspiracy?

By far the most notable AA-themed release of the 1980s was *Hangar 18* – arguably Hollywood's first UFO conspiracy movie and one that incorporated into its plot many aspects of the real-life UFO enigma. Intriguingly, the film features specific details from allegedly authentic top secret UFO-related government documentation.

Hangar 18's content continues to provoke discussion in the UFO community, in part for the fact that the film was released in 1980. This was the year that details of the Roswell incident began to filter into the popular consciousness with the publication of Charles Berlitz and William Moore's *The Roswell Incident* – the first book on the Roswell subject.

Equally significant in 1980, and undoubtedly connected to the Roswell developments, was the quiet insertion into the UFO community of the term "MJ-Twelve." This term, along with its variant "Majestic Twelve," has now assumed permanent residency in popular culture, having featured in films, TV shows, comic books and video games (for further discussion of MJ-12, see Chapter Seven).

Hanger contents

Hangar 18 begins in Earth orbit as NASA is preparing to launch a satellite under the watchful eye of the US military. Just as the satellite is launched from the space shuttle, however, it collides with a UFO, killing a NASA astronaut in the launch bay. This is witnessed by the other crew in the shuttle, our heroes Bancroft and Price, (played by Gary Collins and James Hampton). Upon their return to Earth the men seek answers but soon realise their government has instigated a cover-up, and that they, too, are being kept in the dark.

We learn that, following the collision in orbit, the UFO made a controlled landing in the Arizona desert, where it was captured by the US military. The craft is soon transported to the top secret 'Hangar 18' where it is studied by NASA scientists (lead by Darren McGavin). Onboard the craft, the scientists make a series of startling discoveries:

- The alien pilots, although dead, are physically undamaged and are almost exactly human in appearance. The scientists conclude that the aliens visited Earth in ancient times, that they were seen as gods, and that they interbred with Earth women and 'jumpstarted' human life as we know it today.

- A human woman is also onboard the craft in stasis. When removed by doctors, the woman awakens in a state of terror. We assume she is an abductee.

- In the ship's data files, the scientists find glyphs similar to those used by ancient Earth civilizations. The scientists also discover extensive aerial surveillance footage of Earth's power plants, military bases and major cities. The aliens, it seems, have been taking an active interest in our technological capabilities.

Meanwhile, Bancroft and Price are dogged in their pursuit of the truth and are targeted by the government for assassination. Price is killed, but Bancroft survives and eventually finds his way to Hangar 18 and aboard the alien spacecraft. Around this point, the NASA scientists finally decipher the alien glyphs, which indicate that the beings were planning to return to Earth en masse in the near future.

Before any of this information has a chance to sink-in, government agents fly a remote-controlled jet filled with explosives into Hangar 18, the goal being to kill all involved in the cover-up, thereby permanently burying the secret. However, unbeknownst to the government hit squad, several of the NASA scientists, as well as Bancroft, are inside the alien craft when the hanger explodes. The craft, it turns out, is invincible, and the survivors inside decide to let the truth be known. The film ends with UFO Disclosure.

Ancient Astronauts and Christianity

Hangar 18's depiction of human-looking extraterrestrials is particularly interesting, as is the idea that these beings jumpstarted the human race – these very same details were to appear three years later in a 'secret' Air Force report shown to Linda Moulton Howe as part of the filmmaker and journalist's preparation for a documentary on UFOs.

On 9 April 1983, during a meeting at Kirtland Air Force Base in New Mexico, Air Force Office of Special Investigations Officer Richard Doty presented Howe with a document, the front cover of which read:

BRIEFING PAPER
FOR
THE PRESIDENT OF THE UNITED STATES OF AMERICA
ON THE SUBJECT OF
UNIDENTIFIED AERIALVEHICLES (UAVs)

Doty told Howe that she was to read the document at the request of his superiors, but stressed that she was forbidden from taking the document with her and from taking notes of any kind.

The weighty document detailed many aspects of the UFO phenomenon and included a list of UFO crash/retrievals. The list included two separate incidents near the Roswell region in 1947, and another in 1949, which resulted in the capture of a live extraterrestrial that was taken to Los Alamos National Laboratories. Apparently, the being was held captive before it died of unknown causes in 1952. Other crashes listed in the document included Aztec New Mexico, Kingman Arizona, and Loredo Texas.

Most shocking to Howe was a paragraph that said the extraterrestrials had manipulated DNA in an evolving primate species to create Homo sapiens. Elsewhere in the document it was noted that the ETs had created a being on Earth whose purpose was to teach humans about love and non-violence. Howe was astonished: "We are talking about Jesus Christ," she said to Doty, who said nothing in response, but who, she asserts, looked deeply uncomfortable.[15]

The author and researcher Mike Clelland has pointed out that the parallels between the content of *Hangar 18* and the report shown to Linda Moulton Howe are so striking that "The document that Howe saw could very well have been written by Darren McGavin's character from what he learned in the movie." Clelland observes:

We have a reporter [LMH] being shown a secret document by the Air Force in 1983, the conclusion is that they [officialdom] wanted this information floated out to the public. Three years earlier we have the movie *Hangar 18* "floating" out *the same information* in the guise of an action film.[16]

Rising Sunn

In 1971, Sunn Classic Pictures started to produce and distribute feature films and documentaries about UFOs (with an emphasis on Ancient Astronauts) and other paranormal/psychic phenomena. Titles included the aforementioned AA-themed *The Outer Space Connection* (1975), *The Amazing World of Psychic Phenomena* (1976), *The Bermuda Triangle* (1979), based on Charles Berlitz's non-fiction book linking UFOs to the disappearance of ships and aircraft; *Beyond Death's Door* (1979), about life after death; and, in 1980, *Hangar 18*. Sunn Classic Pictures also had a strong focus on religious documentaries, with titles including: *In Search of Noah's Ark* (1976), *In Search of Historic Jesus* (1979), and a TV series that ran from 1978 to 1979 called *Greatest Heroes of the Bible*.

The Mormon connection

Sunn Classic Pictures was established in Utah as a Mormon-run company with Raylan Jensen as its first President. Many of the studio's writers, producers, and directors also were Mormons, including Robert Starling (writer of *In Search of Historic Jesus*, and who in later life would make an educational documentary about the Mormon Church), and Charles E. Sellier Jr., one of Sunn's most successful writer/producers and also a co-founder of the studio with Raylan Jensen. As a producer, Sellier would make only family-friendly G-rated films "out of Mormon conviction."[17] His credits for Sunn notably included *The Bermuda Triangle* and *Hangar 18*. In 1997, Sellier wrote *UFO*, a non-fiction book examining the UFO enigma in the context of a government cover-up.

It makes sense that a Mormon-run film studio should exhibit an interest in UFOs. Mormon cosmology holds that the Earth is not unique, but just one of many inhabited planets, each created by Jesus for the purpose of bringing about immortality and eternal life. Mormon leaders have taught that the inhabitants of these planets are almost identical in appearance to humans – just as the alien beings in *Hangar 18* are extremely human-like (a point dwelt upon in the film's plot).

Also worthy of mention in this discussion is "Kolob," a heavenly body described in Mormon scripture as a star, but which is generally regarded by Mormons as a planet. It is said to be the closest place in the universe to the throne of God. In the context of science-fiction, the popular AA-flavoured TV series *Battlestar Galactica* (1978–1979 and

2004–2009) incorporates many Mormon cosmological beliefs into its overarching narrative. This is because the creator of the show, Glen Larson, was himself a Mormon. In the TV series, the planet Kobol (as opposed to Kolob) is the birth place of the human race where the "Lords of Kobol" are held sacred.

An LDS educational agenda?

In the Mormon text, *Doctrines of Salvation* (1:62), tenth President of the Church of Jesus Christ of Latter-day Saints (LDS), Joseph Fielding Smith, states: "We are not the only people that the Lord has created. We have brothers and sisters on other earths. They look like us because they, too, are the children of God and were created in his image, for they are also his offspring." Smith began his LDS Presidency in 1970, the year prior to the establishment of Sunn Classic Pictures.

Also relevant is a quote by LDS Apostle Neal A. Maxwell. In his book, *A Wonderful Flood of Light* (p.25), Maxwell wrote: "We do not know how many inhabited worlds there are, or where they are. But certainly we are not alone."[18] Between 1970 and 1976, the formative years of Sunn Classic Pictures, Maxwell served as the LDS Commissioner of Church Education, which is responsible for providing religious and secular education for people of all ages, both LDS and non-LDS.[19]

Did Mormon leaders such as Smith and Maxwell merely *believe* in the reality extraterrestrial life, or were their statements based on something more tangible? In a 2005 interview, Dr. Steven Greer of the Disclosure Project said: "The Mormon corporate empire has an enormous interest in this subject; they have much more power than the White House or the Pentagon over this issue."[20] I contacted Greer asking him if he could elaborate on this statement or provide me with some sources to follow up on. He has yet to respond.

The question is...

The key question relating to Sunn Classic Pictures (and one that, for now, remains unanswered) is this: was the studio's alien-themed output simply a reflection of Mormon ideals and beliefs held by the studio's core writers/producers/directors (as well as an attempt on their part to cash in on the ever-popular subject of UFOs), or, was it a more lofty strategy on the part of Mormon Church itself to subtly educate the public about an aspect of the Mormon faith which, in the century of the UFO, was becoming both increasingly taboo and increasingly relevant (i.e. life on other planets and its possible links to humanity)?

Stargates, 'real' and imagined

The 1980s witnessed a waning of public interest in AA theories, and, although a handful of books were published on the subject during this decade, Hollywood showed little enthusiasm. By the mid-1990s, though, extraterrestrial shenanigans in our distant history seemed fresh once again in Tinseltown, and this was owed almost entirely to the surprise success of one movie: *Stargate*.

Released in 1994, Roland Emmerich's movie was one of the first of its decade to neatly package the core ingredients of America's now vibrant UFO-conspiracy subculture: government secrecy, reverse engineering of alien technology, an evil alien from a dying world, and crucially, Ancient Astronauts.

The plot concerns a 10,000 year old headstone discovered in Egypt in 1928 and now under lock and key in a US military installation (clearly modelled on NORAD's Cheyenne Mountain complex). Linguist Daniel Jackson (James Spader) is tasked by project leaders with deciphering the glyphs and symbols that adorn the artifact and deduces from them the existence of a "Stargate," a device capable of forming a traversable wormhole for cosmic explorers.

But the Stargate, it turns out, is already in the hands of the US military, which, until now, has been unable to activate it. Under the steely leadership of Col. Jack O'Neil (Kurt Russell), Jackson accompanies an elite military unit on a reconnaissance mission through the wormhole, which leads them to the interior of a pyramid in a desert landscape. Upon exploring their new environment the team is surprised to discover a human-run mining operation. The primitive miners receive Jackson, O'Neil, and co. as emissaries of their all-powerful god, Ra – the name of the ancient Egyptian sun god on Earth.

Through rudimentary communication with one of the natives, Jackson learns that Ra is a parasitic extraterrestrial who arrived on Earth in its ancient past seeking a cure for his impending death. By inhabiting a human body (that of a teenage boy) Ra found that he could sustain his own life indefinitely. In his new human form, Ra enslaved the boy's tribe and shipped them to a planet in another galaxy where they would mine the precious mineral from which Ra derives his advanced technology.

The film's screenplay was a not-so-subtle endorsement of America's actions during the first Gulf War, pitching a despotic 'foreign' leader against the US military (portrayed here as a liberating rather than invading force) in a battle for the hearts and minds of an oppressed desert people. The film sees the despot destroyed, and the desert folk freed and Americanized in the process, trying cigarettes and Hershey's 5th Avenue chocolate bars along the way, before ending up clad in US military fatigues while proudly saluting Kurt Russell's Colonel O'Neil.

As with almost every AA-themed entertainment product that preceded it, *Stargate* owed a heavy debt to Erich von Däniken. The *Stargate* Ultimate Edition DVD includes a featurette called *Is There A Stargate?*, which chronicles von Däniken's life, from boyhood to AA authority. Although a box-office success upon its release, *Stargate* has yet to spawn a sequel. In 2014, though, MGM and Warner Bros. announced they are teaming-up with Director Roland Emmerich and Producer Dean Devlin for a "re-imagined trilogy" based on the original movie.

Stargate on TV and at the Pentagon

Movies aside, *Stargate* did generate a popular spin-off TV franchise comprised of *Stargate* series *SG-1*, *Atlantis*, and *Universe*, all of which tapped into UFO mythology to varying degrees. In *SG-1* (1997–2007) and *Atlantis* (2004–2009) the iconic Grays feature prominently as a species called the Asgard who in ancient times masqueraded themselves holographically as the gods of Norse mythology and who in 1947 were involved in the Roswell Incident. In the *Stargate* narrative, the Asgards (Grays) are benevolent and actively protect mankind from threats from other alien civilizations. To this end they work hand-in-hand with the US government, sharing their advanced technology with the military and bringing to mind one of the central themes of UFO conspiracy culture. The *SG-1* writers also incorporated specific details from real-life abduction lore. So, *in SG-1*, the Asgards (Grays) are a dying race without the capacity for sexual reproduction, reduced to cloning for perpetuation of their species.

While the producers of the 1994 movie neither sought nor received military assistance, the TV spin-offs received extensive support from the Pentagon, the USAF, and US Space Command (and all the script input that implies), which is perhaps unsurprising considering their overwhelmingly positive portrayals of the armed services.[21] While the secret facility in the movie is *based* on NORAD's Cheyenne Mountain, the facility in the TV show is Cheyenne Mountain itself, filmed with the permission of the Air Force. The USAF was so enthusiastic about the franchise that in season four of *Stargate SG-1* Air Force Chief of Staff Michael E. Ryan made a cameo appearance as himself shortly before his retirement. In the episode "Prodigy" the Jack O'Neil character (played for TV by Richard Dean Anderson) asks Ryan, "Do you really have Air Force Colonels who act the way I do?" To which the real-life General replies: "Yes, and worse!"

Another Air Force Chief of Staff, General John P. Jumper, starred as himself in 'Lost City Part 2,' the final instalment of season seven of *SG-1*, first broadcast in March 2004. Later that same year *SG-1* star Richard Dean Anderson was invited to the Pentagon where he chatted with the Joint Chiefs of Staff before being awarded the title of 'Honorary Brigadier General – USAF' as thanks for *SG-1*'s consistently positive depiction of the US military. The award was bestowed on the actor by General Jumper himself.[22] Three years later, in June 2007, Jumper became a director of Science Applications International Corporation (SAIC), a powerhouse defense contractor long rumored to be one the key players in the reverse-engineering of alien technologies.[23] It is perhaps noteworthy that the *SG-1* episode in which General Jumper appears dealt with an imminent, large-scale invasion of Earth by the Gao'uld aliens. Dialogue in the episode serves to justify huge military spending on the reverse engineering of alien technologies to more effectively combat cosmic threats. Problems inherent in the public disclosure of alien reality are also a running theme in parts one and two of the episode.

A Stargate to Mars?

By the mid-noughties, online UFO discourse had begun to feed more directly from film and TV narratives, many of which were themselves loosely inspired by UFO literature. Indeed, the rich lore of the *Stargate* universe seems to have greatly influenced conspiratorial thinking in the UFO community post-9/11, giving rise to elaborate and supposedly factual narratives from self-described 'whistleblowers' claiming experience with a real-life top secret Stargate program run by elements within the US military-industrial-complex. Take Henry Deacon (pseudonym), for example, who ambiguously claimed to be a physicist with "one of the three letter agencies" and to have worked on classified projects at Lawrence Livermore National Laboratory in California, which is funded by the US Department of Energy. Between 2006 and 2007, Deacon told the online 'whistleblower' hub, Project Camelot, of his inside knowledge of at least two types of Stargate then being used in US government black projects: "(a) the kind where you step through a portal and leave the device behind [as in the *Stargate* movie and TV shows], and (b) the kind where you take the device with you." Of the latter type, Deacon told Camelot: "Think about where you want to go, and you're there."

Additionally, Deacon claimed that Mars is a populated planet, with at least 670,000 people (perhaps not all human) currently living there in a base "at the bottom of an ancient seabed." Apparently this population has waxed and waned over the centuries. The famous "face" on Mars is real, said Deacon, despite NASA's statements and evidence to the contrary. Transport to the red planet is by two means: "Stargates for personnel and small items, and spacecraft for larger items of freight." Deacon also spoke of the Anunnaki described in the work of Zecharia Sitchin. They're real, too, he claimed, and are split into a number of factions, some of which are friendly, others not.[24]

Project Camelot founders Kerry Cassidy and Bill Ryan seemingly were not at all concerned that the pseudonym 'Henry Deacon' is the name of a character in the popular sci-fi TV show *Eureka* (2006–2012), which is set in a fictional town inhabited by scientific geniuses who work on advanced technologies for the US Department of Defense. Clearly, Camelot's Henry Deacon is a man who enjoys his science fiction.

Ideas like those espoused in the testimonies of Deacon and other dubious Camelot 'whistleblowers' had already taken cinematic form, not only in *Stargate*, but in a number of films dating back to the early years of the Cold War. Perhaps fresher in Deacon's mind on the Martian front, though, was Disney's *Mission to Mars* (2000), in which the first manned mission to the red planet meets with disaster and the ensuing rescue team discovers that humans are descended from an ancient race of Martians (who, we learn, constructed the famous Martian 'face' and 'pyramids'). Disney and director Brian De Palma had high hopes for their $100 million epic, but the best it could do was recoup its production costs worldwide, plus a paltry $11 million.[25]

Bizarrely, *Mission to Mars* received assistance from NASA. A notice in the film's closing credits reads: "The National Aeronautics and Space Administration's cooperation and assistance does not reflect an endorsement of the contents of the film or the treatment of the characters depicted therein."

Fresher still in Deacon's mind may have been the sci-fi actioner *Doom*, released in 2005, less than one year prior to his first Camelot interview. An adaptation of the 1990s shoot-em-up video game of the same name, the movie opens with a voice telling us:

> In the year 2026 archaeologists working in the Nevada desert discovered a portal to an ancient city on Mars. They called this portal 'The Arc.' Twenty years later we're still struggling to understand why it was built and what happened to the civilization that built it.

The Arc in *Doom* is a Stargate in almost every respect but name: an ancient technology discovered by archaeologists that enables near instantaneous travel to other worlds (in this case, Mars) where scientists discover fossilized evidence of a human-like civilization. Much like the Stargate in the eponymous movie, the Arc in *Doom* is stored at a top secret underground military facility – in this case Papoose Lake in Nevada, the exact location of the facility described by Area 51 whistleblower Bob Lazar (see Chapter Seven).

Alien + Predator + Ancient Astronauts = disappointment

2004 saw two iconic franchises melded to unmemorable effect in *Alien vs. Predator*, which did exactly what it said on the tin and little more. Directed by Paul W. S. Anderson (*Event Horizon, Resident Evil*) and loosely based on a series of Dark Horse comics, the plot concerns an ancient and ongoing rivalry between the Xenomorphs of the *Alien* franchise and the ruthless big-game-hunting extraterrestrials of the *Predator* movies.

The film follows a group of archaeologists in their discovery and exploration of a pyramid buried 2000 feet beneath the surface of an Antarctic whaling station. Hieroglyphs and sculptures within reveal it to be an ancient hunting ground for Predators who kill Xenomorphs as a rite of passage. The humans soon get caught in the middle of a battle between the two species and desperately attempt to prevent the aliens from reaching the surface and wreaking further havoc. Along the way we learn that the Predators were worshipped as gods by ancient civilizations and that it was they who taught early humans to build pyramids and other sacred structures.

In addition to the *Alien vs. Predator* comic books, Anderson cites a certain Swiss AA theorist as his primary influence. In a promotional featurette, the director states:

> Something that's always fascinated me is the work of Erich von Däniken who [asks] 'how can the ancients have built the pyramids?' And of course Däniken's answer is that humans built the pyramids with alien help, and, of course, we agree with him. In Aztec mythology they believe that their gods came from the skies... that's the backbone of our story.[26]

Anderson has also acknowledged the influence on his film of H. P. Lovecraft, who indirectly inspired von Däniken himself.

Alien vs. Predator received a 2005 Golden Raspberry Award nomination in the category of 'Worst Remake or Sequel.' Bad reviews failed to prevent the 2007 sequel *Alien vs. Predator: Requiem*.

Indiana Jones and the misjudged plot device

Steven Spielberg's continuing fascination with UFOs was evidenced in 2008 in *Indiana Jones and the Kingdom of the Crystal Skull*, which saw the iconic hero in pursuit of an ancient artifact of the fallen Mesoamerican Ugha civilization (modelled on the Mayan civilization). The crystal skull, we come to learn, is that of an interdimensional being, one of many who once were revered as gods by the people of the mystical city of Akator and who bestowed upon their subjects advanced knowledge and technology. In one scene, our hero interprets ancient pictographs inside the Temple of the Crystal Skull, which he estimates to be "as old as the pyramids," depicting beings with enlarged craniums being worshipped by the masses: "Someone came and taught the Ugha farming, irrigation," says Indy.

The film is explicitly UFOlogical. It features direct references to the Roswell Incident. There is even a scene set at a secret military base in the Nevada desert unmistakably modelled on Area 51, as well as a classic flying saucer, which, in the film's finale, transports the interdimensional being, closely resembling a tall alien Gray, "not into space," as Professor Oxley (John Hurt) tells Indy, "but to the space between spaces." All of this was much to the annoyance of *Indiana Jones* fans, who felt that, while supernatural and religious MacGuffins were acceptable staples of the franchise, Ancient Aliens were a step too far.

Despite the fans' disappointment, *Indiana Jones and the Kingdom of the Crystal Skull* went on to gross in excess of $700 million at the worldwide box-office, making it one of Spielberg's most successful films to date.[27]

Aliens and Vikings

2008 also saw the limited cinematic release of *Outlander*, an old-fashioned sci-fi fantasy adventure starring Jim Caviezel as Kainan, an alien who crash-lands in Norway circa 709 AD, accidentally unleashing an alien monster (a "Moorwen") that has been hiding aboard his spaceship. Kainan learns from his ship's computer that he is on Earth, which is classified by his people as an "Abandoned Seed Colony." The implication is clear: humanity is directly descended from extraterrestrials. The plot then plays out Beowulf style with an AA-inspired twist as the heroic Kainan ingratiates himself with the local townsfolk (who call him "Outlander") and battles with the terrifying Moorwen (and its newborn baby). Kainan is able to penetrate the Moorwen's natural armor with a sword specially forged for this purpose made from Kainan's alien metal and Norwegian iron. In the end, with the Moorwen vanquished, Kainan, now a Viking King, decides to remain on Earth with his new family.

Strange territory

The Objective is a 2008 low-budget sci-fi horror directed by Daniel Myrick, who is best known for co-helming the influential found-footage horror, *The Blair Witch Project* (1999). The movie follows a team of US Special Forces soldiers in Afghanistan led by tight-lipped CIA operative Benjamin Keynes (Jonas Ball). Their mission: to locate an important Afghan cleric. Further details are classified top secret and known only to Keynes. As their mission unfolds, it becomes terrifyingly apparent to all involved that otherworldly forces are at play in the harsh

Afghan wilderness. The film grows increasingly surreal as it progresses, incorporating UFO conspiracy theory, esoteric symbolism, and, most notably, the vimanas of ancient Sanskrit literature and AA lore.

In correspondence with the author, director Daniel Myrick described how he had grown up in the 1970s watching TV series and documentaries exploring Ancient Astronauts. Specifically, Myrick cited the 1977 BBC documentary *The Case for Ancient Astronauts* and the aforementioned *In Search of Ancient Astronauts*, narrated by Rod Serling. "Both had big influences on my imagination and world view about earth and the cosmos," Myrick explained.[28]

Curiously, *The Objective*'s screenplay was co-written by Wesley Clark Jr., son of the famous US General, Wesley Clark, former Supreme Allied Commander of NATO in Europe and, in 2004, a candidate for the Democratic Party Presidential nomination. In October of that year, UFO researcher David Rudiak had the opportunity to speak with Clark directly in Reno, Nevada. "When you were in the military, were you ever briefed on the subject of UFOs?" Rudiak asked the General. According to Rudiak, "Clark looked down for a moment and shook his head somewhat chagrined looking like 'Damn it, here it comes!'" Clark then answered: "I heard a bit. In fact, I am going to be in Roswell, New Mexico, tonight." Rudiak followed up: "So, were you briefed?'" General Clark replied: "There are things going on. But we will have to work out our own mathematics." With that, the General was gone.[29]

With this information in mind I asked Myrick to what extent Clark Jr. was involved in scripting *The Objective* and what attracted him to the project in the first place. The director informed me that Clark Jr. had written the initial draft of the script based on Myrick's own original story outline. "From there I revised and eventually produced the shooting version you see in the film," Myrick explained. "My understanding is that Wesley liked the premise and the fact it was dealing with Special Forces operations."

Like many people, Myrick is a firm believer in life elsewhere in the cosmos and is hopeful that contact might be established within his lifetime, although he is far from sold on the extraterrestrial hypothesis for UFOs. He acknowledged in our correspondence:

> Well, there is a 'phenomenon' to be sure. Exactly what is the root cause is more open to speculation. Scientifically, I find it hard to imagine that a race of beings with the capability of space travel over such distances would come all this way only to leave blurry remnants of themselves for us mere mortals to argue over in the ensuing years after their

departure. More likely we'll be making contact via radio telescope or some other technology that has yet to be invented.

Myrick also stated that actual alien intelligences will undoubtedly bear little relation to Hollywood's limited imaginings of them: "If and when [contact] day comes, any preconceptions we may have with regard to alien characteristics will be blown away."[30]

"I don't know, therefore aliens"

AA theory achieved maximum cultural penetration in 2010 with the arrival of *Ancient Aliens*, a TV documentary series first broadcast on The History Channel and later on its sister station H2. In sensationalist style the fast-paced show explored the theories of all the major AA personalities, particularly von Däniken and Sitchin. The biggest star to emerge from the show was Giorgio Tsoukalos, a protégée of von Däniken who featured prominently in every season (his signature hairdo growing wilder with each passing year), passionately insistent that most historical mysteries are attributable to one thing: "Aliens."

Television viewers couldn't get enough of the show, which, at its peak in 2011, boasted more than two million viewers each week. Then came the memes. Today, an Internet search of 'Georgio Tsoukalos' will retrieve literally hundreds of images of the follically flamboyant TV personality anchored by captions such as: "I don't know, therefore aliens," "I'm not saying it was aliens, but it was aliens," and "I didn't hear your question, but the answer is aliens." The show was spoofed in a November 2011 episode of *South Park*, titled 'A History Channel Thanksgiving,' in which it is revealed that aliens were present at the original harvest feast of 1621. *Ancient Aliens* had become a joke, but all the more influential for it, as Jason Colavito observes:

> Because of the outrageousness of *Ancient Aliens* and the various Internet memes that it has spawned – particularly the ones of Giorgio Tsoukalos – it has a much larger impact than just the raw numbers would suggest because it has exposed a whole new generation to the AA theory and has created a sort of entertaining version of it that has become something that celebrities are now interested in, celebrities like Katy Perry and Megan Fox, who have talked publicly about their love of *Ancient Aliens*.[31]

A Marvel-ous Ancient Astronaut

With the overwhelming popularity of *Ancient Aliens* on the small screen, Hollywood producers saw immediate potential at the box-office, leading to two major AA-inspired releases in 2011 alone. In May, and with a budget of $150 million, came *Thor*, a Marvel production starring Chris Hemsworth as the eponymous hero, Tom Hiddleston as his treacherous adopted brother Loki, and Anthony Hopkins as their imposing father, Odin.

In the movie, Thor, the bullish crown prince of the mythical realm of Asgard, is exiled to Earth by his disapproving father. It is on our planet that Thor meets beautiful astrophysicist Jane Foster (Natalie Portman), who helps him stop his brother Loki from seizing the crown of Asgard and waging war across the universal realms.

One of the film's opening sequences depicts the Norse people of early Scandinavia at the mercy of alien beings (the frost giants). In a voice-over, Odin tells us: "Once, mankind accepted a simple truth – that they were not alone in this universe. Some worlds Man believed to be home to their gods; others they knew to fear..."

In the Marvel universe, Thor and other gods of old are aliens – or rather inter-dimensional beings. In the movie they travel between worlds (or "realms") by way of wormhole technology known as a Bifrost Bridge, which references the Bifrost of Norse mythology – a burning rainbow bridge that reaches between Midgard (our world) and Asgard, the realm of the gods. Seeking to ground their fantasy in solid scientific theory, director Kenneth Brannagh and his screenwriters liaised with scientists from the Science & Entertainment Exchange, among them Kevin Hand, who, at a NASA panel discussion in 2014, predicted that extraterrestrial life would be found within the next 20 years. It was through discussion with the Exchange that wormholes came to feature as a major plot device in the movie, with the characters accurately recognizing the Bifrost as being an "Einstein–Rosen bridge."

Thor was well received by critics and proved a hit at the box-office, raking in just shy of $450 million worldwide.[32]

Weird, weird West

Two months later, in July of 2011, stars Harrison Ford and Daniel Craig got in on the AA scene. Based on a graphic novel by Scott Mitchell

Rosenberg, the Spielberg-produced *Cowboys & Aliens* sees a generic 1870s frontier town besieged by monstrous aliens who are mining the regional gold and abducting humans in an effort to discover their weaknesses. The screenplay taps into UFOlogy with references to missing time, cattle mutilations, and, in the form of its gold-seeking aliens, the Anunnaki of AA-lore. "They want gold," we are told by one of the characters, "it's as rare to them as it is to you."

Acknowledging the film's debt to AA-lore, in the documentary *Cowboys & Aliens: An Inside Look with Steven Spielberg* (2011), Spielberg remarks: "A lot of people have come to believe that visitors from outer space have something to do with the pyramids, and so it just seemed that if the Egyptians had an [alien] interaction, couldn't pioneers of the West?"[33]

Perhaps they could. In January 1878, *The Denison Daily* newspaper of Texas reported that a local farmer, Mr. John Martin, had witnessed "a dark object high in the northern sky" of such unusual shape and velocity as to make him stop and stare. As he stared, the object grew considerably in size and moved in his direction until it was "almost overhead." The object was reported as "going through space at a wonderful speed," and, significantly, "was the size of a large saucer."[34]

Despite the huge talent involved in the production, and a huge budget ($163 million), *Cowboys & Aliens* somehow missed its mark, failing to connect with critics and returning a disappointing $176 million at the worldwide box-office.[35]

"A challenge to the gods"

The *Alien* franchise was further expanded in 2012 when director Ridley Scott returned to the helm with *Prometheus*, the long awaited, much-hyped prequel to his 1979 classic.

In 2089, archaeologists Elizabeth Shaw (Noomi Rapace) and Charlie Holloway (Logan Marshall-Green) discover a starmap in remote Scotland that matches others from multiple unconnected ancient cultures across the globe. The starmap is interpreted as an invitation from humanity's extraterrestrial creators, the "Engineers," and a corporate funded mission to the distant moon LV-223 is soon underway aboard the spaceship Prometheus. This is a film in which humans quite literally meet their makers. Unfortunately for the crew, their makers are harsh masters, and humanity is revealed to be but one of many genetic experiments to have been conducted by the Engineers across the galaxy. The Engineers' real area of interest is bio-weapons, and their greatest achievement is the Xenomorph of the *Alien* franchise – the ultimate biological killing machine.

In advance of the film's release, Ridley Scott spoke repeatedly about the influence of Erich von Däniken, and of his own personal belief in the existence of intelligent alien life and visitation. While at the CineEurope expo in 2011, Scott said of *Prometheus*:

> The (space) journey, metaphorically, is about a challenge to the gods... NASA and the Vatican agree that is almost mathematically impossible that we can be where we are today without there being a little help along the way. That's what we're looking at (in the film), at some of Erich von Däniken's ideas of how did we humans come about.[36]

Scott further 'outed' himself as an AA proponent when he told *Empire* magazine:

> In the '60s there was a guy called Erich von Däniken who did a very popular book called *Chariots of the Gods?*, and he proposed pre-visitation, which we all pooh-poohed. But the more we get into it, the more science accepts the fact that we're not alone in this universe, and there's every feasible chance that there's more of us, not exactly as we are, but creatures that are organically living in other parts of this particular galaxy.

When asked by *Empire* if he personally believes Earth has been visited by extraterrestrials in its ancient past, Scott replied:

> I think it's entirely logical. The idea that we've been here three billion years and nothing happened until 75,000 years ago is absolute nonsense. If something happened here two billion years ago, if there was a civilization at least equal to ours, there would be nothing left after two billion years. It would be carbon. We talk about Atlantis and cities under water that have long gone, long submerged, but they're in the relatively recent past. I'm talking about one-and-a-half-billion years ago – was this planet really empty? I don't think so.[37]

In addition to AA theory, *Prometheus* also makes a very specific, albeit oblique, reference to abduction lore. In Ridley Scott's 1979 movie

Alien, after the crew of the spaceship Nostromo has awakened from their hyper-sleep, the ship's navigator, Lambert (Veronica Cartwright), states their location as "just short of Zeta II Reticuli."

Zeta Reticuli, as any self-respecting UFO buff knows, is a binary star system in the constellation of Reticulum located approximately 39 light-years from Earth. The UFO buff knows this because Zeta Reticuli is thought by many to be the home system of the so-called "Gray" aliens – an idea that has its roots in the 1961 Hill abduction incident in which Betty and Barney Hill were allegedly taken aboard an extraterrestrial spacecraft in rural New Hampshire and subjected to medical tests.

When the Hills underwent regression hypnosis several years after their abduction experience, Betty recalled being shown a starmap by the ETs, which she later sketched from memory at the urging of her psychiatrist. That starmap was interpreted by amateur astronomer Marjorie Fish as a depiction of the Zeta Reticuli star system and quickly entered UFO lore.

During the marketing campaign for *Prometheus*, Ridley Scott made explicit reference to Zeta II Reticuli. In a promotional featurette, the director said: "The planet where they [the crew of the Prometheus] go is called Zeta II Reticuli... This story kind of walks around the truth of what there may be out there... It presents some big questions."[38]

The implication of Scott's statement was that the UFOlogical significance of Zeta II Reticuli would receive greater emphasis in *Prometheus* than it did in *Alien*. However, when the movie finally hit cinemas it contained no spoken reference whatsoever to Zeta II Reticuli. Still, we can be certain that Zeta II Reticuli was indeed the crew's destination based on an early scene in the movie in which a prehistoric cave painting depicts a human figure pointing skyward to what is interpreted by the scientists as a star constellation. Its configuration matches Betty Hill's starmap, proving that *Prometheus* did go to Zeta II Reticuli and that the movie drew inspiration in this regard directly from imagery from the Hill abduction case.[39]

Prometheus opened strong at the box-office but received mixed reviews from critics, who praised Scott's typically stunning aesthetics but savaged the film's confused plot. A sequel is now in the works.

J. J.'s AAs

In 2013, director J.J. Abrams impressed audiences with his second instalment of the newly rebooted *Star Trek* movie franchise. *Star Trek into Darkness* was essentially a re-imagining of the 1982 classic, *Star Trek II: The Wrath of Khan*, in which the crew of the USS Enterprise face-off against a ruthless, genetically engineered human (Khan) hell-bent on exacting his revenge against Starfleet.

The film's opening sequence plunges us into the brilliant crimson forests of an alien world where Captain James T. Kirk (Chris Pine) and Doctor Leonard McCoy (Karl Urban) are fleeing a primitive humanoid tribe. The Starfleet officers are in disguise so as to prevent the tribes-people from seeing their human (i.e. alien) faces and shattering their embryonic philosophical and religious paradigm. Kirk and McCoy are, as any Trekkie will appreciate, seeking to uphold their prime directive: to avoid at all costs any overt interference with the internal development of an alien civilization – especially one that is "barely out of the stone age" and which views its own culture as the center of the universe.

This idea of non-interference between alien cultures is frequently discussed in the UFO and scientific communities. Some scientists consider it entirely plausible that any advanced extraterrestrial civilizations in our galaxy would seek to avoid drawing the attention of inhabitants of more primitive worlds for fear of sparking civilizational collapse. Many in the UFO community insist this is why ET has not yet landed on the White House lawn.

Numerous alleged contactees have claimed that benevolent space folk have actually saved humanity from destruction on occasion throughout history by quietly preventing potentially catastrophic natural disasters. *Star Trek into Darkness* explores these UFOlogical concepts in its opening scenes. The reason Kirk and McCoy (and also Commander Spock) are on the alien planet in the first place is to attempt to covertly prevent the eruption of a super volcano that would wipe-out the fledgling civilization. The Starship Enterprise is hidden from the aliens' view beneath hundreds of feet of water off the coastline as Kirk and McCoy attempt to blend in with the natives. Things don't go according to plan, however, as not only are the two astronauts rumbled, but their starship is witnessed by the awe-struck tribespeople rising majestically from the ocean. We know in that moment that their civilizational path has been dramatically altered as, soon after, they begin drawing and worshipping a crude pictogram of the Enterprise. A religion is born.

As if these UFOlogical allusions weren't sufficient, the fictional alien planet of our discussion is actually called 'Nibiru.' As mentioned previously, Nibiru is a theoretical planet thought by Zecharia Sitchin to pass by Earth every 3,600 years, allowing its inhabitants, the Anunna-ki, to interact with humanity. According to Sitchin, these beings were the first gods worshipped by Man.

These filmic nods to UFOlogy should come as small surprise when we consider that the screenwriters for *Star Trek into Darkness* are Alex Kurtzman, Roberto Orci, and Damon Lindelof. Between them, these men have written and/or produced the likes of *Transformers*, *Cowboys and Aliens*, and *Prometheus* – all of which owe a heavy debt to UFO literature. Orci, for one, has made no secret of his personal interest in the UFO subject. In July 2011, the screenwriter was asked by *The Wrap* if he believed in aliens. He replied in the affirmative and added: "I think the evidence clearly indicates that the government's lying about what the hell's going on."[40]

AAs far from extinct at the box-office

At the time of writing, the most recent major film to tap the AA mythos is *Transformers: Age of Extinction* (2014), the fourth instalment of the Spielberg-produced *Transformers* franchise. It is worthy of mention here for its depiction of an advanced alien race known as "The Creators," who wiped out the dinosaurs 65 million years ago in order to re-seed our planet with their own technology to use Earth as a construction site for the Transformers. Early on in the movie we see spectacular scenes of prehistoric animals fearfully looking skyward as giant alien ships position themselves overhead before attacking.

Transformers: Age of Extinction was panned by critics but still grossed in excess of $1 billion worldwide. It is currently the thirteenth most successful film of all time.[41]

Conclusion

The takeaway from this chapter, if nothing else, should be the over-whelming influence of one man on AA-themed entertainment prod-ucts: Erich von Däniken. Equally, it is important to remember that von Däniken's non-fiction works were heavily influenced by fiction literature dating to the early years of 20th Century and to religio-philosophical notions of the century prior. As Jason Colavito notes: "There's this very close interconnection between fact and fiction as the lines move back and forth. What we hear of in non-fiction becomes grist for movies and TV shows, which in turn inspire new non-fiction ideas."[42] While cultural feedback loops often are frustratingly indistinct when examining other UFOlogical facets, with Ancient Astronauts a bold line can be drawn from the theosophical ideas of the late-1800s, through fiction literature of the 1920s and 1930s, to von Däniken's non-fiction *Chariots of the Gods?* in the late-1960s and the many books and documentaries it inspired in the 1970s, to the dense fictional narratives of the 1990s and noughties in the form of the *Stargate* franchise, *Prometheus*, and beyond.

Perhaps more so than any other UFOlogical facet, Ancient Astronaut theory has struck a chord with the public at large, having demonstrated its enduring appeal not only to the UFO crowd, but to those typically less inclined towards belief in the seemingly impossible. Jason Colavito convincingly accounts for this:

> If you say that you saw a UFO or that you were abducted by aliens you personally would be labelled a kook and a crazy person because in most people's daily life and experience that's not the kind of the thing that happens and it's rather difficult to believe that it happens to any given person. On the other hand, setting all of this back thousands of years it sort of falls behind the veil of history and you can look at it and say 'well maybe it did happen back then – that was a long time ago when things were different.' And it benefits from a sort of residual belief that people have that in ancient times there were gods, monsters and miracles. It's harder to imagine these almost supernatural events occurring today in the world in which we live and interact with others, but to set them in a sort of semi-mythical past becomes something that's more plausible, if only because people know less about it and can fill in the gaps of their ignorance with myth.[43]

However, although the AA theory is tenuous in its specific assertions, the general theory of ancient alien visitation is far from ludicrous. In August 2011, Professor Paul Davies, Chair of SETI's Post-Detection Science and Technology Task Group, suggested that "a very advanced [alien] technology might leave... subtle footprints requiring sophisticated scientific methods to uncover." In a paper titled 'Footprints of Alien Technology,' Davies insists: "We must not overlook the possibility that alien technology has impacted our immediate astronomical environment, even Earth itself, but probably a very long time ago. This raises the question of what traces, if anything, might remain today..." Davies then goes on to consider the possibilities of biological, geological and physical traces, and how we might search for them.[44]

Debates surrounding the origin and construction of ancient civilizations around the globe will assuredly continue for decades to come, and, for many people, satisfactory answers will remain elusive. But so long as Hollywood sees fit to mine and develop AA-lore, it's a safe bet that Ancient Astronaut theory will be captivating the public at large long after Erich von Däniken departs our world on his own heavenly chariot.

CHAPTER SEVEN

NEED TO KNOW

"The human race has been drip-fed images of my face,
on lunchboxes and T-shirts and shit..."

– Paul, the Gray alien (Seth Rogen), *Paul* (2011)

This final chapter brings us to UFO conspiracy movies and TV
shows – entertainment products in which a cover-up of extraterrestrial visitation is central or significant to the plot. Governments in these narratives are usually depicted as nefarious entities
acting above the law in order to protect their explosive UFO secrets.

Here we look at the emergence of conspiracy lore in the UFO field
and how the subcultural notion of a grand UFO cover-up was gradually adopted and popularized by Hollywood. A detailed production
history of the 1994 TV movie *Roswell* is presented as a key illustration
of this cultural process.

Also considered is the idea that Hollywood has been exploited to
encourage a belief within conspiracy communities that officialdom is
actually deeply knowledgeable about UFOs and is on a level pegging
with alien intelligences. In this context, particular emphasis is placed on
three productions: 1. *UFO Cover-Up?: Live!* (1988), which was targeted
for monitoring and manipulation by intelligence agencies, or else was
created from the outset as tool in a psychological warfare campaign; 2.

The Disney documentary *Alien Encounters from New Tomorrowland* (1995), which may also have been produced for UFO disinformation purposes; and 3. *Dark Skies* (1996–1997), Bryce Zabel's sci-fi TV show, which again appears to have been targeted for narrative subversion by shadowy agencies.

The first chapter of this book presents clear evidence of high levels of official UFO secrecy in the United States dating back to the earliest years of the phenomenon. Many thousands of now declassified files pertaining to UFOs from the US and other governments are testament to the seriousness with which officialdom has long regarded unidentified objects in the skies of Earth. Most of these files took decades to find their way into the public domain. For the first thirty years of the flying saucer phenomenon, the American public was assured repeatedly that, when it came to UFOs, there was nothing to see and certainly nothing to hide. Public interest was quelled (or not) by repeated USAF statements about flocks of geese, weather balloons, and swamp gas. Still, the sightings continued.

Early secrecy and its depictions

Amidst the official debunkery of the time, one (ex-) military man stood out boldly for his outspoken views on flying saucers. Major Donald Keyhoe was publicly adamant that the phenomenon was not only real, but was likely interplanetary in nature and that this was known full well to the US government. Keyhoe presented these views in a widely-read article for *True* magazine in January 1950. Later that same year he expanded his article into a book, *The Flying Saucers Are Real*, which sold more half a million copies in paperback. UFOs and official secrecy were now entrenched firmly together in popular debate.[1]

The summer of 1952 saw the national defense apparatus in a state of high panic following mass UFO sightings over Washington D.C., the underlying reality of which was supported by official radar returns. In a crowded press conference held on 29 July 1952, USAF Major Generals John Samford and Roger Ramey attributed the sightings to a combination of "temperature inversions" and misidentified stars and meteors.

By this point Hollywood had already begun to engage with the phenomenon with the likes of *The Flying Saucer* (1950), and, more notably, in *The Day the Earth Stood Still* and *The Thing from Another World* (both 1951). The first movie attracted the attention of the USAF for its director's sensationalist claims that he was in possession of real UFO footage, while the latter movies were the first to depict official engagement with UFOs as extraterrestrial vehicles. A cover-up is out of the question in *The Day the Earth Stood Still* as the saucer's arrival is so conspicuous, but in *The Thing from Another World*, the crash of a saucer and its occupant is cause for grave concern to USAF officers, who wish to bury the alien and the story. Both of these movies may have been covertly manipulated by the CIA, as discussed in Chapters Two and Three.

The 1957 movie *Invasion of the Saucer Men* was notable for drawing inspiration from the 1955 'Kentucky farm siege' case, but also for dialogue alluding to real-world government secrecy surrounding the UFO phenomenon. When the eponymous saucer men begin their small-town siege, military personnel show up to investigate, remarking at the sight of a grounded saucer, "Amazing! One of them actually landed intact!" The implication is that saucer wrecks have been recovered by authorities in the past. Observing the saucer, one of the military men states, "Only us and the President will know," which suggests that his unit is tasked specifically to UFO-related matters. There is even an allusion to compartmentalization of classified information in dialogue referring to "other secret units covering-up other secret things."

Continuing denials and official disengagement

Despite witnesses claiming clandestine visits from government UFO spooks, the official line remained unchanged – UFOs were of no concern to officialdom and the phenomenon was unworthy of secrecy.

In 1966 two USAF officers sat for a televised interview to discuss the history and function of Project Blue Book. The officers in question were Lt Colonel Laurence Tacker, formerly the chief spokesman of Blue Book, and Major Hector Quintanilla, the then head of the USAF UFO project. Both men looked uncomfortable throughout and delivered clearly rehearsed answers to softball questions. At one point their interviewer asks the officers to respond to allegations of a USAF UFO cover-up. "These charges are absolutely untrue," states

Col. Tacker. "There is nothing to hide?" He is prompted. "There is nothing to hide at all," Tacker replies sternly, before staring awkwardly into the camera.

Major Quintanilla is then asked: "Is there anything in the files, either classified or unclassified that would indicate that there may be extraterrestrial visitors?" To which the answer comes: "First of all, the project is completely unclassified and there is nothing in the record that would indicate that we have been visited by an alien civilization."[2]

Three years later, in 1969, Blue Book was closed forever and the USAF wiped its hands of the UFO issue. Officially, at least. By this point the Freedom of Information Act had been created, and throughout the 1970s and 1980s UFO researchers would seek out and acquire reams of formerly secret UFO-related documentation from every branch of the US military, as well as from the CIA and other intelligence agencies. Slowly, a very different picture began to emerge than that historically painted by officialdom. UFOs clearly had been a constant source of puzzlement, concern, and frustration for the US government. While there was no 'smoking gun' for alien visitation in the files, there was plenty of cumulative evidence to support the theory that some UFOs might be of non-human origin.

Blue Book onscreen

Almost a decade after it closed, Project Blue Book would get its very own unofficial TV show. Airing between 1978 and 1979, *Project U.F.O.* drew direct inspiration from real Blue Book files, which had recently been declassified. The episodes revolved around two UFO investigators from the Foreign Technology Division at Wright Patterson Air Force Base (played by William Jordan and William Caskey Swaim) who travel around the country seeking explanations for reported UFO sightings and encounters. The show served as significant inspiration for *The X-Files*, which was created 14 years after the cancellation of *Project U.F.O.*

In reality, the Blue Book officers went to great lengths to avoid exotic conclusions in their investigations. In the show, however, a considerable number of the cases examined are strongly suggestive of alien visitation. Boasting former Pentagon spokesman Col. William Coleman as a producer and technical advisor, the show can perhaps be read as an unofficial (and thus politically safe) DoD endorsement of the extraterrestrial hypothesis. A few years earlier, Coleman had appeared in Robert Emenegger's Pentagon-backed pro-UFO documentary *UFOs: Past Present and Future*, in which he spoke open-mindedly about the ETH. He would further subtly support the ETH the following decade in the broadcast of *UFO Cover-Up?: Live!* (1988), discussed later in this chapter.

Also worthy of note in the context of Blue Book is the cult TV series *Twin Peaks* (1990-1991), which explored a range of paranormal phenomena, synchronicities, and the occasional UFO sighting in the fictional town of Twin Peaks in Washington State. Blue Book featured significantly in the second season of the show. The character of Blue Book officer Major Garland Briggs (played by Don S. Davis, who would later go on to play a very a similar role in *Stargate SG-1*), reveals to the show's protagonist, FBI agent Dale Cooper (Kyle MacLachlan), that the USAF has been intercepting transdimensional radio signals from an otherworldly realm inhabited by beings who feed on human pain and suffering. This idea would later become central to David Icke's elaborate reptilian conspiracy narrative.

Privileged contact

Spielberg's UFO epic *Close Encounters of the Third Kind* was released in 1977. The movie depicted the USAF and NASA as permanently one step behind the UFO phenomenon, pursuing its rapidly accelerating manifestations around the world while attempting to guess its next move in the hopes of meeting the alien intelligences face-to-face, which ultimately they do, covertly. The public at large is kept in the dark throughout. In one scene, clearly modeled on televised UFO dismissals from Blue Book personnel in decades prior, a USAF representative addresses concerned citizens and reporters, assuring them that UFOs are non-existent. Holding up a convincing photograph of a UFO, the rep, Major Benchley, declares: "Ladies and gentlemen, this is a flying saucer." Then, picking up a silver pie plate, he continues, "It's made of pewter, made in Japan, and thrown across the lawn by one of my children."

Elaborate cover stories are also put in place, as when a compliant media falsely reports a chemical spill near Devils Tower, requiring total civilian evacuation of the area so no one can witness the government/alien contact.

In Spielberg's movie, UFO disclosure is for the privileged few only, namely those in officialdom and a handful of contactees who have been compulsively drawn to the site of contact, much to the annoyance of the secret-keepers. What happens after Roy Neary departs on the mothership is never hinted at, but, given the secret nature of alien-human communion we have just witnessed, it is safe to assume that the lid will stay firmly shut on UFO reality in the wider world.

Evidence of historical UFO secrecy was presented throughout the 1980s in a number of popular books, including Lawrence Fawcett and Barry Greenwood's *Clear Intent* (1984) and Timothy Good's bestselling *Above Top Secret* (1987).

In *Clear Intent* the authors describe how the CIA successfully infiltrated and gradually dismantled the National Investigations Committee on Aerial Phenomena (NICAP) – a major civilian UFO research organization established in the 1950s with Donald Keyhoe on its board of governors. The first director of the CIA, Roscoe Hillenkoetter, would later join NICAP as a governor, and more men with Agency ties would join in years to come. Fawcett and Greenwood explained how these individuals came to control NICAP from within during the 1960s and 1970s as Keyhoe was pushing ever harder for government disclosure of UFO reality. Eventually Keyhoe was ousted as NICAP Director by Joseph Bryan, former chief of the CIA's psychological warfare staff. From here on in, NICAP became notably less active and competent as a scientific UFO investigations group. By 1980 it was defunct.[3]

The CIA's take-over of NICAP was significant for it established a clear historical intent on the part of intelligence agencies to infiltrate the UFO community and to influence it from within. This was an ongoing strategy that would invisibly steer the direction of UFO research in the following decades.

Wavelength

In the early-to-mid 1980s Roswell had yet to break big in pop-culture, or even the UFO community. However, at least one Hollywood production from this time period took inspiration from the incident.

The low-budget, little-seen 1983 movie *Wavelength* concerns a UFO being shot down with a laser by the USAF and its friendly alien occupants being held captive at a top secret facility in the desert. The aliens in the movie are played by children, as Spielberg's were in *Close Encounters* a few years earlier. The beings here, although far more humanlike than Spielberg's, also call to mind those reported by Roswell witnesses and in later abduction accounts with their small stature and bald heads. There is even a scene in which a dead alien is autopsied by military doctors, which anticipated the infamous 'Alien Autopsy' footage widely released in 1995, which purported to show the dissection of a real Roswell alien in 1947. The footage was later exposed as a hoax.[4]

Wavelength was written and directed by Mike Gray, who had penned the screenplay for *The China Syndrome* (1979). Artist and UFO researcher David Sankey wrote to Gray in 2009 seeking a response to a rumor in the UFO community that his film had been produced in collaboration with the government and was inspired not by Roswell, but by an alleged incident in which the US military shot down a UFO in California in the early 1970s.

Sankey wrote to Gray:

> Over the years in my role as researcher I have come across many references to statements by a variety of people that the basic storyline plot to *Wavelength* was actually based on a factual account or incident which took place at 'Hunter Liggett' 90 miles south-south-east of Monterey, California. With this in mind, I would like to be direct and ask if there is any truth in these statements and were you influenced in any way by other parties in preparation for the original *Wavelength* screenplay? By other parties I mean specifically governmental or military personal who may have approached you in an advisory capacity to see that specific details and information should be contained within the film structure.

Gray wrote back to Sankey that same day. His email read, in part:

> It was totally my idea without any input from ex-government officials. I simply took the story of the Roswell incident and asked, "What if they were just tourists?" The whole thing was fiction from start to finish. On the other hand, I've always been convinced that the government was hiding something about Roswell.[5]

Here come the Men in Black

The 1984 movie *The Brother from Another Planet* was the first ever to feature the Men in Black of UFO lore.

In numerous accounts over the decades, mysterious black-suited men have been described as harassing UFO witnesses, often visiting them at their homes and demanding details of their saucer sightings. Sometimes the men attempt to silence the witnesses through intimidation. Sometimes they show official-looking identification badges for various government or military agencies. In many cases, however, the Men in Black seem barely human, having been described as almost alien in their actions and appearance, often speaking and moving robotically and appearing distinctly out of place in an Earthly environment. The UFO literature is littered with such accounts. In his book *On the Trail of the Saucer Spies*, author Nick Redfern writes:

> Since the early 1950s, the mysterious Men in Black (MIB) have been a persistent part of UFO lore, as have their attempts to silence UFO witnesses. Precisely who they are and what lies behind their sinister activities provokes controversy to this day. Time after time the Men in Black are described as being dressed in black suits, black hats, black ties, and white shirts. They are often short in stature, extremely thin, with slightly Asian features. They also seem to have a tenuous grasp of the English language, with some even exhibiting a monotone-style of speaking, and they are glaringly unaware of our most basic customs and conventions.[6]

While a number of UFO movies in previous decades had featured black-suited government spooks investigating saucer sightings, it was not until *The Brother from Another Planet* that the Men in Black were depicted precisely as described in the literature.

In the movie, the MIBs (played by John Sayles and David Strathairn) are gaunt, pale-faced figures clad entirely in black, whose behaviour is threatening, robotic, and bizarre, and with good reason – they are alien bounty hunters in search of the Brother. In the film's closing credits they are even listed as "Men in Black."

Sayles wrote his film in the early-1980s after having worked on the script for Spielberg's aborted alien horror movie *Night Skies*, elements of which would ultimately be used in the Spielberg productions *E.T. The Extraterrestrial* (1982), *Poltergeist* (1982), and *Gremlins* (1984). Evidently,

Sayles had at some point familiarized himself with the details of MIB lore, likely during his research for *Night Skies*, which itself was directly inspired by the 1955 Kelly-Hopkinsville incident, one of the most famous cases of alleged alien contact in UFO literature.

In *The Brother from Another Planet*, Sayles paid close attention to the bizarre physical motion of his MIBs. In order to convey their otherworldliness, the director filmed their entrance and exit scenes entirely in reverse and with the camera upside down. The effect is subtle, but creepy.

Spies, lies, and perception management

In 1980, intelligence operatives launched an ambitious disinformation campaign through the UFO community. It began with researcher William Moore, whose co-authored book *The Roswell Incident* had been published earlier that year. Moore knew full well that he was being used by US intelligence – he was told so explicitly by those who were using him. Moore was fine with this, though, as he had made a secret deal with them.

Moore's original intelligence contact was an enigmatic individual who went unnamed for many years. He was eventually revealed by author Greg Bishop to have been Harry Rositzke (now deceased), a former high-ranking CIA officer brought out of retirement.[7] Moore referred to Rositzke publicly only as 'Falcon.' In his book, *Project Beta*, Greg Bishop describes how Falcon (Rositzke) told Moore that "he represented a group of intelligence agents in the US government who were tired of the secrecy surrounding the UFO subject and were eager to release more accurate information to the public. They wanted to do this through a reputable researcher." Moore, apparently, was their man. Or one of them, at least.

There was a catch, though. "To get at the UFO info, he would have to agree to give the government people something in return."[8] This "something" was to help the intelligence operatives plant particular ideas into the UFO community, sowing truth with fiction, and to monitor and report back on how this information was being received, interpreted, and spread. "Moore was an asset, and nothing more," writes Bishop. "He was just another game piece on Falcon's board."[9]

Enter Richard Doty

In October of 1980 Falcon introduced Moore to Richard Doty, a Special Agent with the Air Force Office of Special Investigations at Kirtland Air Force Base in New Mexico. Doty would thereafter become Moore's primary intelligence contact. In other words, Doty became Moore's handler. But Doty was handled by Falcon (Rositzke), who was himself almost certainly acting on the authority of the CIA, or elements within it.

It got even more complicated, as Greg Bishop observes:

> Within a few years, Moore and his colleagues would begin to assign code names to their growing coterie of contacts so that they could talk freely about developments without fear of identification if they were overheard. All were given the names of birds, and were collectively referred to as the 'Aviary'.[10]

Moore would eventually confess to his role as an intelligence asset in spectacular fashion at the annual MUFON conference in 1989. Instead of delivering his scheduled UFO talk, he described how he had made a deal with the intelligence community, but that his plan all along had been to "play the disinformation game and to get his hands just dirty enough to lead those directing the process into believing that he was doing exactly what they wanted him to do. All the while he would continue to burrow his way into the defense and intelligence matrix to learn who was directing it and why."[11]

The UFO community was outraged at Moore's confession, and Moore knew better than to stick around. He left the stage quickly that night, and the UFO field too. Other researchers had little inclination to pick up the pieces, and the disinformation campaign was far from over.

In 1983, three years after his first meeting with William Moore, Richard Doty invited journalist and cattle mutilation researcher Linda Moulton Howe to Kirtland Air Force Base, where he showed her what he said were top secret documents concerning UFO crash/retrievals and ancient alien visitation. The documents suggested that aliens from Zeta Reticuli were the creators of our species. Doty implied to Howe that the powers that be were now ready to release some of this information to the public at large, and that she was to play a role in the acclimation process.

A few months prior to Howe's visit with Doty, New York Attorney Peter Gersten, the legal advisor for Citizen's Against UFO Secrecy

(CAUS), had also been given 'inside' information by Doty. Howe later summarized this meeting: "Doty claimed the government and ETs have made an agreement. The aliens could conduct animal mutilations and human abductions in exchange for teaching U.S. experts about alien advanced technologies."[12]

MJ-12

The following year, in December 1984, Hollywood producer Jamie Shandera, research partner to intelligence asset William Moore, received a roll of undeveloped film, which, when processed, showed photos of documents discussing a purported saucer crash near Roswell, New Mexico, in 1947. The documents described how the saucer crash led to the establishment of 'Majestic 12,' or 'MJ-12,' a group of twelve top-tier science and military men charged by the president with secretly managing the UFO issue and understanding the true nature and purpose of the phenomenon, especially the advanced technologies involved.[13]

In the following years other MJ-12 documents were quietly 'discovered.'[14] The content of the newer documents supported that of the originals, convincing Shandera and Moore that MJ-12 was the real deal, and that elements within the US government had been involved in hands-on research and development of alien technologies dating back to the late-1940s and had even established treaties with the UFO occupants. The men sat on the MJ-12 documents for three years before Moore shared them with the broader UFO community in June of 1987. He did so on the advice of Falcon (Rositzke). British UFO writer Timothy Good had also independently received the MJ-12 documents in 1987 and later that same year published a handful of them in his bestselling book *Above Top Secret*.[15]

The MJ-12 documents have since been subjected to extensive forensic examination, including by the FBI, and have been convincingly shown to be fraudulent. Still, it is agreed that whoever created them went to a great deal of trouble to do so. In short, the documents realistically could only have been the product of a laborious counterintelligence operation. This has not stopped the majority of UFO researchers from accepting the MJ-12 story in essence. As noted by George P. Hansen in his book *The Trickster and the Paranormal*, from the 1980s onwards, "MJ-12, or a similar group by any other name, became a centerpiece of theorizing by UFOlogists. It established a governing paradigm for many researchers. They gathered snippets of evidence and tried fitting them into this framework."[16] It was a framework built around Roswell and the tantalizing notion that officialdom had an intimate understanding and firm control of the UFO issue.

UFOs go live

This emerging narrative was further enriched and popularized on 14 October 1988, with the broadcast of *UFO Cover-up?: Live!*, a nationally televised two-hour live special examining the history of UFOs and UFO secrecy. Hosted by actor Mike Farrell, the show was billed as the ultimate exposé of the UFO cover-up. It featured interviews with former Blue Book head Col. Robert Friend and former Pentagon spokesman Col. William Coleman, as well as filmmaker Robert Emenegger and Holloman Air Force Base security officer Paul Shartle (who claimed to have seen the alien landing footage which was promised but never delivered to Emenegger in the 1970s). A number of high-profile UFO witnesses were also interviewed.

The stars of the show were William Moore and Jamie Shandera, who here introduced the world to their Aviary 'informants,' Falcon and Condor, who appeared in the show only in silhouette and with their voices electronically distorted. As if things weren't mysterious enough already, the silhouetted 'Falcon' was not the real Falcon, but was in fact Richard Doty, who was standing in for his boss, Harry Rositzke. It was later learned that Rositzke was sat in the studio audience all along, silently watching the whole thing unfold.[17] 'Condor' would later be revealed to be former USAF Captain Robert Collins, who, like Doty, had also been stationed at Kirtland Air Force Base.[18]

Between them, Moore, Shandera, 'Falcon' (Doty), and Condor discussed MJ-12, UFO crash retrievals (including Roswell), and the relationship between the US government and two Extraterrestrial Biological Entities or "EBEs," dubbed EBE-1 and EBE-2, as well as alien biology and culture (including the EBEs' love of strawberry ice cream and ancient Tibetan music!). In its pop-cultural 'blink-and-you-miss-it' debut, Area 51 was also fleetingly mentioned in text form. This was no accident, as the following year Area 51 would serve as the focus of the next chapter of the secret keepers' finely tailored overarching UFOlogical narrative. In the show, Falcon (Doty) also introduced the idea that the government's UFO research programs ultimately operate under the control of US Naval Intelligence. Again, this was an important detail that would resurface in the years to come. More on this later.

UFO Cover-Up?: Live! served to crystalize and synthesize all elements of the emerging UFO 'core story' which had been sown into the UFO community by government spooks up to that point.

The show was produced by Michael B. Seligman, who for years had been a key organizer of Academy Awards ceremonies. He was and is a man of considerable influence in Hollywood. Also involved as a producer was Tracy Tormé, screenwriter of *Fire in the Sky* and *Intruders*. In a 2014 interview, Tormé explained to me his involvement in *UFO Cover-Up?: Live!* and the bizarre events that unfolded during its development and production.

The inside story

"I get this call from these producers, and they're doing this thing called *UFO Cover-Up?: Live!* and they'd like me to be a producer on it," Tormé told me. "There was a producer named Kurt Bruebaker, and there was Michael B. Seligman, who had been a long time 'second banana' on the Academy Awards shows. So I met all these people and at first there were some really high hopes for this project. It was going to be two hours long, it was going to be live, they were going to spare no expense, they were going to get to the bottom of all this, and they wanted to expose the cover-up of UFOs and everything, and it all got off to a pretty good start."

Things began to get weird when the enigmatic William Moore forced himself on the project. At this point Moore had yet to confess his longstanding role as a controlled asset for the US intelligence community. That confession would come the following year. "Bill Moore wanted to get involved in the project because he'd heard all about it," Tormé recalled. "So he came in and it was very, very cloak and dagger. He insisted on meeting the producers behind closed doors, and they couldn't tell any of us what they had discussed." Before long, Moore flew the producers out to an island in the middle of the Great Lakes where he introduced them to his inside informants, 'Falcon' (Doty, not Rositzke) and 'Condor' (Robert Collins).

"After this meeting took place on a power boat in the middle of one of the great lakes, Michael Seligman came back and was scared of his own shadow," Tormé continued. "I mean, it was just kind of unbelievable to see the change in him. He was very, very uptight suddenly. He was very, very nervous. He was paranoid. He would constantly be telling people to keep their voices down when we were talking in the offices. He was obviously worried someone was listening to us."

After hearing tales of MJ-12 and who knows what else from 'Falcon' and Condor, Seligman showed signs of cracking. "He just went completely off the deep end," said Tormé, "he started making a lot of really irrational decisions. We were doing a completely live show, but Michael insisted that every person that appeared on camera during the two hours have to read off cue cards. His reasoning was that he didn't want anyone saying anything he wasn't expecting. He wanted to know what they were going to say. So what ended up happening was that every interview had this wooden, artificial, stupid quality to it."

I asked Tormé if he felt the TV show had been targeted and hijacked for UFO disinformation purposes. "At that time there were people who were intentionally spreading disinformation to a select group of researchers, including Bill Moore, Jamie Shandera, Linda Moulton Howe, amongst others." Tormé acknowledged. "False information was being funnelled to these people. Obviously Richard Doty was one of the disinformants, and he was also involved in *UFO Cover-Up?: Live!* So there is a certain amount of truth to the conspiracy rumours. There may have been outside efforts to exert some control over the project through Mike Seligman, who was so weak-kneed by that point, and so freaked out by whatever it was that he had been told, that we were rudderless. We had no one in charge of this project."

When I asked what could have caused such an extreme reaction from Seligman, Tormé speculated that, "They probably told him something that sounded very ominous, like we were headed towards an alien invasion, or something like that. And Seligman just bought it, hook, line, and sinker."[19]

In the context of *UFO Cover-Up?:Live!* and the disinformative events leading up to it beginning in the early-1980s, George Hansen astutely observes that:

> Any legitimate analysis that tries to explain belief about UFOs must recognize that the UFO subculture is awash in disinformation spread by government personnel, and that this has played an enormous role in shaping the subculture. Virtually all UFO investigators who make regular public presentations are from time to time approached by people who claim to have seen materials or documents while

in military service that confirmed that the government has UFO projects... These low-profile informants are a major source of UFO beliefs held by millions of people. Their information circulates quietly throughout the culture... [20]

This is demonstrably the case. But the next 'informant' was far from low-profile. This one would shout from the rooftops, and his testimony would become a central pillar of modern UFO conspiracy theory.

Bob Lazar and Area 51

In November of 1989, a thirty-year-old scientist by the name of Bob Lazar was interviewed exclusively by the respected investigative reporter George Knapp for the Las Vegas-based KLAS TV station. The topic of the interview was Lazar's alleged recent employment at a top secret facility called S-4, which was located close to another top secret facility called Area 51 (unknown to the public at the time). The story Lazar told was jaw-dropping, if true, which it appeared to be, based on his scientific knowledge and cool demeanour, and on supporting circumstantial evidence for his claims that had been gathered by Knapp.

Lazar's story has now been extensively documented in countless articles, books, and TV documentaries. The story he told Knapp in 1989 has not changed at all to this day. I, for one, am absolutely confident in stating that Lazar was, and is, telling the truth as he saw it. In other words, he has not consciously spoken untruths in his recollections of Area 51 and S-4. However, the story that he tells is almost certainly untrue. Or, rather, many of the circumstances and events that constitute the story were carefully orchestrated and staged specifically for Lazar as part of a sophisticated and ongoing UFO perception management campaign (which likely has counterintelligence purposes far beyond the UFO subject).

As has been documented by Knapp and others, there is every reason to believe that Lazar really did work at and/or near Area 51 for a short time in the late 1980s. But it appears he was cherry picked for his job based on his psychological profile and his spotty personal and business history.[21] In other words, it was known and desired that he would blow the whistle when the time came, and that it would be easy to publicly discredit him after he did so, ensuring that his story would not be accepted by all, but by just enough to engrain into a rapidly expanding subcultural belief system.

Lazar described to Knapp how he had been recruited to work at S-4 for just a few weeks in 1988 and 1989. Everything was cloaked in secrecy and the atmosphere at the base was oppressive. Information was shared there strictly on a need-to-know basis and his every move was closely monitored by armed security personnel.

Lazar claimed that he was tasked with helping his employers at S-4 to understand the propulsion system of a highly advanced air/space vehicle, which was being stored in one of nine camouflaged hangars at the facility. When Lazar first set eyes on the craft – which was classic saucer-shaped and which he later dubbed 'the sports model' – he assumed it was man-made. He had not been a believer in flying saucers; at least not of the alien variety. As the days and weeks went by, however, Lazar came to the conclusion that the craft must have been extraterrestrial in origin. Its technology was far too advanced to have been of human design, and, furthermore, its seats were far too small to accommodate human adults. They were child-sized, he said. At one point, Lazar actually bore witness to a test flight of the craft at the base. It simply lifted off the ground and returned vertically to its original position. But it did so in absolute silence without any form of thrust propulsion, which impressed Lazar greatly.

While at S-4 on another occasion, Lazar was taken into an office and shown weighty briefing documents, which he was told to study. They described how aliens from Zeta Reticuli – the classic Grays – had been interacting with humanity for at least 10,000 years. Literally everything Lazar read in the documents regarding human history, alien biology, and political events, supported the claims of Falcon, Condor, and the content of the MJ-12 documents and of the documents shown to Linda Moulton Howe.

The question is, why was Lazar, who was supposedly employed strictly on a need-to-know basis as a physicist with one very specific technical task, given access to top secret documentation which had literally no bearing on that task. The answer can only be that Lazar was being deliberately seeded with disinformation and was expected to later share it with the public. The nature of this disinformation was totally in-keeping with that already spread through the likes of Bill Moore and Jamie Shandera via Richard Doty and his superiors. Lazar was even issued with an ID badge which read "U.S. Department of Naval Intelligence." Also prominently featured on the badge was the word "MAJ" – an abbreviation of Majestic. All the pieces seemed to fit.

UFO Cover-Up?: Live! aired in October of 1988. Lazar began his employment at S-4 just two months later in December of that year. Lazar, it seems, was the next phase of the plan – just another pawn in an epic UFOlogical chess game.

As a final thought on the orchestrated nature of his Area 51 experience, Lazar described how, on one of his final nights at S-4, he set eyes on an alien entity working quite literally side-by-side with human scientists. At least, that is what he was meant to *believe* he saw. On the night in question, Lazar was being escorted down a hallway by armed security personnel who had instructed him to keep his eyes forward at all times. With this instruction in mind, as they passed a doorway, naturally Lazar peeked momentarily to one side. His peripheral vision detected what he thought in that moment was one of the Gray aliens he had read about in the briefing documents. The small figure was stood between two men in lab coats. The three of them were looking at a computer console with their backs to the door. Lazar's glimpse was so fleeting that no fine details were distinguishable. He was then pushed further along the corridor by one of the guards who instructed him once again to keep his eyes forward. Even in his telling of his story in 1989, Lazar was of the opinion that this particular incident was staged specifically for him, speculating that someone was playing mind games with him and that what he had seen was actually a doll or a dummy.

Bob Lazar's story went global, fast. Although it quickly became the new central focus of the UFO community, it was a few years before Hollywood had time to assimilate the Area 51 story and work it into its sci-fi narratives. Once that process started, however, there was no stopping it.[22]

Trust no one

No entertainment product has so tantalisingly explored notions of UFO secrecy as *The X-Files*, which ran from 1993 to 2002. The righteous pursuit of 'UFO truth' was embodied in the character of Fox Mulder, who was just one step away from unravelling his government's UFO conspiracy and understanding the aliens' ultimate agenda. This was at the heart of the series' overarching narrative – the truth was "out there" to be discovered, and individual obsession to the point of religious devotion was key to its discovery. This idea held tremendous appeal for the UFO community. UFOlogy had always been a New Age religion, but this was never quite so evident as in the age of Fox Mulder.

In the show, as in pre-established UFO lore, UFO secrecy is maintained not by the government per se, but by rogue elements within it. The show's iconic human antagonist, 'the smoking man', is a long-time member of the Syndicate, an MJ-12-style control group which operates above and beyond all laws in its efforts to conceal from the public an extraterrestrial agenda to colonize and repopulate our planet.

The X-Files' conspiracy narrative calls to mind the complimentary stories spun through the MJ-12 documents and through the aforementioned 'leakers' and 'whistle-blowers' of the time. The show engaged with and furthered almost every aspect of existing UFO mythology, particularly ideas of UFO crashes (including Roswell) and hands-on government access to alien technology (specifically at Area 51, which also featured in the series). With this in mind it is important to note that none other than Richard Doty claims to have worked as a consultant on *The X-Files* from 1994 to 1996, and even to have ghost-written an episode of the series,'The Blessing Way,' which aired on September 22, 1995. The episode featured the MJ-12-style 'Syndicate' and men in black, as well as alien abduction and implants. Doty further claims to have been an extra (again uncredited) in two episodes that same year: 'Anasazi,' and 'Paper Clip,' the stories for which were both directly related to 'The Blessing Way.'[23]

Assimilation of the core story continues

1993 saw the TV broadcast of Bryce Zabel's small-screen movie *Official Denial*, an ambitious exploration of UFO conspiracy lore featuring all elements of the emerging UFO core story, from MJ-12 and UFO crash-retrievals, to an alien in US government custody. It even anticipated reports to follow of military abductions of UFO experiencers (known in UFOlogy as 'MILABs'). *Official Denial* was perhaps the most explicitly UFOlogical movie ever produced at that point. Unfortunately, its ambitions greatly exceeded its limited budget, and its special effects were severely dated even at the time of its broadcast. It was not widely seen and has yet to receive a DVD release. We will return to *Official Denial* shortly.

The following year another TV movie would have far greater impact on popular perceptions of UFO history: *Roswell* (1994). Starring Kyle MacLachlan as whistle-blower Jesse Marcel, the Showtime movie was the first Hollywood entertainment product to focus exclusively on the still relatively unknown Roswell Incident of 1947. In a 2013 interview, writer/producer Paul Davids explained to me how his movie came to be.

Fate

"My daughter screamed at me: 'Daddy, get upstairs! I see a flying saucer!'" Even by phone, it was clear that Paul Davids was almost re-living the event. On 25 February 1987, Davids was at home in his office, working on the script for what would become *Starry Night* – his whimsical fantasy film about Vincent van Gogh.

"My daughter was in her room on the second floor. My son was home. She was nine. He was six," Davids recalled. His daughter's initial flying saucer alert was dismissed out of hand. His daughter became hysterical. "She said: 'Daddy, get up here! I mean it! It's a flying saucer, I mean it! Get up here right now!' Davids did as he was told.

Before that day, Davids had not been a believer in UFOs. "It wasn't until the moment that I set my eyes on it that I took anything seriously about this at all. But when I saw it, my reaction was 'Oh, my God.'" Davids and his children stepped out onto the roof together, awestruck. "It was there," he said, "descending from a high dramatic cloud. It approached us when we were out on the roof. And then it hovered above our two front trees out over the road in front of our house. It was at least the size of the cockpit of a helicopter."

Disc-shaped? I asked. "Yes. Absolutely classic saucer. Very clear. It was sort of a dull gray, and it had a dome on top meeting like an upside-down plate. No portholes. It did not make a sound." Davids and his children watched the object for several minutes and felt that whoever was piloting it was staring right back at them. "It seemed to be aware of us by its movements," he explained. "It took a position in a little space between the leaves of the trees, but there was still eye contact. It seemed deliberate, and it hovered there." The object came to within 500 feet of their position before it "swooped down" across the valley. "Then, in the blink of an eye it was gone... It just wasn't there anymore."

Fate had dealt Davids his hand. "That was how it started," he said, "that day, at four o'clock, my life changed." His sighting that afternoon would start a seven-year chain reaction involving long-buried truths and Hollywood legends, and that would eventually play a major role in the popularization of a word that has since captured the imagination of millions: Roswell.

"I couldn't dislodge it from my mind," said Davids of his saucer sighting. "It became a focus of my attention for the months that followed. By the end of that summer I think I had bought and read a couple hundred UFO books." Though he didn't know it yet, Davids was already on his personal road to Roswell. For further input about his sighting, Davids spoke with Roy Thinnes, the star of the iconic 1960s UFO-themed TV show *The Invaders*. Thinnes had developed a real-life interest in UFOs during the course of playing his TV role, and the actor duly prepared a report about Davids' sighting and sent it to the J. Allen Hynek Center for UFO Studies in Chicago where it was received by UFO investigator Don Schmitt – one of only a small handful of people in the world at that point (including UFO researcher Stanton Friedman) who were taking an active interest in the long-dormant Roswell case. The Air Force had officially explained the mysterious crash as a "weather balloon," but the residents of Roswell had for years been whispering a more interesting story.

"Don came to visit me on his next trip to Los Angeles," Davids continued, "and he told me that he and his friend Kevin Randle were going to reinvestigate the Roswell Incident - go down to Roswell and try to get to the bottom of it. And they asked me: 'are you interested in a movie deal about this?'" It turned out Schmitt and Randle had a seventeen–page treatment for an unwritten book about the Roswell Incident. The book, they said, could be movie gold if only someone would option it. A mere $25 sealed the deal between Schmitt, Randle, and Davids.

Davids accompanied Schmitt and Randle on a number of their visits to Roswell to interview the town's old-time residents. "I drove them from witness to witness," he explained. "I heard from the townspeople, from the former military people, from the people who'd been involved in the radio broadcasts at that time, from people who knew the rancher Mack Brazel [who discovered the wreckage]. Believe me, it's convincing. It is really, really convincing that a flying saucer from another world did crash in Roswell in 1947 and the people there were coerced into silence."

Schmitt and Randle's book, *UFO Crash at Roswell*, was published in 1991, by which point Davids had already spent two years pitching his movie adaptation to studios and TV networks. "Everyone said no," he sighed. I enquired on what grounds the suits were rejecting his pitch. "A lot of them said 'this Roswell Incident never could have happened or I would have heard of it.' They also were afraid of getting egg on their face, so to speak. And they were afraid somebody connected with it would say that it was all made up. So they backed away and wouldn't give us a deal."

Finally, after around forty rejections, Davids' Roswell pitch was picked up by HBO, only to be dropped again after 18 months of script development by Arthur Kopit, one of Davids' co-writers on the film. As the production moved into its casting stage, the plug was unceremoniously pulled. Davids and his core team were summoned before HBO bosses and told, "Sorry guys, we gotta let you know we've decided not to make the movie."

But where one door closed, another one opened, as the premium cable network Showtime enthusiastically added Roswell to its production slate. "And that was the turning point," said Davids, "because they really wanted to make it, and they poured resources into it. It was fabulous."

Davids played a major role in shaping the film's narrative structure, central to which are themes of time and memory. "I came up with the whole concept about this being a reunion at the military base – it would all be done as a flashback. Jesse Marcel [the original Roswell whistleblower], all these years later, he's going back and meeting with all the different people he knew then, trying to put together pieces of the puzzle." It was a formulaic approach, but it served well the complex and controversial source material. For Davids, the purpose of his movie was not just to entertain, but to educate, to bring the Roswell Incident to wider public attention in a powerful and comprehensible form.

Roswell is also noteworthy as being one of the first movies to feature a direct reference to Area 51. The base shows up fleetingly in a sequence in which a mysterious Falcon-style government leaker (played by Martin Sheen) describes to Jesse Marcel the events that unfolded in the months and years following the saucer crash. He reveals the existence of MJ-12 and of their attempts to communicate with one of the captured Roswell aliens. "And then there are the stories if Area 51," says Sheen's mystery man. "What is Area 51?" Asks Marcel. Sheen replies: "That's where people swear they've actually seen recovered alien craft and that we're working with them right now."

The production process for *Roswell* was relatively smooth, although not without its share of intrigue. Suspicious happenings were evident even before Showtime accepted the project. "While we were under development at HBO, I began to notice strange goings-on with my phone," Davids explained. "Weird clicking during conversations about the film; on several occasions obvious sounds of a third party being on the line; and, most notably, a call being abruptly disconnected during a conversation about the evidence for alien bodies."

Don Schmitt had told Davids at the outset that he believed his line was tapped, and Davids felt that he, too, had become a surveillance target. "The weird phone activity seemed to spread from Don, to me, and others involved in the film." More troubling to Davids were the inquisitive strangers. "There were people who 'popped into my life' trying to become new close friends as quickly as possible and who seemed to be trying to lift sensitive information about the production from me in suspicious ways." On one occasion, some strange men in a car snapped some "quick stolen photos" of Davids and Schmitt while they were driving together. "These were not paparazzi," he insisted, "the circumstances were suspicious yet done in an obvious way as if someone wanted us to know we were being watched."

Davids' sighting that fateful day in 1987 opened his eyes to a world hidden from public view. "I think the whole cover-up is a disgrace," he fumed. "I'm opposed to it from top to bottom. So that's why I made the film."

The film was a huge success, both commercially and critically, not only significantly increasing Showtime's subscriber base, but also garnering a Golden Globe nomination for best television movie. "I think the impact was considerable," said Davids of *Roswell*. "It was enormous. Millions of people saw it. Millions."

I asked Davids if the word 'Roswell' would be so culturally resonant today had he not so memorably contextualized it in his 1994 movie. "Not as much," he replied, without hesitation, although he acknowledged that *The X-Files*, which premiered a year before his movie, also played a major role. "But *The X-Files* wasn't just about Roswell," he stressed, "it was all over the place dealing with a lot of different things. Roswell was just a little part of it." Other entertainment products throughout the 1990s also contributed to the popularization of the Roswell story, most significant among which, according to Davids, were *Independence Day* (1996), *Dark Skies* (1996–1997), and *Men in Black* (1997). "By that time, Roswell was a national institution," Davids observed. "If it's a myth, which I don't believe it is for one minute, it is now a national myth massively engrained into the public consciousness, as much as any other story from the history of our country."[24]

It is hard to argue with that statement, and it is harder still to underestimate the seminal role Paul Davids played in that engraining process.

The *Roswell* movie is the perfect demonstration of the cultural dynamic between a real and mysterious phenomenon and its creative utilization by the entertainment industry. A man has a real UFO experience. This experience inspires him to make a movie about a then-little-known UFO incident. The movie is then viewed by millions of people around the world for whom this little-known incident is simultaneously actualized *and* fictionalized. The question of whether or not aliens crashed in New Mexico in 1947 is now meaningless. Aliens definitely *did* crash, because we saw it in a movie. But they definitely *didn't* crash, because we saw it in a movie. This is the effect of cinema.

Kubrick and Roswell

Roswell was now beginning to sink itself into the cultural bedrock, even capturing the attention of Stanley Kubrick. Although Kubrick was a firm believer in intelligent life elsewhere in the universe, as time wore on he became less convinced that the UFO phenomenon was representative of ET visitation. In the mid-1990s, as Roswell fever was sweeping the world in the form of books, TV shows, and movies, Kubrick was prompted to speculate as to the true nature of the Roswell Incident. The director was troubled by the fact that the USAF's official report on Roswell belatedly and begrudgingly acknowledged original witness descriptions of "bodies" associated with the crash. To Kubrick, the USAF seemed to be backtracking. The truth was indeed being buried, he surmised, but aliens had nothing to do with it.

In his book *Are We Alone?: The Stanley Kubrick Extraterrestrial Intelligence Interviews*, Kubrick's former assistant, Anthony Frewin, recalls the director's reasoning on Roswell:

> SK and I developed a theory in conversation that, we felt, explained what really went on... We would not have thought twice about the 1994 report were it not for one small item that set off alarm bells: the USAF's mention of anthropomorphic 'test dummies'... Here, for the first time, the government acknowledges that there were bodies, yes, but they were test dummies... Not far away from Roswell is the White Sands Missile Range where rockets were being tested from 1945 onwards. Could it be that what was going up in them were test humans, not dummies? The chances of fatalities were high, so we can discount the military seeking volunteers from the services when 'expendable' humans were freely available. And who were these expendable humans? How about 'mental defectives' from state asylums? If the reader thinks this too

farfetched one can point to innumerable cases of state-sponsored abuse of unwitting citizens in the twentieth century.[25]

UFOs and Disney

1995 saw the broadcast of a documentary titled *Alien Encounters from New Tomorrowland*, which officially was produced with the sole purpose of promoting Disneyworld's then-new 'ExtraTERRORestrial Alien Encounter' ride in Orlando. The content of this 'promotional' documentary reinforced ideas thus far sown into the conspiracy community by disinformation operatives. It may or may not have been intended as a furtherance of covert efforts to encourage particular beliefs within the UFO community and the public at large. In any case, it seems worthy of discussion here.

Throughout the documentary's forty-minute run-time, the presenter/narrator, Robert Urich, makes numerous declarative statements to the effect that UFOs are one-hundred-percent real and extraterrestrial in origin. Such statements include: "For nearly fifty years, officials have been documenting routine alien encounters here on earth," "More than one alien craft crashed and was recovered for secret US military research. The most famous case took place in July of 1947 just outside the community of Roswell, New Mexico," and "Indications are that government, military and scientific leaders will soon release nearly a half-century of official documentation of ongoing alien encounters on earth."

The 'ExtraTERRORestrial' ride itself received very little screen-time, with the vast majority of the documentary's content being focused on UFOs and extraterrestrials as a factual reality. The ride itself seemed like an afterthought.

The documentary was aired in only a handful of US cities at seemingly random times on selected dates in February and March 1995 with no advance notice – an incredibly odd marketing strategy considering its purpose was to promote a major theme park ride for families.

For the above reasons, many in the UFO research field came to believe that Disney's *Alien Encounters* documentary was an effort by the powers that be to prepare us for UFO disclosure.

I interviewed the documentary's writer/director, Andrew Thomas, in 2011. Thomas told me how he had been selected by Disney for the documentary project based on his background in reality television, having been the original producer of the phenomenally successful TV show, *Cops*. "Making things exceptionally real was the line of work that I was in at the time," he said. Thomas had also worked for Columbia Pictures as head of special marketing on Spielberg's *Close Encounters*.

Thomas told me that Disney had requested a documentary "about the history of mankind and aliens. Not a film history, but more of a realistic approach... a special about the history of UFO sightings." Disney's only stipulation was that "the last five minutes had to focus on the ride." Thomas confirmed to me that, instead of giving the documentary network time, Disney's plans from the outset were to "seed it into independent television stations across the country."

But why did Thomas' documentary take such a strong stance in favor of UFO/ET reality? He summed-up his approach as follows:

> I figured, instead of asking people to question 'could it be possible?' to just adopt the point of view that alien visitation has been going on for 50 years, and everybody's known about it. I thought it fit with the ultra-realistic nature of the ride that we were eventually trying to promote. I did it kind of naively. I said to myself 'okay, I'm going to believe everything and I'm going to collect all this stuff and construct what would be a documentary if we all just had a consensus that the UFO phenomenon was real...' We didn't make up anything, but it certainly surprised the people at Disney.

Thomas claims to have written the script in just a few hours while flying back from Florida to his home in Los Angeles. "There was nothing to it," he said, "it just kind of came out, it was easy." Furthermore, Thomas claims to have conducted the vast majority his research at the National Archives and stressed that, beyond these archival visits, "there was no direct government contact" on the production. "I didn't get any special access from anybody," he said.

These statements from Thomas punch sizable holes in the idea that the Disney documentary was anything other than a promo for a theme park ride. However, there were aspects of the *Alien Encounters* project that Thomas considered strange. Disney CEO Michael Eisner took a direct interest in the documentary, personally vetting its content and even filming his own introduction for the piece. Thomas mused:

> I thought it was really odd because this was kind of a minor marketing project, but Disney put a lot of weight into it. I mean, Eisner doesn't have to stop walking down the street to pick up a twenty-dollar-bill – it's not

worth his time. But they had him look through this. And he filmed this intro to the show. He had his own film crew take him out to a sound stage and film his own intro, which I thought was just really surprising.

Also surprising to Thomas was Disney's inexplicable TV schedul-ing for the documentary, which he described as "completely counter-intuitive" because "it played on independent stations in the afternoon at like 2 o'clock or 3 o' clock, or some horrible time when no one would be watching it."[26]

Why was Michael Eisner so personally invested in what, on the sur-face at least, was a minor TV marketing project? And why the bizarre and "totally counter-intuitive" TV scheduling for the documentary?

Indulging the conspiratorial interpretation of events, if powerful UFO-related interests were involved in the documentary – perhaps having recommended Thomas knowing what he would produce based on his sophisticated viral work on Spielberg's *Close Encounters* – then Thomas himself would likely be oblivious to this fact. He would have been a pawn in a much larger game. I will be the first to admit that this interpretation seems farfetched, but it is not beyond the realms of possibility. Disney maintains close historical ties with the DoD and was highlighted specifically by the CIA Robertson Panel in the 1950s as being an ideal conduit in its UFO perception management efforts. In 1994, one year prior to the *Alien Encounters* documentary, Disney had worked closely with the Pentagon during the production of *In the Army Now* (1994). The Pentagon gave this pro-military movie its full cooperation, providing Disney with expensive military hardware and on-set advice from DoD personnel.[27]

Still, I would be inclined to disregard Disney's *Alien Encounters* documentary entirely as any kind of psychological operation if not for the fact that it was tied directly to another, more baffling Disney UFO project.

Disney UFO conference

A few months before the broadcast of its *Alien Encounters* docu-mentary, in January of 1995, Disney made the unprecedented move of staging a major UFO conference at its Orlando resort. As with the documentary, the official purpose of the conference was to help promote its new ExtraTERRORestrial ride. Disney sought to bring together the world's leading UFO experts for no less that two full weeks. These included major names of the time including Budd Hopkins, George Knapp, Don Schmitt, Kevin Randle, and Zecharia Sitchin, among others. Such a line-up at the height of UFO hysteria in America would ordinarily have attracted many hundreds, if not thousands, of attendees. Strangely, though, Disney chose not to advertise their costly two-week event. As a result, the world's leading UFO speakers spoke to almost no one at all.

The man tasked with organizing the conference for Disney was Don Ecker, Director of Research at *UFO Magazine*, then the world's most popular UFO publication. I interviewed Ecker in 2015. "In a way, the Disney conference is kind of a murky legendary incident in the history of UFOs in the United States. But this is one of the only times I've ever been queried about it," he told me. Ecker recalled:

> This was going to be a two-week event and Disney wanted me to host it. They would fly me down to Orlando. I would be the person choosing all the speakers and organizing the line-up. There were two groups of speakers that came in. One group for week one, the second group for week two. Disney had set aside an auditorium for this whole thing.

It wasn't until the conference began that Ecker learned of Disney's non-promotion of the event. He told me, still in disbelief:

> Disney never gave it an ounce of promotion. They did not promote it *at all*. In the two weeks that we were there the most highly attended day for speakers in an auditorium that could have seated several hundred, we may have had 10 or 12 attendees at most. We had virtually no audience at all. That Disney didn't promote it made no sense to me then, and it makes no sense to me now.

Ecker said that abduction researcher Budd Hopkins was particularly outraged by the lack of attendees. "He just upped and left in the middle of the week," Ecker recalled. "Didn't even say goodbye or thanks." Despite the almost total lack of attendees, the other speakers (approximately twenty in total) still delivered their prepared lectures each day based on their current research.

The conference could not have been cheap. "These speakers had received airline tickets to fly in, free room, board, and meals for two weeks, everything paid for by Disney," said Ecker.

On the final evening, during a goodbye meal at the resort, Ecker received an official thank you from Disney World. Ecker told me with disgust:

> They presented me with a 'Mousker'. This Disney drone - this gofer kid - came running up to me and said, 'Mr Ecker, we have something we want to present you with.' So I followed him literally into a hallway behind one of the big rooms. A Disney executive came up to me, along with another kid carrying a cardboard box. The kid reached into the box, pulled out this statue of Mickey Mouse and they presented it to me. That was their way of saying thanks for the job I did for two weeks putting this thing together. Looking at it in retrospect, I really felt like they took me to the shower, dropped the soap in front of me, and asked me to bend over and pick it up.

The whole thing seem to defy logic from a marketing standpoint. Disney had created a costly alien-themed attraction and claimed to want to promote it through a two-pronged marketing campaign consisting of a two-week conference at Disney World and a tie-in documentary (*Alien Encounters from New Tomorrowland*). Yet, inexplicably, Disney promoted neither the conference nor the documentary, rendering both of them entirely useless as marketing tools. "It was basically like Disney taking tens-of-thousands of dollars and burning it on a bonfire," said Ecker.[28]

Perhaps there was an ulterior motive behind the conference. It was held in the mid-1990s, before the global dominance of the Internet and email, before UFOlogists began sharing all their work online. With this in mind, the conference may have been an orchestrated opportunity for intelligence agencies to assemble under one roof the leading figures in UFOlogy for an extended period of time in order to simply take the current pulse of the UFO research field. This is speculation, of course, but there would seem to be no other logical reason for the conference. It was not promoted. It was not attended. It served no obvious purpose, unless its purpose was for intelligence-gathering. Given Disney's previously stated ties to official power structures, this theory may hold at least some measure of water.

Area 51 and Roswell clear up at the box-office

1996 was a big year for UFO conspiracy theory onscreen. In August of that year, some seven years after its name was first dripped into the mainstream media in *UFO Cover-Up?: Live!*, Area 51 would serve as a central plot device in the highest grossing film of the year – *Independence Day*. The Roswell Incident, popularized two-years earlier in Paul Davids' 1994 TV movie, would also feature significantly in *Independence Day*.

The following month, Area 51, Roswell, and literally every other aspect of UFO lore would combine to drive the narrative of an ambitious new TV show – *Dark Skies*.

History as a lie

No Hollywood product has so actively sought to blur the boundaries between UFO fact and fantasy as the NBC TV show *Dark Skies*, which ran from September 1996 to May 1997.

Created by Bryce Zabel and Brent Friedman, the series presented an alternate history of 20th Century America. Its tagline read: "History as we know it is a lie." In this case, it was a lie sprung from and built around a secret extraterrestrial presence on Earth and the US government's covert efforts to understand and control the alien threat.

The narrative begins with the Roswell Incident (here a deliberate military shoot-down of an alien craft) and the establishment of the top secret working group, Majestic, which, as in the literature, is tasked with overseeing the rapidly escalating UFO problem in the United States.

We then jump forward to 1961 where the show's protagonists, John Loengard (Eric Close) and Kim Sayers (Megan Ward), a young couple with political aspirations in Washington D.C., find themselves drawn into the shadowy world of Majestic 12, headed by the imposing Frank Bach (J.T. Walsh). Whereas *The X-Files'* Fox Mulder was forever on the outside of the cover-up attempting to look in, *Dark Skies'* John Loengard was on the inside looking out. *Dark Skies* was a detailed architectural blueprint of a theoretical UFO conspiracy, but with its details drawn meticulously from real UFO literature and debate.

Each episode saw John and Kim attempting to understand and combat not only the Gray aliens, known in the series as 'The Hive', but Majestic themselves, whose motives and actions are morally dubious at best. All of this plays out against the backdrop of real historical events of the 20th Century, including the Cuban missile crisis, the assassination of JFK, the death of Marilyn Monroe, the Watts riots of 1965, and the north-east black out of that same year. Numerous cultural icons show up throughout the series, including The Beatles, Jim Morrison, Ed Sullivan, and Timothy Leary, as well as real-life figures from politics, science, and UFOlogy, such as Harry Truman, Allen Dulles, Nelson Rockefeller, J. Edgar Hoover, J. Allen Hynek, and Carl Sagan.

It is worth noting the show's Gray aliens are not innately hostile, but are being used as a slave species by parasitic aliens known as 'Ganglions,' which can infest and control any host body.

The pitch

Zabel and Friedman pitched their series to networks in the form of a faux 'Top secret' briefing file, modelled on the MJ-12 documents. The thick, ring-bound file, which they referred to as the 'Dark Skies Bible,' contained enough rich UFO lore intertwined with official history to comfortably fuel five full series of the prospective show, which had been the original plan. The file was fronted by a one-page letter 'written by' the show's fictional hero, John Loengard. It was dated 2 January 1995 and was addressed to his real-world creators. It read:

Bryce and Brent,

The truth must be told. You have been chosen as instruments to achieve this objective.
The truth, however, must <u>not</u> be represented as truth. Too many people who are needed in the struggle will die.
The cover of <u>fiction</u> must be used to present this truth. Those who fear the light will not want to bring attention to you by allowing your death. This is the only way.
Do not be afraid.
The fight for humanity demands your courage.

[SIGNED]

John Loengard.

The *Dark Skies* Bible, and the Loengard letter in particular, exemplified the now complete inseparability and symbiosis of UFOlogical 'fact' and Hollywood fantasy. Loengard's statement to his creators that they had been chosen as instruments to tell the truth about UFOs under the cover of fiction would later ring disturbingly true for Zabel and Friedman, as we shall see.

Inside Dark Skies

In 2015, Bryce Zabel shared with me his recollections of *Dark Skies*, and of his 1993 TV movie, *Official Denial*. We discussed their development, production, and reception.

I began by asking Bryce what inspired him to write *Official Denial*. He recalled:

> Like a lot of people, I had read *The Interrupted Journey* [the Hill Abduction book] when I was a kid, and I'd read *Chariots of the Gods*, but I wasn't fanatical, or militant, or political about the subject. I think Whitley Strieber's *Communion* book was very important. That encouraged me to read more on the subject, and after a year or so I thought to myself, 'I don't know if this stuff is true, but whether it's true or not, it's a damn good story and I should write about it.'

Bryce began writing the script for what would become *Official Denial* in 1988. He had a number of ideas for a UFO movie, but one in particular he knew he had to get down on paper: military abductions of UFO witnesses (MILABs, as they would later be known):

> I thought, wouldn't it be interesting if someone like Whitley Strieber or some other abductee was being monitored by the government, so that they could use the abductee as a tripwire to shoot down a UFO. To the best of my knowledge these ideas were pretty original when I was thinking of them. I don't know if they were *completely* original – maybe someone had written about them in *True* magazine or something, but certainly I'd never read about military abductions.

Whether or not MILABs were being discussed in the UFO community prior to *Official Denial*, it is safe to say the Bryce's movie was the first to give focused attention to the idea. The movie was also original in its theorizing that the aliens might not be aliens at all, but rather humans from our distant future. This idea had not featured prominently in UFO literature prior to *Official Denial*, but it would become increasingly popular in the years that followed, particularly among a number of self-proclaimed 'whistle-blowers' in the new millennium who would speak of multiple "timelines" relating to time-travelling UFOs and their trans-human occupants.

Official Denial was a passion project for Bryce, and so its less-than-perfect onscreen realization disappointed him greatly:

> The sadness of my life is that I didn't sell the script to a large film studio who would have spent 30 or 40 million dollars making the perfect version of it. Instead it got sold to a small company, which sold it to the Sci-Fi Channel [now The SyFy Channel], which made it for around $2 million. The result was that I couldn't even watch the finished product. The alien was a twelve-year-old ballerina in a plastic costume, and the effects were bad, and the acting was bad. It just wasn't on film what it was in my mind.

It was the partial failure of *Official Denial* that prompted Bryce to embark on his next UFO-themed project. "I just felt I needed to sell something to somebody who had more money so that we can do these aliens right," he recalled. The development of *Dark Skies* began in late-1994 while Bryce was working at Universal as a writer on *M.A.N.T.I.S*, Sam Raimi's short-lived TV show about an African-American super hero. "My assistant on that show introduced me to her husband, who was Brent Friedman. Brent and I started talking UFOs and it turned out he had been told certain things by a government insider."

Friedman has described this incident as follows:

> A good family friend of ours when I was just getting out of high school was working at a very high level in the Reagan administration. One night he took me aside and told me some of the things he was doing in the government, and he ended up telling me some pretty shattering stories. He knew that I'd always been into science-fiction, fantasy, and comic books, and he very casually just threw out there that 'aliens are real, they're here, and I've seen them.' At the time I was just absolutely shocked. This was a person that I grew up with and absolutely trusted, and it just rocked my world.

With their mutual interest established, Bryce and Brent set about developing what would become their *Dark Skies* Bible. "Our show was really about blending the UFO phenomenon into documented, accepted world history," Bryce told me. "Everything I had read in UFO literature ended up in *Dark Skies*, from Betty and Barney Hill to Majestic-12, you name it. I tried to weave it all in there."

Here come the real Men in Black

The inclusion of such intricate UFOlogical detail in *Dark Skies* apparently attracted the attention of real government UFO spooks.

The series pilot premiered on NBC on 21 September 1996. That same night, Bryce threw a wrap party at his Los Angeles home for his cast and crew - some 200 people in total. They would watch the pilot live together. It was a private party, invitation only. All invited guests were issued in advance with a faux Majestic-12 ID badge (loosely modeled on Bob Lazar's Area 51 ID badge) which they were required to wear throughout the evening. One man at the party that evening wore no ID badge.

"A guy showed up here," Bryce recalled. "Nicely dressed, young. Nobody recognized him. He approached Brent and myself and he told us, "We've seen your pilot." This was strange, because at that point in evening the pilot had yet to air. "Nobody else had seen it, other than a few people in Hollywood," said Bryce. The man stated again, "We've seen your pilot and we think you get a lot right, but we want to help you with the rest."

The mystery man suggested to the producers that their show could benefit from inside information on UFOs, and that he could provide them with this information. Here, then, was John Loengard sprung to life from Bryce and Brent's fictional letter, choosing them as conduits to share the truth disguised as fiction. The producers initially suspected a prank, but their *Dark Skies* pitch had been private. No one had seen their Loengard letter but for a handful of network executives in Hollywood. What's more, based on his detailed knowledge of its plot, the mystery man seemed to have really seen the unaired *Dark Skies* pilot, as he claimed. He even knew details about episodes that hadn't been filmed yet.

"Who *are* you?" the producers asked. "That's really not important right now," came the reply. "But I work with people who have an interest in what you're doing and what you're putting out." The mystery man then proceeded to grab a napkin and scrawl something on it. "It was a bunch of symbols and stuff," said Bryce. The man handed the napkin to Brent, who naturally enquired as to its meaning. "The secrets of the universe," said the man, enigmatically. "Sound, light, and frequency." I asked Bryce where the napkin is now. "I haven't seen it in years," he told me. "Brent has it locked in a safe some place."

The man and his napkin were undeniably intriguing, but this was bad timing. Bryce was playing host to 200 people. "I didn't really have time to stand around talking to this guy. But Brent invited him to our office at NBC to come and talk to us some more at a later date."

That meeting happened a few days later, and it would prove both confusing and unsettling.

Bryce described the meeting to me:

> The guy from the party shows up with two other people, older men, who he said were his bosses in Naval Intelligence. They sat around a table with us and they spoke for around two hours. They certainly had a well-constructed alternate world. They had lots of details, and they weren't shy. Actually they were a little condescending to us, saying things like, 'You guys think you're such hotshots because you're in Hollywood, but the truth is that you don't even know what you're playing with. Yes, you've stumbled into getting most of it right, but there are some things that you haven't got right.'

Cemetery at midnight

Things were about to get even stranger: "At one point the guy puts a little vile on the table and says 'you don't have this in your show.' And we're looking at it and we say 'what is this?', and he says 'this is what this is all about.' It was a vile of gold, or fool's gold, I'm not sure which." Were Bryce and Brent meant to infer that aliens were after our gold, like the Anunnaki of Ancient Astronaut lore? Or were they supposed to think the vile contained some alien element, perhaps used to fuel a flying saucer? It is impossible to know, but certainly the mystery men were intent on confusing and provoking the producers. "Their whole tone was like, 'You fucking idiots! This is what it's about! You don't even have the truth!' It was just weird."

Bryce asked again precisely who these men were. "So one of them said, 'look. We're with Naval Intelligence and if you really want us to read you in you're going to have to meet the big guy. There's a ship down in Long Beach right now and we can arrange for you to meet him. But you can't meet him on the ship."

One of the men then provided Bryce and Brent with the location of a cemetery in Long Beach, where they could meet the big guy at midnight on a given date. Bryce was now thoroughly perturbed. He had heard enough. "That's when I pushed back from the table and said 'Okay, I'm done. I have a show to run, and I have three children, and I am not meeting you or anyone else in a cemetery at midnight. Good day.'" That was the last Bryce heard from them.

What can we make of these events? Certainly they would appear to be neatly in line with disinformative strategies employed previously against UFO researchers and through entertainment media. Did intelligence operatives get wind of a new *X-Files*-style TV show utilizing factual UFOlogical detail and see it as great new opportunity to sow its content with self-serving UFO conspiracy mythology, or even simply to manage and guide the show's existing mythology? "It was very intricate," said Bryce of the whole affair. "It felt like it was staged for us. Like it was all built around us. It seems to be that we had been targeted for some elaborate disinformation job."

I asked Bryce if he felt the men were the real deal, and if there is any chance it was all just a prank by some amateur tricksters:

> Do I think they were really going to read us into a secret UFO program? No. But it did seem like they really were part of some official organization. One of the guys said he was a SEAL, and, I have to say, all of these guys looked like *very* hardcore military guys. They didn't look like soft fanboys pulling a prank on us. They didn't look like guys you'd see at Comic Con. They looked and spoke like military guys.

I asked Bryce if he believed in UFOs at the time of *Dark Skies'* development and if his intention with the show was to educate and inform the public about the subject. He replied:

> Did I intend to inform? No. I intended to entertain. But did I believe in UFOs and alien visitation? Yes. I believed strongly at the time of *Dark Skies* that Roswell was a real event and that it was probably unearthly in nature. I still believe that today. Whether or not I believed the Majestic 12 documents were real or faked was irrelevant. I just used the name because it was on people's minds. But I did feel that if MJ-12

didn't exist, then another group like it by another name probably did. Somebody had to be working on the UFO problem.

Dark Skies arrived on TV in 1996, and comparisons to a certain other UFO conspiracy show were inevitable. Bryce said:

> People accused us at the time of ripping off *The X-Files*. But actually we didn't like what *The X-Files* was doing, which was teasing everybody. We wanted to do the opposite. We wanted to say 'we're not going to tease you about the cover-up. We're going to take you inside the cover-up and let our character be your tour guide through these events of history.' It was more direct than *The X-Files*.

Dark Skies was cancelled before the end of its first season due to low ratings, which may have been a result of its inopportune weekly scheduling. The show was dark in name, dark in themes, and dark in visual content, with violent and intense scenes in most episodes. Despite this, *Dark Skies* was broadcast at 8pm on Saturday evenings – peak viewing time for families (for whom the show was not entirely suitable), and peak going-out time for teens and young adults. Today *Dark Skies* retains a cult fanbase, and Bryce is proud of what he and Brent achieved with the show. "It's about 90 percent faithful to what I set out to do back in 1994, and it certainly succeeds in twisting UFOlogy and history and tying them into this knot. It's one of the most subversive TV shows ever produced."[29]

Back in black

The line between documented UFOlogical fact and speculative pop-cultural fiction continued to blur in 1997 with the release of the hugely successful *Men in Black*. As mentioned previously, civilian encounters with the enigmatic MIB have been documented for decades in relation to UFOs, and those who have been unfortunate enough to attract the attention of these black-clad mystery-men typically describe them as creepy, imposing, and outright threatening in their behaviour. But Steven Spielberg's big-budget production (based on the comic book by Lowell Cunningham) re-spun MIB-lore in favor of the *Men in Black* themselves and of government secrecy surrounding the UFO phenomenon. It was a message encapsulated by Will Smith's Grammy

Award-winning title rap for the movie's soundtrack, which character-ized the MIBs as good guys acting covertly to protect humanity from the worst scum of the universe. If the MIBs show at your door it's for your own protection, the song assures us.

In the minds of the many unfamiliar with UFOlogy, Men in Black would now and forever be associated exclusively with a movie and a song of the same name. Moreover, MIBs went from being sinister witness-harassers to heroic "galaxy-defenders." Such is the power of entertainment.

The *Men in Black* franchise may not be movie propaganda in the traditional sense, in that it was not pushed into production by the state for political ends, but it serves the UFO-related interests of officialdom nonetheless in its presentation of a just cover-up of extraterrestrial vis-itation orchestrated by a shadowy, yet entirely righteous organization that, by necessity, operates without legal oversight for the good of all mankind.

If the time ever comes when the US President is called upon by his citizens to justify the historical UFO cover-up, he need not prepare an elaborate speech, but say, simply: "Go watch *Men in Black*."

Men in Black spawned sequels in 2002 and 2012, both of which failed to live up to the first movie. During the promotional campaign for *Men in Black 3*, Will Smith told BBC Radio 1 host Chris Moyles that his 13-year-old son Jayden (himself a Hollywood star) had put President Obama on the spot during a recent private tour of the White House. The subject of Jayden's presidential enquiry was aliens. Strangely, Obama anticipated Jayden's question before the young star even had chance to ask it, and the President's response was suitably tantalizing. Obama said:

> The aliens, right? OK, I can neither confirm nor deny the existence of extraterrestrials but I can tell you if there had been a top secret meeting and if there would have had to have been a discussion about it, it would have taken place in this room.[30]

Disclosure

As the new millennium dawned, the Internet helped turn the idea of UFO disclosure into a meme. Disclosure (now with a capital D) be-came not only a buzzword, but a core concept of UFOlogy, and its ul-timate goal. Like all memes, it was highly infectious. On 9 May 2001,

Dr. Steven Greer, founder of the Disclosure Project, held a press conference at the National Press Club in Washington DC. The objective was to force congress to hold open, secrecy-free hearings on the alleged alien presence on and around Earth, and to encourage an official investigation into advanced technologies related to the UFO phenomenon.

The event was hosted by famous White House Press Corps reporter Sarah McClendon and in attendance were journalists and camera crews representing international news networks, including CNN, Fox News, and the BBC, among others. Flanking Greer on both sides were some 20 men and women selected from a larger witness pool of named and ranked professionals in the fields of military, intelligence, science, and aviation, each claiming firsthand knowledge of or experiences with UFOs, extraterrestrials, ET technology, and a UFO cover-up.[31]

Despite the significant press turn out, mainstream news media failed to follow up on what Greer had pitched to them as the biggest story of all time. Still, the 'Disclosure' meme spread quickly via the Internet and the term is now synonymous with government secrecy surrounding UFOs.

The rise of exopolitics

The rise of the Internet and the birth of the modern Disclosure movement coincided with, and rapidly accelerated, the evolution of traditional UFOlogy into 'exopolitics,' a term like 'Disclosure,' now central to debate among proponents of the Extraterrestrial Hypothesis. If UFOlogy had been the study of lights in the sky and endless speculation as to their possible origins, then exopolitics was the acceptance that most 'true' UFOs are attributable to extraterrestrial intelligences, and, moreover, that Earth's ET visitors maintain a permanent presence on and around our planet. Exopolitics has operated from the outset on shared assumptions among its figureheads about the inherent benevolence of extraterrestrial civilizations. Little allowance has been made for the possibility of hostile ET intent, much less for the notion that UFO phenomena may represent realities substantially more profound and challenging than mere extraterrestrials.

The first use of the term "exopolitics" in the context of UFOs was made in 2000 by Alfred Lambremont Webre, a former Senior Policy Analyst at the Center for the Study of Social Policy at Stanford Research Institute, who in 1977, directed a proposed Extraterrestrial

Communication Study for the Carter White House. He has since become a fringe figure even within UFOlogy, apparently taking any and all 'whistle-blower' claims at face value and sharing them enthusiastically through his articles and video blogs. Webre referred to exopolitics as, "the study of politics, government, and law in the Universe."[32] Before the middle of the decade the term had entered the UFOlogical lexicon, having been adopted and popularized by a handful of single-minded individuals seeking Disclosure. The most prominent among these were lobbyist Stephen Bassett, founder of the Paradigm Research Group (an online hub linking exopolitical organizations in dozens of countries)[33] and Dr. Michael Salla, founder of the popular website Exopolitics.com.[34]

Down to Earth

In 2003, director Lawrence Kasdan's *Dreamcatcher* (adapted from the Steven King novel) drew inspiration from the murkier annals of UFO conspiracy lore. In the film, an elite UFO crash-retrieval unit, codenamed 'Blue Boy,' has been operating secretly for decades to secure and capture downed alien spacecraft around the world. Naturally, the aliens are hostile and so the unit's secrecy is justified on the familiar grounds of "National Security." Most cinema-goers likely will be oblivious to the fact that the film's fictional project Blue Boy is actually inspired by its one-time real life equivalents, Blue Fly and Moon Dust – Air Force intelligence projects whose personnel were employed "on a quick reaction basis to recover or perform field exploitation of Unidentified Flying Objects."[35] Beyond this vague description, however, and outside of a handful of declassified USAF documents which mention Moon Dust and Blue Fly in the context of historical efforts to retrieve downed celestial objects around the world,[36] little information is available publicly concerning these mysterious Air Force units. It was mainly through Disclosure Project witness Sgt. Clifford Stone that Blue Fly and Moon Dust entered the UFO debate. In September 2000, Stone told Steven Greer what he would repeat in essence to the world's news media the following year during the aforementioned Disclosure Project press conference:

> In short, under Moon Dust and under Blue Fly, we have recovered alien debris not of this Earth... we saw living and dead bodies of entities that were not born on this planet. We have contact with aliens not

originating from some foreign country but from some other solar system. And I have been a party to that.[37]

Project Moon Dust also served to influence Disney's *Race to Witch Mountain* (2009). The movie's primary antagonist is Henry Burke (Ciaran Hinds), a specialist in UFO crash-retrieval situations. When we are introduced to Burke he is seen carrying a thick ring-bound document displaying, in bold lettering, the words: "PROJECT MOON DUST: CLASSIFIED." Project Moon Dust appealed to the film's director, Andy Fickman, because, he told me, "it was coming new to the [UFO] mythology." In our 2010 interview, Fickman remarked: "It's fun for me to talk to you, because you're somebody who recognizes the Project Moon Dust folder and you can really appreciate that there's some historical truth to it, or at the very least some historical reporting of it, whereas to a lot of people it was just a prop."[38]

Filling the gaps in our knowledge

Following its utilization as a major plot device in *The X-Files* and *Independence Day*, Area 51 was now an iconic (albeit invisible) American landmark.

A comical use of Area 51 came in 2003 in director Joe Dante's *Loony Toons Back in Action*, which mixed live action and animation to bring Warner Bros.' classic cartoon characters to new audiences in the 21st century. In a pivotal scene, the film's human protagonists (played by Brendan Fraser and Jenna Elfman), along with Bugs Bunny and Daffy Duck, stumble across a top secret military base in the Nevada desert where they see live alien creatures sealed in giant glass jars. The self-reflexive twist here is that all of these specimens are iconic 'monsters' or characters from science-fiction cinema and television – the eponymous Robot Monster and the *Man from Planet X*, Daleks from *Doctor Who*, a Mutant from *This Island Earth*, and Warner Bros.' very own Marvin the Martian. The odd one out alongside these fantastical celluloid creations is a typical alien Gray from UFO-lore stretched out on a medical table. This supposedly fact-based rendering is effectively fictionalized by its association with the line-up of schlock Hollywood creatures that precedes it.

"So, this is Area 51, right, the secret military base where they keep the aliens?" asks Bugs Bunny, to which a scientist (played by Joan Cusack) replies, "No, Area 51 is actually a paranoid fantasy we concocted to hide the true identity of this facility." Behind the characters, a bold red sign clearly reads: "AREA 52: KEEPING THINGS FROM THE AMERICAN PEOPLE SINCE 1947."

In a 2008 interview, director Joe Dante told me that the decision to call the base "Area 52" in his film was purely a comedic one, apparently unaware that a site bearing this name really does exist. Located in the Nevada desert approximately 70 miles northwest of Area 51, the Tonopah Test Range is designated by the US Department of Energy as "Area 52," and, like its infamous sister site, it has long been a testing ground for top secret military technologies, including the F-117A Nighthawk, more commonly known as the Stealth Fighter.[39]

According to Dante, his film's corporate overseers attempted to have the Area 52 scene removed in its entirety. Warner Bros.' concerns were not political, said Dante, but artistic: "There was pressure to take the scene out of the picture, but it was because the studio thought the monsters were stupid, it wasn't because they had any issues with Area 51." When I told Dante that the Pentagon had denied its cooperation to *Independence Day* in 1996 due in part to the film's Area 51 plotline, he replied, "Well the cat is out of the bag, I'm afraid. I mean it's a little late for the Pentagon to be worrying about that. Area 51 has entered folklore."[40] It certainly has, and Dante can now count himself among the small group of filmmakers who have helped push America's most enigmatic military base firmly and forever into folkloric territory.

Cinematic simulations of Area 51 are more real to most of us than the place itself. The real Area 51 is so far removed from prying eyes, so remote in its desert locale that it may as well not exist. Indeed, it does not exist for almost all who know of it, except onscreen. It is as Ken Russell said: "Hollywood fills the gaps in our knowledge of the world."[41] This seems especially true not only of our knowledge of Area 51, but also of Roswell, and of the UFO phenomenon more broadly.

Monsters vs. Aliens.

UFO conspiracy ideas featured obliquely in the hugely successful 2010 DreamWorks animation *Monsters vs. Aliens*. In the movie, the US government, for decades, behind a thick wall of secrecy, has maintained its own "monster" agency. To anyone broadly versed in UFO conspiracy lore it is immediately apparent that this "monster" agency is actually a thinly veiled UFO agency. Its history, as told by the character of General W. R. Monger (voiced by Kiefer Sutherland), mirrors the cover-up narrative central to UFO-lore.

Monger explains:

> In 1950 it was decided that Jane and Joe Public could not handle the truth about monsters and should focus on more important things like paying taxes. So the government convinced the world that monsters were the stuff of myth and legend and then locked them away in this here facility... This place is an X-file, wrapped in a cover-up and deep fried in a paranoid conspiracy.

The "facility" to which Monger refers is based on Area 51. In one scene, set in the government's War Room, the facility is described as "so secret that the very mention of its name is a federal offence." At this point, a military officer leans into another and asks, "Is he referring to Area 5...?" But the man is rendered unconscious by a dart to the back of the neck before finishing his sentence.

Super 8

Spielberg returned again to UFO lore in 2011 as executive producer of *Super 8*, an affectionate pastiche of Spielbergian themes and imagery directed by J. J. Abrams. Set in 1979, the movie follows a group of young friends in a small Ohio town who witness a train crash and become embroiled in the mystery that ensues. The train, it turns out, is owned by the USAF and is transporting a captive alien from Area 51 to Wright Patterson Air Force Base in Ohio. When the train crashes, the monstrous alien escapes and wreaks havoc on the small town. We later learn it was acting out of fear and self-defense. It is not hostile at heart, but has become aggressive through decades of ill-treatment at the hands of the US military at Area 51.

Paul

2011 also saw the release of *Paul*, a comedy in which two British sci-fi geeks, Graham and Clive (Simon Pegg and Nick Frost), embark upon a UFO road trip across America with the goal of hitting all the key tourist attractions, including Roswell and Area 51. While in the Nevada desert en route to the famous Area 51 perimeter (by now a real-world tourist attraction), Graham and Clive stumble across a Gray alien named Paul (voiced by Seth Rogen) who has just escaped from the base, where he had been a "guest" (prisoner) since 1947. Graham and Clive agree to help the benevolent but foul-mouthed Paul flee his Men in Black pursuers and eventually return to his home planet.

This witty movie utilizes almost every element of modern UFO conspiracy lore to enrich its plot, from Roswell and aliens in US government custody, to aliens inspiring Earthly technological developments, to Men in Black. It even draws conscious attention to the interplay between UFOs and Hollywood and makes light of the idea that pop-culture has been deliberately seeded with alien imagery in an effort to prepare the masses for open contact. At one point in the movie, Clive remarks of Paul's archetypal appearance, "He looks too obvious!" Paul responds: "There's a reason for that, Clive! Over the last 60 years, the human race has been drip-fed images of my face, on lunchboxes and T-shirts and shit. It's in case our species do meet, you don't have a fucking spaz attack!"

Later in the movie it is revealed that, while at Area 51, Paul worked closely with Hollywood creatives, inspiring iconic movie and TV characters, including Fox Mulder and Spielberg's E.T. In a flashback scene set in 1980, we see Paul at Area 51 on the phone to Steven Spielberg (appearing as himself in voice form only), who is seeking Paul's advice on a future movie about a friendly little alien. The conversation plays out as follows:

Paul: Okay Steven, how about cellular revivification?
Spielberg: I don't know what that is.
Paul: Oh. Restoration of damaged tissue through telepathic manipulation of intrinsic field memory.
Spielberg: What's that mean?
Paul: It means healing, Mr. Spielberg.
Spielberg: Yeah right, healing. Like by touch or something like that. Like maybe his finger lights up on the end when he reaches out and touches?
Paul: Maybe... You know, sometimes I find less is more.
Spielberg: Hey, trust me.

Escape from Planet Earth

Hollywood returned to Area 51 in 2013 in *Escape from Planet Earth*, which again saw captive aliens breaking out of the base in the hope of returning to their own planets. In this animated children's adventure, alien astronaut Scorch Supernova (a little blue man, instead of a little green one) flies to Earth, and to Area 51 specifically, in response to a mysterious SOS, only to be captured by the evil General Shanker Saunderson (voiced by William Shatner), who controls the top secret facility. While a prisoner at Area 51, Scorch meets other aliens of different species, all of whom have been captured by the 'US Department of Global Defense' and forced to work as technological innovators for the military-industrial-complex and for other corporations. One alien invented the Internet search engine, one invented social networking, and another invented touch screen technology. "He rips off our technology and sells it to the world," says one disgruntled alien of General Saunderson. "He's got deals with everybody... Apple, Facebook, them Google guys... you think humans could build this stuff? I don't think so! Who do you think invented the Internet, cell phone, computer animation? We did!"

Gray aliens also feature in the movie. Small, telepathic, and telekinetic, they have been working at Area 51 since 1947 and are referred to as "guests of the US government." This is a reference to terminology used by Falcon (Doty) in *UFO Cover-Up?: Live!* in 1988, who spoke of Zeta Reticulan Grays as being "guests" of his government.

Conclusion

For decades, UFO secrecy was something of a side-note in Hollywood's flying saucer movies, but by the mid-1990s, with products like *The X-Files, Dark Skies, Roswell, Independence Day,* and *Men in Black,* the idea of a UFO cover-up had become a driving narrative force in sci-fi entertainment. When depicting UFO secrecy, as ever, Hollywood borrowed liberally from UFOlogy, incorporating fine details from officially declassified UFO documentation, from 'whistle-blower' testimonies, and particularly from the MJ-12 documents, which were almost certainly entirely fraudulent and central to an ambitious and successful UFO perception management campaign dating back to the early-1980s.

Recognizing that the public at large was resolute in believing in UFOs and associating the phenomenon specifically with extraterrestrials and government conspiracies, efforts were made not to debunk these notions (which would be have been futile), but rather to manage and steer an underlying belief system to create a schizophrenic paradigm in which millions of people deeply distrust officialdom while simultaneously looking to officialdom for the truth, and ultimately, for salvation and enlightenment. Controlled disinformative 'leaks' that began as trickles in the UFO community, became raging torrents through popular media outlets. The narrative that emerged was one of American officialdom having hands-on access to alien technology and the know-how to successfully reverse-engineer it. Crucially, this narrative gave the impression that American elites and ultra-advanced alien intelligences were engaged in mutually-beneficial treaties, that American leaders were on a level pegging with UFO intelligences, and that historical UFO secrecy was justified because the intelligences were/are potentially hostile, but not to worry as the powers that be have a firm handle on the situation.

Another, more obvious goal for American officialdom in its creation of the UFO 'core story' relates to psychological warfare, not against the American UFO community, but against any number of enemy foreign powers, and particularly the Soviet Union, which at the time was frozen solid in its Cold War with America. What better way to scare potential aggressors than to make them suspect you are in possession of super-advanced alien technologies and are even allied with the aliens themselves? Like their American counterparts, various branches of the Soviet military had been secretly studying UFOs for decades and were well aware that the phenomenon was genuinely anomalous in nature, perhaps even representative of non-human intelligences. It would not have been a huge leap for them to believe that the Americans truly might have been in possession of exotic technologies and bodies. This psychological warfare angle seems especially plausible given the intriguing fact that *UFO Cover-Up?: Live!*, which was pivotal in bringing the UFO core story to a mass audience, was broadcast live in America and the Soviet Union simultaneously. Soviet UFOlogists appear on camera a number of times live from Moscow, one of whom is the Science Secretary of a UFO working group in the state-funded USSR Academy of Sciences. Early on in the show, host Mike Farrell stresses the significance of this Soviet participation, describing it as "The first UFO glasnost in television history." Later in the show, Farrell, still reading from his teleprompter, says to one of the Soviet UFOlo-gists, "Thanks for opening a new channel of communication between the US and the USSR."

Whatever its ultimate purpose, the UFO core story has proven so popular in the UFO community because it has a clear resolution, and one that requires minimum effort on our part.......Disclosure. All we need do is keep talking about UFOs and aliens and occasionally send a petition to the White House. Eventually, our leaders (whom we deeply distrust, but whose statements we will unquestioningly believe on Dis-closure day) will see fit to share with us their world-changing informa-tion and technologies, ushering in a new era of cosmic consciousness.

It is a myth. Spun partly by external design, and partly by the UFO community's deep need to believe that universal truth is within arm's reach.

The problem with the Disclosure mindset is that it declares an end to the UFO enigma. It says, in essence, we know what 'they' are – extra-terrestrial spacecraft – end of story. All the while the movement looks to officialdom as a sort of unfair parent figure, and it tugs incessantly at the leg of power. But power isn't listening, and, more importantly, power doesn't have the answers.

It seems likely that elements within official power structures have more pieces of the UFO puzzle at their fingertips than do the rest of us, but it is extremely improbable that they have succeeded in solving the puzzle. Despite appearances and the power of their egos, in a uni-verse that is some 13 billion years old, the secret-keepers are monkeys like the rest of us, flailing around for answers in the early years of the 21st century on a planet whose dominant trend is war. It is doubtful that the powers that be can even comprehend the underlying nature of UFO phenomena, much less explain it. What can our elite parent figures possibly divulge to us without appearing ignorant and con-fused, without losing a huge weight of their authority? It is better to stay silent, while subtly encouraging a belief that they indeed have all the answers, that they're all-knowing.

Should officialdom ever 'come clean' on the UFO issue, we should all be immediately and extremely suspicious. UFO truth by way of of-ficial power structures will not be truth at all. It will, by necessity, be whatever truth least vilifies and incriminates the secret-keepers, whose primary concern is not to bring about world peace through the disclosure of cosmic secrets, but rather to avoid at all costs being lynched by angry mobs for having withheld from the public incomprehensible data concerning the nature of our reality, and to maintain our existing global system – a system in which the activities of the privileged few are concealed from the distracted masses. The illusion of democracy.

If and when the day comes that the layers of our reality are peeled back and humanity collectively finds itself in a new world, it will not be for one signature too many on a Disclosure petition. Disclosure, if we must insist on using the term, is best viewed as a slow process of personal awakening on a mass scale.

The ultimate irony of the Disclosure movement is that, by imagining all answers to the UFO mystery to be out of public reach, deep in the bowels of the national security state, it actually places power into hands of officialdom, while disempowering the individual.

Modern UFOlogy, characterized by exopolitics, is no longer about asking challenging questions. Rather it is about fitting predetermined answers into an established quasi-religious belief system.

Disclosure has become *the* focus of UFOlogy, its alluring 'fast-track to UFO truth' marginalizing more esoteric approaches to the phenomena. If the day ever comes when humanity can claim an understanding of the UFO phenomenon, it seems unlikely that politics, 'exo' or otherwise, will have played any significant role in this enlightenment.

The kind of revolutionary change many hope will be triggered by UFO Disclosure can only ever occur from a bottom-up level, and over a considerable expanse of time. Enlightenment is earned slowly by the individual, it is not handed to her on a saucer-shaped platter. But then, it is easier to demand of a faceless bureaucracy than it is to demand of oneself.

Understanding UFOs and related phenomena is a glacially slow process in its fetal stages. UFOlogy would do well to accept and appreciate this. Therein lies the freedom to explore, and to learn.

CONCLUSION

UFOS AND HYPERREALITY

Between 1947 and the time of this writing, UFOs have gone from being a tangible national security concern to increasingly impalpable cultural artifacts. As 'real' phenomena, they continue flit in and out of our perception, sometimes profoundly affecting individual lives. Meanwhile, they permeate our culture as iconographic entertainment products. UFOs are real, and they are unreal. This dichotomy demands some focused attention here before signing off.

The literary critic and philosopher Walter Benjamin saw in the cinematic medium a "unique faculty to express by natural means and with incomparable persuasiveness all that is fairylike, marvellous, supernatural."[1] Benjamin died in 1940, seven years prior to the birth of the modern UFO phenomenon. Had he lived to experience the age of the flying saucer and of saucer movies, his observation would likely have been extended to include the "alien."

The transcendent, actualizing power of cinema has been similarly noted by the artist Valie Export, who suggests that films are "expansions of our structures of time and space, of our experiential structures... they are expansions of our reality and our independent consciousness." Through cinema, says Export, "the past is made visible, space and time can be transported... the boundaries between artificial and natural reality, between actual and possible reality... between man and object are transcended."[2]

The spectacle and the hyperreal

The social theorist Guy Debord spoke of the 'spectacular society,' in which "the real world changes into simple images... and the simple images become real." In our spectacular society, said Debord, "the image matters more than the object, in fact, much more so than mere objective truth."[3] The image replaces the truth – it is truth, it is reality. The resultant state, in postmodern theory, is 'hyperreality.'

By its most popular definition, hyperreality is:

> An inability of consciousness to distinguish reality from a simulation of reality, especially in technologically advanced postmodern societies... [it is] a condition in which what is real and what is fiction are seamlessly blended together so that there is no clear distinction between where one ends and the other begins.[4]

Something that is hyperreal, then, is simultaneously real *and* unreal, fact *and* fantasy.

The key words in the above definition are "technologically advanced." Technologies of reproduction (mechanical and digital) have ushered in the age of the hyperreal; an age where simulations of reality threaten to dissolve the boundaries between 'fact' and 'fantasy,' between 'true' and 'false,' 'real' and 'imaginary.'[5] It is my contention that cinematic simulations of UFOlogical history have all but consumed the history itself through the process of replication – just as humans were consumed and replicated as 'pod people' in genre classics such as *Invasion of the Body Snatchers* (1956) or John Carpenter's *The Thing* (1982).

The power of cinema

Cinema has an essential mystical ability to completely detach us from our physical environment and transport us to another, more vivid, realm of perception; a realm where everything is at once illusory, yet strangely real.

In film studies, anything that exists within the world of the film is known as diegesis. The cinema screen separates *their* fictional world from our 'real' world. But, actually, the diegesis seeps through the screen into our world, into our subconscious. It becomes part of our reality.

Key to cinema's power is that movies, in their slick, neatly packaged, self-contained way, serve to narrativize and contextualize the events, debates, and processes that constitute our frustratingly non-narrative world. Life rarely makes sense, but movies usually do, and in that we take comfort and, therein lies the problem – movies, no matter how realistic they are in the events they depict, are *not* real life. They are, at best, reflections of our reality, snapshots of it, simulations of it, skewed and distorted through the ideological framework of those who have made them.

Movies masquerade as the final word on a given topic. No matter what the subject, and regardless of how much that subject has already been written about and debated, once it is committed to film – once it has received the full Hollywood treatment – it is embedded firmly and forever into the popular consciousness. Imprinted on our psyche. Plunged into the deep wells of memory and imagination.

UFO reality

Unidentified Flying Objects are 'real,' which is to say they exist independently of cinema, and of pop-culture more broadly. UFOs have been investigated by governments around the world for almost seven decades. What the phenomenon represents is open for debate, and various theories have been propounded – from secret military aircraft, to natural phenomena, otherworldly intelligences, and even untapped human potential. The point is that even in a world without movies, people would continue to report UFOs. People were reporting UFOs, and flying saucers specifically, long before Hollywood got in on the act.

UFOlogy informs Hollywood more than Hollywood informs UFOlogy, which is to say that Hollywood engages with UFO lore in a parasitic fashion, sucking dry the pulsing veins of a seventy year old subculture. The industry grabs hold of fringe ideas and popularizes them through the science-fiction genre: Men in Black, Close Encounters of the Third Kind, The Fourth Kind, Area 51. Hollywood didn't create these terms, they were all part of the common language of UFOlogy decades before Hollywood lifted them.

In Hollywood's UFO movies, broadly speaking, art imitates life. If the opposite were true, then following the release of James Cameron's

Avatar, the highest grossing film of all time, we might reasonably have expected thousands of people to have begun reporting ten-foot-tall blue aliens. This did not happen; just as Hollywood's forceful projection of the 'little green men' meme has failed to result in mass sightings of little green men (although reports of such entities do lightly pepper the UFO literature).

When it comes to UFOs, Hollywood produces depictions, albeit not entirely faithful ones, of what people actually report. This is not to say that what's reported is necessarily true or accurate, but merely that Hollywood sees dramatic potential in these reports.

My position is this: Hollywood draws extensively from fact-based discourse on UFOs – a phenomenon whose existence is already rejected by consensus reality. The presentation of this UFO discourse on-screen (and particularly within the context of the sci-fi genre) serves to blur the boundaries between UFO fact and fantasy.

UFOs and the Hyperreal process

Cinematic simulations of UFOlogical history (UFO movies and TV shows) simultaneously actualize *and* fictionalize their underlying subject matter – it becomes *hyperreal*, both real *and* unreal. We can unpack this concept into what I consider to be the three phases of UFOlogical hyperreality:

Phase One

SIMULATION

In which a film or TV show is produced that
reflects a basic UFOlogical reality.

Phase Two

RECEPTION

In which the basic UFOlogical reality is screened as spectacle for
mass consumption, and, in the process, is masked and perverted

through the cultural value of the medium (in this case film or TV, but we could also extend it to video games, comic books, etc.).

Phase Three

HYPERREALITY

In which reality and simulation are experienced as without difference, or rather, the image has come to mean more to us than any underlying reality.

Essentially, then, the hyperreality of the UFO phenomenon has arisen primarily through processes of mass media simulation. The blurring of true and false, real and imaginary, through that most mystical of mediums (cinema) and within the context of that most fantastical of genres (science fiction) engenders our acceptance of the UFO as just that: a fictional media construct with little or no grounding in our lived historical reality. And yet, thanks to their permanent residency in the popular imagination, UFOs are no less real to us as a result.

It boils down to this...

In our hyperreal world, a world where Roswell is better understood as a plot device and Area 51 is a tourist attraction – a UFOlogical Disneyland – debates surrounding official 'Disclosure' of UFO reality (whatever that reality might be) are meaningless. How does one Disclose what is already *hyper*-real? The hyperreality of the UFO phenomenon in the popular imagination nullifies its potential to be either real *or* unreal, because it is now, and perhaps always will be, both.

Of course, this hyperreality model does not offer a solution to the UFO enigma, because it does not address what UFOs are at an ontological level. But it does, I believe, go a very long way towards explaining *why* UFOs continue to defy acceptance within our consensus reality.

And so, one last time, if you care about UFOs, you should care a great deal about UFO movies. They have shaped your perceptions of the phenomenon, often without conscious intent, but sometimes wilfully. With this in mind, when next we encounter a silver screen saucer, let us all take a moment to peer up from our popcorn, and to separate the fact from the fantasy. We can but try.

ENDNOTES

CHAPTER ONE

1   Lynne Kirby, *Parallel Tracks: The Railroad and Silent Cinema* (Duke University Press, 1997), 62.

2   See: "Avatar-Induced Depression: Coping with the Intangibility of Pandora (VIDEO)," *Huffington Post*, 18 March 2010, http://www.huffingtonpost. com/2010/01/12/avatar-induced-depression_n_420605.html

3   Jo Piazza, "Audiences experience 'Avatar' blues," *CNN*, 11 Jan. 2010, http:// edition.cnn.com/2010/SHOWBIZ/Movies/01/11/avatar.movie.blues/index. html

4   Ibid.

5   Walter Murch, *In the Blink of an Eye, 2ⁿᵈ Edition* (Los Angeles: Silman James Press, 2001), 122.

6   Colin McGinn, *The Power of Movies: How Screen and Mind Interact* (New York: Vintage, 2005), 22.

7   Ibid, 38.

8   Martin Scorsese, *A Personal Journey with Martin Scorsese through American Movies*, 1995. Directors: Martin Scorsese, Michael Henry Wilson. DVD, BFI.

[9] See: Richard Dolan, *UFOs and the National Security State: Chronology of a Cover-up 1941–1973* (Virginia: Hampton Roads, 2002), xvii – xviii, 5–7.

[10] For a selection of early press reports detailing Arnold's sighting, see: "UFO Reports – 1947," *Project 1947*: http://www.project1947.com/fig/1947b.htm. The first use of the "flying saucer" term features in the report titled: "Harassed Saucer-Sighter Would Like to Escape Fuss," *Boise, Idaho Statesman*, 27 Jun. 1947.

[11] The Estimate of the Situation was first mentioned in print in 1956 by former Project Blue Book Head Captain Edward Ruppelt. Its conclusions so alarmed Chief of Staff General Hoyt S. Vandenberg that he ordered all copies of the document incinerated; a few survived, however, one of which was examined by Ruppelt. See: Edward Ruppelt, *The Report on Unidentified Flying Objects* (Middlesex: The Echo Library, 2007), 45.

[12] Air Material Command, "Flying Discs," 23 Sept. 1947, Letter to Commander of the Army Air Forces, in Timothy Good, *Beyond Top Secret: The Worldwide UFO Security Threat* (London: Sidgwick and Jackson, 1996), 313–315. Document also viewable at: http://www.nicap.org/twining_letter_docs.htm

[13] Smith obtained this information via the Canadian Embassy in Washington DC. See: Wilbert Smith, "Memorandum to the Controller of Telecommunications," Top Secret Confidential Department of Transport, Intradepartmental Correspondence, Ottowa, Ontario, 21 Nov. 1950, http://www.roswellproof.com/Smith_11_21_50.html

[14] In 2010, the Argentine Air Force announced its creation of a commission to investigate UFOs. See: "On the Hunt for UFOs," *TN*, 29 Dec. 2010, http://www.tn.com.ar/sociedad/128489/la-caza-de-ovnis

[15] The Uruguayan Air Force has been active in UFO investigations for decades and began declassification of its UFO files in 2009. See: Daniel Isgleas, "There are still 40 cases of unexplained UFO[sic]," *El Pais*, 7 Jun. 2009, http://www.elpais.com.uy/090607/pnacio-421863/nacional/hay-aun-40-casos-de-ovnis-sin-explicacion/

[16] The Peruvian Air Force's Office for the Investigation of Anomalous Activity (known as OIFFA) was established in 2001. See: Leslie Kean, *UFOs: Pilots Generals and Government officials go on the Record*, (New York: Harmony Books, 2010), 189.

[17] The Chilean government's Committee for the Study of Anomalous Aerial Phenomena (known as CEFAA) was established in 1997 under the

jurisdiction of its civil aviation department and works closely with the aviation branch of the Chilean Army. Ibid, 190.

[18] In 2010 the Brazilian government ordered its Air Force to officially record all UFO sightings and to register them with the national aerospace defense command. All sighting reports are now stored in the national archives in Rio de Janiro and made available to researchers. See: "Brazil Air Force to Record UFO Sightings, *BBC News, Latin America and Caribbean*, 12 Aug. 2010, http://www.bbc.co.uk/news/world-latin-america-10947856

[19] Operating within the framework of the French national space agency (CNES) the Group for the Study of Information on Unidentified Aerospace Phenomena (known as GEIPAN) is generally recognized as the most scientific and efficiently organized official UFO investigations body in the world, having operated continuously for over thirty years. See: http://www.cnes-geipan.fr/

[20] In 2010, The New Zealand government declassified approximately two thousand pages of UFO sighting reports collected by its military between 1954 and 2009. See: "New Zealand Releases UFO Government Files," *BBC News, Asia-Pacific*, 22 Dec. 2010, http://www.bbc.co.uk/news/world-asia-pacific-12057314

[21] The Danish Tactical Air Command's historical UFO archives were made available to the public in 2009 and are accessible at: http://forsvaret.dk/FRK/Nyt%20og%20Presse/Pages/UFO.aspx

[22] Canada's UFO files have been available to the public through its national archives since 2007. See: http://www.collectionscanada.gc.ca/databases/ufo/index-e.html

[23] In 2009, the Russian Navy declassified its records of encounters with UFOs and USOs (Unidentified Submerged Objects). See: "Russian Navy UFO Records Say Aliens Love Oceans," *Russia Today*, 21 Jul. 2009: http://rt.com/news/russian-navy-ufo-records-say-aliens-loveoceans/

[24] MoD UFO files viewable at: http://www.nationalarchives.gov.uk/ufos/

[25] Air Command, UK Ministry of Defence, *UAP in the UK Air Defence Region: Executive Summary (Full). Ministry of Defence*, Dec. 2000, 6–7, http://webarchive.nationalarchives.gov.uk/20121026065214/http://www.mod.uk/DefenceInternet/FreedomOfInformation/PublicationScheme/SearchPublicationScheme/UapInTheUkAirDefenceRegionExecutiveSummary.htm

[26] Ibid, 4.

[27] Ibid, 10.

[28] "NASA: Alien life may be found within 10 years on other planets," *BBC Newsbeat*, 8 Apr. 2015, http://www.bbc.co.uk/newsbeat/article/32216869/nasa-alien-life-may-be-found-within-10-years-on-other-planets

[29] Kaku even suggests that advanced extraterrestrials may be using our own moon as an operations base for their reconnaissance of Earth. See: Michio Kaku, *Physics of the Impossible: A Scientific Exploration of the World of Phasers, Force Fields, Teleportation and Time Travel* (London: Penguin, 2008), 152.

[30] Kaku first laid out his theories of hyperspace (and potential human and extraterrestrial uses of it) in 1994. See: Michio Kaku, *Hyperspace: A Scientific Odyssey through Parallel Universes, Time Warps, and the 10th Dimension* (Oxford University Press, 1994).

[31] Richard Dolan, "Twelve Government Documents That Take UFOs Seriously," *Richard Dolan Press*, http://www.richarddolanpress.com/#!twelve-government-documents/cg96

[32] Ibid.

[33] Ibid.

[34] Ibid.

[35] Colonel Salgado speaking in the 2010 documentary, *UFOs in South America: Disclosure has Begun*, available at: http://www.youtube.com/watch?v=ojyP88bY61I

[36] Billy Cox, "Three Cheers for Uruguay," *Herald Tribune, De Void*, 7 Feb. 2012, http://devoid.blogs.heraldtribune.com/12766/three-cheers-for-uruguay/

[37] An English Translation of The COMETA Report is downloadable in full at: http://www.ufoevidence.org/topics/cometa.htm

[38] COMETA, *UFOs and Defense: What Should We Prepare For?* Institute of Higher Studies for National Defense, 1999, 34, http://www.ufoevidence.org/newsite/files/COMETA_part2.pdf. The report originally appeared in a special issue of the magazine VSD in France, Jul. 1999.

[39] Ibid, 71.

[40] Ibid, 85.

41 "Behind the scenes, high-ranking Air Force officers are soberly concerned about the UFOs. But through official secrecy and ridicule, many citizens are led to believe the unknown flying objects are nonsense. To hide the facts, the Air Force has silenced its personnel." Vice Admiral Roscoe Hillencoetter as quoted in: "Air Forge [sic] Order On 'Saucers' Cited; Pamphlet by the Inspector General Called Objects a 'Serious Business,'" *New York Times*, 27 Feb. 1960, http://select.nytimes.com/gst/abstract. html?res=F50A12F9345D1A728DDDA10A94DA405B808AF1D3. See also: Kean, *UFOs: Generals, Pilots and Government Officials Go on the Record*, 143.

42 "I do know that the CIA and the US government have been concerned over the UFO phenomenon for many years and that their attempts, both past and recent, to discount the significance of the phenomenon and to explain away the apparent lack of official interest in it have all the earmarks of a classic intelligence cover-up... My theory is that we have, indeed, been contacted – perhaps even visited – by extraterrestrial beings, and that the US government, in collusion with other national powers of the Earth, is determined to keep this information from the general public." Victor Marchetti, "How the CIA Views the UFO Phenomenon," *Second Look*, May 1979, 2–5.

43 In an official United States Senate letter dated 28 Mar. 1975, Goldwater responded to an enquiry regarding his publicly stated interest in UFOs: "About ten or twelve years ago I made an effort to find out what was in the building at Wright Patterson Air Force Base where the [UFO] information is stored that has been collected by the Air Force, and I was understandably denied this request. It is still classified above Top Secret." In another Senate letter, dated 19 Oct. 1981, Goldwater further stated: "I have had one long string of denials from chief after chief, so I have given up... this thing [the UFO issue] has gotten so highly classified... it is just impossible to get anything on it." See: Kean, *UFOs: Generals, Pilots and Government Officials go on the Record*, 243.

44 "For many years I have lived with a secret, in a secrecy imposed on all specialists and astronauts. I can now reveal that every day, in the USA, our radar instruments capture objects of form and composition unknown to us... I feel that we need to have a top-level, coordinated program to scientifically collect and analyze data from all over the Earth concerning any type of encounter, and to determine how best to interface with these visitors in a friendly fashion." Gordon Cooper, Col. USAF (Ret.), letter to

Ambassador Griffith, Mission of Grenada to the United Nations, New York, 9 Sept. 1978. See: Gordon Cooper and Bruce Henderson, *Leap of Faith: An Astronaut's Journey into the Unknown* (New York: Harpertorch, 2002), 219–225.

45 "The [UFO] evidence is now so consistent and so overwhelming that no reasonably intelligent person can deny that something unexplained is going on in our atmosphere... there is... a cover-up: in the United States on a massive scale, in Great Britain, and in several other countries." Admiral of the Fleet the Lord Hill Norton is his foreword to: Good, *Beyond Top Secret*, xii–xiii.

46 In a 1995 letter addressed to Bill Clinton, as part of a sustained dialogue with the White House on the issue of UFO disclosure, Rockefeller requested that the President "personally and specifically direct a review of current government information policy concerning Extraterrestrial Intelligence (ETI), including Unidentified Flying Objects (UFOs)." Rockefeller wrote: "It is widely believed that various agencies of the federal government have substantial information concerning the existence or nonexistence of UFOs, and that it has been unnecessarily withheld from the public as classified. If the information were released, it would be received as evidence of a new spirit of partnership between government and its citizens." Lawrence S., Rockefeller, "Lifting Secrecy on Information about Extraterrestrial Intelligence as part of the Current Classification Review," letter to President Clinton, 23 Aug. 1995.

47 "I happen to have been privileged enough to be in on the fact that we've been visited on this planet and the UFO phenomena is real... It's been well covered up by all our governments for the last 60 years or so, but slowly it's leaked out and some of us have been privileged to have been briefed on some of it... I've been in military and intelligence circles, who know that beneath the surface of what has been public knowledge, yes – we have been visited." Edgar Mitchell as quoted in: "Apollo 14 astronaut claims aliens HAVE made contact – but it has been covered up for 60 years," *The Daily Mail*, 24 Jul. 2008: http://www.dailymail.co.uk/sciencetech/article-1037471/Apollo-14-astronaut-claims-aliens-HAVE-contact--covered-60-years.html

48 "The time has come to lift the veil of secrecy and let the truth emerge so that there can be a real and informed debate about one of the most important problems facing our planet today... but it is quite impossible to have that kind of informed debate about a problem that doesn't officially exist." Paul Hellyer speaking at a symposium on UFO disclosure, 25 Sept. 2005.

49 "There are many high-ranking military, aviation and government officials who share my concerns [about UFOs]. While on active duty, they have either witnessed a UFO incident or have conducted an official investigation into UFO cases relevant to aviation safety and national security... We want the government to stop putting out stories that perpetuate the myth that all UFOs can be explained away in down-to-earth conventional terms. Investigations need to be re-opened, documents need to be unsealed and the idea of an open dialogue can no longer be shunned... When it comes to [UFO] events... that are still completely unsolved, we deserve more openness in government, especially our own. See: Fife Symington, "Symington: I Saw a UFO in the Arizona Sky," *CNN*, 9 Nov. 2007, http://edition.cnn.com/2007/TECH/science/11/09/simington.ufocommentary/

50 In response to a question about UFOs during a press conference on 20 December 2007, Ishiba stated: "There are no grounds for us to deny there are unidentified flying objects and some life-form that controls them." See: Stuart Biggs, "Defense Minister Ishiba Considers Japan's Options in UFO Attack," *Bloomberg*, 21 Dec. 2007, http://www.bloomberg.com/apps/news?pid=newsarchive&sid=apLM6RsqojXY

51 The press conference took place on 22 Oct. 2002 and was organized by the coalition for Freedom of Information. Video of Podesta's statement available at: http://www.youtube.com/watch?v=smwQau3HtKM

52 Ken Russell, "Seeing is Believing – If the Special Effects Work," *The Times*, Times2, 27 March 2008.

CHAPTER TWO

1 Dolan, *UFOs and the National Security State: Volume 1*, 209–10.

2 Ibid.

3 Richard H. Hall, "Armstrong Circle Theatre: Air Force Censorship of TV Broadcast about UFOs Stirred Controversy in 1958," *Journal of UFO History*. Vol. 1, No. 6 (Jan/Feb 2005), 5, http://www.nicap.org/jufoh/JournalUFOHistoryVol1No6.pdf

4 Ibid.

5 David L. Robb, *Operation Hollywood: How the Pentagon Shapes and Censors the Movies* (New York: Prometheus, 2004), 91–93.

6   Ibid, 42–45.

7   Ibid, 29–30.

8   "RAAF Captures Flying Saucer on Ranch in Roswell Region: No Details of Flying Disk are Revealed," *Roswell Daily Record*, 8 Jul. 1947, 1. For further details see: http://www.wired.com/thisdayintech/2010/07/0708army-announces-roswell-new-mexico-ufo-sighting/

9   Associated Press, "Gen. Ramey Empties Roswell Saucer," *Roswell Daily Record*, 9 Jul. 1947.

10 Headquarters United States Air Force, "The Roswell Report: Fact versus Fiction in the New Mexico Desert," US Government Printing Office, 1995.

11 Headquarters United States Air Force, "The Roswell Report: Case Closed," US Government Printing Office, 1997, http://contrails.iit.edu/History/Roswell/roswell.pdf

12 Central Intelligence Agency, *Report of Scientific Advisory Panel on Unidentified Flying Objects Convened by Office of Scientific Intelligence, CIA: January 14–18, 1953*, http://www.cufon.org/cufon/robert.htm. See also: Dolan, *UFOs and the National Security State: Volume 1*, 122–131.

13 Ibid.

14 Ibid.

15 Thornton Page, Letter to Frederick Durant, 8 Sept. 1966, Smithsonian Institution Archives, Record Unit 398, Box 61, Folder No. 4, cited in: Terry Hansen, *The Missing Times: News Media Complicity in the UFO Cover-up* (Self Published, 2000), 254, 330.

16 Robert Barrow, "U.F.O. Revisited," *Official UFO Magazine*, 1976, http://www.nicap.org/ufochop1.htm. See also: Paul Meehan, *Saucer Movies: A UFOlogical History of the Cinema* (Maryland: Scarecrow, 1998), 66–67.

17 James H. Farmer and John Ellis, DVD commentary, *The Complete Steve Canyon on TV Volume 1*, Episode 7: "Project UFO," NBC First Run Tuesday 19 May 1959, DVD released through Milton Caniff Estate.

18 Ibid.

19 John Ellis, telephone interview with the author, 1 June 2009.

20 David Haft, interview with John Ellis, 17 Aug. 2006. Ellis relayed Haft's account to the author during a telephone interview, 1 June 2009.

21 Ibid.

22 Draft script supplied by John Ellis to the author, 27 May 2009, courtesy of the Milton Caniff Estate.

23 Ibid.

24 Ibid.

25 Ibid.

26 James H. Farmer and John Ellis, DVD commentary, *The Complete Steve Canyon on TV Volume 1*, Episode 7: "Project UFO," NBC First Run Tuesday 19 May 1959, DVD released through Milton Caniff Estate.

27 Ibid.

28 Lawrence Suid, "Lights! Camera! NASA!" *Space World*, Jun. 1987, 16.

29 Nick Redfern, "The Flying Saucer That Never Was," *Intermediate States: The Anomalist*, Vol. 13, (Oct. 2007), 51.

30 Ibid.

31 Suid, "Lights! Camera! NASA!" 16.

32 For details on the history and operating procedure of Project Grudge, see Edward Ruppelt, *The Report on Unidentified Flying Objects*, 58–66.

33 Lawrence Suid, *Guts and Glory: The Making of the American Military Image in Film, Revised and Expanded Edition* (University Press of Kentucky, 2002), 223.

34 For information on Blue Book files stored at the US National Archives, see: http://www.archives.gov/research/military/air-force/ufos.html

35 Suid, *Guts and Glory*, 494.

36 Suid, "Lights! Camera! NASA!" 20.

37 Gail Heathwood, "Steven Spielberg," *Cinema Papers* (April/June 1978), 320. Requests to NASA, the Pentagon, and Spielberg for a copy of the letter have proved unsuccessful.

38 Suid, *Guts and Glory*, 588.

39 Ibid.

40 Ibid.

41 Ibid, 590.

42 Ibid, 588–89.

43 The film's primary military advisor, Pentagon film liaison Phil Strub, justified the DoD's involvement as follows: "We just wanted the case made that the Marines [depicted onscreen] understood that they were not going to prevail, but they were nobly sacrificing so the civilians... could escape." See: John Herrman, "How America's Proudest Technological Achievements Become Movie Props," *Smart planet,* 5 Oct. 2010.

44 Larry A. Simmons, "'Transformers' put Airmen, Aircraft on Big Screen," *Af.mil,* 3 Jul. 2007, http://www.af.mil/News/ArticleDisplay/tabid/223/Article/126378/transformers-put-airmen-aircraft-on-big-screen.aspx

45 Transformers box-office data at: http://www.imdb.com/title/tt0418279/business

46 Simmons, "'Transformers' put Airmen, Aircraft on Big Screen."

47 1st Lt. Kinder Blacke, "Tinker Airmen make mark in 'Transformers: Revenge of the Fallen,'" *Af.mil,* 26 June 2009, http://www.af.mil/News/ArticleDisplay/tabid/223/Article/119899/tinker-airmen-make-mark-in-transformers-revenge-of-the-fallen.aspx

48 See: Capt. Kristen D. Duncan, "'Transformers: Dark of the Moon' filmed at Hurlburt; Airmen included as extras," *Af.mil,* 30 Jun. 2011, http://www.af.mil/News/ArticleDisplay/tabid/223/Article/112921/transformers-dark-of-the-moon-filmed-at-hurlburt-airmen-included-as-extras.aspx. See also: Steven Siceloff, "NASA Adds Unique Touch to Transformers," *Nasa.gov,* 29 Jun. 2011, http://www.nasa.gov/centers/kennedy/news/transformerspremiere.html

49 Erin McCarthy, "How Real Marines Made Battle: Los Angeles More Accurate," *Popular Mechanics,* 7 March 2011, http://www.popularmechanics.com/culture/movies/a6677/how-the-marines-made-battle-los-angeles-more-accurate/. For behind the scenes photos of the movie's shoot at Camp Pendleton, see: David Strick, "Behind the Scenes of 'Battle: Los Angeles,'" *The Hollywood Reporter,* 3 Mar. 2011.

50 For a detailed accounting of the Battle of Los Angeles UFO incident, see: "The Battle of Los Angeles," *Saturday Night Uforia,* http://www.saturdaynightuforia.com/html/articles/articlehtml/thebattleoflosangeles.html. See also: Jeff Rense, "The 1942 'Battle of Los Angeles,'" *UFO Evidence,* http://www.ufoevidence.org/cases/case509.htm

51 *Battleship* featurette: "Real Heroes," viewable at: http://www.youtube.com/watch?v=yldtkUcLkI8&feature=player_embedded

52 See: Travis Walton, *Fire in the Sky: The Walton Experience* (New York: Marlowe and Company, 1996), 242.

53 In addition to on-set technical advice, the USAF's involvement in *Transformers* also extended to "script research" and "dialogue assistance." See: "Air Force Entertainment Liaison Office (Motion Pictures)," *Af.mil*, http://www.airforcehollywood.af.mil/portfolio/index.asp

54 DoD Entertainment Liaison office addresses listed at: *U.S. Department of Defense*, "U.S. Military Assistance in Producing Motion Pictures, Television Shows, Music Videos," http://www.defense.gov/faq/pis/pc12film.aspx

55 Linda Moulton Howe, telephone interview with the author, 8 Oct. 2008.

56 See: Peter B. Flint, "Edmund H. North, 79, a Writer; He Shared an Oscar for 'Patton,'" *The New York Times*, Obituaries, 31 Aug. 1990, http://www.nytimes.com/1990/08/31/obituaries/edmund-h-north-79-a-writer-he-shared-an-oscar-for-patton.html

57 See: Leonard Mosley, *Zanuck* (Boston, MA, 1984), 195–244.

58 See: Tony Shaw, *Hollywood's Cold War* (Edinburgh University Press, 2007), 115. For the full list of the NCFE's original members and Executive Officers, see: Central Intelligence Agency, "National Committee for Free Europe," memo dated 4 Aug. 1949, *Cia.gov*, accessed on 14. Jun. 2012 at: http://www.foia.cia.gov/docs/DOC_0000238872/DOC_0000238872.pdf. See also: Tim Weiner, "Legacy of Ashes" (Doubleday, 2007), 36.

59 See: Frances Stonor Saunders, *Who Paid the Piper? The CIA and the Cultural Cold War* (London: Granta, 2000), 146–147. See also: "Jackson, C. D.: Papers, 1931–1967," *Eisenhower Archives* (online), http://eisenhower.archives.gov/Research/Finding_Aids/pdf/Jackson_CD_Papers.pdf

60 See: Stonor Saunders, *Who Paid the Piper?* 289–290.

61 See: Rudy Behlmer (ed.), *Memo from Darryl F. Zanuck: The Golden Years at Twentieth Century-Fox* (New York: Grove Press, 1993), 192.

62 Ibid, 191.

63 Ibid.

64 Ibid, 192.

[65] Cited in: Shaw, *Hollywood's Cold War*, 9.

[66] Stanton Friedman, 'Re: The UFO/Disney Connection,' email to Grant Cameron, March 17 2000. Friedman was present when Kimball revealed the story and confirmed to researcher Grant Cameron that: "It was at the Saturday Night program of the July 1979 MUFON Symposium in San Francisco. Kimball spoke first, then Allen Hynek, and then me." Incidentally, Kimball's enduring fascination with UFOs was well known during his later years. His involvement in space-themed educational films for Disney and the political significance of these is also well established. See: Mike Wright, "The Disney-Von Braun Collaboration and Its Influence on Space Exploration," Nasa.gov, http://history.msfc.nasa.gov/vonbraun/disney_article.html

[67] Philip J. Corso and William J. Birnes, *The Day After Roswell* (New York: Pocket Books, 1997), 84–85.

[68] Dan Vergano, "Searching for Signs of ET life in the Universe," *USA Today*, 19 Mar. 2002, http://www.usatoday.com/news/science/2002-03-19-et-signs.htm

[69] Lawrence Suid, email correspondence with Matthew Alford, 10 Feb. 2012.

[70] Robert Emenegger, telephone interview with the author, 28 Oct. 2008.

[71] Details from Robert Emenegger's resume, dated 13 Dec. 1968, held by the National Archives and obtained by Grant Cameron through FOIA.

[72] Ibid.

[73] Letter from President-elect Richard M. Nixon to Robert Emenegger, dated 2 Dec. 1968. Provided to Grant Cameron by Robert Emenegger.

[74] Robert Emenegger, telephone interview with the author, 28 Oct. 2008.

[75] Ibid.

[76] Ibid.

[77] Ibid.

[78] Ibid.

[79] See "Veteran Intelligence Officers for Sanity," *Sourcewatch.org*, 6 Jul. 2004, http://www.sourcewatch.org/wiki.phtml?title=Veteran_Intelligence_Professionals_for_Sanity

[80] Andy Fickman, telephone interview with the author, 2 Sept. 2010.

81 Ibid.

82 Ibid.

83 Ibid.

84 Ibid.

85 Paula Weiss, email response to the author, 9 Aug. 2010. After having conducted the interview with Fickman the following month, I sought further response from Weiss, who on 7 Sept. 2010, replied via email: "We have no knowledge of any CIA officer having assisted with this film... It's very easy for outsiders, including Hollywood film people, to assume any US intelligence officer is CIA when in fact he could be from DIA, NSA, NGA, etc. Sorry I can't resolve this for you based on the available information."

86 Andy Fickman, telephone interview with the author, 2 Sept. 2010.

87 Ibid.

88 Ibid.

89 See: Tricia Jenkins, *The CIA in Hollywood: How the Agency Shapes Film and Television* (University of Texas Press, 2012), 73.

90 Central Intelligence Agency, *Task Force Report on Greater CIA Openness*, 20 Dec. 1991, 6. Report accessible through George Washington University National Security Archive at: http://www.gwu.edu/~nsarchiv/NSAEBB/ciacase/EXB.pdf

91 See: Wesley Britton, *Spy Television* (Connecticut: Praeger, 2004), 247.

92 Robert Burns, AP Military Writer, "Usually Closed CIA Welcomes Hollywood," *The AP*, 13 Oct. 1999, Wednesday, Section: Washington Dateline.

93 "CIA Hosts Screening of 'In the Company of Spies,'" *CIA.gov*, 14 Oct. 1999, https://www.cia.gov/news-information/press-releases-statements/press-release-archive-1999/pr101499.html

94 Bill Cosford, "Hollywood Brings CIA spooks back in from the cold," *Toronto Star*, 24 Jun. 1992, Wednesday final edition, C8.

95 Katharine Q. Seelye, "When Hollywood's big guns come right from the source," *New York Times*, 10 Jun. 2002, Monday late edition – final, 1.

96 Wesley Britton, *Beyond Bond: Spies in Fiction and Film* (Connecticut: Praeger, 2005), 229.

[97] Michael Frost Beckner, personal interview with Tricia Jenkins, 2 Dec. 2009 (transcript supplied to Matthew Alford and shared with the author). For further details see: Jenkins, *The CIA in Hollywood*, 66–70.

[98] See: David Eldridge, "'Dear Owen': The CIA, Luigi Luraschi, and Hollywood, 1953," *Historical Journal of Film, Radio and Television* 20, no. 2 (June 2000).

[99] Ibid, 159.

[100] Daniel J. Leab, *Orwell Subverted: The CIA and the Filming of Animal Farm* (Pennsylvania State University Press, 2007), 145.

[101] Jenkins, *The CIA in Hollywood*, 3.

[102] Ibid.

[103] Ibid.

[104] Ibid.

[105] Ibid.

[106] Ibid.

[107] Ibid.

[108] See: Carl Bernstein, "The CIA and the Media," *Rolling Stone*, 20 Oct. 1977. Accessible at: http://www.carlbernstein.com/magazine_cia_and_media.php

[109] Ibid.

[110] Ibid.

[111] Ibid.

[112] Bryson was a director of the Boeing Company from 1995 to 2011, and a director of the Disney Company from 2000 to 2011. He stepped down from both posts to be sworn in as the US government's 37th Secretary of Commerce on 21 Oct. 2011. See: Joe Flint, "John Bryson resigns from Disney board," *The Los Angeles Times*, 25 Oct. 2011, http://latimesblogs.latimes.com/entertainmentnewsbuzz/2011/10/john-bryson-resigns-from-disney-board.html. See also: Mark Drajem, "Obama Nominee Bryson Sides with Republicans on Taxes, Rules," *Bloomberg*, 21 Jun. 2011, http://www.bloomberg.com/news/2011-06-21/bryson-says-u-s-needs-businesses-in-a-less-taxed-position-.html

[113] See: Dolan, "Twelve Government Documents That Take UFOs Seriously," *Richard Dolan Press*, http://www.richarddolanpress.com/#!twelve-government-documents/cg96

[114] Robert Baer, telephone interview with the author, July 2008.

[115] McGinn, *The Power of Movies*, 4.

[116] Ibid, 200–201.

[117] Paul Barry was CIA Entertainment Liaison from 2007–2008. See: Tricia Jenkins, "Get Smart: A Look at the Current Relationship between Hollywood and the CIA," *Historical Journal of Film, Radio and Television*, Vol. 29, no. 2 June, 2009, 234.

CHAPTER THREE

[1] "Stephen Hawking: Alien Life is Out There, Scientist Warns," *The Telegraph*, 25 Apr. 2010, http://www.telegraph.co.uk/news/science/space/7631252/Stephen-Hawking-alien-life-is-out-there-scientist-warns.html

[2] Springer's interview was recorded April 8 2012. Viewable at: https://www.youtube.com/watch?v=dUSgkoYSEqo

[3] Full transcript of Reagan's speech available at: http://www.reagan.utexas.edu/archives/speeches/1987/092187b.htm. Video available at: https://www.youtube.com/watch?v=dL6PlM24JBQ

[4] CNN News Room, 19 Jul. 2012. Kaku's interview viewable at: https://www.youtube.com/watch?v=MpaIWPmiS5w

[5] Jack Mirkinson, "Paul Krugman: Fake Alien Invasion Would End Economic Slump," *The Huffington Post*, 15 Aug. 2011, http://www.huffingtonpost.com/2011/08/15/paul-krugman-fake-alien-invasion_n_926995.html

[6] Lee Spiegel, "Paul Krugman's Alien Invasion Defense Idea To Save Economy Gets Brickbats, Bouquets From Experts," *The Huffington Post*, 21 Jun. 2012, http://www.huffingtonpost.com/2012/06/21/paul-krugman-alien-invasion_n_1612973.html

[7] Travis S. Taylor, Bob Boan, R.C. Anding, T. Conley Powell, *An Introduction to Planetary Defense: A Study of Modern Warfare Applied to Extra-Terrestrial Invasion* (Brown Walker Press, 2006), 13.

8   For a detailed examination of the *Foo Fighter* mystery, see: Keith Chester, *Strange Company: Military Encounters with UFOs in WWII* (Anomalist Books, 2007).

9   For more information on the Mantell Incident, see: Jerome Clark, *The UFO Book: Encyclopedia of the Extraterrestrial* (Visible Ink Press, 1998), 351–356.

10 For a collection of articles on the Kelly-Hokinsville case, see: http://www.ufoevidence.org/cases/case524.htm. See also: Ronald D. Story (ed.), *The Mammoth Encyclopedia of Extraterrestrial Encounters* (Constable and Robinson, Ltd, 2001), 353–354.

11 Good, *Beyond Top Secret*, 539–540.

12 Ibid.

13 Ibid, 168–179.

14 *St. Petersburg Times*, Gallup Poll, 15 Aug. 1947. See: https://news.google.com/newspapers?nid=feST4K8JoscC&dat=19470815&printsec=frontpage&hl=en

15 Paul J. Davids, "Hollywood's Aliens: A One Hundred Billion Dollar Enterprise," *Silver Screen Saucers* (blog), 14 May 2011, http://silverscreensaucers.blogspot.co.uk/2011/05/guest-blogger-paul-davids.html

16 Ibid.

17 Jerome Clark, *The UFO Book*, 653–662.

18 *Invaders from Mars* scene viewable at: https://www.youtube.com/watch?v=wU8jmoiSqeg

19 Hermann Oberth, "Flying Saucers Come from a Distant World," *American Weekly*, 24, Oct. 1954.

20 Vallee's analysis of the 200 cases appears in: Charles Bowen (ed.), *The Humanoids* (Neville Spearman, 1969), 27–76.

21 Peter Biskind, *Seeing is Believing: Or How Hollywood Taught Us to Stop Worrying and Love the 50s* (Bloomsbury, 2000), 107.

22 Christine Cornea, *Science Fiction Cinema: Between Fantasy and Reality* (Edinburgh University Press, 2007), 70.

23 Kenn Thomas, "Earth vs. Flying Saucers with Cloudbusters," *Silver Screen Saucers* (blog), 29 Oct. 2011, http://silverscreensaucers.blogspot.co.uk/2011/10/guest-blogger-kenn-thomas.html

24 Meehan, *Saucer Movies*, 64–65.

25 For details of Project Twinkle, see: Clark, *The UFO Book*, 261–262.

26 Edward Ruppelt, *The Report on Unidentified Flying Objects* (The Echo Library, 2007), 45.

27 See: Good, *Beyond Top Secret*, 409–411.

28 Ibid, 196–201.

29 Richard H. Hall, *The UFO Evidence: Volume II, A Thirty Year Report* (Scarecrow Press, 2001), 250–254.

30 See: NICAP, http://www.nicap.org/jemhearing.htm

31 Good, *Beyond Top Secret*, 440.

32 United Nations Office for Outer Space Affairs, "Treaty on Principles Governing the Activities of States in the Exploration and Use of Outer Space, including the Moon and Other Celestial Bodies," 14, available at: http://www.unoosa.org/oosa/en/ourwork/spacelaw/treaties/introouterspacetreaty.html. See also: Nick Redfern, "Night of the Living Virus," *Mysterious Universe*, 19 Sept. 2013, http://mysteriousuniverse.org/2013/09/night-of-the-living-virus/

33 U.S. Air Force Fact Sheet, Unidentified Flying Objects and Air Force Project Blue Book, available at: http://archive.is/20120719123429/ http://www.af.mil/information/factsheets/factsheet_print. asp?fsID=188&page=1#selection-31.0-42.2

34 See: Christopher O'Brien, *Stalking the Herd: Unravelling the Cattle Mutilation Mystery* (Adventures Unlimited Press, 2014).

35 For a UFOlogical discussion of *Endangered Species*, see: Linda Moulton Howe, "When Hollywood Wanted 'A Strange Harvest,'" *Silver Screen Saucers* (blog), 17 May 2011, http://silverscreensaucers.blogspot.co.uk/2011/05/guest-blogger-linda-moulton-howe.html

36 Lewis Beale, "Horrors! Yuppies Vs. The Homeless 'They Live' Carpenter's Allegory of Doom & Politics," *Los Angeles Daily News*, 8 Nov. 1988, available at: http://articles.philly.com/1988-11-08/news/26245703_1_john-carpenter-alien-invasion-homeless-people

37 Keith David's comments feature in a 'making of' documentary on the Region 2 DVD release (Momentum, 2002).

38 Janet Maslin, "They Live (1988) Review/Film; A Pair of Sunglasses Reveals a World of Evil," *The New York Times*, 4 Nov. 1988.

[39] Richard Harrington, "They Live," *The Washington Post*, 5 Nov. 1988.

[40] Good, *Beyond Top Secret*, 478–483.

[41] *Independence Day* box-office data at: http://www.the-numbers.com/movies/franchise/Independence-Day

[42] "Interview with Tom Brokaw of MSNBC's 'InterNight,'" *The American Presidency Project*, 15 Jul. 1996, http://www.presidency.ucsb.edu/ws/?pid=53067

[43] *Signs* box-office data at: http://www.the-numbers.com/movie/Signs#tab=summary

[44] Peter Biskind, *Seeing Is Believing: How Hollywood Taught Us to Stop Worrying and Love the 50s* (Bloomsbury, 2001), 102.

[45] "Hello, ET? Web site sends texts into space," *MSNBC*, 12 Aug. 2009: http://web.archive.org/web/20090814175357/http://www.msnbc.msn.com/id/32391717/ns/technology_and_science-space/. See also: "Hello from Earth," https://en.wikipedia.org/wiki/Hello_from_Earth

[46] "Stephen Hawking: Alien Life is Out There, Scientist Warns," *The Telegraph*, 25 Apr. 2010.

[47] Antonio Huneeus, "Russian navy declassifies UFO records," *Open Minds*, 13 Oct. 2009, http://www.openminds.tv/russian-navy-declassifies-ufo-records/160

[48] See: The Science and Entertainment Exchange, *Facebook*, https://www.facebook.com/pages/The-Science-and-Entertainment-Exchange/41869161471?q=about

[49] See: George Andrews, *MKULTRA: The CIA's Top Secret Program in Human Experimentation and Behavior Modification* (Healthnet Pr, 2001).

[50] See: Paul H. Smith, *Reading the Enemy's Mind: Inside Star Gate—America's Psychic Espionage Program* (Forge, 2005).

[51] CNN News Room, 19 Jul. 2012.

[52] Richard Dolan and Bryce Zabel, *A.D. After Disclosure: The People's Guide to Life After Contact* (Keyhole Publishing, 2010), 150.

[53] CNN News Room, 19 Jul. 2012.

CHAPTER FOUR

1   See: Timothy Good, *Alien Base: Earth's Encounters with Extraterrestrials* (Century, 1998), 100–155. See also: George Adamski and Desmond Leslie, *Flying Saucers Have Landed* (Werner Laurie, 1953), 185–216.

2   See: Nick Redfern, *Contactees: A History of Alien-Human Interaction* (Career Press, 2009), 69–83.

3   Ibid, 47–55.

4   See: Good, *Alien Base*, 177–195.

5   Ibid, 240–248.

6   See: Jim Marrs, *Alien Agenda: The Untold Story of Extraterrestrials Among Us* (Harper Collins, 1998), 201–212.

7   See: Good, *Alien Base*, 41–44.

8   Letter to the author, 19 Mar. 2007.

9   Telephone conversation between author and witness, 21 Mar. 2007.

10   Paul Davids, telephone interview with the author, 5 Aug. 2013.

11   Lecture given by Robert Dean at the Civic Theatre, Leeds, England, 24 Sept. 1994. See also: Nick Redfern, *Contactees*, 125–126.

12   See: Good, *Alien Base*, 223–227.

13   Ibid, 292–299.

14   See: National Film Preservation Board: http://www.loc.gov/programs/national-film-preservation-board/film-registry/complete-national-film-registry-listing/

15   Full transcript of Reagan's speech available at: http://www.reagan.utexas.edu/archives/speeches/1987/092187b.htm. Video viewable at: https://www.youtube.com/watch?v=dL6PlM24JBQ

16   See: Grant Cameron, "Ronald Reagan's UFO Sightings," *The Presidents UFO Website*, 13 Aug. 2009, http://www.presidentialufo.com/ronald-reagan/204-ronald-reagans-ufo-sightings

17   Grant Cameron, "Klaatu Barada Nikto," *Silver Screen Saucers* (blog), 10 Jun. 2011, http://silverscreensaucers.blogspot.co.uk/2011/06/guest-blogger-grant-cameron.html

18 See: "President Obama Mum on Aliens During Roswell Visit (video),
    LiveLeak, 24 Mar. 2012, http://www.liveleak.com/view?i=f91_1332617625.
    See also: Devin Dwyer, "In Oil and UFO Country, Obama Says 'I Come
    in Peace,'" *ABC News*, 21 Mar. 2012, http://abcnews.go.com/blogs/
    politics/2012/03/in-oil-and-ufo-country-obama-says-i-come-in-peace/

19 Paul Davids, telephone interview with the author, 5 Aug. 2013.

20 See: Good, *Alien Base*, 57–78. See also: Daniel W. Fry, *The White Sands
    Incident: A Technician Talks with a Spaceman and Rides in a Flying Saucer*
    (New Age Publishing, 1954).

21 Ibid, 166–168. A video interview with Jesse Roestenburg is viewable at:
    https://www.youtube.com/watch?v=npCZ3W7Qtz4

22 Meehan, *Saucer Movies*, 60.

23 See: Lawrence H. Suid and Dolores A. Haverstick, *Stars and Stripes on Screen:
    A Comprehensive Guide to Portrayals of American Military on Film*, 155.

24 Meehan, *Saucer Movies*, 113–114.

25 See: Gene D. Phillips (ed.), *Stanley Kubrick: Interviews* (University Press
    of Mississippi, 2001), 50.

26 See: Meehan, *Saucer Movies*, 140– 41.

27 See: Marrs, *Alien Agenda*, 201–212.

28 See box-office data for *War of the Worlds* at: http://www.the-numbers.
    com/movie/War-of-the-Worlds#tab=summary and *Indiana Jones and
    the Kingdom of the Crystal Skull* at: http://www.the-numbers.com/movie/
    Indiana-Jones-and-the-Kingdom-of-the-Crystal-Skull#tab=summary

29 Joe Alves, telephone interview with the author, 26 Nov. 2013.

30 Jacques Vallee in: *Heretic Among Heretics: Jacques Vallee Interview*, http://
    www.ufoevidence.org/documents/doc839.htm

31 Bob Balaban, *Close Encounters of the Third Kind Diary* (Paradise Press,
    Inc., 1998), 110.

32 Joe Alves, telephone interview with the author, 26 Nov. 2013.

33 Richard Combs, "Primal Scream: An Interview with Steven Spielberg,"
    Sight and Sound, Spring 1977, in: Lester D. Friedman and Brent Notbohm,
    Steven Spielberg Interviews (University Press of Mississippi, 2000), 31–32.

34 *Close Encounters* promotional interview, 1977, available at: http://www. youtube.com/watch?v=P9TY6yg4ejM&feature=related

35 Andrew Thomas, telephone interview with the author, 10 Feb. 2011.

36 *Close Encounters* promotional interview, 1977, available at: http://www. youtube.com/watch?v=BACQX-WzWeA

37 *Phoenix Gazette*, 18 Mar. 1978.

38 See: Grant Cameron, "Jimmy Carter UFO," *The Presidents UFO Website*, 1 Aug. 2009, available at: http://www.presidentialufo.com/ jimmy-carter/93-jimmy-carter-ufo

39 For detailed information on Carter's sighting, see: "President Jimmy Carter's UFO Sighting," at: http://www.ufoevidence.org/cases/case294.htm

40 For full details of Project Serpo, including rumours relating to *Close Encounters of the Third Kind*, see *Serpo.org, The Zeta Reticuli Exchange Program*, http://www.serpo.org/

41 *Close Encounters* box-office details at: http://www.the-numbers.com/movie/ Close-Encounters-of-the-Third-Kind#tab=summary

42 See *Public Opinion Surveys and Unidentified Flying Objects 50+ years of Sampling Public Opinions*, January, 2000, 14.

43 See: Anthony Breznican, "Steven Spielberg: The EW Interview," *Entertainment Weekly*, 2 Dec. 2011, http://www.ew.com/article/2011/12/02/ steven-spielberg-ew-interview/4

44 Suid and Haverstick, *Stars and Stripes on Screen*, 221.

45 Joe Alves, telephone interview with the author, 26 Nov. 2013.

46 See: *Public Opinion Surveys and Unidentified Flying Objects 50+ years of Sampling Public Opinions*, January, 2000, 14.

47 'UFO' landing at 1984 Olympic closing ceremony viewable at: https://www. youtube.com/watch?v=io_3RNjuKSk

48 See: Good, *Alien Base*, 356–357.

49 Paul Mayo, telephone interview with the author, 15 May, 2010.

50 Suid and Haverstick, *Stars and Stripes on Screen*, 47.

51 Paul Mayo, telephone interview with the author, 15 May, 2010.

[52] Vivian Sobchack, *Screening Space: The American Science Fiction Film*, Second, Enlarged Edition (Rutgers University Press, 2004), 293.

[53] *Life Force and Cocoon* were both released 21 Jun. 1985. The former grossed $12 million domestically, and the latter $76 million. Source: http://www.the-numbers.com/

[54] See: *Dan Aykroyd Unplugged on UFOs*, dir. David Sereda (2005). Viewable at: https://www.youtube.com/watch?v=oVCd5oLXPGY

[55] *Phenomenon* box-office data at: http://www.the-numbers.com/movie/Phenomenon#tab=summary

[56] *Contact* box-office date at: http://www.the-numbers.com/movie/Contact#tab=summary

[57] James V. Hart has been a long-time supporter of UFO conspiracy guru David Wilcock, providing praise for Wilcock's book *The Source Field Investigations* (Plume, 2012), and personally introducing Wilcock as a speaker at the 2012 Conscious Life Expo in Los Angeles. Wilcock and Hart were, for a time, collaborating on a screenplay exploring the latter's work, central to which are ideas relating to UFOs and alien intelligences. See: http://divinecosmos.com/start-here/davids-blog?hc_location=ufi&start=79

[58] See: Meehan, *Saucer Movies*, 298. For Clinton's full statement, made 7 Aug. 1996, see: "President Clinton Statement Regarding Mars Meteorite Discovery," http://www2.jpl.nasa.gov/snc/clinton.html

[59] Clinton's Roswell remarks in Belfast viewable at: https://www.youtube.com/watch?v=wSMhNk8wSng. See also: Grant Cameron, "Bill Clinton and the UFO Crash at Roswell," *The Presidents UFO Website*, 24 Aug. 2009, http://www.presidentialufo.com/bill-clinton/244-bill-clinton-and-the-ufo-crash-at-roswell

[60] Andrew Russell, "The Silbury Hill Stargate," *The official Website of Colin Andrews*, http://www.colinandrews.net/UFO-PoliceSergeant-SilburyHill.html

[61] "Mayan 'apocalypse' crop circle appears at Silbury Hill," *The Telegraph*, 8 Jul. 2009, http://www.telegraph.co.uk/news/newstopics/howaboutthat/5777580/Mayan-apocalypse-crop-circle-appears-at-Silbury-Hill.html

[62] See: Good, *Alien Base*, 216.

[63] Andy Fickman, telephone interview with the author, 2 Sept. 2010.

[64] See: Good, *Alien Base*, 217.

65 See: Richard Alleyne, "Aliens are likely to look and behave like us," *The Telegraph*, 25 Jan. 2010, http://www.telegraph.co.uk/news/science/science-news/7071013/Aliens-are-likely-to-look-and-behave-like-us.html

66 See: Good, *Alien Base*, 216.

67 See: "SETI Institute's Jill Tarter takes issue with Stephen Hawking, MIB3, Prometheus and Battleship," *SETI Institute*, http://www.seti.org/node/1288

CHAPTER FIVE

1   For discussion of abduction-like experiences pre-dating the modern UFO era, see: Time Life, *Alien Encounters* (Time Life, 2004), 43–51. See also: Clark, *The UFO Book*, 51; and Keith Thompson, *Angels and Aliens* (Fawcett Columbine, 1991), 151.

2   See: Story (ed.), *The mammoth Encyclopedia*, 5.

3   Clark, *The UFO Book*, 214.

4   See: Story (ed), *The Mammoth Encyclopedia*, 5. See also: Clark, *The UFO Book*, 214–215.

5   See: Story (ed.), *The Mammoth Encyclopedia*, 6. See also: David M. Jacobs, *Secret Life: Firsthand Accounts of UFO Abductions* (BCA, 1992); and: David M. Jacobs, *The Threat: Revealing the Secret Alien Agenda* (Fireside, 1999).

6   See: Story (ed.), *The Mammoth Encyclopedia*, 6. See also: Andrea Pritchard (ed.), *Alien Discussions: Proceedings of the Abduction Study Conference* (North Cambridge Press, 1995); and C. D. B. Bryan, *Close Encounters of the Fourth Kind: Alien Abduction and UFOs – Witnesses and Scientists Report* (Orion, 1995).

7   John E. Mack M.D., *Abduction: Human Encounters with Aliens* (Macmillan, 1994).

8   Audio file of Mack's full statement freely accessible at MakeMagic Productions website, http://makemagicproductions.com/

9   *Oprah* episode viewable at: https://www.youtube.com/watch?v=kfBODQZTQRo.

10 See: Jacques Vallee, "Physical Analysis in Ten Cases of Unexplained Aerial Objects with Material Samples," *Journal of Scientific Exploration*. Vol. 12, No. 3. 1998, 359–375.

[11] Meehan, *Saucer Movies*, 60.

[12] See: Marrs, *Alien Agenda*, 196–197.

[13] See: Clark, *The UFO Book*, 274–292. See also: John G. Fuller, *The Interrupted Journey: Two Lost Hours Aboard a Flying Saucer* (The Dial Press, 1966).

[14] See: Clark, *The UFO Book*, 291.

[15] See: Story (ed.), *The Mammoth Encyclopedia*, 629–633.

[16] See: Clark, *The UFO Book*, 445–450.

[17] Mike Clelland, "Foreshadowing, unexplainable pregnancies, hybrid children and the creative process," *Hidden Experience*, 14 Oct. 2012, http://hiddenexperience.blogspot.co.uk/2012/10/the-stranger-within.html

[18] Jeffrey J. Kripal, *Mutants and Mystics: Science Fiction, Super Hero Comics, and the Paranormal* (University of Chicago Press, 2011), 11.

[19] Ibid, 54

[20] Ibid.

[21] For a detailed study of the Travis Walton case, see: Clark, *The UFO Book*, 627–652. For Walton's personal accounting of events, see: Travis Walton, *Fire in the Sky: The Walton Experience* (Marlowe and Company, 1996).

[22] See: Mike Clelland, "Owls and the UFO Abductee," *Hidden Experience*, 3 July 2013, http://hiddenexperience.blogspot.co.uk/2013/07/owls-and-ufo-abductee.html. See also: Mike Clelland, *The Messengers: Owls, Synchronicity, and the UFO Abductee* (Richard Dolan Press, 2015).

[23] Whitley Strieber, *Communion* (Arrow Books, 1997), 30–31.

[24] Whitley Strieber, audio interview with guest Catherine Austin Fitts, Dreamland radio show, 1 May 2015.

[25] Clelland, *The Messengers* (from the manuscript, in advance of publication).

[26] For an overview of the Jordan-Kauble case, including a position statement from Jordan-Kauble herself, see: Story (ed.), *The Mammoth Encyclopedia*, 341–344.

[27] Information provided to the author by Peter Robbins, former assistant to Budd Hopkins, and by Will Bueché of John Mack Archives LLC.

[28] Tracy Tormé, telephone interview with the author, 11 April 2014.

29 Roger Ebert's *Fire in the Sky* Review dated 15 March, 1993, available at: http://www.rogerebert.com/reviews/fire-in-the-sky-1993

30 James Berardinelli's *Fire in the Sky* review available at: http://www.imdb.com/reviews/18/1824.html

31 Carter met with Mack on a number of occasions to discuss the abduction phenomenon in the context of *The X-Files*. Carter even observed a number of Mack's private sessions with an abductee, who was a friend and colleague of Carter's. Mack later said of Carter: "I liked him a lot and I thought he was very creative but I came to the conclusion that we were really operating in different audiences, in different relationships to reality, different purposes...We stayed in touch a little after that but it didn't seem like we had any place to go after that. So, that was that." Mack discusses his meetings with Chris Carter in the documentary *Touched* (dir. Laurel Chiten, Blind Dog Films, 2003). Additional info on Mack's relationship with Carter provided to the author by Will Bueché of the John E. Mack Archives LLC.

32 *Taken* budget details at: http://www.imdb.com/title/tt0289830/

33 Jeff Richardson, "Alaska Newspapers, Movie Studio Reach Settlement over 'Fourth Kind," *Fairbanks Daily News Miner*, 11 Nov. 2009.

34 *The Fourth Kind* box-office data at: http://www.the-numbers.com/movies/2009/4KIND.php

35 *Dark Skies* box-office data at: http://www.the-numbers.com/movie/Dark-Skies#tab=summary

36 Matty Beckerman, audio interview with Alejandro Rojas, *Open Minds UFO Radio*, posted online 5 May 2014, available at: http://www.openminds.tv/matty-beckerman-director-alien-abduction-may-5-2014/27412

37 See: Steven Jones, *An Invitation to the Dance: The Awakening of the Extended Human Family* (Little Star Publishing, 2010). Available at: http://www.amazon.co.uk/An-Invitation-The-Dance-Awakening/dp/0956689507

38 See: Bret Oldham, *Children of the Greys* (House of Halo, 2013), available through Bret's website: http://childrenofthegreys.com/

39 Brigitte Barclay describes her experiences in a lecture delivered 7 Aug. 2011 at the 3rd Annual British Exopolitics Expo at the University of Leeds. Viewable at: https://www.youtube.com/watch?v=3ZVigcmemNE

40 Chris Bledsoe describes his experiences in great detail in an interview with Mel Fabregas for Veritas Radio, recorded 1 Mar. 2013, available at: http://www.veritasradio.com/guests/2013/03mar/VS-130301-cbledsoe.php For MUFON's investigation into Chris Bledsoe's case, see: *UFOs Over Earth: The Fayetteville Incident* (dir. Robert M. Wise, 2008). Viewable at: https://www.youtube.com/watch?v=icW3iZZQAzo

41 For more information on Peter Faust, see his website: http://www.peterfaust.com. Peter's appearance on *Oprah* is viewable at: https://www.youtube.com/watch?v=kfBODQZTQRo. See also the documentary *Touched* (dir. Laurel Chiten, Blind Dog Films, 2003), in which Peter features prominently.

CHAPTER SIX

1 See: Jacques Vallee and Chris Aubeck, *Wonders in the Sky: Unexplained Aerial Objects from Antiquity to Modern Times* (Tarcher Penguin, 2010), 29–30.

2 Ibid, 32–35.

3 See: Story (ed.), *The Mammoth Encyclopedia*, 220.

4 Peter Brookesmith, *UFO: The Complete Sightings Catalogue*, (Cassell, 1996) 12.

5 Erich von Däniken, *Chariots of the Gods? Unsolved Mysteries of the Past* (Putnam, 1968).

6 See, by Zecharia Sitchin: *The 12th Planet* (Stein and Day, 1976); *The Stairway to Heaven* (Avon Books, 1980); and *The Wars of Gods and Men* (Avon Books, 1985).

7 Jason Colavito, Skype interview with the author, 11 Feb. 2015. For further reading on the Cthulhu Mythos, see: Daniel Harms, *The Cthulhu Mythos Encyclopedia* (Elder Signs Press, 2008). See also: Jason Colavito (ed.), *Theosophy on Ancient Astronauts, Studies in Ancient Astronautics Vol. 1* (JasonColavito.com, 2012); and: Colavito, *The Cult of Alien Gods: H.P. Lovecraft and Extraterrestrial Pop Culture* Prometheus Books, 2005).

8 See: Richard C. Hoagland and Mike Bara, *Dark Mission: The Secret History of NASA* (Feral House, 2007, 2009). More of Hoagland's theories at his website: http://www.enterprisemission.com/

9   Meehan, *Saucer Movies*, 138–139.

10 Ibid, 139–140.

11 See: Ian Sample, "We should scour the moon for ancient traces of aliens, say scientists," *The Guardian*, 25 Dec. 2011, http://www.theguardian.com/science/2011/dec/25/scour-moon-ancient-traces-aliens. Davies and Wagner's paper, "Searching for Alien Artifacts on the Moon," available at: http://www.sciencedirect.com/science/article/pii/S0094576511003249

12 See: *Room 237*, dir. Roger Ascher (IFC Films, 2012).

13 Jason Colavito, Skype interview with the author, 11 Feb. 2015.

14 *Mysteries of the Gods* (1976), viewable in full at: https://www.youtube.com/watch?v=VnUy-naDoYw

15 See: Alejandro Rojas, "UFO disclosure at Kirtland Air Force Base," *Open Minds*, 7 Jun. 2010, http://www.openminds.tv/ufo-discosure-afb/

16 Mike Clelland, "Hangar 18 and predictive weirdness," *Hidden Experience*, 4 Nov. 2012, http://hiddenexperience.blogspot.co.uk/2012/11/hanger-18-and-predictive-weirdness.html

17 "And Gallup Said Unto Sellier, 'Thou Shalt Make a Film About Noah,'" *People*, 4 Apr. 1977, Vol. 7, No. 13, http://www.people.com/people/archive/article/0,,20067599,00.html. See also: Variety Staff, "Charles Sellier, creator of 'Grizzly Adams,' dies at 67," *Variety*, 2 Feb. 2011. http://variety.com/2011/scene/news/charles-sellier-creator-of-grizzly-adams-dies-at-67-1118031462/

18 Neal A. Maxwell, *A Wonderful Flood of Light* (Bookcraft, 1990), 25.

19 See: "Church Educational System," *Wikipedia*, https://en.wikipedia.org/wiki/Church_Educational_System

20 Steven Greer interviewed by Jean-Noel Bassior, "UFOs: What the Government Really Knows," *Hustler*, Nov. 2005, 54. Scan available at: http://www.disclosureproject.org/transcripts/JeanNoelBassior3.htm

21 Pentagon, USAF, and U.S. Space Command cooperation in *SG-1* is acknowledged in the series' closing credits.

22 See: Anna Sokol, "Richard Dean Anderson – A Day of Honors," 1 Oct. 2004, http://www.rdanderson.com/archives/2004-10-01.htm

23 See: "SAIC Announces CEO Succession," *PR Newswire*, 1 Mar. 2012, http://www.prnewswire.com/news-releases/saic-announces-ceo-succession-139806803.html

24 See: "A further update from 'Henry Deacon,'" *Project Camelot*, 2 May 2007, http://projectcamelot.org/livermore_physicist_3.html

25 *Mission to Mars* box-office data at: http://www.the-numbers.com/movie/ Mission-to-Mars#tab=summary

26 *Alien vs. Predator featurette*, Apple Inc. 2004, http://web.archive.org/ web/20080107231134/http://www.apple.com/trailers/fox/avp/featurette/

27 *Indiana Jones and the Kingdom of the Crystal Skull* box-office data at: http://www.the-numbers.com/movie/Indiana -Jones-and-the-Kingdom-of-the-Crystal-Skull#tab=summary

28 Daniel Myrick, email correspondence with the author, 17 Mar. 2014.

29 Documented by Grant Cameron. See: "Is there a UFO Cover-Up?" White House UFO, 23 Feb. 2012, http://whitehouseufo.blogspot.co.uk/2012/02/ is-there-ufo-cover-up.html

30 Daniel Myrick, email correspondence with the author, 17 Mar. 2014.

31 Jason Colavito, Skype interview with the author, 11 Feb. 2015.

32 *Thor* box-office data at: http://www.the-numbers.com/movie/Thor#tab=summary

33 *Cowboys & Aliens: An Inside Look with Steven Spielberg* viewable at: https:// www.youtube.com/watch?v=IINvwOBdwBU

34 See: Brookesmith, *UFO*, 19.

35 *Cowboys & Aliens* box-office data at: http://www.the-numbers.com/movie/ Cowboys-and-Aliens#tab=summary

36 See: Scott Roxborough, "Ridley Scott, Michael Fassbender, Noomi Rapace Tease 'Prometheus' at CineEurope," *The |Hollywood Reporter*, 28 Jun. 2011, http://www. hollywoodreporter.com/news/ridley-scott-michael-fassbender-noomi-206321

37 See: *Empire* magazine, Issue 274, Apr. 2012.

38 Scott makes the statements in: *Prometheus Exclusive Featurette: Origins* (2012). See: Robbie Graham, "'Prometheus' headed for Zeta Reticuli," *Silver Screen Saucers* (blog), 10 May 2012, http://silverscreensaucers.blogspot. co.uk/2012/05/prometheus-headed-for-zeta-reticuli.html

39 See: Robbie Graham "Prometheus did go to Zeta Reticuli, after all," *Silver Screen Saucers* (blog), 27 Jan. 2013, http://silverscreensaucers.blogspot. co.uk/2013/01/prometheus-did-go-to-zeta-reticuli.html

[40] See: Jake Weintraub, 'Cowboys & Aliens' Writer Roberto Orci: 'The Government's Lying!' *The Wrap*, 23 Jul. 2011, http://www.thewrap.com/cowboys-aliens-writer-roberto-orci-aliens-governments-lying-29399/. See also: Robbie Graham, "'Cowboys and Aliens' writer alleges UFO cover-up," *Silver Screen Saucers* (blog), 26 Jul. 2011, http://silverscreensaucers.blogspot.co.uk/2011/07/cowboys-and-aliens-writer-alleges-ufo.html

[41] *Transformers: Age of Extinction* box-office ranking at: http://www.the-numbers.com/movie/records/All-Time-Worldwide-Box-Office

[42] Jason Colavito, Skype interview with the author, 11 Feb. 2015.

[43] Ibid.

[44] See: Davies, P.C.W, "Footprints of Alien Technology," *Acta Astronautica*, Volume 73, April–May 2012, 250–257, available at: http://www.sciencedirect.com/science/article/pii/S0094576511002323

CHAPTER SEVEN

[1] See: Clark, *The UFO Book*, 326.

[2] The Blue Book interview was produced by the US Department of Defense and is viewable at: https://www.youtube.com/watch?v=mNAkFRNPrvU&feature=youtu.be. Full transcript available at: http://www.vidqt.com/id/UlmwakUTo3M?lang=en

[3] See: George P. Hansen, *The Trickster and the Paranormal* (Xlibris, 2001), 221–223. See also: Lawrence Fawcett and Barry J. Greenwood, *Clear Intent: The Government Cover-Up of the UFO Experience* (Prentice Hall, 1984), 206–208.

[4] See: Philip Mantle, "Alien Autopsy End Game," *Open Minds*, 23 Dec. 2009, http://www.openminds.tv/alien-autopsy-end-game-answering-the-final-question-concerning-the-alien-autopsy-movie/1337

[5] Email correspondence between David Sankey and Mike Gray, 16 Jan. 2009.

[6] Nick Redfern, *On the Trail of the Saucer Spies* (Anomalist Books, 2006), 49.

[7] Bishop revealed Falcon's identity as Harry Rositzke during a live streaming event called the Alternate Universe I-Conference on 30 June 2012. Rositzke was a man of considerable standing and influence in the CIA. He died

in 2002, aged 91. For his obituary, see: Paul Lewis, "Harry Rositzke, 91, Linguist and American Spymaster," *The New York Times*, 8 Nov. 2002, http://www.nytimes.com/2002/11/08/us/harry-rositzke-91-linguist-and-american-spymaster.html

8   Greg Bishop, *Project Beta: The Story of Paul Bennewitz, National Security, and the Creation of a Modern UFO Myth*, (Paraview Pocket Books, 2005), 60.

9   Ibid, 66.

10   Ibid, 64.

11   Ibid, 60

12   See: Hansen, *The Trickster and the Paranormal*, 229.

13   See: Bishop, *Project Beta*, 210–211. See also: Timothy Good, *Above Top Secret: The Worldwide UFO Cover-Up* (Harper Collins, 1993), 250–252, 540–547.

14   The most famous of these documents is the 'Cutler-Twining memo,' dated Jul. 14, 1954. It was 'discovered' by Moore, Shandera, and Stanton Friedman in 1985 in the National Archives. It is now generally agreed that the document was planted there for them as part of the ongoing MJ-12 disinformation program. More MJ-12 documents surfaced between 1992 and 1994. See: Stanton T. Friedman, *Top Secret/Majic* (Michael O'Mara Books, 1997), 86–102. For the National Archives' description of the Cutler-Twining memo, see: "Unidentified Flying Objects - Project BLUE BOOK," Military Records, *National Archives*, http://www.archives.gov/research/military/air-force/ufos.html#mj12

15   See: Bishop, *Project Beta*, 211.

16   Hansen, *The Trickster and the Paranormal*, 225.

17   See: Bishop, *Project Beta*, 211–212.

18   Ibid, 212. Collins describes his role in the Aviary and in *UFO Cover-Up?: Live!* In: Robert M. Collins with Richard C. Doty, *Exempt from Disclosure: The Black World of UFOs* (Peregrine Communications, 2012).

19   Tracy Tormé, telephone interview with the author, 11 Apr. 2014.

20   Hansen, *The Trickster and the Paranormal*, 245.

21   Lazar openly admitted that he and his first wife, Carol, had owned a legal brothel in Northern Nevada in the early-1980s. He was later given a three

year suspended sentence for assisting a friend with an illegal brothel in Las Vegas, helping with computer software and accounting. See: Timothy Good, *Alien Liaison, The Ultimate Secret* (Arrow, 1992), 178–179.

[22] George Knapp's first video interview with Lazar was broadcast in May of 1989, when Lazar appeared in silhouette under the pseudonym 'Denis.' He revealed his true name and face in another interview with Knapp for KLAS TV in November 1989. For a detailed accounting of the Bob Lazar-Area 51 story, see: Timothy Good, *Alien Liaison*, 130–186. For a 2014 KLAS TV retrospective on the Lazar story see: "George Knapp Interviews Bob Lazar 25 Years after His 1st Historic interview – KLAS," 14 May 2014, viewable at: https://www.youtube.com/watch?v=auuVZWx-LXI. George Knapp shared his personal views on the Lazar case during an Oct. 2014 lecture in Copenhagen for Exopolitics Denmark, viewable at: https://www.youtube.com/watch?v=K1viG6PRjiw

[23] See: Bishop, *Project Beta*, 83.

[24] Paul Davids, telephone interview with the author, 5 Aug. 2013.

[25] Anthony Frewin (ed.), *Are We Alone? The Stanley Kubrick Extraterrestrial-Intelligence Interviews* (Elliott & Thompson, 2005), 25–26.

[26] Andrew Thomas, telephone interview with the author, 10 Feb. 2011.

[27] See: Suid and Haverstick, *Stars and Stripes on Screen*, 119,

[28] Don Ecker, Skype interview with the author, 3 Feb. 2015.

[29] Bryce Zabel, interview with the author, 8 June 2015.

[30] Will Smith described the meeting with President Obama to radio host Chris Moyles on 16 May 2012. Video viewable at: http://silverscreensaucers.blogspot.co.uk/2012/05/president-obama-tells-will-smiths-son-i.html

[31] Video of the full Disclosure Project 2001 National Press Club conference viewable at: https://www.youtube.com/watch?v=8i-48LpRB9c. See also: Steven M. Greer, *Disclosure: Military and Government Witnesses reveal the Greatest Secrets in Modern History* (Crossing Point, 2001).

[32] Alfred L. Webre, "Towards a Decade of Contact: Preparing for re-integration into Universe Society," *Exopolitics Journal*, Jun. 2000, Updated 30 Jun. 2007, 142.

[33] See the Paradigm Research Group website: http://www.paradigmresearchgroup.org/

[34] See Michael Salla's biography at his website: http://exopolitics.org/about/founder/

[35] See: Dolan, *UFOs and the National Security State: Volume 1*, 257–258.

[36] Project Moon Dust documents dated between 1967 and 1979 accessible in PDF format at: http://www.majesticdocuments.com/official.documents.foia.php

[37] See: Greer, *Disclosure*, 327–330.

[38] Andy Fickman, telephone interview with the author, 2 Sept., 2010.

[39] The Tonopah Test Range is referred to as "Area 52" on page 34 of a 1998 US Department of Energy document entitled: 'Closure Report for Corrective Action Unit 426: Cactus Spring Waste Trenches, Tonopah Test Range, Nevada,' available in PDF format, here: http://www.osti.gov/bridge/purl.cover.jsp;jsessionid=0A1103EA281777397F3B071F77508E55?purl=/10152-bE9iaX/webviewable/

[40] Joe Dante, telephone Interview with the author, 11 Jul. 2008.

[41] Ken Russell, "Seeing is Believing – If the Special Effects Work," *The Times*, *Times2*, 27 Mar. 2008.

CONCLUSION

[1] Walter Benjamin, "The Work of Art in the Age of Mechanical Reproduction," 1936, *Marxists Internet Archive*. Available at: http://www.marxists.org/reference/subject/philosophy/works/ge/benjamin.htm

[2] Valie Export, "Expanded Cinema as Expanded Reality," *Senses of Cinema* (May/Jun. 2003).

[3] Guy Debord, "Society of the Spectacle," 1967, *Marxists Internet Archive*. Available at: http://www.marxists.org/reference/archive/debord/society.htm

[4] See: http://en.wikipedia.org/wiki/Hyperreality

[5] See: Jean Baudrillard, "Simulacra and Simulations," in Mark Poster (ed.), *Jean Baudrillard, Selected Writings* (Stanford University Press, 1998), 166–184.

INDEX

Paperbacks also available from
White Crow Books

Elsa Barker—*Letters from a Living Dead Man*
ISBN 978-1-907355-83-7

Elsa Barker—*War Letters from the Living Dead Man*
ISBN 978-1-907355-85-1

Elsa Barker—*Last Letters from the Living Dead Man*
ISBN 978-1-907355-87-5

Richard Maurice Bucke—*Cosmic Consciousness*
ISBN 978-1-907355-10-3

Arthur Conan Doyle—*The Edge of the Unknown*
ISBN 978-1-907355-14-1

Arthur Conan Doyle—*The New Revelation*
ISBN 978-1-907355-12-7

Arthur Conan Doyle—*The Vital Message*
ISBN 978-1-907355-13-4

Arthur Conan Doyle with Simon Parke—*Conversations with Arthur Conan Doyle*
ISBN 978-1-907355-80-6

Meister Eckhart with Simon Parke—*Conversations with Meister Eckhart*
ISBN 978-1-907355-18-9

D. D. Home—*Incidents in my Life Part 1*
ISBN 978-1-907355-15-8

Mme. Dunglas Home; edited, with an Introduction, by Sir Arthur Conan Doyle—*D. D. Home: His Life and Mission*
ISBN 978-1-907355-16-5

Edward C. Randall—*Frontiers of the Afterlife*
ISBN 978-1-907355-30-1

Rebecca Ruter Springer—*Intra Muros: My Dream of Heaven*
ISBN 978-1-907355-11-0

Leo Tolstoy, edited by Simon Parke—*Forbidden Words*
ISBN 978-1-907355-00-4

Leo Tolstoy—*A Confession*
ISBN 978-1-907355-24-0

Leo Tolstoy—*The Gospel in Brief*
ISBN 978-1-907355-22-6

Leo Tolstoy—*The Kingdom of God is Within You*
ISBN 978-1-907355-27-1

Leo Tolstoy—*My Religion: What I Believe*
ISBN 978-1-907355-23-3

Leo Tolstoy—*On Life*
ISBN 978-1-907355-91-2

Leo Tolstoy—*Twenty-three Tales*
ISBN 978-1-907355-29-5

Leo Tolstoy—*What is Religion and other writings*
ISBN 978-1-907355-28-8

Leo Tolstoy—*Work While Ye Have the Light*
ISBN 978-1-907355-26-4

Leo Tolstoy—*The Death of Ivan Ilyich*
ISBN 978-1-907661-10-5

Leo Tolstoy—*Resurrection*
ISBN 978-1-907661-09-9

Leo Tolstoy with Simon Parke—*Conversations with Tolstoy*
ISBN 978-1-907355-25-7

Howard Williams with an Introduction by Leo Tolstoy—*The Ethics of Diet: An Anthology of Vegetarian Thought*
ISBN 978-1-907355-21-9

Vincent Van Gogh with Simon Parke—*Conversations with Van Gogh*
ISBN 978-1-907355-95-0

Wolfgang Amadeus Mozart with Simon Parke—*Conversations with Mozart*
ISBN 978-1-907661-38-9

Jesus of Nazareth with Simon Parke—
Conversations with Jesus of Nazareth
ISBN 978-1-907661-41-9

Thomas à Kempis with Simon
Parke—*The Imitation of Christ*
ISBN 978-1-907661-58-7

Julian of Norwich with Simon
Parke—*Revelations of Divine Love*
ISBN 978-1-907661-88-4

Allan Kardec—*The Spirits Book*
ISBN 978-1-907355-98-1

Allan Kardec—*The Book on Mediums*
ISBN 978-1-907661-75-4

Emanuel Swedenborg—*Heaven and Hell*
ISBN 978-1-907661-55-6

P.D. Ouspensky—*Tertium Organum:
The Third Canon of Thought*
ISBN 978-1-907661-47-1

Dwight Goddard—*A Buddhist Bible*
ISBN 978-1-907661-44-0

Michael Tymn—*The Afterlife Revealed*
ISBN 978-1-970661-90-7

Michael Tymn—*Transcending the
Titanic: Beyond Death's Door*
ISBN 978-1-908733-02-3

Guy L. Playfair—*If This Be Magic*
ISBN 978-1-907661-84-6

Guy L. Playfair—*The Flying Cow*
ISBN 978-1-907661-94-5

Guy L. Playfair —*This House is Haunted*
ISBN 978-1-907661-78-5

Carl Wickland, M.D.—
Thirty Years Among the Dead
ISBN 978-1-907661-72-3

John E. Mack—*Passport to the Cosmos*
ISBN 978-1-907661-81-5

Peter & Elizabeth Fenwick—
The Truth in the Light
ISBN 978-1-908733-08-5

Erlendur Haraldsson—
Modern Miracles
ISBN 978-1-908733-25-2

Erlendur Haraldsson—
At the Hour of Death
ISBN 978-1-908733-27-6

Erlendur Haraldsson—
The Departed Among the Living
ISBN 978-1-908733-29-0

Brian Inglis—*Science and Parascience*
ISBN 978-1-908733-18-4

Brian Inglis—*Natural and Supernatural:
A History of the Paranormal*
ISBN 978-1-908733-20-7

Ernest Holmes—*The Science of Mind*
ISBN 978-1-908733-10-8

Victor & Wendy Zammit —*A Lawyer
Presents the Evidence For the Afterlife*
ISBN 978-1-908733-22-1

Casper S. Yost—*Patience
Worth: A Psychic Mystery*
ISBN 978-1-908733-06-1

William Usborne Moore—
Glimpses of the Next State
ISBN 978-1-907661-01-3

William Usborne Moore—
The Voices
ISBN 978-1-908733-04-7

John W. White—
The Highest State of Consciousness
ISBN 978-1-908733-31-3

Stafford Betty—
The Imprisoned Splendor
ISBN 978-1-907661-98-3

Paul Pearsall, Ph.D. —
Super Joy
ISBN 978-1-908733-16-0

**All titles available as eBooks, and selected titles available in Hardback and
Audiobook formats from www.whitecrowbooks.com**

CPSIA information can be obtained
at www.ICGtesting.com
Printed in the USA
BVOW08s1842071216
R7685400001B/R76854PG469695BVX2B/2/P